The Cultural Politics of Emotion

The Cultural Politics of Emotion

SECOND EDITION

Sara Ahmed

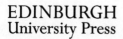

EDINBURGH
University Press

© Sara Ahmed, 2004, 2014

First edition published by Edinburgh University Press in 2004

Second edition 2014

Edinburgh University Press Ltd
The Tun – Holyrood Road
12 (2f) Jackson's Entry
Edinburgh EH8 8PJ

www.euppublishing.com

Typeset in 11 on 13 pt Ehrhardt by
SNP Best-set Typesetter Ltd, Hong Kong, and
new material by Servis Filmsetting Ltd, Stockport, Cheshire
Printed and bound in Great Britain by
CPI Group (UK) Ltd, Croydon CR0 4YY

A CIP record for this book is available from the British
Library

ISBN 978 0 7486 9113 5 (paperback)
ISBN 978 0 7486 9114 2 (webready PDF)
ISBN 978 0 7486 9115 9 (epub)

Contents

Acknowledgements

I wrote this book whilst I was co-director and then director of the Institute for Women's Studies at Lancaster University between 2000 and 2003. Thanks to all colleagues and students at Lancaster who helped me stay motivated during a challenging time, especially: Jackie Stacey (who shared the directorship with me for two years, and did much more than lighten the load); Rosemary Betterton; Claudia Castañeda; Alison Easton; Anne-Marie Fortier; Gerry Harris; Maureen McNeil; Lynne Pearce; Celia Roberts; Mimi Sheller; Vicky Singleton; Elaine Swan and Imogen Tyler. Thanks to Lauren Berlant whose visits to Lancaster generated much debate about 'feelings in public', from which I have greatly benefited. Thanks to Janet Hartley and Sandra Irving for continual and good-humoured support. My appreciation to Yuko Ogawo who gave me wonderful assistance in the preparation of the final manuscript and to Sarah Franklin, Nicole Vittelone, and Mimi Sheller who offered really helpful feedback on an earlier draft. Thanks to Jackie Jones for her excellent editorial advice throughout and her patience towards the end of the project. And my appreciation to Martha Elisa Bojórquez for kindly giving permission to use her beautiful art work for the cover.

I have been lucky to edit the book whilst on study leave in Australia. Thanks to the Arts and Humanities Research Board who funded this leave. I am very grateful to Elspeth Probyn and staff and students in the Department of Gender Studies, Sydney University, for providing such a stimulating environment in which to work. Thanks to my family, for being nearby in this past year, and for living under the sun. A special thanks to Sarah Franklin and Imogen Tyler for helping me change directions more than once.

Earlier versions of chapters have appeared as follows, and I thank publishers for permission to reprint here: (2001) 'The Organisation of Hate' in *Law and Critique* 13 (3): 345–65, with kind permission of Kluwer Academic Publishers; (2002) 'Contingency of Pain' in *Parallax* 8 (1): 17–34 (http://www.tandf.co.uk/journalsroutledge/13534645.html; (2003) 'The Politics of Fear in the Making of Worlds' in *International Journal of Qualitative Studies in Education* 16 (3): 377–98 (http://www.tandf.co.uk); (2003) 'Feminist Futures' in M. Eagleton (ed.), *The Concise Companion to Feminist Theory*, Blackwell. Permission to quote from *Bringing Them Home* was granted by the Human Rights and Equal Opportunity Commission, Australia.

Acknowledgements for the Second Edition

With thanks to Jackie Jones for suggesting and supporting a second edition of this book and to the editorial team at Edinburgh University Press for their help and efficiency. My appreciation to those with whom I have conversed about affect and emotion in the past decade including Lauren Berlant, Lisa Blackman, Kristyn Gorton, Sneja Gunew, Jin Haritaworn, Carolyn Pedwell, Elspeth Probyn, Divya Tolia-Kelly and Imogen Tyler. Thanks to my now-not-so-new colleagues at Goldsmiths for creating such a friendly and lively space to work; and to those who helped set up our new Centre for Feminist Research especially Sarah Kember, Angela McRobbie, Beverley Skeggs, and Natalie Fenton. And my heartfelt thanks to Sarah Franklin for travelling with me on this intellectual journey.

Introduction: Feel Your Way

> Every day of every year, swarms of illegal immigrants and bogus
> asylum seekers invade Britain by any means available to them . . .
> Why? They are only seeking the easy comforts and free benefits in
> Soft Touch Britain. All funded by YOU – The British Taxpayer!
> (British National Front Poster)[1]

How does a nation come to be imagined as having a 'soft touch'? How does
this 'having' become a form of 'being', or a national attribute? In *The
Cultural Politics of Emotion*, I explore how emotions work to shape the 'surfaces' of individual and collective bodies. Bodies take the shape of the very
contact they have with objects and others. My analysis proceeds by reading
texts that circulate in the public domain, which work by aligning subjects with
collectives by attributing 'others' as the 'source' of our feelings. In this quote
from the British National Front, 'the others', who are named as illegal immigrants and bogus asylum seekers, threaten to overwhelm and swamp the
nation. This is, of course, a familiar narrative, and like all familiar narratives,
it deserves close and careful reading. The narrative works through othering;
the 'illegal immigrants' and 'bogus asylum seekers' are those who are 'not us',
and who in not being us, endanger what is ours. Such others threaten to take
away from what 'you' have, as the legitimate subject of the nation, as the one
who is the true recipient of national benefits. The narrative invites the reader
to adopt the 'you' through working on emotions: becoming this 'you' would
mean developing a certain rage against these illegitimate others, who are represented as 'swarms' in the nation. Indeed, to feel love for the nation, whereby
love is an investment that should be returned (you are 'the taxpayer'), is also
to feel injured by these others, who are 'taking' what is yours.

It is not the case, however, that anybody within the nation could inhabit
this 'you'. These short sentences depend on longer histories of articulation,

which secure the white subject as sovereign in the nation, at the same time as they generate effects in the alignment of 'you' with the national body. In other words, the 'you' implicitly evokes a 'we', a group of subjects who can identify themselves with the injured nation in this performance of personal injury. Within the British National Front, the 'we' of the nation is only available to white Aryans: 'We will reinstate the values of separatism to our racial kindred. We will teach the youth that one's country is the family, the past, the sacred race itself . . . We live in a nation that is historically Aryan'.[2] This alignment of family, history and race is powerful, and works to transform whiteness into a familial tie, into a form of racial kindred that recognises all non-white others as strangers, as 'bodies out of place' (Ahmed 2000).[3] The narrative is addressed to white Aryans, and equates the vulnerability of the white nation with the vulnerability of the white body. 'YOU' will not be soft! Or will you?

What is so interesting in this narrative is how 'soft touch' becomes a national character. This attribution is not specific to fascist discourses. In broader public debates about asylum in the United Kingdom, one of the most common narratives is that Britain is a 'soft touch': others try and 'get into' the nation because they can have a life with 'easy comforts'.[4] The British Government has transformed the narrative of 'the soft touch' into an imperative: it has justified the tightening of asylum policies on the grounds that 'Britain will not be a soft touch'. Indeed, the metaphor of 'soft touch' suggests that the nation's borders and defences are like skin; they are soft, weak, porous and easily shaped or even bruised by the proximity of others. It suggests that the nation is made vulnerable to abuse by its very openness to others. The soft nation is too emotional, too easily moved by the demands of others, and too easily seduced into assuming that claims for asylum, as testimonies of injury, are narratives of truth. To be a 'soft touch nation' is to be taken in by the bogus: to 'take in' is to be 'taken in'. The demand is that the nation should seal itself from others, if it is to act on behalf of its citizens, rather than react to the claims of immigrants and other others. The implicit demand is for a nation that is less emotional, less open, less easily moved, one that is 'hard', or 'tough'. The use of metaphors of 'softness' and 'hardness' shows us how emotions become attributes of collectives, which get constructed as 'being' through 'feeling'. Such attributes are of course gendered: the soft national body is a feminised body, which is 'penetrated' or 'invaded' by others.

It is significant that the word 'passion' and the word 'passive' share the same root in the Latin word for 'suffering' (*passio*). To be passive is to be enacted upon, as a negation that is already felt as suffering. The fear of passivity is tied to the fear of emotionality, in which weakness is defined in terms of a tendency to be shaped by others. Softness is narrated as a proneness to injury. The association between passion and passivity is instructive. It works as a reminder of how 'emotion' has been viewed as 'beneath' the faculties of thought and reason. To be emotional is to have one's judgement affected: it is to be reactive rather than active, dependent rather than autonomous. Feminist philosophers have shown us how the subordination of emotions also works to subordinate the feminine and the body (Spelman 1989; Jaggar 1996). Emotions are associated with women, who are represented as 'closer' to nature, ruled by appetite, and less able to transcend the body through thought, will and judgement.

We can see from this language that evolutionary thinking has been crucial to how emotions are understood: emotions get narrated as a sign of 'our' pre-history, and as a sign of how the primitive persists in the present. The Darwinian model of emotions suggests that emotions are not only 'beneath' but 'behind' the man/human, as a sign of an earlier and more primitive time. As Darwin puts it:

> With mankind some expressions, such as the bristling of the hair
> under the influence of extreme terror, or the uncovering of the teeth
> under that of furious rage, can hardly be understood, except on the
> belief that man once existed in a much lower and animal-like
> condition. (Darwin 1904: 13–14)

Such an evolutionary model allows us to return to the 'risk' of emotions posited through the attribution of 'soft touch' as a national characteristic. The risk of being a 'soft touch' for the nation, and for the national subject, is not only the risk of becoming feminine, but also of becoming 'less white', by allowing those who are recognised as racially other to penetrate the surface of the body. Within such a narrative, becoming less white would involve moving backwards in time, such that one would come to resemble a more primitive form of social life, or a 'lower and animal like condition'.

The hierarchy between emotion and thought/reason gets displaced, of course, into a hierarchy between emotions: some emotions are 'elevated' as signs of cultivation, whilst others remain 'lower' as signs of weakness. The story of evolution is narrated not only as the story of the triumph of reason, but of the ability to control emotions, and to experience the 'appropriate' emotions at different times and places (Elias 1978). Within contemporary culture, emotions may even be represented as good or better than thought, but only insofar as they are re-presented as a form of intelligence, as 'tools' that can be used by subjects in the project of life and career enhancement (Goleman 1995). If good emotions are cultivated, and are worked on and towards, then they remain defined against uncultivated or unruly emotions, which frustrate the formation of the competent self. Those who are 'other' to me or us, or those that threaten to make us other, remain the source of bad feeling in this model of emotional intelligence. It is not difficult to see how emotions are bound up with the securing of social hierarchy: emotions become attributes of bodies as a way of transforming what is 'lower' or 'higher' into bodily traits.

So emotionality as a claim *about* a subject or a collective is clearly dependent on relations of power, which endow 'others' with meaning and value. In this book, I do not want to think about emotionality as a characteristic of bodies, whether individual or collective. In fact, I want to reflect on the processes whereby 'being emotional' comes to be seen as a characteristic of some bodies and not others, in the first place. In order to do this, we need to consider how emotions operate to 'make' and 'shape' bodies as forms of action, which also involve orientations towards others. Emotions, for the British National Front, may pose a danger to the national body of appearing soft. But the narrative itself is an emotional one: the reading of others as bogus is a reaction to the presence of others. *Hardness is not the absence of emotion, but a different emotional orientation towards others.* The hard white body is shaped by its reactions: the rage against others surfaces as a body that stands apart or keeps its distance from others. We shouldn't look for emotions 'in' soft bodies.[5] Emotions shape the very surfaces of bodies, which take shape through the repetition of actions over time, as well as through orientations towards and away from others. Indeed, attending to emotions might show us how all actions are reactions, in the sense that what we do is shaped by the contact we have with others. In Spinoza's terms, emotions shape what bodies can do, as 'the modifications of the body by which the power of action on the body is increased or diminished' (Spinoza 1959: 85).

So rather than asking 'What are emotions?', I will ask, 'What do emotions do?' In asking this question, I will not offer a singular theory of emotion, or one account of the work that emotions do. Rather, I will track how emotions circulate between bodies, examining how they 'stick' as well as move. In this introduction, my task will be to situate my account of the 'cultural politics' of emotion within a very partial account of the history of thinking on emotions. I will not offer a full review of this history, which would be an impossible task.[6] It is important to indicate here that even if emotions have been subordinated to other faculties, they have still remained at the centre of intellectual history. As a reader of this history, I have been overwhelmed by how much 'emotions' have been a 'sticking point' for philosophers, cultural theorists, psychologists, sociologists, as well as scholars from a range of other disciplines. This is not surprising: what is relegated to the margins is often, as we know from deconstruction, right at the centre of thought itself. In the face of this history, my task is a modest one: to show how my thinking has been informed by my contact with some work on emotions.

EMOTIONS AND OBJECTS

One way of reflecting on this history of thinking about emotion is to consider the debate about the relation between emotion, bodily sensation and cognition.[7] One could characterise a significant 'split' in theories of emotion in terms of whether emotions are tied primarily to bodily sensations or to cognition. The former view is often ascribed to Descartes and David Hume. It would also be well-represented by the work of William James, who has the following formulation: 'The bodily changes follow directly the perception of the exciting fact . . . and that our feeling of the same changes as they occur IS the emotion' (James 1890: 449). Emotion is the feeling of bodily change. The immediacy of the 'is' suggests that emotions do not involve processes of thought, attribution or evaluation: we feel fear, for example, *because* our heart is racing, our skin is sweating. A cognitivist view would be represented by Aristotle, and by a number of thinkers who follow him (Nussbaum 2001: 10). Such theorists suggest that emotions involve appraisals, judgements, attitudes or a 'specific manner of apprehending the world' (Sartre 1962: 9), which are irreducible to bodily sensations. Some theorists have described emotions as being judgements (Solomon 1995), whilst others might point to how they involve judgements: the emotion of anger, for example, implies a judgement that something is bad, although we can be wrong in our judgement (Spelman 1989: 266). Of course, many theorists suggest that emotions involve sensations or bodily feeling as well as forms of cognition. But as Alison M. Jaggar has suggested, the shift towards a more cognitive approach has often been at the expense of an attention to bodily sensations (Spelman 1989: 170). Or when emotions are theorised as being about cognition as well as sensation, then these still tend to be presented as different aspects of emotion (Jaggar 1996: 170).

To begin a rethinking of the relation between bodily sensation, emotion and judgement we can turn to Descartes' 'The Passions of the Soul'. Whilst this little book may be full of problematic distinctions between mind and body, its observations on emotions are very suggestive. Descartes suggests that objects do not excite diverse passions because they are diverse, but because of the diverse ways in which they may harm or help us (Descartes 1985: 349). This is an intriguing formulation. Some commentators have suggested that Descartes argues that emotions are reducible to sensations insofar as they are caused by objects (Brentano 2003: 161; Greenspan 2003: 265). But Descartes offers a critique of the idea that objects have causal properties, suggesting that we don't have feelings for objects because of the nature of objects. Feelings instead take the 'shape' of the contact we have with objects (see Chapter 1). As he argues, we do not love and hate because objects are good or bad, but rather because they seem 'beneficial' or 'harmful' (Descartes

1985: 350). Whether I perceive something as beneficial or harmful clearly depends upon how I am affected by something. This dependence opens up a gap in the determination of feeling: whether something is beneficial or harmful involves thought and evaluation, at the same time that it is 'felt' by the body. The process of attributing an object as being or not being beneficial or harmful, which may become translated into good or bad, clearly involves reading the contact we have with objects in a certain way. As I argue in Chapter 1, whether something feels good or bad *already* involves a process of reading, in the very attribution of significance. Contact involves the subject, as well as histories that come before the subject. If emotions are shaped by contact with objects, rather than being caused by objects, then emotions are not simply 'in' the subject or the object. This does not mean that emotions are not read as being 'resident' in subjects or objects: I will show how objects are often read as the cause of emotions in the very process of taking an orientation towards them.

If the contact with an object generates feeling, then emotion and sensation cannot be easily separated. A common way of describing the relation between them is as a form of company: pleasure and pain become companions of love and hate, for example, in Aristotle's formulation (2003: 6, see also Spinoza 1959: 85). The idea of 'companions' does not do the trick precisely, given the implication that sensation and emotion can part company. Instead, I want to suggest that the distinction between sensation and emotion can only be analytic, and as such, is premised on the reification of a concept. We can reflect on the word 'impression', used by David Hume in his work on emotion (Hume 1964: 75). To form an impression might involve acts of perception and cognition as well as an emotion. But forming an impression also depends on how objects impress upon us. An impression can be an effect on the subject's feelings ('she made an impression'). It can be a belief ('to be under an impression'). It can be an imitation or an image ('to create an impression'). Or it can be a mark on the surface ('to leave an impression'). *We need to remember the 'press' in an impression.* It allows us to associate the experience of having an emotion with the very affect of one surface upon another, an affect that leaves its mark or trace. So not only do I have an impression of others, but they also leave me with an impression; they impress me, and impress upon me. I will use the idea of 'impression' as it allows me to avoid making analytical distinctions between bodily sensation, emotion and thought as if they could be 'experienced' as distinct realms of human 'experience'.

So how do we form such impressions? Rethinking the place of the object of feeling will allow us to reconsider the relation between sensation and emotion. Within phenomenology, the turn away from what Elizabeth V. Spelman calls the 'Dumb View' of emotions (Spelman 1989: 265), has involved an emphasis on intentionality. Emotions are intentional in the sense that they are 'about' something: they involve a direction or orientation towards an object (Parkinson 1995: 8). The 'aboutness' of emotions means they involve a stance on the world, or a way of apprehending the world. Now, I want to bring this model of the object as 'about-ness' into dialogue with the model of contact implicit in Descartes.[8] Emotions are both about objects, which they hence shape, and are also shaped by contact with objects. Neither of these ways of approaching an object presumes that the object has a material existence; objects in which I am 'involved' can also be imagined (Heller 1979: 12). For example, I can have a memory of something, and that memory might trigger a feeling (Pugmire 1998: 7). The memory can be the object of my feeling in both senses: the feeling is shaped by contact with the memory, and also involves an orientation towards what is remembered. So I might feel pain when I remember this or that, and in remembering this or that, I might attribute what is remembered as being painful.

Let's use another example. The example that is often used in the psychological literature on emotions is a child and a bear.[9] The child sees the bear and is afraid. The child runs away. Now, the 'Dumb View' would be that the bear makes the child afraid, and that the bodily symptoms of fear are automatic (pulse rate, sweating, and so on). Functionalist models of emotion, which draw on evolutionary theory, might say that the fear has a function: to protect the child from danger, to allow survival. Fear in this situation could be an *instinctual reaction* that has enhanced successful adaptation and thus selection.[10] Fear would also be an action; fear would even be 'about' what it leads the child to do.[11] But the story, even in its 'bear bones', is not so simple. Why is the child afraid of the bear? The child must 'already know' the bear is fearsome. This decision is not necessarily made by her, and it might not even be dependent on past experiences. This could be a 'first time' encounter, and the child still runs for it. But what is she running from? What does she see when she sees the bear? We have an image of the bear as an animal *to be feared*, as an image that is shaped by cultural histories and memories. When we encounter the bear, we already have an impression of the risks of the encounter, as an impression that is felt on the surface of the skin. This knowledge is bodily, certainly: the child might not need time to think before she runs for it. But the 'immediacy' of the reaction is not itself a sign of a lack of mediation. It is not that the bear *is* fearsome, 'on its own', as it were. It is fearsome *to* someone or somebody. So fear is not in the child, let alone in the bear, but is a matter of how child and bear come into contact. This contact is shaped by past histories of contact, unavailable in the present, which allow the bear to be apprehended as fearsome. The story does not, despite this, inevitably lead to the same ending. Another child, another bear, and we might even have another story.

It is not just that we might have an impression of bears, but 'this bear' also makes an impression, and leaves an impression. Fear shapes the surfaces of bodies in relation to objects. Emotions are relational: they involve (re)actions or relations of 'towardness' or 'awayness' in relation to such objects. The bear becomes the object in both senses: we have a contact with an object, and an orientation towards that object. To be more specific, the 'aboutness' of fear involves a reading of contact: the child reads the contact as dangerous, which involves apprehending the bear as fearsome. We can note also that the 'reading' then identifies the bear as the cause of the feeling. The child becomes fearful, and the bear becomes fearsome: the attribution of feeling to an object (I feel afraid because you are fearsome) is an effect of the encounter, which moves the subject away from the object. Emotions involve such affective forms of reorientation.

Of course, if we change the bear to a horse, we might even get to the father.[12] If the object of feeling both shapes and is shaped by emotions, then the object of feeling is never simply before the subject. How the object impresses (upon) us may depend on histories that remain alive insofar as they have already left their impressions. The object may stand in for other objects, or may be proximate to other objects. Feelings may stick to some objects, and slide over others.[13] In this book, I offer an analysis of affective economies, where feelings do not reside in subjects or objects, but are produced as effects of circulation (see Chapter 2). The circulation of objects allows us to think about the 'sociality' of emotion.

INSIDE OUT AND OUTSIDE IN

What do I mean by the sociality of emotion? Before I can answer this question, we must firstly register what might seem too obvious: the everyday language of emotion is based on the presumption of interiority. If I was thinking about emotions, I would probably assume that I need to look inwards, asking myself, 'How do I feel?' Such a model of emotion as interiority is crucial to psychology. Indeed, the emergence of psychology as a discipline had significant consequences for theories of emotion: by becoming an 'object lesson' for psychology, emotions have been psychologised (White 1993: 29). In a psychological model, I have feelings, and they are mine. As K. T. Strongman states, 'Above all, emotion is centred internally, in subjective feelings' (Strongman 2003: 3). I may express my feelings: I may laugh, cry, or shake my head. Once what is inside has got out, when I have expressed my feelings in this way, then my feelings also become yours, and you may respond to them.[14] If you sympathise, then we might have 'fellow-feeling' (Denzin 1984: 148). If you don't understand, we might feel alienated from each other

(Scheff 1994: 3).[15] The logic here is that I have feelings, which *then* move outwards towards objects and others, and which might then return to me. I will call this the 'inside out' model of emotions.

In critiquing this model, I am joining sociologists and anthropologists who have argued that emotions should not be regarded as psychological states, but as social and cultural practices (Lutz and Abu-Lughod 1990; White 1993: 29; Rosaldo 1984: 138, 141; Hochschild 1983: 5; Kemper 1978: 1; Katz 1999:2; Williams 2001: 73; Collins 1990: 27). I want to offer a model of sociality of emotion, which is distinct from this literature, as well as informed by it. Take Durkheim's classic account of emotions. He argues in *The Rules of Sociological Method* that sociology is about recognising constraint: 'Most of our ideas and our tendencies are not developed by ourselves but come to us from without. How can they become a part of us except by imposing themselves upon us?' (Durkheim 1966: 4). Here, the sociological realm is defined as the imposition of 'the without' on the individual subject. This demarcation of 'the sociological' becomes a theory of emotion as a social form, rather than individual self-expression. Durkheim considers the rise of emotion in crowds, suggesting that such 'great movements' of feeling, 'do not originate in any one of the particular individual consciousnesses' (Durkheim 1966: 4). Here, the individual is no longer the origin of feeling; feeling itself comes from without. Durkheim's later work on religion suggests that such feelings do not remain 'without'. As he notes: 'This force must also penetrate us and organise itself within us; it thus becomes an integral part of our being and by that very fact this is elevated and magnified' (Durkheim 1976: 209). For Durkheim, then, emotion is not what comes from the individual body, but is what holds or binds the social body together (Collins 1990: 27).

This argument about the sociality of emotions takes a similar form to the psychological one, though with an obvious change of direction. The 'inside out' model has become an 'outside in' model. Both assume the objectivity of the very distinction between inside and outside, the individual and the social, and the 'me' and the 'we'. Rather than emotions being understood as coming from within and moving outwards, emotions are assumed to *come from without and move inward*. An 'outside in' model is also evident in approaches to 'crowd psychology', where it is assumed that the crowd *has* feelings, and that the individual gets drawn into the crowd by feeling the crowd's feelings as its own. As Graham Little puts it: 'Emotions run the other way, too: sometimes starting "out there" – and Diana's death is a prime example of this – but linking up with something in us so that we feel drawn in and become personally involved' (Little 1999: 4). The example of Diana's death is useful. An outside in model might suggest that feelings of grief existed in the crowd, and only then got taken on by individuals, a reading which has led to accusations that such grief was inauthentic, a sign of being 'taken in'.[16]

Indeed the 'outside in' model is problematic precisely because it assumes that emotions are something that 'we have'. The crowd becomes like the individual, the one who 'has feelings'. Feelings become a form of social presence rather than self-presence. In my model of sociality of emotions, I suggest that emotions create the very effect of the surfaces and boundaries that allow us to distinguish an inside and an outside in the first place. So emotions are not simply something 'I' or 'we' have. Rather, it is through emotions, or how we respond to objects and others, that surfaces or boundaries are made: the 'I' and the 'we' are shaped by, and even take the shape of, contact with others. To return to my argument in the previous section, the surfaces of bodies 'surface' as an effect of the impressions left by others. I will show how the surfaces of collective as well as individual bodies take shape through such impressions. In suggesting that emotions create the very effect of an inside and an outside, I am not then simply claiming that emotions are psychological *and* social, individual *and* collective. My model refuses the abbreviation of the 'and'. Rather, I suggest that emotions are crucial to the very constitution of the psychic and the social as objects, a process which suggests that the 'objectivity' of the psychic and social is an effect rather than a cause.

In other words, emotions are not 'in' either the individual or the social, but produce the very surfaces and boundaries that allow the individual and the social to be delineated as if they are objects. My analysis will show how emotions create the very surfaces and boundaries that allow all kinds of objects to be delineated. The objects of emotion take shape as effects of circulation. In suggesting emotions circulate, I am not offering a model of emotion as contagion (see Izard 1977: 106). The model of emotional contagion, which is often influenced by Silvan S. Tomkins' work, is useful in its emphasis on how emotions are not simply located in the individual, but move between bodies.[17] After all, the word 'contagion' derives from the Latin for 'contact'. In this model, it is the emotion itself that passes: I feel sad, because you feel sad; I am ashamed by your shame, and so on. In suggesting that emotions pass in this way, the model of 'emotional contagion' risks transforming emotion into a property, as something that one has, and can then pass on, as if what passes on is the same thing. We might note that the risk is not only a theoretical one. I have experienced numerous social occasions where I assumed other people were feeling what I was feeling, and that the feeling was, as it were, 'in the room', only to find out that others had felt quite differently. I would describe such spaces as 'intense'. Shared feelings are at stake, and seem to surround us, like a thickness in the air, or an atmosphere. But these feelings not only *heighten tension*, they are also *in tension*. Emotions in their very intensity involve miscommunication, such that even when we feel we have the same feeling, we don't necessarily have the same relationship to the feeling. Given that shared feelings are not about feeling the same feeling, or feeling-in-common, I suggest that it is the objects of emotion that circulate, rather than emotion as such. My argument still explores how emotions can move through the movement or circulation of objects. Such objects become sticky, or saturated with affect, as sites of personal and social tension.

Emotions are after all moving, even if they do not simply move between us. We should note that the word 'emotion' comes from the Latin, *emovere*, referring to 'to move, to move out'. Of course, emotions are not only about movement, they are also about attachments or about what connects us to this or that. The relationship between movement and attachment is instructive. What moves us, what makes us feel, is also that which holds us in place, or gives us a dwelling place. Hence movement does not cut the body off from the 'where' of its inhabitance, but connects bodies to other bodies: attachment takes place through movement, through being moved by the proximity of others. Movement may affect different others differently: indeed, as I will suggest throughout this book, emotions may involve 'being moved' for some precisely by fixing others as 'having' certain characteristics. The circulation of objects of emotion involves the transformation of others into objects of feeling.

My argument about the circulation of objects draws on psychoanalysis and Marxism (see Chapter 2). I consider, for example, that the subject does not always know how she feels: the subject is not self-present and emotions are an effect of this splitting of experience (Terada 2001: 30). From Freud onwards, this lack of self-presence is articulated as 'the unconscious'. Working with Freudian psychoanalysis, I will show how objects get displaced, and consider the role of repression in what makes objects 'sticky'. But I also suggest that the lack of presence does not always return to the subject, or to the 'scene' of trauma (castration), upon which much psychoanalytic theory rests. Drawing on Marx, I argue that emotions accumulate over time, as a form of affective value. Objects only seem to have such value, by an erasure of these histories, as histories of production and labour. But whilst Marx suggests that emotions are erased by the value of things (the suffering of the worker's body is not visible in commodity form), I focus on how emotions are produced.[18] It is not so much emotions that are erased, as if they were already there, but the processes of production or the 'making' of emotions. In other words, 'feelings' become 'fetishes', qualities that seem to reside in objects, only through an erasure of the history of their production and circulation.

Holding together these different theoretical traditions is a challenge.[19] There is no glue, perhaps other than a concern for 'what sticks'. Indeed, the question, 'What sticks?', is one that is posed throughout this study. It is a reposing of other, perhaps more familiar, questions: Why is social transformation so difficult to achieve? Why are relations of power so intractable and enduring, even in the face of collective forms of resistance? This book attempts to answer such questions partially by offering an account of how we become invested in social norms. The work to which I am most indebted is the work of feminist and queer scholars who have attended to how emotions can attach us to the very conditions of our subordination (Butler 1997b; Berlant 1997; Brown 1995). Such scholars have shown us how social forms (such as the family, heterosexuality, the nation, even civilisation itself) are effects of repetition. As Judith Butler suggests, it is through the repetition of norms that worlds materialise, and that 'boundary, fixity and surface' are produced (Butler 1993: 9). Such norms appear as forms of life only through the concealment of the work of this repetition. Feminist and queer scholars have shown us that emotions 'matter' for politics; emotions show us how power shapes the very surface of bodies as well as worlds. So in a way, we do 'feel our way'.

This analysis of how we 'feel our way' approaches emotion as a form of cultural politics or world making. My argument about the cultural politics of emotions is developed not only as a critique of the psychologising and privatisation of emotions,[20] but also as a critique of a model of social structure that neglects the emotional intensities, which allow such structures to be reified as forms of being. Attention to emotions allows us to address the question of how subjects become *invested* in particular structures such that their demise is felt as a kind of living death. We can see this investment at work in my opening quote: the nation becomes the object of love precisely by associating the proximity with others with loss, injury and theft (see also Chapter 6). The presence of non-white others is even associated by the British National Front with death: 'Britain is Dying: How long are you just going to watch?'[21] To become the 'you' addressed by the narrative is to feel rage against those who threaten not only to take the 'benefits' of the nation away, but also to destroy 'the nation', which would signal the end of life itself. Emotions provide a script, certainly: you become the 'you' if you accept the invitation to align yourself with the nation, and against those others who threaten to take the nation away.

THE EMOTIONALITY OF TEXTS

But there is still more. For a book on emotions, which argues that emotions cannot be separated from bodily sensations, this book may seem very orientated towards texts.[22] I offer close readings of texts, with a concern in particular with metonymy and metaphor: my argument will suggest that 'figures of speech' are crucial to the emotionality of texts. In particular, I examine how different 'figures' get stuck together, and how sticking is dependent on past histories of association that often 'work' through concealment. The emotionality of texts is one way of describing how texts are 'moving', or how they generate effects.

I will also consider the emotionality of texts in terms of the way in which texts name or perform different emotions. Naming emotions often involves differentiating between the subject and object of feeling. When we name an emotion we are not simply naming something that exists 'in here'. So a text may claim, 'the nation mourns'. We would pause here, of course, and suggest the 'inside out/outside in' model of emotion is at work: the nation becomes 'like the individual', a feeling subject, or a subject that 'has feelings'. But we would also need to ask: *What does it do to say the nation mourns?* This is a claim both that the nation has a feeling (the nation is the subject of feeling), but also that generates the nation as the object of 'our feeling' (we might mourn on behalf of the nation). The feeling does simply exist before the utterance, but becomes real as an effect, shaping different kinds of actions and orientations. To say, 'the nation mourns' is to generate the nation, *as if it were a mourning subject*. The 'nation' becomes a shared 'object of feeling' through the orientation that is taken towards it. As such, emotions are performative (see Chapter 4) and they involve speech acts (Chapter 5), which depend on past histories, at the same time as they generate effects.

When we talk about the displacement between objects of emotion, we also need to consider the circulation of words for emotion. For example, the word 'mourns' might get attached to some subjects (some bodies more than others represent the nation in mourning), and it might get attached to some objects (some losses more than others may count as losses for this nation). The word 'mourns' might get linked to other emotion words: anger, hatred, love. The replacement of one word for an emotion with another word produces a narrative. Our love might create the condition for our grief, our loss could become the condition for our hate, and so on (see Chapter 6). The emotion does its work by 'reading' the object: for example, others might get read as the 'reason' for the loss of the object of love, a reading which easily converts feelings of grief into feelings of hate (see Chapter 7).

So I am not discussing emotion as being 'in' texts, but as effects of the very naming of emotions,[23] which often works through attributions of causality. The different words for emotion do different things precisely because they involve specific orientations towards the objects that are identified as their cause. As such, my archive is full of words. But the words are not simply cut off from bodies, or other signs of life. I suggest that the work of emotion involves the 'sticking' of signs to bodies: for example, when others become 'hateful', then actions of 'hate' are directed against them (see Chapter 2). My archive is perhaps not 'an archive of feelings' to use Ann Cvetkovich's beautiful formulation. Cvetkovich's method involves 'an exploration of cultural texts as repositories of feelings and emotions' (2003b: 7). Feelings are not 'in' my archive in the same way. Rather, I am tracking how words for feeling, and objects of feeling, circulate and generate effects: how they move, stick, and slide. We move, stick and slide with them.

The texts that I read circulate in the public domain, and include web sites, government reports, political speeches and newspaper articles. Although the book involves close readings of such texts, it is not 'about' those texts. They do not simply appear as texts in my reading. Clearly, I have chosen these texts and not others. The texts evoke what we could call 'cases'. Three cases inform my choices of texts: reconciliation in Australia (Chapters 1 and 5 on pain and shame); responses to international terrorism (Chapters 3 and 4 on fear and disgust), and asylum and immigration in the UK (Chapters 2 and 6 on hate and love). Each of these cases shows us the very public nature of emotions, and the emotive nature of publics.[24] They are also cases in which I am involved, which matter to me, in my contact with the world.

To name one's archive is a perilous matter; it can suggest that these texts 'belong' together, and that the belonging is a mark of one's own presence. What I offer is a model of the archive not as the conversion of self into a textual gathering, but as a 'contact zone'. An archive is an effect of multiple forms of contact, including institutional forms of contact (with libraries, books, web sites), as well as everyday forms of contact (with friends, families, others). Some forms of contact are presented and authorised through writing (and listed in the references), whilst other forms of contact will be missing, will be erased, even though they may leave their trace. Some everyday forms of contact do appear in my writing: stories which might seem personal, and even about 'my feelings'. As a 'contact writing', or a writing about contact, I do not simply interweave the personal and the public, the individual and the social, but show the ways in which they take shape through each other, or even how they shape each other. So it is not that 'my feelings' are in the writing, even though my writing is littered with stories of how I am shaped by my contact with others.[25]

The book has a shape of its own, of course. It does not take shape around each of these cases, as if they could be transformed into objects, or moments in the progression of a narrative. I have instead taken different emotions as points of entry. Even though I am challenging the idea that there simply 'are' different emotions, 'in here', or 'out there', I also want to explore how naming emotions involves different orientations towards the objects they construct. In this sense, emotions may not have a referent, but naming an emotion has effects that we can describe as referential. So each chapter takes a different emotion as a starting point, or point of entry, and does not 'end' with the emotion, but with the work that it does.

The book begins with pain, which is usually described as a bodily sensation. I begin here in order to show how even feelings that are immediate, and which may involve 'damage' on the skin surface, are not simply feelings that one has, but feelings that open bodies to others. My analysis introduces the concept of 'intensification' to show how pain creates the very impression of a bodily surface. I also consider how pain can shape worlds as bodies, through the ways in which stories of pain circulate in the public domain, with specific reference to the report on the stolen generation in Australia, *Bringing Them Home*. The second chapter turns to hate, exploring how feelings of injury get converted into hatred for others, who become read as causing 'our injury'. In examining this conversion, I consider how hate circulates through signs, introducing the concept of 'affective economies'. I show how hate works by sticking 'figures of hate' together, transforming them into a common threat, within discourses on asylum and migration. My analysis examines how hate crime works within law, and asks how the language of hate affects those who are designated as objects of hate.

The following four chapters work to refine and develop these concepts about emotions in embodiment and language, showing how fear, disgust, shame and love work as different kinds of orientations towards objects and others, which shape individual as well as collective bodies. In Chapter 3, I show how fear is attributed to the bodies of others, and how fear is intensified by the possibility that the object of fear may pass us by. My analysis examines the spatial politics of fear and the way fear restricts the mobility of some and extends the mobility of others. Responses to terrorism work as 'an economy of fear', in which the figure of the terrorist gets associated with some bodies (and not others), at the same time as the terrorist 'could be' anyone or everywhere. In Chapter 4, I analyse how disgust works to produce 'the disgusting', as the bodies that must be ejected from the community. Working with a model of disgust as stickiness, I suggest that disgust shapes the bodies of a community of the disgusted through how it sticks objects together. My analysis examines speech acts, which claim 'that's disgusting!' in response to September 11, exploring how cohesion (sticking together) demands adhesion (sticking to), but also how the object of disgust can get unstuck.

In Chapters 5 and 6 on shame and love, I show how objects of emotion not only circulate, but also get 'taken on' and 'taken in' as 'mine' or 'ours'. In Chapter 5, I examine how expressions of shame, in speech acts of 'apologising', can work as a form of nation building, in which what is shameful about the past is covered over by the statement of shame itself. Shame hence can construct a collective ideal even when it announces the failure of that ideal to be translated into action. With reference to reconciliation in Australia, and the demand that governments apologise for histories of slavery and colonialism, I also show how shame is deeply ambivalent: the exposure of past wounds can be a crucial part of what shame can do. In Chapter 6, I examine how love can construct a national ideal, which others fail. By considering how multiculturalism can work as an imperative to love difference, I show that love can work to elevate the national subject insofar as it posits the other's narcissism as the cause of injury and disturbance. Love is conditional, and the conditions of love differentiate between those who can inhabit the nation, from those who cause disturbance. In both these chapters, I examine how the objects of emotions can be 'ideals', and the way in which bodies, including bodies of nations, can take shape through how they approximate such ideals.

The final two chapters ask how emotions can work within queer and feminist politics, as a reorientation of our relation to social ideals, and the norms they elevate into social aspirations. Different feelings seem to flow through these chapters: discomfort, grief, pleasure, anger, wonder, and hope. The focus on attachments as crucial to queer and feminist politics is itself a sign that transformation is not about transcendence: emotions are 'sticky', and even when we challenge our investments, we might get stuck. There is hope, of course, as things can get unstuck.

This book focuses on emotions. But that does not make emotions the centre of everything. Emotions don't make the world go round. But they do in some sense go round. Perhaps, unlike the saying, what goes round does not always come round. Focusing on emotions is what will allow me to track the uneven effects of this failure of return.

NOTES

1. The poster was downloaded from the following web site:
   http://members.odinsrage.com/nfne/nf_bogus_asylum_nfne.a6.pdf The British National Front web site can be found on: http://www.nf.co.uk Accessed 30 September 2003.
2. See http://www.nfne.co.uk/intro.html Accessed 21 February 2004.
3. In *Strange Encounters* (2000), I offer an approach to 'othering' by examining how others are recognised as strangers, as 'bodies out of place', through economies of vision and touch. I will be building on this argument in *The Cultural Politics of Emotion*, by focusing on how relations of othering work through emotions; for example, othering takes place through the attribution of feelings to others, or by transforming others into objects of feeling. In making such claims, I am drawing on a long history of Black and critical race scholarship, which contests the model of race as a bodily attribute, by examining discourses of racialisation in terms of othering (hooks 1989; Lorde 1984; Said 1978; Fanon 1986; Bhabha 1994).
4. We might assume that in government rhetoric in the UK, the nation is not imagined as being white in the way that it is in the British National Front, especially given the

official endorsement of a policy of multiculturalism. The differences between fascism and neo-liberalism should be acknowledged, but we should not assume the difference is absolute. As I will argue in Chapter 6, the nation is still constructed as 'being white' in multiculturalism, precisely as whiteness is reimagined as the imperative to love difference ('hybrid whiteness').

5. It also follows that we should not look for emotions only where the attribution of 'being emotional' is made. What is posited as 'unemotional' also involves emotions, as ways of responding to objects and others. I will not be equating emotionality with femininity. See Campbell (1994) for an important critique of how women are 'dismissed' through being seen or 'judged' as being emotional.

6. I can direct you to the following texts, which I found useful. For an interdisciplinary collection on emotions see Lewis and Haviland (1993). For an interdisciplinary approach to emotions see Lupton (1998). For a review of psychological approaches, see Strongman (2003). For sociological collections on emotions, see Kemper (1990) and Bendelow and Williams (1998). For an anthropological approach to emotions see Lutz (1988). For a philosophical collection see Solomon (2003). And for a historical approach to emotions, see Reddy (2001).

7. The analysis in this paragraph simplifies the debate for the purpose of argument. I should acknowledge that the meaning of each of the crucial terms – sensation, emotion, affect, cognition and perception – is disputed both between disciplines and within disciplines.

8. Solomon argues that emotions are caused (as reactions), but that objects of emotion must be distinguished from the cause (Solomon 2003: 228). I am making a different claim, which is made possible by my distinction of 'contact' from the attribution of causality: the object with which I have contact is the object that I have a feeling 'about'. *The 'aboutness' involves a reading of the contact.*

9. This is a 'primal scene' in the psychology of emotions (for a recent review of this literature see Strongman 2003). The fact that the subject of the story is a child is crucial; the figure of the child does important work. 'The child' occupies the place of the 'not-yet subject', as the one whose emotions might allow us to differentiate between what is learnt and what is innate. The investment in the child's 'innocence' is vital to this primal scene. See Castañeda (2002) for an excellent reading of how the figure of 'the child' is produced within theory.

10. My critique of the 'Dumb View' of emotions, which follows from the work of Alison Jaggar (1996) and Elizabeth V. Spelman (1989) is also a critique of the assumption that emotions are innate or biological. I have avoided positioning myself in the debate between biological determinism and cultural or social constructionism, as the posing of the debate along these terms had delimited the field by creating false oppositions (aligning the biological with what is fixed, universal and given, and the cultural with what is temporary, relative and constructed). I would argue that emotions involve the materialisation of bodies, and hence show the instability of 'the biological' and 'the cultural' as ways of understanding the body. See Wilson (1999) for an interesting account of the importance of the biological to understanding emotions. Whilst I offer a different approach, which does not identify 'the biological' or 'the cultural' as separate spheres, I support her emphasis on the importance of the bodily dimensions of emotions, which she elaborates through a careful reading of Freud's model of the role of somatic compliance in hysteria.

11. To this extent, functionalist approaches would share my preference for the question, 'What do emotions do?', rather than 'What are emotions?' (Strongman 2003: 21–37). In

such approaches, which consider emotions in terms of their physiological effects, the function of fear may be flight, and with it, the survival of the individual organism, and the survival of the species. In my account, however, the 'doing' of emotions is not reducible to individual actions (though it involves action) and is not governed by the logic of reproduction of the human.

12. In Freud's reading of the little Hans case, the fear of the horse is read as a displacement of the fear of the father (see Chapter 3).

13. It may be useful to compare my approach on the relation between emotions and objects to Tomkins' (1963) theory of affect. As others have commented, Tomkins' attention to affect as opposed to drive emphasises the 'freedom' of emotion from specific objects (Izard 1977: 52; Sedgwick 2003: 19). I am also suggesting that emotions are 'free' to the extent that they do not reside within an object, nor are they caused by an object. But the language of 'freedom' is not one I will use in this book. I will argue instead that the association between objects and emotions is contingent (it involves contact), but that these associations are 'sticky'. Emotions are shaped by contact with objects. The circulation of objects is not described as freedom, but in terms of sticking, blockages and constraints.

14. My critique of the 'inside out' model is also an implicit critique of the expressive model of emotions, which assumes that emotional expressions comprise the externalisation of an internal feeling state, which is distinct and given (see Zajonc 1994: 4–5).

15. Both Denzin and Scheff are writing about emotions as social and not psychological forms. Despite this, both use an 'inside out' model. The former suggests emotions are 'self-feelings' (Denzin 1984: 50–1), even though others are required to experience the feeling. Scheff has a very problematic account of the sociality of emotions. He describes emotions in terms of the social bond, and suggests pride involves a 'secure bond' and shame a 'damaged bond'. He uses war and divorce as examples of alienation (see Chapter 5, and the conclusion to this book, which critique this idealisation of the social bond). Scheff's model not only idealises the social bond, but also creates a model of 'the social' premised on a liberal model of the self, as 'being whole', or 'at one with itself'.

16. The critique of the inauthenticity of grief for Diana was clear in public commentary around her death as Graham Little (1996) shows in his analysis of public emotions. As he argues, such critiques are also by implication critiques of femininity and hysteria, in which women in particular are seen as having been 'taken in'. It is important to note here that 'the crowd' is itself an unstable object: early work on crowds considers the crowd as a mob, which is physically co-present 'on the street'. More recent work considers 'the crowd' not necessarily as a physical mass, but as the perception of a mass, which is affected by the media, and other technologies of connection, which allow 'feelings with', without physical proximity. For a summary of debates in crowd psychology, see Blackman and Walkerdine 2002.

17. See Gibbs (2001) for an excellent example of the use of 'emotional contagion' to understand political affect.

18. In his early writings, Marx describes 'man's feeling' as 'truly ontological affirmations of his essence' (Marx 1975: 375). In this view, alienation is a form of estrangement: the transformation of labour into an object (the objectification of labour) hence effects an estrangement from the material realm of feelings. See Cvetkovich (1992) for a reading of Marx and emotion.

19. The challenge is also to work across or between disciplines, many of which now claim emotions as a sub-discipline. It is a rather frightening task. Doing interdisciplinary

work on emotions means accepting that we will fail to do justice to all of the intellectual histories drawn upon by the texts we read. It means accepting the possibility of error, or simply getting some things wrong. For me, this is a necessary risk; emotions do not correspond to disciplinary objects (the social, cultural, historical and so on), and tracking the work of emotions means crossing disciplinary boundaries.

20. Emotions are also relegated to the private sphere, which conceals their public dimension and their role in ordering social life. For an excellent analysis of the publicness of emotions see Berlant (1997).

21. 'Britain Suffers from Alien-Made Laws – the Flame', http//:www.nfne.co.uk/aleinlaws.html Accessed 12 January 2004.

22. It might be tempting to contrast this model of 'the emotionality of texts' with sociological, anthropological or psychological research, which involves interviewing people about their emotional lives. A good example of such work is Katz (1999). The difference between my research and interview based work is not that I am reading texts. It is important to state that interviewing people about emotions still involves texts: here, interviewees are prompted to talk before an interviewer ('the interview'), as a form of speech that is translated or 'transcribed' into a written text; the researcher then becomes the reader of the text, and the writer of another text about the text. The distinction between my research and interview based research on emotions is in the different nature of the texts generated; the texts I read are ones that already exist 'out there' in the public, rather than being generated by the research itself. My own view is that research on emotions should embrace the multiple ways emotions work, whether in public culture or everyday life, and this means working with a range of different materials, which we can describe in different ways (as texts, data, information). We need to avoid assuming that emotions are 'in' the materials we assemble (which would transform emotion into a property), but think more about what the materials are 'doing', how they work through emotions to generate effects.

23. Importantly, words that name a specific emotion do not have to be used for texts to be readable in terms of that emotion. The 'publicness' of emotions means that we learn to recognise their signs, which can include actions, gestures, intonation. So my opening quote did not have to name its rage: the physicality of how the statement 'rejects' the presence of others, and names that presence as injury, is a performance of rage. In particular, Chapter 4 on disgust explores how words can involve forms of action, by showing how statements of disgust are physical acts of recoiling from alien bodies.

24. But just as I argue that we shouldn't look for emotions in soft bodies, I would also suggest we shouldn't assume emotional publics are a particular kind of public; emotional publics are not only publics that display emotions in ways that we recognise as emotional. So, for instance, it is not that publics become emotional when politicians cry or 'express their feelings'. Publics organised around the values of thought or reason, or indeed of 'hardness' or detachment, also involve emotional orientations towards objects and others.

25. Thanks to Mimi Sheller for encouraging me to think again about the personal nature of archive.

CHAPTER 1

The Contingency of Pain

Landmines. What does this word mean to you? Darkened by the horrific injuries and countless fatalities associated with it, it probably makes you feel angry or saddened. *I'm sure you will be interested in the success stories that your regular support has helped to bring about . . . Landmines.* Landmines are causing pain and suffering all around the world, and that is why Christian Aid is working with partners across the globe to remove them . . . *Landmines.* What does this word mean to you now? I hope you feel a sense of empowerment. (Christian Aid Letter 9 June 2003)[1]

How does pain enter politics? How are lived experiences of pain shaped by contact with others? Pain has often been described as a private, even lonely experience, as a feeling that I have that others cannot have, or as a feeling that others have that I myself cannot feel (Kotarba 1983: 15). And yet the pain of others is continually evoked in public discourse, as that which demands a collective as well as individual response. In the quote above from a Christian Aid letter, the pain of others is first presented through the use of the word 'landmines'. The word is not accompanied by a description or history; it is assumed that the word itself is enough to evoke images of pain and suffering for the reader.[2] Indeed, the word is repeated in the letter, and is transformed from 'sign' to the 'agent' behind the injuries: 'Landmines are causing pain and suffering all around the world.' Of course, this utterance speaks a certain truth. And yet, to make landmines the 'cause' of pain and suffering is to stop too soon in a chain of events: landmines are themselves effects of histories of war; they were placed by humans to injure and maim other humans. The word evokes that history, but it also stands for it, as a history of war, suffering and injustice. Such a letter shows us how the language of pain operates through signs, which convey histories that involve injuries to bodies, at the same time as they conceal the presence or 'work' of other bodies.

The letter is addressed to 'friends' of Christian Aid, those who have already made donations to the charity. It focuses on the emotions of the reader who is interpellated as 'you', as the one who 'probably' has certain feelings about the suffering and pain of others. So 'you' probably feel 'angry' or 'saddened'. The reader is presumed to be moved by the injuries of others, and it is this movement that enables them to give. To this extent, the letter is not about the other, but about the reader: the reader's feelings are the ones that are addressed, which are the 'subject' of the letter. The 'anger' and 'sadness' the reader should feel when faced with the other's pain is what allows the reader to enter into a relationship with the other, premised on generosity rather than indifference. The negative emotions of anger and sadness are evoked as the reader's: the pain of others becomes 'ours', an appropriation that transforms and perhaps even neutralises their pain into our sadness. It is not so much that we are 'with them' by feeling sad; the apparently shared negative feelings do not position the reader and victim in a relation of equivalence, or what Elizabeth V. Spelman calls co-suffering (Spelman 1997: 65). Rather, we feel sad *about* their suffering, an 'aboutness' that ensures that they remain the object of 'our feeling'. So, at one level, the reader in accepting the imperative to feel sad about the other's pain is aligned with the other. But the alignment works by differentiating between the reader and the others: their feelings remain the object of 'my feelings', while my feelings only ever approximate the form of theirs.

It is instructive that the narrative of the letter is hopeful. The letter certainly promises a lot. What is promised is not so much the overcoming of the pain of others, but the empowerment of the reader: 'I hope you feel a sense of empowerment.' The pain of the other is overcome, but it is not the object of hope in the narrative; rather, the overcoming of the pain is instead a means by which the reader is empowered. So the reader, whom we can name inadequately as the 'Western subject', feels better after hearing about individual stories of success, narrated as the overcoming of pain as well as the healing of community. These stories are about the lives of individuals that have been saved: 'Chamreun is a survivor of a landmine explosion and, having lost his leg, is all the more determined to make his community a safer place in which to live.' These stories of bravery, of the overcoming of pain, are indeed moving. But interestingly the agent in the stories is not the other, but the charity, aligned here with the reader: through 'your regular support', you have 'helped to bring about' these success stories. Hence the narrative of the letter ends with the reader's 'empowerment'. The word 'landmines', it is suggested, now makes 'you' feel a sense of empowerment, rather than anger or sadness.

This letter and the charitable discourses of compassion more broadly show us that stories of pain involve complex relations of power. As Elizabeth V. Spelman notes in *Fruits of Sorrow*, 'Compassion, like other forms of caring, may also reinforce the very patterns of economic and political subordination responsible for such suffering' (Spelman 1997: 7). In the letter, the reader is empowered through a detour into anger and sadness about the pain of others. The reader is also elevated into a position of power over others: the subject who gives to the other is the one who is 'behind' the possibility of overcoming pain. The over-representation of the pain of others is significant in that it fixes the other as the one who 'has' pain, and who can overcome that pain only when the Western subject feels moved enough to give. In this letter, generosity becomes a form of individual and possibly even national character; something 'I' or 'we' have, which is shown in how we are moved by others. The transformation of generosity into a character trait involves fetishism: it forgets the gifts made by others (see Diprose 2002), as well as prior relations of debt accrued over time. In this case, the West gives to others only insofar as it is forgotten what the West has already taken in its very *capacity* to give in the first place. In the Christian Aid letter, feelings of pain and suffering, which are in part effects of socio-economic relations of violence and poverty, are assumed to be alleviated by the very generosity that is enabled by such socio-economic relations. So the West takes, then gives, *and in the moment of giving repeats as well as conceals the taking*.

But is the story 'about' pain, whether in the form of 'our sadness' or the other's suffering? My reading of this letter has involved reading *claims* to pain as well as sadness and suffering. But what does it mean to be *in* pain or indeed to *have* it? It is difficult to talk about the experience of pain. As Elaine Scarry suggests in her powerful book, *The Body in Pain*, pain is not only a bodily trauma, it also resists or even 'shatters' language and communication (Scarry 1985: 5). So that which seems most self-evident – most there, throbbing in its thereness – also slips away, refuses to be simply present in speech, or forms of testimonial address. And yet, as we have seen, claims to pain and suffering on behalf of myself or others are repeated in forms of speech and writing. There is a connection between the over-representation of pain and its unrepresentability. So, for example, I may not be able to describe 'adequately' the feelings of pain, and yet I may evoke my pain, again and again, as something that I have. Indeed, I may repeat the words 'pain' or 'hurts' precisely given the difficulty of translating the feeling into descriptive language. The vocabularies that are available for describing pain, either through medical language that codifies pain (see Burns, Busby and Sawchuk 1999: xii) or through metaphor that creates relations of likeness (see Scarry 1985), seem inadequate in the face of the feeling.

What claims of pain are doing must be linked in some way to what pain does to bodies that experience pain. Rather than assuming that pain is unrepresentable, this chapter explores how the labour of pain and the language of pain work in specific and determined ways to affect differences between bodies. I will return to the question of how pain enters politics after reflecting on the lived experiences of pain.

PAIN SURFACES

We could begin by asking: What is pain? What does it mean to be in pain? Pain is usually described as a sensation or feeling (Cowan 1968: 15). But it is of course a particular kind of sensation. The International Association for the Study of Pain has adopted the following definition:

(a) pain is subjective; (b) pain is more complex than an elementary sensory event; (c) the experience of pain involves associations between elements of sensory experience and an aversive feeling state; and (d) the attribution of meaning to the unpleasant sensory events is an intrinsic part of the experience of pain. (Chapman 1986: 153)

This definition stresses how pain, as an unpleasant or negative sensation, is not simply reducible to sensation: how we experience pain involves the attribution of meaning through experience, as well as associations between different kinds of negative or aversive feelings. So pain is not simply the feeling that corresponds to bodily damage. Whilst pain might seem self-evident – we all know our own pain, it burns through us – the experience and indeed recognition of pain *as pain* involves complex forms of association between sensations and other kinds of 'feeling states'.

In medical discourse, it is taken for granted that there is not a simple relationship or correspondence between an external stimulus and the sensation of pain (leading to the development, for example, of the gateway theory of pain) (see Melzack and Wall 1996). Pain is not only treated as symptomatic of disease or injury: for instance, chronic pain is treated as a medical condition with its own history (Kotarba 1983). There are many instances when the relationship between the intensity of pain and the severity of injury is not proportional (Melzack and Wall 1996: 1). In the classic medical textbook on pain, *The Challenge of Pain*, Melzack and Wall suggest that pain:

is not simply a function of the amount of bodily damage alone. Rather, the amount and quality of pain we feel are also determined by our previous experiences and how well we remember them, by our ability to understand the cause of the pain and to grasp its consequences. (Melzack and Wall 1996: 15)

If pain is not simply an effect of damage to the body, then how can we understand pain?

Rather than considering how the feeling of pain is determined (by, for example, previous experiences), we can consider instead what the feeling of pain *does*. The affectivity of pain is crucial to the forming of the body as both a material and lived entity. In *The Ego and the Id*, Freud suggests that the ego is 'first and foremost a bodily ego' (Freud 1964b: 26). Crucially, the formation of the bodily ego is bound up with the surface: 'It is not merely a surface entity, but is itself the projection of a surface' (Freud 1964b: 26). Freud suggests that the process of establishing the surface depends on the experience of bodily sensations such as pain. Pain is described as an '*external and internal perception*, which behaves like an internal perception even when its source is in the external world' (Freud 1964b: 22, emphasis added). It is through sensual experiences such as pain that we come to have a sense of our skin as bodily surface (see Prosser 1998: 43), as something that keeps us apart from others, and as something that 'mediates' the relationship between internal or external, or inside and outside.

However, it is not that pain *causes* the forming of the surface. Such a reading would ontologise pain (and indeed sensation more broadly) as that which 'drives' being itself.[3] Rather, it is through the flow of sensations and feelings that *become* conscious as pain and pleasure that different surfaces are established. For example, say I stub my toe on the table. The impression of the table is one of negation; it leaves its trace on the surface of my skin and I respond with the appropriate 'ouch' and move away, swearing. It is through such painful encounters between this body and other objects, including other bodies, that 'surfaces' are felt as 'being there' in the first place. To be more precise *the impression of a surface is an effect of such intensifications of feeling*. I become aware of my body as having a surface only in the event of feeling discomfort (prickly sensations, cramps) that become transformed into pain through an act of reading and recognition ('it hurts!'), which is also a judgement ('it is bad!'). The recognition of a sensation as being painful (from 'it hurts' to 'it is bad' to 'move away') also involves the reconstitution of bodily space, as the reorientation of the bodily relation to that which gets attributed as the cause of the pain. In this instance, having 'felt' the surface as hurtful, I move my toe away from its proximity to the surface of the table. I move away from what I feel is the cause of the pain, and it feels like I am moving away from the pain.

Such an argument suggests an intimate relationship between what Judith Butler has called 'materialisation' – 'the effect of boundary, fixity and surface' (Butler 1993: 9) – and what I would call *intensification*. It is through the intensification of pain sensations that bodies and worlds materialise and take shape, or that the effect of boundary, surface and fixity is produced. To say that feelings are crucial to the forming of surfaces and borders is to suggest that what 'makes' those borders also unmakes them. In other words, what separates us from others also connects us to others. This paradox is clear if we think of the skin surface itself, as that which appears to contain us, but as where others *impress* upon us. This contradictory function of skin begins to make sense if we unlearn the assumption that the skin is simply already there, and begin to think of the skin as a surface that is felt only in the event of being 'impressed upon' in the encounters we have with others. As Rose-lyne Rey puts it: 'Through his [sic] skin – the boundary between the self and the world . . . every human being is subject to a multitude of impressions' (Rey 1995: 5).

This surfacing of bodies involves the over-determination of sense perception, emotion and judgement. It is through the recognition or inter-pretation of sensations, which are responses to the impressions of objects and others, that bodily surfaces take shape. I am not saying here that emo-tions are the same thing as sensations, but that the very intensity of percep-tion often means a slide from one to another, as a slide that does follow as a sequence in time. Hence whilst sensation and emotion are irreducible, they cannot simply be separated at the level of lived experience.[4] Sensations are mediated, however immediately they seem to impress upon us. Not only do we read such feelings, but how the feelings feel in the first place may be tied to a past history of readings, in the sense that the process of *recognition* (of this feeling, or that feeling) is bound up with what we *already know*. For example, the sensation of pain is deeply affected by memories: one can feel pain when reminded of past trauma by an encounter with another. Or if one has a pain one might search one's memories for whether one has had it before, differentiating the strange from the familiar. Indeed, even before I begin my search, the sensation may impress upon me in a certain way, bypassing my consciousness. Only later will I realise that the hurt 'hurts' *because* of this or that. Even though pain is described by many as non-intentional, as not 'about' something, it is affected by objects of percep-tion that gather as one's past bodily experience. Indeed, Lucy Bending suggests that although pain may not be about something, it is still 'because something', and this 'because' involves acts of attribution, explanation and narration, which function as the object of pain (Bending 2000: 86). It is not just that we interpret our pain as a sign of something, but that how pain feels in the first place is an effect of past impressions, which are often hidden from view. The very words we then use to tell the story of our pain also work to reshape our bodies, creating new impressions. The slide between sensations of pain and other kinds of 'negative feeling states' is bound up with the work that pain is doing in creating the very surfaces of bodies.

It may seem counter-intuitive to say that pain is crucial to the formation of the body as a perceiving surface. For example, don't I already have a sense of where my body is *before* I feel it as 'being hurt'? Isn't that knowledge necessary to the very ability to feel that pain *as* a pain in different parts of the body? How else would it be possible for me to say, 'I have pain in my toe'? Of course, in some ways I do already have a sense of my body surface. After all, life experience involves multiple collisions with objects and others. It is through such collisions that I form a sense of myself as (more or less) apart from others, as well as a sense of the surfaces of my body. Such a sense of apartness may be crucial for bodily survival (for those who lack the ability to feel pain-like sensations, the world is very dangerous),[5] though it may be felt differently by different bodies. So I do have a sense of myself as body, before I encounter an object. But what is crucial is that although I have a sense of my body before each new encounter, my body seems to *disappear from view*; it is often forgotten as I concentrate on this or on that.

This process is described beautifully by Drew Leder in *The Absent Body*. He suggests that 'the body is "absent" only because it is perpetually outside itself, caught up in a multitude of involvements with other people' (Leder 1990: 4). And so, experiences of dysfunction (such as pain) become lived as a return to the body, or a rendering present to consciousness of what has become absent: 'Insofar as the body tends to disappear when functioning unproblematically, it often seizes our attention most strongly at times of dysfunction' (Leder 1990: 4). The intensity of feelings like pain recalls us to our body surfaces: pain seizes me back to my body. Leder also suggests that pain can often lead to a body that *turns in on itself*, while pleasure tends to open up bodies to other bodies (Leder 1990: 74–5; see also Chapter 7). Indeed, bodies in pain might come to our attention in this very process of turning in; their 'forming' is a 'reforming'. Bodily surfaces become reformed not only in instances when we might move away from objects that cause injury, but also in the process of *moving towards the body and seeking to move away from the pain*. In my experiences of period pain,[6] for example, I feel a dull throbbing that makes me curl up. I try and become as small as possible. I hug myself. I turn this way and that. The pain presses against me. My body takes a different shape as it tries to move away from the pain, even though what is being moved away from is felt within my body.

However, I would not use the terms 'absent' and 'present' to describe embodiment as Leder does, as it implies the possibility that bodies *can* simply appear or disappear. Rather, I would point to the economic nature of intensification, and suggest that one is more or less aware of bodily surfaces depending on the range and intensities of bodily experiences. The intensity of pain sensations makes us aware of our bodily surfaces, and points to the *dynamic nature of surfacing itself* (turning in, turning away, moving towards, moving away). Such intensity may impress upon the surfaces of bodies through negation: the surface is felt when something is felt 'against' it. As Elaine Scarry suggests, the experience of pain is often felt as negation: something from outside presses upon me, even gets inside me (Scarry 1985: 15). When there is no external object, we construct imaginary objects or weapons to take up their empty place: we might use expressions like 'I feel like I have been stabbed by a knife' (Scarry 1985: 55). It is this perceived intrusion of something other within the body that creates the desire to re-establish the border, to push out the pain, or the (imagined, material) object we feel is the 'cause' of the pain. Pain involves the violation or transgression of the border between inside and outside, and it is through this transgression that I feel the border in the first place.

In the example of period pain discussed above, I also create an imagined object. The pain is too familiar – I have felt it so many times before. I remember each time, anew. So I know it is my period, and the knowledge affects how it feels: it affects the pain. In this instance, the blood becomes the 'object' that pushes against me, which presses against me, and that I imagine myself to be pushing out, as if it were an alien within. I want the pain to leave me; it is not a part of me, even though it is in my body that I feel it. So pain can be felt as something 'not me' within 'me': *it is the impression of the 'not' that is at stake*. It is hence not incidental that the sensation of pain is often represented – both visually and in narrative – through 'the wound' (a bruised or cut skin surface). The wound functions as a trace of where the surface of another entity (however imaginary) has impressed upon the body, an impression that is felt and seen as the violence of negation.

It is these moments of intensification that define the contours of the ordinary surfaces of bodily dwelling, surfaces that are marked by differences in the very experience of intensities.[7] As pain sensations demand that I *attend* to my embodied existence, then I come to inhabit the surfaces of the world in a particular way. The tingles, pricks and then cramps return me to my body by giving me a sense of the edge or border, a 'sense' that is an experience of intensification and a departure from what is lived as ordinary. The ordinary is linked in this way to the absence of perception, rather than the absence of the body (see Chapter 8). As Elizabeth Grosz puts it, in the case of pain: 'The effected zones of the body become enlarged and magnified in the body image' (Grosz 1994: 76). Such enlarged sensations of the limits of our bodies may also involve an impression of the *particularity* of how they occupy time and space. In other words, I become aware of bodily limits *as* my bodily dwelling or dwelling place when I am in pain. Pain is hence bound up with how we inhabit the world, how we live in relationship to the surfaces, bodies and objects that make up our dwelling places. Our question becomes not so much what *is* pain, but what *does* pain do.

Notably, Jean-Paul Sartre describes pain as 'a contingent attachment to the world' (Sartre 1996: 333). For Sartre, the lived experience of pain as 'being there' is dependent on what bodies are doing (reading, writing, sleeping, walking) on *how they might be arranged*. Or, in my terms, pain sensations might rearrange bodies, which huddle or shudder into different shapes, shapes that take shape here or there, in this place or that. So the experience of pain does not cut off the body in the present, but attaches this body to the world of other bodies, an attachment that is contingent on elements that are absent in the lived experience of pain.

The contingency of pain is linked both to its dependence on other elements, and also to touch. The word 'contingency' has the same root in Latin as the word 'contact' (Latin: *contingere: com*, with; *tangere*, to touch). Contingency is linked in this way to the sociality of being 'with' others, of getting close enough to touch. But we must remember that not all attachments are loving. We are touched differently by different others (see Ahmed 2000: 44–50) and these differences involve not just marks on the body, but different intensities of pleasure and pain. So what attaches us, what *connects us* to this place or that place, to this other or that other is also what we find most touching; it is that which makes us feel. The differentiation between attachments allows us to align ourselves with some others and against other others in the very processes of turning and being turned, or moving towards and away from those we feel have caused our pleasure and pain.

For example, to be touched in a certain way, or to be moved in a certain way by an encounter with another, may involve a reading not only of the encounter, *but of the other that is encountered as having certain characteristics*. If we feel another hurts us, then that feeling may convert quickly into a reading of the other, such that *it* becomes hurtful, or is read as *the impression of the negative*. In other words, the 'it hurts' becomes, 'you hurt me', which might become, 'you are hurtful', or even 'you are bad'. These affective responses are readings that not only create the borders between selves and others, but also 'give' others meaning and value in the very act of apparent separation, a giving that temporarily fixes an other, through the movement engendered by the affective response itself. Such responses are clearly mediated: materialisation takes place through the 'mediation' of affect, which may function in this way as readings of the bodies of others.[8]

THE SOCIALITY OF PAIN

Such a model of pain as contingent, as that which attaches us to others through the very process of intensification, might seem counter-intuitive. As I pointed out in the opening of this chapter, pain is often represented within

Western culture as a lonely thing (Kleinman, Das and Lock 1997: xiii). For example, Kotarba describes how pain experience is 'inherently private and remains unnoticed by others unless actively disclosed by the sufferer' (Kotarba 1983: 15). But even when the experience of pain is described as private, that privacy is linked to the experience of being with others. In other words, it is the apparent loneliness of pain that requires it to be disclosed to a witness. Melzack and Wall suggest that: 'Because pain is a private, personal experience, it is impossible for us to know precisely what someone else's pain feels like' (Melzack and Wall 1996: 41). We can see that the impossibility of inhabiting the other's body creates a desire to know 'what it feels like'. To turn this around, it is because no one can know what it feels like to have my pain that I want loved others to acknowledge how I feel. The solitariness of pain is intimately tied up with its implication in relationship to others.

So while the experience of pain may be solitary, it is never private. A truly private pain would be one ended by a suicide without a note. But even then one seeks a witness, though a witness who arrives after the anticipated event of one's own death. Perhaps the over-investment in the loneliness of pain comes from the presumption that it is always 'my' pain that we are talking about – a presumption that is clear, for example, in the phenomenological and existential writings on pain (Merleau-Ponty 1962; Sartre 1996). But we can ask Wittgenstein's (1964) question: What about the pain of others? Or, how am I affected by pain when I am faced by another's pain? Because we don't inhabit her body, does that mean that her pain has nothing to do with us? For me, these are personal questions. I would say that my main experiences of living with pain relate to living with my mother's pain. My mother was diagnosed with multiple sclerosis just after I was born. I was sent away to Pakistan and they thought she was dying. I lived in Pakistan for over a year (there are pictures of me with grandparents I now struggle to recall), while my mother pulled through. She lived, she lives on. In fact, decades later they realised they had got it wrong and they changed her diagnosis to transverse myelitis. It meant that her illness isn't degenerative. But it doesn't mean an end to her pain. And the change in diagnosis gave her a different kind of pain.

You might note that I said 'living with' my mother's pain. You might question this. It is my mother who has pain. She has to live with it. Yet, the experience of living with my mother was an experiencing of living with her pain, as pain was such a significant part of her life. I would look at her and see her pain. I was the witness towards whom her pleas would be addressed, although her pleas would not simply be a call for action (sometimes there would be nothing for me to do). Her pleas would sometimes just be for me to bear witness, to recognise her pain. Through such witnessing, I would grant her pain the status of an event, a happening in the world, rather than just the 'something' she felt, the 'something' that would come and go with her coming and going. Through witnessing, I would give her pain a life outside the fragile borders of her vulnerable and much loved body. But her pain, despite being the event that drew us together (the quiet nights in watching classical movies; it was a life together that hummed with sentimentality), was still shrouded in mystery. I lived with what was, for me, the unliveable.

Pain, which is often experienced as 'already there', is difficult to grasp and to speak about, whether in the event of talking about pain in the past or pain in the present. When we talk of the experience of pain we assume it is 'my pain' because I cannot feel the other's pain. I may experience my pain as too present and the other's as too absent. And yet, others are in pain; I *read* her body as a sign of pain. I see you grimace, or your face, white and drawn. I watch sadly as your body curls up, curls away. I want to reach you, to touch you. Love is often conveyed by wanting to feel the loved one's pain, to feel the pain on her behalf (see Chapter 6 for an analysis of love). I want to have her pain so she can be released from it, so she doesn't have to feel it. This is love as empathy: I love you, and imagine not only that I can feel how you feel, but that I could feel your pain *for you*. But I want that feeling only insofar as I don't already have it; the desire maintains the difference between the one who would 'become' in pain, and another who already 'is' in pain or 'has' it. In this way empathy sustains the very difference that it may seek to overcome: empathy remains a 'wish feeling', in which subjects 'feel' something other than what another feels in the very moment of imagining they could feel what another feels.[9]

The impossibility of feeling the pain of others does not mean that the pain is simply theirs, or that their pain has nothing to do with me. I want to suggest here, cautiously, and tentatively, that an ethics of responding to pain involves being open to being affected by that which one cannot know or feel. Such an ethics is, in this sense, bound up with the sociality or the 'contingent attachment' of pain itself. Much of the thinking on pain, however, contrasts the ungraspability of the other's pain with the graspability of my own pain. Elaine Scarry makes this contrast in her analysis of pain and torture (1985: 4). Certainly, there is something ungraspable about the other's pain, and this is not just because I do not feel it. But my pain, even when I feel it, is not always so graspable. So in some sense, as I respond to this other's pain, as I touch her cheek, I come to feel that which I cannot know. It is the ungraspability of her pain, in the face of the thereness of my own, that throws me into disbelief. But it is not her pain that I disbelieve. I believe in it, more and more. I am captured by the intensity of this belief. Rather it is my pain that becomes uncertain. I realise that my pain – it seems so there – is unliveable to others, thrown as they are into a different bodily world. The ungraspability of her pain calls me back to my body, even when it is not in pain, to feel it, to explore its surfaces, to inhabit it. In other words, the ungraspability of my own pain is brought to the surface by the ungraspability of the pain of others. Such a response to her pain is not simply a return to the self (how do I feel given that I don't know how she feels?): this is not a radical egoism. Rather, in the face of the otherness of my own pain, I am undone, before her, and for her.

The sociality of pain – the 'contingent attachment' of being with others – requires an ethics, an ethics that begins with your pain, and moves towards you, getting close enough to touch you, perhaps even close enough to feel the sweat that may be the trace of your pain on the surface of your body. Insofar as an ethics of pain begins here, with how you come to surface, then the ethical demand is that I must act about that which I cannot know, rather than act insofar as I know. I am moved by what does not belong to me. If I acted on her behalf only insofar as I knew how she felt, then I would act only insofar as I would appropriate her pain as my pain, that is, appropriate that which I cannot feel. To return to my introduction to this chapter, it is the very assumption that we know how the other feels, which would allow us to transform their pain into our sadness.

THE POLITICS OF PAIN

Pain involves the sociality of bodily surfaces (including the surfaces of objects) that 'surface' in relationship to each other. Some of these encounters involve moments of collision. Here, the surface comes to be felt as an intense 'impression' of objects and others. Not all pain involves injuries of this sort. Even in instances of pain that is lived without an external injury (such as psychic pain), pain 'surfaces' in relationship to others, who bear witness to pain, and authenticate its existence.

But to talk about the lived experiences of pain in such general terms may seem problematic. Isn't there a danger of 'flattening' out the differences in pain experience, or turning the sociality of pain into a new form of universalism? In this section, I want to talk about the politics of pain: how pain is involved in the production of *uneven* effects, in the sense that pain does not produce a homogeneous group of bodies who are together in their pain. A political model of pain cannot gather together all the different pain experiences (this is my point). In the first instance, I want to restrict my model of pain to its association with 'injury' and thereby link what you might consider rather banal experiences of injury from an external object, with experiences of feeling injured by others.

How does pain enter politics? Does pain become political only through speech, or through claims for compensation? Pain has been considered by some as a very problematic 'foundation' for politics. Working with Nietzsche's model of *resentiment*, for example, Wendy Brown argues that there has been a fetishisation of the wound in subaltern politics (Brown 1995: 55, see Nietzsche 1969). Subaltern subjects become invested in the wound, such that the wound comes to stand for identity itself. The political claims become claims of injury against something or somebody (society, the state, the middle classes, men, white people and so on) as a reaction or negation (Brown 1995: 73). Following Nietzsche, Brown suggests that reactions to injury are inadequate as a basis of politics since such reactions make action impossible: 'Revenge as a "reaction", a substitute for the capacity to act, produces identity as both bound to the history that produced it and as a reproach to the present which embodies that history' (Brown 1995: 73).[10] Brown's reworking of Nietzsche shows how an over-investment in the wound, 'come[s] into conflict with the need to give up these investments' (Brown 1995: 73).

I agree that the transformation of the wound into an identity is problematic. One of the reasons that it is problematic is precisely because of its fetishism: the transformation of the wound into an identity cuts the wound off from a history of 'getting hurt' or injured. It turns the wound into something that simply 'is' rather than something that has happened in time and space. The fetishisation of the wound as a sign of identity is crucial to 'testimonial culture' (Ahmed and Stacey 2001), in which narratives of pain and injury have proliferated. Sensational stories can turn pain into a form of media spectacle, in which the pain of others produces laughter and enjoyment, rather than sadness or anger. Furthermore, narratives of collective suffering increasingly have a global dimension. As Kleinman, Das and Lock argue, 'Collective suffering is also a core component of the global political economy. There is a market for suffering: victimhood is commodified' (Kleinman, Das and Lock 1997: xi). This commodification of suffering does not mean that all narratives have value or even equal value: as I show in Chapters 6 and 7, following Judith Butler (2002b), some forms of suffering more than others will be repeated, as they can more easily be appropriated as 'our loss'. The differentiation between forms of pain and suffering in stories that are told, and between those that are told and those that are not, is a crucial mechanism for the distribution of power.

We can reflect critically on the culture of compensation, where all forms of injury are assumed to involve relations of innocence and guilt, and where it is assumed that responsibility for all injuries can be attributed to an individual or collective. The legal domain transforms pain into a condition that can be quantified as the basis for compensation claims. The problem of wound fetishism is the equivalence it assumes between forms of injury. The production of equivalence allows injury to become an entitlement, which is then equally available to all others. It is no accident then that the normative subject is often secured through narratives of injury: the white male subject, for example, has become an injured party in national discourses (see Chapter 2), as the one who has been 'hurt' by the opening up of the nation to others. Given that subjects have an unequal relation to entitlement, then more privileged subjects will have a greater recourse to narratives of injury. That is, the more access subjects have to public resources, the more access they may have to the capacity to mobilise narratives of injury within the public domain.

How should we respond to this transformation of injury into an entitlement that secures such forms of privilege? I would suggest that our response should not simply be to critique the rhetorical use of injury or wounds, but to attend to the different ways in which 'wounds' enter politics. Not all narratives of pain and injury work as forms of entitlement; so for example, to read the story of white male injury as the same as stories of subaltern injury would be an unjust reading. Whilst we cannot assume that such differences are essential, or determined 'only' by the subject's relation to power, we also cannot treat differences as incidental, and as separated from relations of power. The critique of wound culture should not operate as generalised critique, which would mean 'reading' different testimonies as symptomatic. As Carl Gutiérrez-Jones argues, the critique of injury needs to recognise the different rhetorical forms of injury as signs of an uneven and antagonistic history (Gutiérrez-Jones 2001: 35).

So a good response to Brown's critique would not be to forget the wound or indeed the past as the scene of wounding. Brown does 'part company' with Nietzsche by suggesting that 'the counsel of forgetting . . . seems inappropriate if not cruel' for subjugated peoples who have yet to have their pain recognised (Brown 1995: 74). I would put this more strongly: forgetting would be a repetition of the violence or injury. To forget would be to repeat the forgetting that is already implicated in the fetishisation of the wound. Our task might instead be to remember how the surfaces of bodies (including the bodies of communities, as I will suggest later) came to be wounded in the first place. Reading testimonies of injury involves rethinking the relation between the present and the past: an emphasis on the past does not necessarily mean a conservation or entrenchment of the past (see Chapter 8).[11] Following bell hooks, our task would be 'not to forget the past but to break its hold' (hooks 1989: 155). In order to break the seal of the past, in order to move away from attachments that are hurtful, we must first bring them into the realm of political action. Bringing pain into politics requires we give up the fetish of the wound through different kinds of remembrance. The past is living rather than dead; the past lives in the very wounds that remain open in the present.

In other words, harm has a history, even though that history is made up of a combination of often surprising elements that are unavailable in the form of a totality. Pain is not simply an effect of a history of harm; it is the *bodily life of that history*. To think through how pain may operate in this way we can consider the document, *Bringing Them Home*, which is a report of the National Inquiry into the Separation of Aboriginal and Torres Strait Islander Children from their Families (1996). *Bringing Them Home* reports on the Stolen Generation in Australia, a generation of indigenous children who were taken away from their families as part of a brutal and shocking policy of assimilation. Generations of indigenous children grew up with little or no contact with their families, or with their community and culture. They were often taken from their homes in a violent manner.

When considering the damage to the bodies of indigenous Australians, we can think about not just the individual's skin surface, but the skin of the community. The violence was not simply inflicted upon the body of the individual who was taken away, but also on the body of the indigenous community, which was 'torn apart'. Here, the community is damaged insofar as 'attachments' with loved ones are severed. As Kai Erikson suggests, collective trauma involves 'a blow to the basic tissues of social life that damages the bonds attaching people together' (Erikson 1995: 187). The skin of the community is damaged, but it is a damage that is felt on the skin of the individuals who make up that community. *Bringing Them Home* is made up of individual testimonies of this pain of separation, this hurt, this bereavement, and this loss from which recovery is so difficult. The testimonies were gathered together, and together form the document.

Such stories of pain must be heard. But what are the conditions of possibility for hearing them? Within the context of Australian politics, the compiling of this document does not necessarily mean that the stories of pain are heard. Or, if they are being heard, it does not mean that they are being heard justly. *Bringing Them Home* is concerned with a process of healing, in which the 'wound' caused by the invasion of Australia and tragedies of the Stolen Generation is healed: 'That devastation cannot be addressed unless the whole community listens with an open heart and mind to the stories of what has happened in the past and, having listened and understood, commits itself to reconciliation.'[12] The document emphasises the importance of recovering rather than forgetting the traumas of the past, which are defined as both 'personal' and 'national'.

Importantly, the testimonies given by indigenous men and women are introduced by the document as demanding national shame rather than personal guilt:

> That is not to say that individual Australians who had no part in
> what was done in the past should feel or acknowledge personal guilt.
> It is simply to assert our identity as a nation and the basic fact that

national shame, as well as national pride, can and should exist in
relation to past acts and omissions. (Governor-General of Australia,
Bringing Them Home, 1996)

The question of who is doing the healing and who is being healed is a troubling one. The preface suggests that the response to the pain of indigenous
Australians should be the shame of the white nation, which is, paradoxically,
not made up of white individuals. The burden of the document falls
unequally: indigenous Australians tell their personal stories, but white
readers are allowed to disappear from this history, having no part in what was
done. Reconciliation becomes, in this narrative, the reconciliation of indigenous individuals into the white nation, which is now cleansed through its
expression of shame (see also Chapter 5). As Fiona Nicoll (1998) has argued,
reconciliation has a double meaning. It can suggest coming to terms with,
but it can also refer to passivity, in which one seeks to make the other passive
(to reconcile her to her fate). In Australian politics, the narrative of reconciliation – and with it, of hearing the other's pain – is too often bound up
with making indigenous others fit into the white nation or community.

In the expression of emotional responses to the stories, the non-
indigenous hearings of indigenous testimonies can involve forms of appropriation. The recognition of the wound of the stolen generation provides, in
the terms of the document, 'our identity as a nation'. The acknowledgement
of their pain hence slides easily into the claiming of national pain. In this way,
the healing of wounds is represented as the healing of the nation: the covering over of the wound caused by the theft of indigenous Australians allows
the nation to become one body, sealed by its skin. In such forms of responding to pain, the national body takes the place of the indigenous bodies; it
claims their pain as its own. As I have already argued, to hear the other's pain
as my pain, and to empathise with the other in order to heal the body (in this
case, the body of the nation), involves violence. But our response to how the
other's pain is appropriated as the nation's pain, and the wound is fetishised
as the broken skin of the nation, should not be to forget the other's pain. Our
task instead is *to learn how to hear what is impossible*. Such an impossible
hearing is only possible if we respond to a pain that we cannot claim as our
own. Non-indigenous readers do need to take it personally (we are part of this
history), but in such a way that the testimony is not taken away from others,
as if it were about our feelings, or our ability to feel the feelings of others.

So I read through the document. Admittedly, it hurts to read the words,
they move on me and move me. The stories, so many of them, are stories of
grief, of worlds being torn apart. So cruel, this world. It is a world that I
lived in. I remind myself of that. Yet I also lived in a very different world.
Each story brings me into its world. I am jolted into it. I try and turn away,

but you hold my attention. These are stories of separation and loss. These are stories of pain. My response is emotional: it is one of discomfort, rage and disbelief. The stories hit me, hurtle towards me: unbelievable, too believable, unliveable and yet lived.

Knowing that I am part of this history makes me feel a certain way; it impresses upon me, and creates an impression. Of course, these impressions are not only personal. It is not just me facing this, and it is certainly not about me. And yet, I am 'in it', which means I am not 'not in it'. Here I am, already placed and located in worlds, already shaped by my proximity to some bodies and not others. If I am here, then I am there: the stories of the document are shaped by the land I had been taught to think of as my own. The 'knowledge' of this history as a form of *involvement* is not an easy or obvious knowledge. Such knowledge cannot be 'taken in' – it cannot be registered as knowledge – without feeling differently about those histories, and without inhabiting the surfaces of bodies and worlds differently. I cannot learn this history – which means unlearning the forgetting of this history – and remain the same. Knowing one's implication in this history is about accepting the violence as a form of 'un-housing'. The house in which I grew up, and to which I am attached through memory, is on indigenous land. To 'feel' differently about this land, as belonging to others, is not about generosity; it is not premised on giving up one's home, but on recognising that where one lived was not one's home to give or to give up in the first place (see Ahmed 2000: 190). The reading cannot then be about my feelings: to be affected by the story as a form of 'un-housing' is to be affected by that which cannot be 'taken' or 'taken back' as 'mine'.

The testimonies of pain that gather in the form of the document involve more than one story: many stories, placed alongside each other, weave the document together. Each story is readable, as the story of this other, a singular other, as a singularity that is irreducible to 'the one'. This other is touched by other others, and other stories of pain and suffering. So one story, I will read with you, but I will not read this story *as* one. It is Fiona's story.[13] That is all I have to start with, your first name. I say it out, quietly, softly. Fiona. I say it again, even more gently, Fiona. You start with a date: '*1936 it was. I would have been five.*' You draw me into a past, into a time and space I have not inhabited before. You say *would have been* not *was*. This wording makes your past seem open. Would have been. *What would you have been if you hadn't been taken away?* The question shocks me. The past is no longer past, but the theft of a different kind of future. What would you have been? I move uneasily. I cannot help but read on: '*We had been playing all together, just a happy community and the air was filled with screams because the police came and mothers tried to hide their children and blacken their children's faces and tried to hide them in caves.*' The event unfolds before me. I close my eyes. It becomes a scene. But the desperation of the mothers who are about to lose their children cuts through the scene and obscures it. I blink. I cannot see this before me. As I close my eyes, I come to hear. Sounds, screams. My ears tremble with the force of hearing those screams. Hearing the screams makes me shudder. The sounds of Fiona being taken away. The cries of Fiona's mother. She is addressed as such by the poetics of this testimony:

> *My mother had to come with us . . . I remember that she came in the truck with us curled up in the foetal position. We can understand that, the trauma of knowing that you're going to lose all your children? We talk about it from the point of view of our trauma but – our mother – to understand what she went through, I don't think anyone can really understand that.*

Already, in telling the story of her mother, the daughter tells of a pain she cannot understand; she cannot write the story from the point of view of the mother's trauma. Even the daughter cannot be with her. There is a gulf that cannot be overcome by empathy, even by somebody in the story, connected by a bond of love; even by the daughter whose pain is also part of the story, whose pain throbs the story into its difficult life. The impossibility of communicating this loss is echoed in the life of these bodies, curled as they are into their different bodily worlds, shuddering with the intensity of a pain that surfaces as loss: *'curled up in the foetal position'*. Bodies, kept apart, moving away from each other, from the reader: *'We got there in the dark and then we didn't see our mother again. She just kind of disappeared into the darkness.'* The pain of this mother's disappearance takes the shape of a darkness that overwhelms. The darkness is the edge of the story, signalling what the reader cannot see and feel.

The daughter's story, Fiona's story, is one of a body being reformed, being made into another body. She surfaces differently, made white as another form of violence: *'From there we had to learn to eat new food, have our heads shaved.'* It is a story of violence, in which the body is turned into an instrument. Words can only tell the story in a way that confirms the violence: *'You forbad us to speak our own language.'* But it is not an embittered story. Indeed, the others who committed this violence – the missionaries, the state – on the body of the community and on Fiona's body are treated with a care that is a torture to read: *'You hear lots and lots of the criticisms of the missionaries but we only learnt from being brought up by missionaries. They took some of that grief away in teaching us another way to overcome the grief and the hurt and the pain and the suffering.'* Faced with this, my anger unfolds and refolds before you. I want to hear your rage; I want you to allow me to be angry with them. They did this. They did this. I want you to say it. But no 'them' appears to allow me the safety of such projection. You refuse to blame those whom I feel caused your injury. And yet, in that refusal, you do not express the language of forgiveness. Rather, you just say that those who were responsible, and they are evoked in such terms, were responsible for more than the experience of pain, but also for your ability to move away from it, to allow it to be taken from you, in the way you were taken from them. My anger at this story, at the possibility of this story, does not find an object; it cannot be contained by an external object. In not having a 'them' to blame in the story, my anger seeps outwards, towards all that makes the story possible.

To those who were responsible for your pain, you can express only a certain kind of attachment. This does not replace your grief, nor does it resolve it. You don't forget the hurt. But they do not become the other against which you define yourself. They become part of the body you now inhabit – the different body, the different community made up of bodies that are with other bodies, and with them in a certain way. Even though this body confirms the loss of 'what would have been', it is a body which speaks to your survival. But your mother is not with you in this body. Your survival is afforded in the pain and violence of this loss. The injury surfaces in the forming of a different kind of body. The scars on your skin both attach you to a past of loss and a future of survival. This is not a healing. But you've moved on.

And so, throughout, it is your mother's loss that you address; it is her loss that keeps open the wound of being taken away:

> I guess the government didn't mean it as something bad but our mothers weren't treated as people having feelings. Naturally a mother's got a heart for her children and for them to be taken away, no-one can ever know the heartache. She was still grieving when I met her in 1968.

The mother's feelings. They are announced from the perspective of the daughter who is now a mother herself. They are the feelings that were negated by those who committed the injustice; they are the feelings that made that injustice so unjust. And yet still, before her mother, Fiona recognises the limits of her own feelings and the impossibility of feeling the feelings of others: 'no-one can ever know the heartache'. The mother's pain is here evoked as unfeelable both for those who are with her, and for those who read the story. We can't feel her pain, her ache; and yet, we are moved by the story. It is a hurt that refuses to keep us apart, but also does not bring us together. I know enough of this pain to know the limits of what I can know, reading as I am in this time and this place, with this body, arranged as it is, here, now. And then: 'All the years that you wanted to ask this and ask that, there was no way we could ever regain that. It was like somebody came and stabbed me with a *knife.'* The experience of pain – the feeling of being stabbed by a foreign object that pierces the skin, that cuts you into pieces – is bound up with what cannot be recovered, with something being taken away that cannot be returned. The loss is, in some sense, the loss of a 'we', the loss of a community based on everyday conversations, on the coming and goings of bodies, in time and in space: *'every morning as the sun came up the whole family would wail'*. Out of the cutting of this body and this community, surfaces a different body, formed as it is by the intensity of the pain. A community that cries together, which *comes together in this gesture of loss*, and which comes together in the painful feeling that togetherness is lost. The language of pain aligns this body with other bodies; the surface of the community comes to be inhabited differently in the event of being touched by such loss.

The testimonies of pain by indigenous Australians work not as appeals to sympathy; they give flesh to feelings that cannot be felt by others. The stories of pain that cover these pages are stories of separation, of losses that cannot be undone. In Fiona's testimony, the pain takes the form of the separation of mothers from daughters, daughters from mothers. The pain of such women is not evoked or sentimentalised as the true burden of community, but moves the story on, as a sign of the persistence of a connection, a thread between others, in the face of separation. The connection is not made as a form of fellow-feeling, and it is not about feeling the other's pain. Pain is evoked as that which even our most intimate others cannot feel. The impossibility of 'fellow feeling' is itself the confirmation of injury. The call of such pain, as a pain that cannot be shared through empathy, is a call not just for an attentive hearing, but for a different kind of inhabitance. It is a call for action, and a demand for collective politics, as a politics based not on the possibility that we might be reconciled, but on learning to live with the impossibility of reconciliation, or learning that we live with and beside each other, and yet we are not as one.

NOTES

1. Thanks to Sarah Franklin who brought this letter to my attention.
2. In due course I will examine how words have associations that do not need to be made explicit as key to the emotionality of language. I will consider such words as 'sticky signs' in Chapters 2, 3 and 4.
3. In fact, psychoanalysis offers a radical critique of the model in which pain and pleasure become individual and social 'drivers'. We can identify this model as utilitarian. Take Bentham's classic formulation: 'Nature has placed mankind under the governance of two sovereign masters, pain and pleasure. It is for them alone to point out what we ought to do, as well as to determine what we shall do' (cited in McGill 1967: 122). My emphasis on sensation as crucial to the surfacing of bodies is not about making pain and pleasure 'sovereign masters'. I am suggesting that pain and pleasure cannot be

separated from the attribution of value to objects, but that the value of objects is not determined by sensation. So whilst pain and pleasure may affect how bodies are orientated towards others, this does not mean we simply calculate pain and pleasure as if they were properties, as if they 'have', or even 'are' value.

4. I am hence departing from the recent tendency to separate sensation or affect and emotion, which is clear in the work of Massumi (2002). Certainly, the experience of 'having' an emotion may be distinct from sensations and impressions, which may burn the skin before any conscious moment of recognition. But this model creates a distinction between conscious recognition and 'direct' feeling, which itself negates how that which is not consciously experienced may itself be mediated by past experiences. I am suggesting here that even seemingly direct responses actually evoke past histories, and that this process bypasses consciousness, through bodily memories. Sensations may not be about conscious recognition and naming, but this does not mean they are 'direct' in the sense of immediate. Further, emotions clearly involve sensations: this analytic distinction between sensation or affect and emotion risks cutting emotions off from the lived experiences of being and having a body. Pain may be a very good example to challenge the distinction between sensation and emotion: it has regularly been described as both, or as a special category between sensation and emotion. See Trigg (1970) for an analysis of pain as both sensation and emotion and Rey for a critique of this distinction in models of pain (Rey 1995: 6).

5. People who do not experience the sensation of pain – who suffer from *congenital analgesia* – are prone to injuries, which can be serious, and indeed are often fatal (Melzack and Wall 1996: 3). This reminds us that some pain sensations can function as warnings as well as reactions that help bodies to navigate their way through the world.

6. Period pain is not a pain that has been written about within the context of existentialism or phenomenology, even by feminists working in these traditions. Yet many women suffer from period pain in a way that affects what they can do with their lives. It is important to write the lived experience of period pain into our theorising of embodiment. The discomfort we might feel in writing such pain into a philosophical body is like many discomforts: it is caused by not quite fitting the body (in this case, the philosophical body) we inhabit. See Chapter 7 for an analysis of discomfort.

7. Of course, with chronic pain, the intense sensation becomes not a departure from the ordinary (which defines the ordinary in the event of the departure), but the ordinary itself. As such, attending to the body surface becomes part of the structure of ordinary experience (see Kotarba 1983).

8. Given the emphasis here on the subject's perceptions and readings in the making of objects and others, is this a radical form of subjectivism? It is important for me to indicate how this argument is not subjectivist, but one that undermines the distinction between the subject and the object. I am suggesting that 'no thing' or 'no body' has positive characteristics, which exist *before contact with others*. So it is not that a subject 'gives' meaning and value to others. Rather, subjects as well as objects are shaped by contact. Such forms of contact do not make something out of nothing: subjects as well as objects 'accrue' characteristics over time (a process which shows precisely how these characteristics are not a positive form of residence) that makes it possible to speak of them as prior to contact. So my argument that the subject's perception and reading of objects and others is crucial does not necessarily exercise a radical form of subjectivism; it does not posit the subject's consciousness as that which makes the world. The subject materialises as an effect of contact with others and has already materialised given such histories of contact.

9. There are different forms of what Robert C. Solomon has called 'fellow-feeling' (1995, see also Denzin 1984: 148; Scheler 1954: 8–36). They include compassion, as well as empathy, sympathy and pity. These different forms cannot be equated. For example Spelman differentiates between compassion, as suffering *with* others, from pity, as sorrow *for* others (Spelman 1997: 65). All of these forms of fellow-feeling involve fantasy: one can 'feel for' or 'feel with' others, but this depends on how I 'imagine' the other already feels. So 'feeling with' or 'feeling for' does not mean a suspension of 'feeling about': *one feels with or for others only insofar as one feels 'about' their feelings in the first place.*

10. See Chapter 8 for a critique of the distinction between reaction and action.

11. Although Brown refuses to echo Nietzsche's call to forget, her conclusion is to replace the language of being ('I am') with the language of desire ('I want'). I suggest that we should also challenge Nietzsche's presumption that the future is open, and that the past – and the present – is what holds or binds the subject. We need to think about how the past remains open in the present, such that the story of the 'I am', or 'how did I come to be', is a story that also opens up the future of the subject. See also Chapter 8.

12. The report is available on the following web site: http://www.austlii.edu.au/au/special/rsjproject/rsjlibrary/hreoc/stolen/ Last accessed on 20 February 2004.

13. Confidential evidence, Case 305. My copy of the report does not have page numbers, but Fiona's testimony is the last one in Chapter 8 on South Australia.

CHAPTER 2

The Organisation of Hate

*The depths of Love are rooted and very deep in a real White
Nationalist's soul and spirit, no form of 'hate' could even begin to
compare. At least not a hate motivated by ungrounded reasoning. It is not
hate that makes the average White man look upon a mixed racial couple
with a scowl on his face and loathing in his hear [sic]. It is not hate that
makes the White housewife throw down the daily jewspaper in repulsion
and anger after reading of yet another child-molester or rapist sentenced
by corrupt courts to a couple short years in prison or on parole. It is not
hate that makes the White workingman curse about the latest boatload of
aliens dumped on our shores to be given job preference over the White
citizens who built this land. It is not hate that brings rage into the heart
of a White Christian farmer when he reads of billions loaned or given
away as 'aid' to foreigners when he can't get the smallest break from an
unmerciful government to save his failing farm. No, it is not hate. It is
Love.* (The Aryan Nations' Website)[1]

How do emotions such as hate work to secure collectives through the way in
which they read the bodies of others? How does hate work to align some subjects with some others and against other others? In this chapter, I consider
the role of hate in shaping bodies and worlds through the way hate generates its object as a defence against injury. We can see such defensive uses of
hate within fascist discourse. It is a common theme within so-called hate
groups to declare themselves as organisations of love on their web sites. This
apparent reversal (we do and say this because we love, not because we hate)
does an enormous amount of work as a form of justification and persuasion.
In the instance above, it is the imagined subject of both party and nation (the
White nationalist, the average White man, the White housewife, the White
workingman, the White Citizen and the White Christian farmer) who is

hated, and who is threatened and victimised by the law and polity. Hate is not simply present as the emotion that explains the story (it is not a question of hate being *at its root*), but as that which is affected by the story, and as that which enables the story to be affective.

Such narratives work by generating a subject that is endangered by imagined others whose proximity threatens not only to take something away from the subject (jobs, security, wealth), but to take the place of the subject. The presence of this other is imagined as a threat to the object of love. This narrative involves a rewriting of history, in which the labour of others (migrants, slaves) is concealed in a fantasy that it is the white subject who 'built this land'.[2] The white subjects claim the place of hosts ('our shores'), at the same time as they claim the position of the victim, as the ones who are damaged by an 'unmerciful government'. The narrative hence suggests that it is love for the nation that makes the white Aryans feel hate towards others who, in 'taking away' the nation, are taking away their history, as well as their future.

We might note that this emotional reading of others as hateful aligns the imagined subject with rights and the imagined nation with ground. This alignment is affected by the representation of the rights of the subject and the grounds of the nation as under threat, as 'failing'. *It is the emotional reading of hate that works to stick or to bind the imagined subjects and the white nation together.* The average white man feels 'fear and loathing'; the White housewife, 'repulsion and anger'; the White workingman 'curses'; the White Christian farmer, feels 'rage'. The passion of these negative attachments to others is redefined simultaneously as a positive attachment to the imagined subjects brought together through the capitalisation of the signifier, 'White'. It is the love of White, or those that are recognisable as White, which supposedly explains this shared 'communal' visceral response of hate. *Because we love, we hate, and this hate is what brings us together.*

This narrative, I would suggest, is far from extraordinary. Indeed, it reveals the production of the ordinary. The ordinary is here fantastic. The ordinary white subject is a fantasy that comes into being through the mobilisation of hate as a passionate attachment closely tied to love. The emotion of hate works to animate the ordinary subject, to bring that fantasy to life, precisely by constituting the ordinary as in crisis, and the ordinary person as the *real victim*. The ordinary becomes that which is *already* under threat by the imagined others whose proximity becomes a crime against person as well as place. As I discussed in the previous chapter, the ordinary or normative subject is reproduced as the injured party; the one that is 'hurt' or even damaged by the 'invasion' of others. The bodies of others are hence transformed into 'the hated' through a discourse of pain. They are assumed to 'cause' injury to the ordinary white subject such that their proximity is read as the origin of bad feeling. Indeed, it is implied that the white subject's good feelings (love) have been 'taken' away by the abuse of such feelings by others.

So who is hated in such a narrative of injury? Clearly, hate is *distributed* across various figures (in this case, the mixed racial couple, the child-molester, the rapist, aliens and foreigners). These figures come to embody the threat of loss: lost jobs, lost money, lost land. They signify the danger of impurity, or the mixing or taking of blood. They threaten to violate the pure bodies; such bodies can only be imagined as pure by the perpetual restaging of this fantasy of violation. Note the work that is being done through this metonymic slide: mixed race couplings and immigration become readable as (like) forms of rape or molestation; an invasion of the body of the nation, evoked here as the vulnerable and damaged bodies of the white woman and child. The slide between figures constructs a relation of resemblance between the figures. What makes them 'alike' may be their 'unlikeness' from 'us'. Within the narrative, hate cannot be found in one figure, but works to create the outline of different figures or objects of hate, a creation that crucially aligns the figures together, and constitutes them as a 'common threat'. Importantly, then, hate does not *reside* in a given subject or object. Hate is economic; it circulates between signifiers in relationships of difference and displacement. To understand such affective economies of hate, I will consider the way in which 'signs' of hate work, and their relation to bodies. My examples will refer specifically to racism as a politics of hatred, and will include an analysis of hate crime as a legal response to racism.

AFFECTIVE ECONOMIES

If hate involves a series of displacements that do not reside positively in a sign or figure, then hate does not originate within an individual psyche; it does not reside positively in consciousness. As such, hate operates at an unconscious level, or resists consciousness understood as plenitude, or what we might call 'positive residence'. My reliance on 'the unconscious' here signals my debt to psychoanalytical understandings of the subject. It is hence important that I clarify how my argument will exercise a concept of the unconscious. In his paper on the unconscious, Freud introduces the notion of unconscious emotions, whereby an affective impulse is perceived but misconstrued, and which becomes attached to another idea (Freud 1964a: 177). What is repressed from consciousness is not the feeling as such, but the idea to which the feeling may have been first (but provisionally) connected. Psychoanalysis allows us to show how emotions such as hate involve a process of movement or association, *whereby feelings take us across different levels of signification, not all of which can be admitted in the present*. This is what I call the 'rippling' effect of emotions; they move sideways (through 'sticky' associations between signs, figures and objects) as well as forwards and backwards (repression always leaves its trace in the present – hence 'what sticks' is bound up with the absent presence of historicity). In the Aryan Nations' quote, we can see how hate slides sideways between figures, as well as backwards, by reopening past associations, which allows some bodies to be read as being the cause of 'our hate'.

Indeed, insofar as psychoanalysis is a theory of the subject as lacking in the present, it offers a theory of emotion as economy, *as involving relationships of difference and displacement without positive value.* That is, emotions work as a form of capital: affect does not reside positively in the sign or commodity, but is produced as an effect of its circulation. I am using 'the economic' to suggest that objects of emotions circulate or are distributed across a social as well as psychic field, borrowing from the Marxian critique of the logic of capital. In *Capital*, Marx discusses how the movement of commodities and money, in the formula (M–C–M: money to commodity to money), creates surplus value. That is, through circulation and exchange 'M' acquires more value (Marx 1976: 248). Or, as he puts it: 'The value originally advanced, therefore, not only remains intact while in circulation, but increases its magnitude, adds to itself a surplus-value or is valorised. *And this movement converts it into capital*' (Marx 1976: 252, emphasis mine). I am identifying a similar logic: the movement between signs or objects converts into affect. Marx does link value with affect through the figures of the capitalist and the miser. He says: 'This boundless drive for enrichment, this passionate chase after value, is common to the capitalist and the miser' (Marx 1976: 254). Here passion drives the accumulation of capital: the capitalist is not interested in the use-value of commodities, but the 'appropriation of ever more wealth' (Marx 1976: 254). What I am offering is a theory of passion not as the drive to accumulate (whether it be value, power or meaning), but as that which is accumulated over time. Affect does not reside in an object or sign, but is an effect of the circulation between objects and signs (= the accumulation of affective value). Signs increase in affective value as an effect of the movement between signs: the more signs circulate, the more affective they become.

Of course, this argument does not respect the important Marxian distinction between use value and exchange value and hence relies on a limited analogy. In some ways, my approach has more in common with a psychoanalytic emphasis on difference and displacement as the form or language of the unconscious, described on page 44. Where my approach involves a departure from psychoanalysis is in my refusal to identify this economy as a psychic one (although neither is it *not* a psychic one), that is, to return these relationships of difference and displacement to the signifier of 'the subject'. This 'return' is not only clear in Freud's work, but also in Lacan's positing of 'the subject' as the proper scene of absence and loss (see Ahmed 1998: 97–8). In contrast, my model of hate as an affective economy suggests that emotions do not positively inhabit *anybody* or *anything*, meaning that 'the subject' is simply one nodal point in the economy, rather than its origin and destination. This is extremely important: it suggests that the sideways and backwards movement of emotions such as hate is not contained within the contours of a subject. The unconscious is hence not the unconscious of a subject, but the failure of presence – or the failure to be present – that constitutes the relationality of subject, objects, signs and others. Given this, affective economies are social and material, as well as psychic. Indeed, as I have shown, if the movement of affect is crucial to the very differentiation between 'in here' and 'out there', then the psychic and the social cannot be installed as proper objects. Instead, I examine how materialisation involves a process of intensification (see Chapter 1).

More specifically, it is the circulation of hate between figures that works to materialise the very 'surface' of collective bodies. We can take as an example the speeches on asylum seekers by one of the previous leaders of the Conservative Party in the UK, William Hague. Between April and June 2000, other speeches were in circulation that became 'stuck' or 'attached' to the asylum seekers speech partly through temporal proximity, but also through the repetition with a difference, of some *sticky words* and language. In the case of the asylum speeches, Hague's narrative is somewhat predictable. Words like 'flood' and 'swamped' are used, which create associations between asylum and the loss of control and hence work by mobilising fear, or the anxiety of being overwhelmed by the actual or potential proximity of others (see also Chapter 3). These words were repeated in 2003 by the current British Home Secretary David Blunkett, who used 'swamped' to describe the effect on others that children of asylum seekers would have if they were taught in local schools. When criticised, he replaced the word 'swamped' with 'overwhelmed'. The assumption here is that 'overwhelmed' resolves the implication of 'swamped', but as we can see, the word still evokes the sensation of being overtaken or taken over by others. The word constructs the nation as if it were a subject, as one who 'could not cope' with the presence of others. Such words generate effects: they create impressions of others as those who have invaded the space of the nation, threatening its existence.

In the earlier speech, Hague differentiates between those others who are welcome and those who are not by differentiating between genuine and bogus asylum seekers. Partly, this enables the national subject to imagine its generosity in welcoming some others. The nation is hospitable as it allows those genuine ones to stay. And yet at the same time, it constructs some others as already hateful (as bogus) in order to define the limits or the *conditions* of this hospitality (see also Chapter 6). The construction of the bogus asylum seeker as a figure of hate also involves a narrative of uncertainty and crisis, but an uncertainty and crisis that *makes that figure do more work*. How can we tell the difference between a bogus and a genuine asylum seeker? It is always possible that we may not be able to tell, and that the bogus may pass their way into our community. Such a possibility commands us (our right, our will) to keep looking, and justifies our intrusion into the bodies of others.

Indeed, the possibility that we may not be able to tell the difference swiftly converts into the possibility that *any* of those incoming bodies may be bogus. In advance of their arrival, they are read as the cause of an injury to the national body. The figure of the bogus asylum seeker evokes the figure of the 'bogey man', as a figure that stalks the nation and haunts its capacity to secure its borders. The 'bogey man' could be anywhere and anyone; a ghost-like figure in the present, who gives us nightmares about the future, as an anticipation of a future injury. We see 'him' again and again. Such figures of hate circulate, and indeed accumulate their affective value, precisely insofar as they do not have a fixed referent. So the figure of the bogus asylum seeker is detached from particular bodies: any incoming bodies *could be* bogus, such that their 'endless' arrival is anticipated as the scene of 'our injury'.[3] The impossibility of reducing hate to a particular body allows hate to circulate in an economic sense, working to differentiate some others from other others, a differentiation that is never 'over', as it awaits others who have not yet arrived. Such a discourse of 'waiting for the bogus' is what justifies the repetition of violence against the bodies of others in the name of protecting the nation.

Hague's speech also generated certain effects through its temporal proximity to another speech about Tony Martin, a man sentenced to life imprisonment for murdering a 16-year-old boy who had attempted, along with one other person, to burgle his house. One sentence of Hague's circulates powerfully. He stated following the sentencing of Martin (but without reference to the Martin case) that the law is 'more interested in the rights of criminals than the rights of people who are burgled'. *Such a sentence evokes a history that is not declared* (this is how attachment can operate as a form of speech, as resistance to literalisation). The undeclared history sticks, and it positions Martin as the victim rather than the criminal, as a person who was burgled, rather than a person who killed. The victim of the murder is now the criminal; the crime that did not happen because of the murder (the burglary) takes the place of the murder as the true crime, and as the real injustice.

The implicit argument that killing in defence of your home makes you a victim acquired more force when Tony Martin was released in August 2003. Tabloids described Tony Martin as an 'ordinary farmer' whose home was ruined during his prison sentence (McGurran and Johnston 2003: 4). The headline on the front page of the *Daily Mirror* sums it up: 'He killed to protect his house . . . but now the memories are too much' (*Daily Mirror*, 9 August 2003). The tragedy of the story is not the death of 'a teenage burglar' but Tony Martin's loss of his home: 'This isn't a home any more. It's a shell' (McGurran and Johnston 2003: 4). The 'shell', an empty and barren place, becomes a sign of the injustice of Martin's prison sentence. The moral of the story becomes: those who defend their property must be defended by the law. In other words, the reversal of the victim/criminal relationship is an implicit and unarticulated defence of the right to kill those who unlawfully enter one's property.

The coincidence of William Hague's words: 'The law is more interested in the rights of criminals than the rights of people who are burgled' in connection with asylum seekers was also affective. The detachment of that sentence allows the two cases to get stuck together, burglary and asylum, which now both become matters of the right to defence. More specifically, the figure of the asylum seeker is aligned with the figure of the burglar. The alignment does important work: it suggests that the asylum seeker is 'stealing' something from the nation. The characteristics of one figure get displaced or transferred onto the other. Or we could say that it is through the association between the figures that they acquire 'a life of their own', as if they contain an affective quality. The burglar becomes a foreigner, and the asylum seeker becomes a criminal. At the same time, the body of the murderer (who is renamed as the victim) becomes the body of the nation; the one whose property and well-being is under threat by the proximity of the other. The sticking together of these speeches produces the following claim: the nation, like Tony Martin, has the right to expel asylum seekers (whatever the means), who as burglars are trying to steal something from the nation, otherwise the nation itself will become 'the shell'. The moral of the story becomes: if we let them in, they will turn the nation 'into a shell', and take the land on which 'we have worked'.

Such a defensive narrative is not explicitly articulated, but rather works through the movement between figures. The circulation does its work: it produces a differentiation between 'us' and 'them', whereby 'they' are constituted as the cause of 'our' feeling of hate. Indeed, we can see how attachment involves a sliding between pain and hate: there is a perceived injury in which the proximity of others (burglars/bogus asylum seekers) is felt as the violence of negation against both the body of the individual (the farmer) and the body of the nation. Bodies surface by 'feeling' the presence of others as the cause of injury or as a form of intrusion. The signs of hate surface by evoking a sense of threat and risk, but one that cannot be simply located or found. This difficulty of location is what makes hate work the way that it does; it is not the impossibility of hate as such, but the mode of its operation, whereby it surfaces in a world made up of other bodies. It is the failure of hate to be located in a given object or figure, which allows it to generate the effects that it does.

HATED BODIES

In this section, I examine how hate works on and through bodies. How does hate involve the spatial reorganisation of bodies through the very gestures of moving away from others that are felt to be the 'cause' of our hate? We need to reflect firstly on the experience of hate. Hate is an intense emotion; it involves a feeling of 'againstness' that is always, in the phenomenological sense, intentional. Hate is always hatred of something or somebody, although that something or somebody does not necessarily pre-exist the emotion. It is possible, of course, to hate an individual person because of what they have done or what they are like. This would be a hate brought about by the particularity of engagement, and one that makes it possible to say, 'I hate you' to a face that is familiar, and to turn away, trembling. It is this kind of hate that is described by Baird and Rosenbaum when they talk of 'seeth[ing] with passion against another human being' (Baird and Rosenbaum 1992: 9). And yet, classically, Aristotle differentiated anger from hatred in that 'anger is customarily felt towards individuals only, whereas hatred may be felt toward whole classes of people' (cited in Allport 1992: 31). Hate may respond to the particular, but it tends to do so by aligning the particular with the general; 'I hate you because you are this or that', where the 'this' or 'that' evokes a group that the individual comes to *stand for* or *stand in for*. Hatred may also work as a form of investment; it endows a particular other with meaning or power by locating them as a member of a group, which is then imagined as a form of positive residence (that is, as residing positively in the body of the individual).

As an investment, hate involves the negotiation of an intimate relationship between a subject and an imagined other, as another that cannot be relegated to the outside. Indeed, a psychoanalytical model used to explain hatred is projection. Here, the self projects all that is undesirable onto another, while concealing any traces of that projection, so that the other comes to appear as a being with a life of its own (see Laplanche and Pontalis 1988: 352). We also have the Kleinian model of projective identification, which is described by Ian Craib as 'a more profound form of projection . . . I behave in such a way as to lead the other person to experience that quality in themselves' (cited in Bird and Clarke 1999: 332). However, this model of projection or projective identification is limited to the extent that it repeats the commonly held assumption that hate moves from inside to outside (pushing what is undesirable out), even if it undermines the objectivity of this distinction. In other words, it takes for granted the existence of negative feelings within the subject, which then become 'the origin' of hatred for others. Whilst there is of course a certain truth within this insistence (bad feelings are crucial to modes of subject formation), negative feelings 'within' might also be effects. The very distinction between inside and outside might be affected by hate. Rather than assuming that hate involves pushing what is undesirable within the self onto others, we could ask: *Why is it that hate feels like it comes from inside and is directed towards others who have an independent existence?*

To consider hatred as a form of intimacy is to show how hatred is ambivalent; it is an investment in an object (of hate) whereby the object becomes part of the life of the subject even though (or perhaps because) its threat is perceived as coming from outside. Hate then cannot be opposed to love. In other words, the subject becomes attached to the other through hatred, as an attachment that returns the subject to itself. Certainly, within psychological theories of prejudice, hate is seen as tied up with love. Or, to put it more precisely, love is understood as the pre-condition of hate. Gordon W. Allport in his classic account *The Nature of Prejudice* suggests that the 'symbiosis and a loving relation always precede hate. There can, in fact, be no hatred until there has been long-continued frustration and disappointment' (Allport 1979: 215). Allport draws on Ian Suttie's *The Origins of Love and Hate*, which argues that hatred 'owes all its meaning to a demand for love' (Suttie 1963: 37), and is bound up with the anxiety of the discovery of the not-self (Suttie 1963: 40). Freud, of course, considers the intimacy of love and hate as affectations for objects throughout the corpus of his work. In *Beyond the Pleasure Principle*, the love for the mother is 'expressed' through a hostile game with a mother-substitute: in the child's game '*fort da*', the child sends an object away, and then pulls it back. The game is partly read as an attempt to convert the passivity of love, in the face of the loved other's departure, with hostile aggression, as if to say 'All right, then, go away!' (Freud 1964c: 16). If the demand for love is the demand for presence, and frustration is the consequence of the necessary failure of that demand, then hate and love are intimately tied together, in the intensity of the negotiation between presence and absence.

It would be problematic to derive all forms of hate from the psychodynamics of the child's relation to its first love, the mother (see Chapter 6). Such a derivation would be a clear instance of the psychologisation of emotions, in which different emotions are always referred back to a primal scene. And yet from the Freudian model, we can begin to grasp the complexity of attachments to objects, and the ways in which such attachments are *sustained* through the conversion of positive to negative feeling. As David Holbrook suggests in *The Masks of Hate*: 'Indifference would manifest our lack of need for the object. Where there is hate there is obviously an *excessive need* for the object' (Holbrook 1972: 36). In other words, hate is opposed to indifference: in hate, the object makes a difference, but cannot satisfy the subject, whose need goes beyond it. However, it is not that the object itself is needed, or that the object is simply determinant. The subject may need the destructive relation to that object: one may be attached to the attachment of hate. Christopher Bollas (1995) differentiates between hate that is destructive, and 'loving hate', which seeks to conserve the object. There is a relation between destructive attachments and conservation: *for the destructive relation to the object to be maintained the object itself must be conserved in some form.* So hate transforms this or that other into an object whose expulsion or incorporation is needed, an expulsion or incorporation that requires the conservation of the object itself in order to be sustained. Such an argument does not presume that one must have first loved an object to hate it (the conversion of hate to love is possible but not necessary), but it does suggest that hate sustains the object through its mode of attachment, in a way that has a similar dynamic to love, but with a different orientation. As Mikkel Borch-Jacobsen puts it, 'Hate wants *to get its hands on* the other; it wants to touch even when it wants to destroy' (Borch-Jacobsen 1993: 10).

Hate is involved in the very negotiation of boundaries between selves and others, and between communities, where 'others' are brought into the sphere of my or our existence as a threat. This other, who may stand for or stand by other others, *presses* against me, threatening my existence. The proximity of the other's touch is felt as a negation. Hate involves a turning away from others that is lived as a turning towards the self. We can now see why stories of hate are *already* translated into stories of love. Of course, it is not that hate is involved in any demarcation between me and not-me, but that some demarcations come into existence through hate, which is felt as coming from within and moving outwards towards others. If hate is felt as belonging to me but caused by an other, then the others (however imaginary) are required for the very continuation of the life of the 'I' or the 'we'. To this extent, boundary formations are bound up with anxiety not as a sensation that comes organically from within a subject or group, but as the effect of this ongoing constitution of the 'apartness' of a subject or group (see Chapter 3).

However, it would be insufficient to posit the story of the 'I' and 'we' as parallel or homologous. Rather, what is at stake in the intensity of hate as a negative attachment to others is how hate creates the 'I' and the 'we' as utterable simultaneously in a moment of alignment. At one level, we can see that an 'I' that declares itself as hating an other (and who might or might not act in accordance with the declaration) comes into existence by also declaring its love for that which is threatened by this imagined other (the nation, the community and so on). But at another level, we need to investigate the 'we' as the effect of the attachment itself; such a subject becomes not only attached to a 'we', but the 'we' is what is affected by the attachment the subject has to itself and to its loved others. Hence in hating another, this subject is also loving itself; hate structures the emotional life of narcissism as a fantastic investment in the continuation of the image of the self in the faces that together make up the 'we'. The attachment to others becomes divided as negative and positive (hate and love) precisely through imaging the faces of the community made up of other 'me's', of others that are loved *as if they were me*.

When Freud suggests in *Group Psychology* (1922) and *The Ego and the Id* (1964b) that we identify with those we love he went some way toward addressing this relationship between ego formation and community. The ego is established by imitating the lost object of love; it is based on a principle of a likeness or resemblance or of *becoming alike* (see Chapter 6 for an extension of this argument). However, I would argue that love does not pre-exist identification (just as hate does not pre-exist dis-identification); so it is not a question of identifying with those we love and dis-identifying with those we hate. Rather, it is through forms of identification that align this subject with this other, that the *character* of the loved is produced as 'likeness' in the first place. Thinking of identification as a form of alignment (to bring into line with ourselves – the subject as 'bringing into line') also shows us how identifications involve dis-identification or an active 'giving up' of other possible identifications (see Butler 1997b). That is, by aligning myself with some others, I am aligning myself against other others. Such a 'giving up' may also produce the character of the hated as 'unlikeness'. What is at stake in the emotional intensities of love and hate, then, is the production of the effect of likeness and unlikeness as characteristics that are assumed to belong to the bodies of individuals. This separation of others into bodies that *can be* loved and hated is part of the work of emotion; it does not pre-exist emotion as its ground – 'I love or hate them *because* they are like me, or not like me.' The effects of the circulation of objects of hate are hence retrospectively evoked as the origin of hate ('I hate them *because* they are unlike us'). So hate works by providing 'evidence' of the very antagonism it effects; we cite the work that it is doing in producing the characteristics of likeness and unlikeness when we show the reasons for its existence. In seeing the other as 'being' hateful, the subject is filled up with hate, which becomes a sign of the 'truth' of the reading.

I have suggested that emotions, which respond to the proximity of others, do not respond the way that they do because of the inherent characteristics of others: we do not respond with love or hate because others are loveable or hateful. It is through affective encounters that objects and others are perceived as having attributes, which 'gives' the subject an identity that is apart from others (for example, as the real victim or as the threatened nation). How does this attribution work on and through bodies? Let's take the following quote from Black feminist Audre Lorde, about her encounter with a white woman on a train:

> *The AA subway train to Harlem. I clutch my mother's sleeve, her arms full of shopping bags, christmas-heavy. The wet smell of winter clothes, the train's lurching. My mother spots an almost seat, pushes my little snow-suited body down. On one side of me a man reading a paper. On the other, a woman in a fur hat staring at me. Her mouth twitches as she stares and then her gaze drops down, pulling mine with it. Her leather-gloved hand plucks at the line where my new blue snowpants and her sleek fur coat meet. She jerks her coat closer to her. I look. I do not see whatever terrible thing she is seeing on the seat between us – probably a roach. But she has communicated her horror to me. It must be something very bad from the way she's looking, so I pull my snowsuit closer to me away from it, too. When I look up the woman is still staring at me, her nose holes and eyes huge. And suddenly I realise there is nothing crawling up the seat between us; it is me she doesn't want her coat to touch. The fur brushes past my face as she stands with a shudder and holds on to a strap in the speeding train. Born and bred a New York City child, I quickly slide over to make room for my mother to sit down. No word has been spoken. I'm afraid to say anything to my mother because I don't know what I've done. I look at the sides of my snowpants secretly. Is there something on them? Some-thing's going on here I do not understand, but I will never forget it. Her eyes. The flared nostrils. The hate.* (Lorde 1984: 147–8)

In this encounter Audre Lorde ends with 'The hate', as an emotion that seems detached from bodies, surrounding the scene with its violence. And yet, the word 'hate' works by working on the surfaces of bodies. This bodily encounter, while ending with 'The hate', also ends with the reconstitution of bodily space. The bodies that come together, that almost touch and co-mingle, slide away from each other, becoming relived in their apartness. The particular bodies that move apart allow the redefinition of social as well as bodily integrity. The emotion of 'hate' aligns the particular white body with the bodily form of the community – the emotion functions to substantiate the threat of invasion and contamination in the body of a particular other, who comes to stand for and stand in for, a group of others. In other words, the hate encounter aligns, not only the 'I' with the 'we' (the white body, the white nation), but the 'you' with the 'them' (the black body, black people).

Does Audre's narrative of the encounter involve her self-designation as the hated; does she hate herself? Certainly, her perception of the cause of the woman's bodily gestures is a misperception that creates an object. The object – the roach – comes to stand for, or stand in for, the cause of 'the hate'. The roach crawls up between them; the roach, as the carrier of dirt, divides the two bodies, forcing them to move apart. Audre pulls her snowsuit, 'away from it too'. But the 'it' that divides them is not the roach. Audre comes to realise that, 'it is me she doesn't want her coat to touch'. What the woman's clothes must not touch is not a roach that crawls between them, but Audre herself. Audre becomes the 'it' that stands between the possibility of their clothes touching. She becomes the roach – the impossible and phobic object – that threatens to crawl from one to the other: 'I don't know what I've done. I look at the sides of my snowpants secretly. Is there something on them?' Hate slides between different signs and objects whose existence is bound up with the negation of its travel. Audre becomes the roach that is then imagined as the cause of the hate. The association between the roach and her body works powerfully. Her body becomes an object of hate through 'taking on' the qualities already attached to the roach: dirty, contaminating, evil. The transformation of *this* or *that* other into an object of hate is over-determined. It is not simply that any body is hated: particular histories of association are reopened in each encounter, such that some bodies are already encountered as more hateful than other bodies. Histories are bound up with emotions precisely insofar as it is a question of *what sticks*, of what connections are lived as the most intense or intimate, as being closer to the skin.

Importantly, then, the alignment of some bodies with some others and against others take place in the *physicality of movement*; bodies are dis-organised and re-organised as they face others who are already recognised as 'the hated'. So the white woman loses her seat to keep the black child at a distance, in the 'speeding' movements of the train. The organisation of social and bodily space creates a border that is transformed into an object, as an effect of this intensification of feeling. The white woman's refusal to touch the black child does not simply *stand for* the expulsion of blackness from white social space, but *actually re-forms that social space through re-forming the apartness of the white body*. The re-forming of bodily and social space involves a process of *making the skin crawl*; the threat posed by the bodies of others to bodily and social integrity is registered on the skin. Or, to be more precise, the skin comes to be felt as a border through the violence of the impression of one surface upon another. In this way, hate creates the surfaces of bodies through the way in which bodies are aligned with and against other bodies. How we feel about others is what aligns us with a collective, which paradoxically 'takes shape' only as an effect of such alignments. It is through how others impress upon us that the skin of the collective begins to take shape.

HATE CRIME

Hate involves the surfacing of bodies through how we encounter others in intimate and public spaces. The politics of racial hatred involves attributing racial others with meaning, a process we can describe as 'the making of unlikeness'. Hatred is a negative attachment to an other that one wishes to expel, an attachment that is sustained through the expulsion of the other from bodily and social proximity. In this section, I want to bring the arguments of the previous two sections together. That is, I will explore how affective economies of hate, where hate circulates in signs that are detached from particular bodies, affect the way bodies take shape. In particular, I will consider how the movement between signs of hate affects the bodies of those who become the objects of hatred.

In order to explore the connection between the language of hate and the surfacing of bodies, I will examine the politics of hate crime. Hate crimes typically are defined when the crime is committed *because of* an individual's group identity (defined in terms of race, religion, sexuality):

> If a person . . . intentionally selects the person against whom the crime . . . is committed or selects the property which is damaged or otherwise affected by the crime . . . *because* of the race, religion, color, disability, sexual orientation, national origin or ancestry of that person or the owner or occupant of the property, the penalties for the underlying crime are increased [Wisconsin v. Mitchell]. (Jacobs and Potter 1998: 3, emphasis added)

What is at stake in hate crime is the *perception* of a group in the body of an individual. However, the way in which it is perception that is at stake is concealed by the word 'because' in hate crime legislation, which implies that group identity is already in place, and that it works only as a cause, rather than also being an effect of the crime.[4] The fact that hate crime involves a perception of a group in the body of the individual does not make the violence any less real or 'directed'; this perception has material effects insofar as it is enacted through violence. That is, hate crime works as a form of violence against groups *through* violence against the bodies of individuals. Violence against others may be one way in which the other's identity is fixed or sealed; the other is *forced* to embody a particular identity by and for the perpetrator of the crime, and that force involves harm or injury.

The legal response to hate crime is one way of dealing with the injustice of violence against minority groups.[5] I suggest that 'hate crime' may be useful as a technology of redress because it can make explicit the role of hate as an intense and negative attachment to others in the politics of racism, as well as other forms of structural violence. As Zillah Eisenstein argues, attending to hate allows us to show how racism involves psychic and bodily investments (Eisenstein 1994: 5–22). For some, this is the risk of hate crime legislation: it can attribute power to psychology, or transform power into psychology. David Theo Goldberg, for example, argues that the use of hate turns racist expression into a psychological disposition (Goldberg 1995: 269). AnnJanette Rosga argues that the use of hate crime as a category has 'a susceptibility to individualised models of oppression through its mobilisation of personal, psychological notions of prejudice and hatred' (Rosga 1999: 149). These critiques are useful, and they remind us of the importance of understanding emotions not as psychological dispositions, but as investments in social norms. Attending to the politics of hate allows us to address the question of how subjects and others become *invested* in norms such that their demise would be felt as a kind of living death. While we need to take care to avoid psychologising power and inequality, we also need to avoid reifying structures and institutions. To consider the investments we have in structures is precisely to attend to how they become meaningful – or indeed, are felt as natural – through the emotional work of labour, work that takes time, and that takes place in time. So 'hate crime' as a category can show us that violence against others involves forms of power that are visceral and bodily, as well as social and structural.

But if hate is part of the production of the ordinary, rather than simply about 'extremists' (perhaps we should say that 'extremes' are part of the production of the ordinary), then we need to ask if it makes any sense to talk about hate as a crime. While it might be important to challenge the narrative which sees hate as something extremists do (which saves the 'ordinary nation', or 'ordinary subjects', from any responsibility for its violence), it is equally important to see that there are different ways in which hate operates. In other words, particular acts (including physical violence directed towards others, as well as name calling and abusive language) do not necessarily *follow* from the uneven effects of hate. Of course, not all subjects hate in the same way. We can demarcate certain actions as wrong and unjustifiable. Such actions can be seen as the responsibility of individuals or groups who commit them. Undermining the distinction between hate and hate crime in the non-opposition between the ordinary and criminal does not mean an emptying out of responsibility for the effects of hate crime.

The terms of my argument about the usefulness of hate crime as a category also suggest its limits: hate crime does not refer to a discrete set of enactments that stand apart from the uneven effects that hate already has in organising the surfaces of the world (though neither does it simply follow from them, as I have suggested). The limits of hate crime then may partly be the limits of the law that seeks to designate the criminal as an ontological category. Insofar as hate enacts the negation that is perceived to characterise the existence of a social group, then we can link hate to injustice, an injustice that is, of course, irreducible to the law, at the same time as it has a relation to it (see Derrida 1992). If hate is always directed to others as a way of *sealing* their fate, then hate may be *about* the effect it has on others. Given this, the introduction of hate crime as a category should be used as a way of making visible the effects of hate, by *listening to the affective life of injustice*, rather than establishing the truth of law.

We can return to Audre Lorde's example. We can ask: How is the black body re-formed in the encounter? What happens to those bodies that are encountered as objects of hate, as having the characteristic of 'unlikeness'? In my earlier reading, I emphasised the effect of the encounter on the white body that becomes lived as apart. What I failed to ask was the role of hate, as a social encounter between others, on the bodies of those who are designated as hated. It is this failure that I take as symptomatic of a tendency to think of hate and hate crime from the point of view of those who hate rather than those who are hated. The destruction of the bodies of the hated is, of course, what is often sought in hate crime itself. To allow such bodies to disappear in our own analysis would be to repeat the crime rather than to redress its injustice.

In the case of Audre's story, Audre's gestures mimic the white woman's. Her gaze is 'pulled down', following the gaze of the white woman. This pulling down of the gaze and the transformation of the black body into an object of its own gaze seems crucial. The hated body becomes hated, not just for the one who hates, but for the one who is hated. This 'taking on' of the white gaze is central to Frantz Fanon's argument in *Black Skin, White Masks*, where he describes how the black body is 'sealed into that crushing objecthood' (Fanon 1986: 109). When Audre's gaze is pulled down with the white woman's, she feels 'afraid'. She comes to recognise herself as the object of the woman's hate: she is 'hailed', in Althusser's (1971) sense, as the hated. The 'doing' of hate is not simply 'done' in the moment of its articulation. A chain of effects (which are at once affects) are in circulation. The circulation of objects of hate is not free. In this instance, bodies that are attributed as being hateful – as the origin of feelings of hate – are (temporarily) sealed in their skins. Such bodies assume the *character of the negative*. That transformation of this body into the body of the hated, in other words, leads to the enclosure or sealing of the other's body within a figure of hate. The white woman who moves away from Audre moves on, of course. *Some bodies move precisely by sealing others as objects of hate.*

Our task may then be to reflect on how it feels to be an object. Mari J. Matsuda's work emphasises the effects of hate on the bodies of the victims. She writes:

The negative effects of hate messages are real and immediate for the victims. Victims of vicious hate propaganda experience physiological symptoms and emotional distress ranging from fear in the gut to rapid pulse rate and difficulty in breathing, nightmares, post-traumatic stress disorder, hypertension, psychosis and suicide. (Matsuda 1993: 24)

The enactment of hate through verbal or physical violence, Matsuda suggests 'hits right at the emotional place where we feel the most pain' (Matsuda 1993: 25). Such lived experiences of pain can be understood as part of the work of hate, or as part of what hate *is doing*. Hate has effects on the bodies of those who are made into its objects; such bodies are affected by the hate that it is directed towards them by others. Hate is not simply a means by which the identity of the subject and community is established (through alignment); hate also works to unmake the world of the other through pain (see Scarry 1985; see Chapter 1). Or hate crimes seek to *crush* the other in what Patricia Williams has called 'spirit murder' (cited in Matsuda 1993: 24).

If the effect of hate crime is affect, and an affect which is visceral and bodily, as Matsuda's work has emphasised, then *the body of the victim is read as testimony*, as a means by which the truth of hate crime is established in law. This poses a particular problem for the incitement to hatred laws as they relate to hate speech. The effects must be seen as fully determined by the crime, a determination that, in a strict sense, is very difficult to establish, without evidence that can be described as bruised skin or other traces of bodily violence. So critics such as Ray Jureidini have mentioned the 'subjectivity' of hate speech laws as a problem: 'Some people are offended by ethnic jokes and name-calling as a problem, some are not' (Jureidini 2000: 13). If the affect and effects of hate speech are not fully determined, then to what extent can 'harm' become evidence for the injustice of hate speech? To what extent can listening to the victim's story become a means of delivering justice?

We can consider here the important critiques made by Wendy Brown (1995) and Lauren Berlant (2000) of 'wound culture', which fetishises the wound as proof of identity (see Chapter 1). Wound culture takes the injury of the individual as the grounds not only for an appeal (for compensation or redress), but as an identity claim, such that 'reaction' against the injury forms the very basis of politics, understood as the conflation of truth and injustice (Brown 1995: 73). What follows from such critiques should not be a refusal to listen to histories of pain as part of the histories of injustice, whereby pain is understood as *the bodily life of such histories*. The fetishising of the wound can only take place by concealing these histories; the greater injustice would be to repeat that fetishisation by forgetting the processes of being wounded by others. I am suggesting the *importance of listening to the affects and effects of hate and hate crime* as a way of calling into question, rather than assuming, the relationship between violence and identity. To say these affects and effects are not fully determined, and that they do not congeal into an identity, is not to suggest that the affects and effects don't matter, and that they are not a form of injustice, even if they cannot function in a narrow sense as evidence or an identity claim. Indeed, to treat such testimonies of injury as evidence would perform its own injustice: the language and bodies of hate don't operate on the terrain of truth, they operate to make and unmake worlds, made up of other bodies. Listening to the affects of hate crime must involve recognising that the affects are not always determined: we cannot assume we know in advance what it feels like to be the object of hate. For some, hate enactments may involve pain; for others, rage. So if the pain of others is the 'intention' of hate crime, then hate crime is not always guaranteed to succeed. We have to have open ears to hear the affects of hate.

But what does the failure of hate as an action against others to determine fully its effects mean for politics? In *Excitable Speech* (1997a) Judith Butler considers the impossibility of deciding in advance the meaning of hate speech for hate crime. She suggests that any signifier can be mobilised in different ways and in new contexts, so that even signs we assume stand for hate (and can only stand for hate), can operate otherwise, such as the burning cross (Butler 1997a: 19). Butler hence criticises the work of Matsuda, amongst others, which she suggests assume that hate resides in particular signs and that the effects of such signs are already determined in advance of their circulation. I am in agreement with Butler. As I have argued in this chapter, hate is economic, and it does not reside positively in a sign or body. But Butler overlooks the relationship between affect and effect that is crucial to Matsuda's own work. Following Matsuda, we need to relate the question of the effect of hate speech with *affect*, which includes the question of how others have been affected by hate speech. Following Butler, we might recognise that the affects are not determined in advance. But if they are not determined in advance, then how do they come to be determined? We need to ask: How do certain signs of hate produce affective responses? Or why are some signs of hate repeated? Is it because such signs are over-determined; is it because they keep open a history which is already open insofar as it is affective?

The fact that some signs are repeated is precisely *not* because the signs themselves contain hate, but because they are effects of histories that have stayed open. Words like 'Nigger' or 'Paki' for example tend to stick; they hail the other precisely by bringing another into a history whereby such names assign the other with meaning in an economy of difference (see Chapter 4, for an extension of this argument about sticky signs). Such words and signs *tend to stick*, which does not mean they cannot operate otherwise. Rather, they cannot simply be liberated from the history of this use as violence or insult, even if they cannot be reduced to that history. Another way of putting this is to say that some words stick because they become attached *through* particular affects. So, for example, someone will hurl racial insults (the white woman who retreats from Audre may mutter under her breath to a compliant witness, 'nigger' and 'roach': an insult that is directed against an other, but mediated by a third party), precisely because they are affective, although it is not always guaranteed that the other will be 'impressed upon' or hurt in a way that follows from the history of insults. It is the affective nature of hate speech that allows us to understand that whether such speech works or fails to work is not really the important question. Rather, the important question is: *What effects do such encounters have on the bodies of others who become transformed into objects of hate?*

This question can only be asked if we consider how hate works as an affective economy; hate does not reside positively in signs, but circulates or moves between signs and bodies. The circulation of signs of hate involves movement and fixity; some bodies move precisely by sealing others as objects of hate. Tracking the history of hate involves reading the surfaces of bodies, as well as listening to those who have been shaped by this history.

NOTES

1. http://www.nidlink.com/~aryanvic/index-E.html Accessed 4 January 2002.
2. Thanks to David Eng for this point.
3. For the British National Party, this argument that 'any' body could be bogus gets translated into 'all' are bogus: 'We will abolish the "positive discrimination" schemes that have made white Britons second-class citizens. We will also clamp down on the flood of "asylum seekers", all of whom are either bogus or can find refuge much nearer their home countries.' See the British National Party website, http://www.bnp.org.uk/policies.html#immigration Accessed 30 July 2003.
4. There are some difficulties around cause and effect here. I would argue with Rosga (1999) that hate crime legislation does tend to reify social groups, by assuming that groups are sealed entities that hate is then directed towards. At the same time, I would question the work of critics such as Jacobs and Potter (1998), who in arguing against the efficacy of the category 'hate crime' suggest that the legislation itself is creating the divisions that the crime is supposed to be a result of. They hence imply that such divisions would not exist if they were not introduced and then exacerbated through hate crime legislation. I cannot go along with this. Rather, I would argue that hate crimes (which I define as forms of violence directed towards others that are perceived to be members of a social group, whereby the violence is 'directed' towards the group) work to effect divisions partly by enforcing others into an identity through violence. This does not mean that others are not aligned with an identity (= identification) before the violence. In other words, the enactment of hate through violence does not 'invent' social

groups out of nothing. Rather, such enactments function as a form of enforcement; hate crimes may work by sealing a particular other into an identity that is *already* affective. The distinction between cause and effect is hence not useful: hate both affects, and is affected by, the sealing of others into group identities. This is why some bodies and not others become the object of hate crimes: hate ties the particular with the group only by reopening a past history of violence and exclusion that allows us to recognise the bodies of some others as *out of place* (see Ahmed 2000: 38–54). Of course, the relevant laws within the UK – the 'incitement to racial hatred' in Part III (ss. 17–29) of the Public Order Act 1986 – are about hate speech rather than hate crime defined in the terms above. Here, racial hatred is not described as the origin of crime, but as the effect (there is criminal liability if a person uses or publishes words or commits acts that are theatening, abusive or insulting, and which are likely to 'stir up' racial hatred). Hence hate speech laws tend to criminalise hate as effect, and hate crime laws to criminalise hate as origin; both of them fail to recognise the role played by hate *in an economy of affects and effects.*

5. In a very interesting article, Muneer Ahmad examines the use of the language of 'hate crime' after September 11, analysing the discourses around the murder of five men. He suggests that 'the hate crime killings before September 11 were viewed as crimes of moral depravity, while the hate killings since September 11 have been understood as crimes of passion' (Ahmad 2002: 108). This shift occurs, he suggests, because the 'hate' that was directed against 'others' was shared by the vast majority of Americans; in other words, the crimes become 'crimes of passion' insofar as a collective anger against the attacks gets displaced into an anger towards racial others. Thanks to David Eng for directing me to Ahmad's article. See Chapter 3 for reflections on racial profiling since September 11.

The Affective Politics of Fear

'Look, a Negro!' It was an external stimulus that flicked over me as I passed by. I made a tight smile.

'Look, a Negro!' It was true. It amused me.

'Look, a Negro!' The circle was drawing a bit tighter. I made no secret of my amusement.

'Mama, see the Negro! I'm frightened! Frightened! Frightened!' Now they were beginning to be afraid of me. I made up my mind to laugh myself to tears, but laughter had become impossible. (Fanon 1986: 111–12)

What makes us frightened? Who gets afraid of whom? The above encounter shows us that it is not simply a question of some body being afraid of some body who passes by. On the contrary, the object of fear is over-determined; here, the Negro is the object of a fear that is declared by a white child, but mediated through the memory traces of the black man. The fear announces itself through an ontological statement, a statement a self makes of itself and to itself – '*I'm* frightened.' Such statements of fear tell the other that they are the 'cause' of fear, in a way that is personal: 'Now they were beginning to be afraid of *me*.' As such the fear signified through language and by the white body does not simply begin and end there: rather the fear works through and on the bodies of those who are transformed into its subjects, as well as its objects. The black body is drawn tighter; it is not just the smile that becomes tighter, and is eventually impossible, but the black body itself becomes enclosed by the fear, and comes to feel that fear as its own, such that it is felt as an impossible or inhabitable body. In this way, fear does not simply come from within and then move outwards towards objects and others (the white child who feels afraid of the black man); rather, fear works to secure the relationship between those bodies; it brings them together and moves them apart through the shudders that are felt on the skin, on the surface that surfaces through the encounter.

And then, the story moves on:

> My body was given back to me sprawled out, distorted, recolored, clad in mourning on that white winter day. The Negro is an animal, the Negro is bad, the Negro is mean, the Negro is ugly; look, a nigger, it's cold, the nigger is shivering, the nigger is shivering because he is cold, the little boy is trembling because he is afraid of the nigger, the nigger is shivering with cold, that cold that goes through your bones, the handsome little boy is trembling because he thinks that the nigger is quivering with rage, the little white boy throws himself into his mother's arms: Mama, the nigger's going to eat me up. (Fanon 1986: 113–14)

The black body is 'given back' through fear only insofar as it has been taken, stolen by the very hostility of the white gaze. For the black man, fear is felt as coldness; it makes the body shiver with a cold that moves from the surface into the depths of the body, as a cold 'that goes through your bones'. Fear envelops the bodies that feel it, as well as constructs such bodies as enveloped, as contained by it, *as if it* comes from outside and moves inward. And yet fear does not bring the bodies together, as a form of shared or fellow feeling. While signs of affect seem to pass between the bodies (the shivering of the Negro becomes the trembling of the little white boy), what passes is not the same affect, and it depends on (mis)reading the other's feelings. The shivering of the black body is misread as a form of rage, and only then as the 'ground' of white fear. In other words, the other is only felt to be fearsome through a misreading, a misreading that is returned by the other through its response of fear, as a fear of the white child's fear. This is not to say that the fear comes from the white child, as if he was the origin of that fear (or even its author); rather the fear opens up past histories of association (in the very rehearsal of childhood fantasies), which allows the white body to be constructed as apart from the black body in the present.

We might note here that fear does something; it re-establishes distance between bodies whose difference is read off the surface, as a reading which produces the surface (shivering, recolouring). Fear involves relationships of proximity, which are crucial to establishing the 'apartness' of white bodies. Such proximity involves the repetition of stereotypes. Fanon begins his reflection on the encounter with stereotypes, as fixed accounts of the other's being that are repeated, as if they come from nowhere: 'the Negro *is*'. Stereo-types seek to fix the meaning of the other, but the very repetition that is required to enable such a fixation renders them a site of insecurity rather than security, as Homi Bhabha (1994) has suggested. Such impossible truths become compelling precisely insofar as they *might be lost on the way*. Fear may also work as an affective economy (see Chapter 2): it does not reside posi-tively in a particular object or sign. It is this lack of residence that allows fear to slide across signs and between bodies. This sliding becomes stuck only temporarily, in the very attachment of a sign to a body, an attachment that is taken on by the body, encircling it with a fear that becomes its own.

Crucially here, we end up with a fantasy in which the white child says to its mother: 'Mama, the nigger's going to eat me up.' Such a cannibalistic fantasy, of being incorporated into the body of the other, is crucial to the politics of fear: fear works by establishing others as fearsome insofar as they *threaten to take the self in*. Such fantasies construct the other as a danger not only to one's self as self, but to one's very life, to one's very existence as a separate being with a life of its own. Such fantasies of the other hence work to justify violence against others, whose very existence comes to be felt as a threat to the life of the white body, but which as a threat to life, may *come to give rather than take life*. Discourses of fear are, in R. D. Laing's terms, con-cerned with the preservation rather than gratification of the subject (Laing 1960: 44). Fear might be concerned with the preservation not simply of 'me', but also 'us', or 'what is', or 'life as we know it', or even 'life itself'.

In this chapter, I consider fear as an 'affective politics', which preserves only through announcing a threat to life itself. First, I consider the relation between fear, anxiety and the loss or 'passing by' of an object. Second, I examine the relationship between fear and the alignment of bodily and social space, in particular, by considering how fear shrinks bodily space and how this shrinkage involves the restriction of bodily mobility in social space. And finally, I reflect on the role of fear in the conservation of power, by consid-ering how narratives of crisis work to secure social norms in the present, with specific reference to the figure of the international terrorist.

FEAR AND ANXIETY

The difference between fear and anxiety is most often represented in terms of the status of the object. Indeed, fear has often been contrasted with anxiety insofar as fear *has* an object. For example, Rachman argues that anxiety can be described as the 'tense anticipation of a threatening but vague event', or a feeling of 'uneasy suspense', while fear is described as an emotional reac-tion 'to a threat that is identifiable' (Rachman 1998: 2–3, see also Fischer

1970). I want to question this model by suggesting that fear is linked to the 'passing by' of the object, even if the absence of the object in fear creates a different impression from the impression it creates in anxiety.

Fear's relation to the object has an important temporal dimension: we fear an object that approaches us. Fear, like pain, is felt as an unpleasant form of intensity. But while the lived experience of fear may be unpleasant in the present, the unpleasantness of fear also relates to the future. Fear involves an *anticipation* of hurt or injury. Fear projects us from the present into a future. But the feeling of fear presses us into that future as an intense bodily experience in the present. One sweats, one's heart races, one's whole body becomes a space of unpleasant intensity, an impression that overwhelms us and pushes us back with the force of its negation, which may sometimes involve taking flight, and other times may involve paralysis. So the object that we fear is not simply before us, or in front of us, but impresses upon us in the present, as an anticipated pain in the future.[1]

Indeed, Heidegger argues that fear is felt in the absence of the object that approaches. As he suggests:

> That which is detrimental, as something that threatens us, is not yet within striking distance, but it is coming close. . . . As it draws close, this 'it can, and yet in the end it may not' becomes aggravated. We say, 'It is fearsome'. This implies that what is detrimental as coming-close close by carries with it the patent possibility that it may stay away and pass us by; but instead of lessening or extinguishing our fearing, this enhances it. (Heidegger 1962: 179–80)

Crucially, Heidegger relates fear to that which is not in the present, in either the spatial or temporal sense of 'the here and the now'. Fear responds to what is approaching rather than already here. It is the futurity of fear which makes it possible that the object of fear, rather than arriving, might pass us by. But the passing by of the object of fear does not mean the over-coming of fear: rather, the possibility of the loss of the object makes what is fearsome all the more fearsome. If fear had an object, then fear could be contained by the object. When the object of fear threatens to pass by, then fear can no longer be contained by an object. Fear in its very relationship to an object, in the very intensity of its directedness towards that object, is intensified by the loss of its object. We could characterise this absence as about being *not quite present* rather than, as with anxiety, being nowhere at all.

But is anxiety nowhere?[2] When Heidegger discusses anxiety he emphasises how it comes from nowhere: 'Accordingly, when something threatening brings itself close, anxiety does not "see" any definite "here" or "yonder" from which it comes. That in the face of which one has anxiety is characterised by the fact that what threatens is *nowhere*' (Heidegger 1962: 231). Or we could consider how anxiety becomes attached to particular objects, which come to life not as the cause of anxiety, but as an effect of its travels. In anxiety, one's thoughts often move quickly between different objects, a movement which works to intensify the sense of anxiety. One thinks of more and more 'things' to be anxious about; the detachment from a given object allows anxiety to accumulate through gathering more and more objects, until it overwhelms other possible affective relations to the world. One becomes anxious as a mode of attachment to objects. In other words, anxiety tends to stick to objects, even when the objects pass by.[3] Anxiety becomes *an approach to objects* rather than, as with fear, *being produced by an object's approach*. This slide between fear and anxiety is affected by the passing by of the object.

Furthermore, fear's relationship to the potential disappearance of an object is more profound than simply a relationship to the object of fear. In other words, it is not just fear that is at stake in fear. For Freud, fears themselves may function as symptoms, as mechanisms for the defence of the ego against danger. In his paper, 'Inhibitions, Symptoms and Anxiety', Freud (1964d) returns to the Little Hans case. Hans had a phobic relationship to horses. Freud argues that this fear is itself a symptom that has been 'put in the place' of another fear, one that much more profoundly threatens the ego: the fear of castration as a fear of the father. Hans can 'manage' his fear of horses through avoidance, in a way in which he could not manage his fear of the father. We might remember that in Freud's model of unconscious emotions, the affect itself is not repressed: rather what is repressed is the idea to which the affect was attached (Freud 1964a: 177; see Chapter 2). The affect of fear is sustained, or is even intensified, through the displacement between objects.

The displacement between objects works to link those objects together. Such linkages are not created by fear, but may already be in place within the social imaginary. In the Freudian model, the movement between objects is intra-psychic, and goes backwards; it refers back to the primary fear of castration. Or, to be more specific, the sideways movement between objects (in this case, between the horse and the father) is itself explained as determined by a repression of the idea to which the affect was originally attached (the threat of castration).[4] I would suggest that the sideways movement between objects, which works to stick objects together as signs of threat, is shaped by multiple histories. The movement between signs does not have its origin in the psyche, but is a trace of how such histories remain alive in the present. We could see this in the encounter described by Fanon. The production of the black man as the object of fear depends on past histories of association: Negro, animal, bad, mean, ugly. The movement of fear between signs is what allows the object of fear to be generated in the present (the Negro *is* an animal, bad, mean, ugly). The movement between signs allows others to be attributed with emotional value, as 'being fearsome'.

Fanon's encounter allows us to explore the links between the displacement of objects of fear and the passing by of the object. In this encounter, fear does become contained in an object: the black body. And yet the containment of fear in an object remains provisional: insofar as the black man is the object of fear, then he may pass by. Indeed, the physicality of this 'passing by' can be associated with the passing of fear between signs: *it is the movement that intensifies the affect*. The black man becomes even more threatening if he passes by: his proximity is imagined then as the possibility of future injury. As such, the economy of fear works to contain the bodies of others, *a containment whose 'success' relies on its failure, as it must keep open the very grounds of fear*.

The sideways movement of fear (where we have a metonymic and sticky relation between signs) is also a backwards movement: objects of fear become substituted for each other over time. This displacement of objects also involves the passing by of the objects from which the subject seems to flee. Fear creates the very effect of 'that which I am not', through *running away from an object*, which nevertheless threatens as it passes by or is displaced. To this extent, fear does not involve the defence of borders that already exist; rather fear makes those borders, by establishing objects from which the subject, in fearing, can flee. Through fear not only is the very border between self and other affected, but the relation between the objects that are feared (rather than simply the relation between the subject and its objects) is shaped by histories that 'stick', making some objects more than others seem fearsome.

Such a model suggests that fear is bound up with more than the loss of the object of fear. Fear is bound up with the loss of the object, as such. For Freud, fear is indeed part of the story of loss in that one also fears the loss of the object of love. As I examined in the previous chapter, Freud, in his analysis of the *fort da* game, shows how the child performs the departure and return of the mother in an attempt to master the impossibility of her love (Freud 1964c: 15–16). Perhaps then anxiety comes in part from love (for the (m)other), as a love that can be taken away, as the taking away of that which secures the subject's relation to the world. Anxiety is then an effect of the impossibility of love; an impossibility that returns in the diminishment of what it is possible to be. The anxiety about the possibility of loss becomes displaced onto objects of fear, which seem to present themselves from the outside as dangers that could be avoided, and as obstacles to the fulfilment of love itself.

Returning to Fanon's encounter, we might note how the white boy's flight from the object of fear, an object that passes him by, takes him into the arms of the mother, which signify a protective and safe form of enclosure, or a transformation of the world into home (being-at-home). In other words, the turning away from the object of fear also involves *turning towards* the object of love, who becomes a defence against the death that is apparently threatened by the object of fear. In this way, we can see that fear *is that which keeps alive the fantasy of love as the preservation of life*, but paradoxically only by announcing the possibility of death. The necessity of the fantasy ('Mama, the nigger's going to eat me up') makes clear that the passing by of the feared object also involves moving towards the loved object, through the forming of a home or enclosure. However, if the flight of fright moves the subject towards the loved other, whose arms provide a second skin, then that enclosure keeps open the possibility of loss. Rather than fear getting in the way of love, we can see that fear allows the subject to get closer to the loved object, though the distance is never quite abolished, and the object of love as well as fear may yet pass by. Indeed, *it is the fear of passing by as a passing away* that seems crucial to the 'turning' that constitutes the subject in the first place. If it is fright that 'brings one to life', then it does so only by announcing the possibility of death. While we may fear that which we cannot contain, through fear, *we may also contain that which cannot be.*

BODIES THAT FEAR

As we have seen from my analysis of Fanon's encounter, fear is an embodied experience; it creates the very effect of the surfaces of bodies. But an obvious question remains: Which bodies fear which bodies? Of course, we could argue that all bodies fear, although they may fear different things in different ways. But I want to suggest that fear is felt differently by different bodies, in the sense that there is a relationship to space and mobility at stake in the differential organisation of fear itself. Certainly, much of the debate on 'fear of crime' has been concerned with the organisation of fear in this spatial sense. A common sense assumption might be that those who are most afraid are those who are most vulnerable; fear could be viewed as a 'reasonable response' to vulnerability, whereby vulnerability itself would be perceived as an inherent quality or characteristic of some bodies. However, as Ditton and Farrall have argued, anxiety about crime is not correlated with degrees of victimisation: 'those least in danger are the most afraid' (Ditton and Farrall 2000: xvi). So fear is not simply a consequence of the 'objectivity' of threats or dangers. Given this, why are some bodies more afraid than others? How do feelings of vulnerability take shape?

Sacco and Glackman describe vulnerability in terms of 'feelings of susceptibility and openness to attack that influence the processes by which definitions of criminal danger are constructed and regarded as salient bases for action' (Sacco and Glackman 2000: 412). Such a definition is useful as it shows us that vulnerability involves a particular kind of bodily relation to the world, in which openness itself is read as a site of potential danger, and as demanding evasive action. Emotions may involve *readings of such openness*, as spaces where bodies and worlds meet and leak into each other. Fear involves reading such openings as dangerous; the openness of the body to the world involves a sense of danger, which is *anticipated as a future pain or injury*. In fear, the world presses against the body; the body shrinks back from the world in the desire to avoid the object of fear. Fear involves shrinking the body; *it restricts the body's mobility precisely insofar as it seems to prepare the body for flight.*

Such shrinkage is significant: fear works to contain some bodies such that they take up less space. In this way, emotions work to align bodily space with social space. It is not that fear begins in a body and then restricts the mobility of that body. For as I have already suggested, the response of fear is itself dependent on particular narratives of what and who is fearsome that are already in place. I have also suggested, following Heidegger, that fear is all the more frightening given the potential loss of the object that it anticipates. The more we don't know what or who it is we fear *the more the world becomes fearsome*. In other words, it is the structural possibility that the object of fear may pass us by which makes everything possibly fearsome. This is an important dimension in the spatial politics of fear: the loss of the object of fear renders the world itself a space of potential danger, a space that is anticipated as pain or injury on the surface of the body that fears. If we return to the racist encounter discussed by Fanon, we can see that the white child's apparent fear does not lead to his refusal to inhabit the world, but to his embrace of the world through the apparently safe enclosure formed by the loved other (being-at-home). Rather, in this case, it is the black subject, the one who fears the white child's fear, who is crushed by that fear, by being sealed into a body that tightens up, and takes up less space. In other words, *fear works to restrict some bodies through the movement or expansion of others*.

Within feminist approaches the question of fear is shown to be structural and mediated, rather than an immediate bodily response to an objective danger. Rather than seeing fear simply as an inevitable consequence of women's vulnerability, feminist critics argue that fear is a response to the *threat* of violence. The threat itself is shaped by the authorisation of narratives about what is and is not threatening, and about who are and are not the appropriate 'objects' of fear. As Elizabeth Stanko (1990) argues, women's access to public space is restricted by the circulation of narratives of feminine vulnerability. Such narratives are calls for action: they suggest women must always be on guard when outside the home. They not only construct 'the outside' as inherently dangerous, but they also posit home as being safe. So women, if they are to have access to feminine respectability, must either stay at home (femininity as domestication), or be careful in how they move and appear in public (femininity as a constrained mobility).[5] Safety here becomes a question of not inhabiting public space or, more accurately, of not moving through that space alone. So the question of what is fearsome as well as who should be afraid is bound up with the politics of mobility, whereby the mobility of some bodies involves or even requires the restriction of the mobility of others. But the production of 'the fearsome' is also bound up with the authorisation of legitimate spaces: for example, in the construction of home as safe, 'appropriate' forms of femininity become bound up with the reproduction of domestic space.

My argument seeks to develop Stanko's work on the effects of the production of feminine bodies as fearful by thinking about the bodily experience of fear. Fear works to contain bodies within social space through the way it shrinks the body, or constitutes the bodily surface through an expectant withdrawal from a world that might yet present itself as dangerous. Or, as Hanmer and Saunders put it in their *Well-Founded Fear*: 'Women's sense of security in public places is profoundly shaped by our inability to secure an undisputed right to occupy that space. The curtailing of movement is a not infrequent response to violent and threatening encounters in public' (Hanmer and Saunders 1984: 39). Fear of 'the world' as the scene of a future injury works as a form of violence in the present, which shrinks bodies in a state of afraidness, a shrinkage which may involve a refusal to leave the enclosed spaces of home, or a refusal to inhabit what is outside in ways that anticipate injury (walking alone, walking at night and so on). Such feelings of vulnerability and fear hence shape women's bodies as well as how those bodies inhabit space. Vulnerability is not an inherent characteristic of women's bodies; rather, it is an effect that works to secure femininity as a delimitation of movement in the public, and over-inhabitance in the private.

In this way, fear works to align bodily and social space: it works to enable some bodies to inhabit and move in public space through restricting the mobility of other bodies to spaces that are enclosed or contained. Spaces extend the mobility of some bodies; their freedom to move shapes the surface of spaces, whilst spaces surface as spaces through the mobility of such bodies. It is the regulation of bodies in space through the uneven distribution of fear which allows spaces to become territories, claimed as rights by some bodies and not others. We can see this process at work in the heterosexualisation of space (see Chapter 7), as well as the racialisation of space (see below). It is no accident that in political rhetoric, freedom and fear are increasingly opposed: the new freedom is posited as the freedom from fear, and as the freedom to move.[6] But which bodies are granted such freedom to move? And which bodies become read as the origin of fear and as threatening 'our' freedom?

GLOBAL ECONOMIES OF FEAR

To address these questions, I want us to think more precisely about the processes through which fear works to secure forms of the collective. My argument is *not* that there is a psychic economy of fear, which then becomes social and collective: rather, as I have already suggested, the individual subject comes into being through its very alignment with the collective. What we need to examine is the complexity of such alignments.

Within political theory, fear has been understood as crucial to the forming of collectives. In Machiavelli's *The Prince and the Discourses*, the prince uses fear as a means of gaining his subject-citizens' consent to the power that he already holds: 'One ought to be both feared and loved, but as it is difficult for the two to go together, it is much safer to be feared than loved' (Machiavelli 1950: 61). Fear is understood as a safer instrument of power than love given its link to punishment: 'fear is maintained by a dread of punishment which never fails' (Machiavelli 1950: 61). Fear makes the subjects of the prince consent to his power as the possibility of dissent is linked to pain and torture. In a different argument, Hobbes (1991) makes fear primary to the emergence of government, arguing that it is fear of anarchy that makes subjects consent to being governed. The fear of anarchy relates to the fear of nature. As William O'Connolly puts it: 'The state of nature is shock therapy. It helps subjects to get their priorities straight by teaching them what life would be like without sovereignty' (cited in Campbell 1998: 57; see also der Derian 1995). In this model, fear works as an imperative for the formation of government: fear would be the 'cost' of anarchy and the promise of civil society is the elimination of fear. As such, subjects consent to being governed: they give up freedom in order to be free from fear. In both models, fear functions as a technology of governance: the sovereign power either uses fear to make others consent to that power, or civil society promises protection, and the elimination of fear, to ensure consent.

Fear has been theorised not just as a technology, but also as a symptom of modern life. It has even been used to describe 'the age in which we live'. Indeed, it has become a commonplace argument that we live in a 'culture of fear' (Furedi 1997) or an 'age of anxiety' (Dunant and Porter 1996). Furedi describes the modern age as inflating dangers and risks not just to the individual, but to life itself: 'When the survival of the human species is said to be at stake, then life itself becomes one big safety issue' (Furedi 1997: 3). He concludes that this positing of life itself as a safety issue is bound up with the weakening of social institutions that link the individual and the social: 'Many of the old routines and traditions of life can no longer be taken for granted' (Furedi 1997: 67). Dunant and Porter suggest that:

> For many people in the western world the unprecedented expansion
> of everything from technology through communication to shopping
> has brought with it not only increased demands of choice (in itself
> something of an anxiety) but also an expanding potential for feeling
> out of control. (Dunant and Porter 1996: xi)

The very existence of fears and anxiety become 'a sign of the times', characterised as they are by rapid transformations and innovations, which have not only eroded old structures and values, but have also led to feelings of loss of control and loss of certainty about the future.

I want to offer a different analysis of the global politics of fear, one which does not assume fear as a symptom of transformation, or as a technology that is used for governance. Rather than fear being a tool or a symptom, I want to suggest that the language of fear involves the intensification of threats, which works to create a distinction between those who are 'under threat' and those who threaten. Fear is an effect of this process, rather than its origin. As David Campbell puts it: 'Danger is not an objective condition. It is not a thing that exists independently of those to whom it may become a threat' (Campbell 1998: 1). Through the generation of 'the threat', fear works to align bodies with and against others. My argument extends Ulrich Beck's position that solidarity is based on 'insecurity' rather than 'need' in the new modernity: it is through the perception of shared risk that communities become a 'binding force' (Beck 1992: 49).

The complexity of the spatial and bodily politics of fear has never been so apparent in the global economies of fear since September 11 2001. We might note that fear is, of course, named in the very naming of terrorism: terrorists are immediately identified as agents of extreme fear, that is, those who seek to make others afraid (less mobile or less free to move) as well as those who seek to cause death and destruction. As the former Australian Prime Minister John Howard put it, Bin Laden's 'hatred' for the United States and for 'a world system built on individual freedom, religious tolerance, democracy, and the international free flow of commerce' means that 'he wants to spread fear, create uncertainty and promote instability, hoping that this will cause communities and countries to turn against each other'. John Howard reads the acts of terror as attacks not only on the mobility of international capital, but also on the bodies of Australians, on their right 'to move around the world with ease and freedom and without fear'.[7] We could argue that terrorist attacks worked to restrict the mobility of the bodies of Americans, Australians and others in the West through the hyper-mobility of the bodies of the terrorists and the technologies or agents they use (including planes as well as biological agents such as anthrax). However, I would like to offer an alternative reading of fear economies, one that differentiates between forms of mobility as well as different kinds of bodily enclosure, containment or detainment.[8]

In the first instance, we can examine how the mobility of the bodies of subjects in the West, while presented as threatened, is also defended, along with the implicit defence of the mobility of capital in the global economy (whereby capital is constructed as 'clean money' and defined against the 'dirty money' of terrorism, which must be frozen or blocked). The most immediate instruction made to subjects and citizens in the West was 'to go about your daily business', 'to travel', 'to spend or consume' and so on, as a way of refusing to be a victim of terror. Indeed, in the United States, citizens were, in effect, asked not to fear, and the nation was represented as not being afraid, as a way of showing the failure of the terrorist attacks to destroy the nation. As George Bush puts it:

It is natural to wonder if America's future is one of fear. Some speak of an age of terror. I know there are struggles ahead, and dangers to face. But this country will define our times, not be defined by them. As long as the United States of America is determined and strong, this will not be an age of terror.[9]

What is clear here is that the nation is constructed as having prevailed through refusing to transform its vulnerability and wounds (terrorism did hurt the nation and there are dangers ahead) into an affective response of fear, a response narrativised as 'determination by terror', rather than self-determination. Bush, then, in an act of self-determination, turns the act of terror into an act of war, which would seek to eliminate the source of fear and transform the world into a place where the mobility of some capital and some bodies becomes the sign of freedom and civilisation. The effect of terror is not containment, but provides the very grounds for remobilisation.

We need, however, to think about this process carefully, without assuming that fear simply brings people together. As I have already noted, the object of fear may pass by and this structural possibility is part of the lived experience of fear. While the events did happen and did constitute an object (however much it passed by, a passing by which was already at stake in the living out of the present given the mediatisation of the event *as event*), that fear slid quickly into anxiety, in which what was at stake was not the *approach of* an object, but an *approach to* an object. The approach to the event – in which it is repeated and transformed into a fetish object – involved forms of alignment, whereby individuals aligned themselves with the nation as being under attack. This, of course, repeats the process of alignment whereby the nation aligned itself with individuals as having been attacked.

Now what is crucial here is not just that this alignment might restrict the mobility of individuals who now feel themselves, in a way that is personal, to be terrorist targets. Rather, given the mediating work of this alignment, experiences of fear became lived as patriotic declarations of love, *which allowed home to be mobilised as a defence against terror*. If subjects stayed at home, then homes became transformed into the symbolic space of the nation through the widespread use of American flags. This is not to say that the meaning of the flags is necessary to its circulation – as if such flags *could only* signify national love. Rather, we can consider how the flag is *a sticky sign*, whereby its stickiness allows it to stick to other 'flag signs', which gives the impression of coherence (the nation as 'sticking together'). The flag as a sign that has historically signified territorial conquest as well as love for the nation (patriotism) has effects, the repetition of the flag sign displays a sense of 'with-ness' and 'for-ness'. George Packer in an article in the *New York Times Magazine* expressed this sentiment well:

> As flags bloomed like flowers, I found that they tapped emotion as quickly as pictures of the missing. To me, these flags didn't represent flabby complacence, but alertness, grief, resolve, even love. They evoked fellow feeling with Americans, for we had been attacked together. (Packer 2001: 16)

The turning away from the object of fear involves a turning towards home, as a 'fellow feeling'. That 'turning towards' involves the repetition or reiteration of signs of 'fellowship'. That turning could even be understood as compulsory: not to display a flag could be read as a sign of a lack of fellowship, as a reading that has obvious risks.[10]

I want to suggest that fear mediated by love as identification with the nation, *which comes to adhere as an effect of signs of love*, does not necessarily shrink bodies. Indeed, fear may even allow some bodies to occupy more space through the identification with the collective body, which stands in for the individual body, and moves on its behalf. The apparent containment of some bodies in the United States can function as a form of mobilisation: staying at home allows the mobilisation of bodies through the symbolic identification with the nation at war. In George Bush's 2002 State of the Union Address the effect of this identification is clear: 'It was as if our entire country looked into a mirror and saw our better selves.'[11] Hence, America is defined as 'caught' by its own reflection in the mirror, a 'catching out' that borders on collective narcissism: self-love becomes a national love that legitimates the response to terror as protection of the loved other, who may be 'with me' by showing signs (such as flags) of being 'like me'.

So if the event of terror – of seeking to cause fear – leads to a defence of the mobility of capital and the mobilisation of some bodies (through both the defence of the home as nation and the identification with the nation), then who is contained through terror? Whose vulnerability is at stake? The events of September 11 have been used to justify the detention of 'any bodies' suspected of being terrorists. Not only was there immediate detention of suspects in the United States and European countries, but governments in the West have responded to the terror by passing new legislation that increases the governments' rights to detain anybody suspected of being a terrorist. The British amendment to the Anti-terrorism, Crime and Security Act 2001 ((Commencement No. 4) Order 2002 (SI 1279)) states that the Secretary of State may issue a certificate if he believes that a person's presence in the UK is a risk to national security or he suspects the person is an international terrorist (p. 10). Here, risk assessment becomes a matter of belief and suspicion itself becomes the grounds for detention. The extension of the powers of detention is not merely symbolic, and nor does it merely relate to the detention of terrorists: given the structural possibility that anybody could be a terrorist, what we have reinstituted and extended is the power of detention, as such.

However, the structural possibility that anyone could be a terrorist does not translate into everybody being affected by the extension of the powers of detention in the same way. It is well documented that people have been detained because of very weak links to terrorist networks, often involving simple connections through names or by places of work or residence. Aristide R. Zolberg considers this process a form of racial profiling, quoting details reported in the *New York Times*: of the 1,147 people detained in the United States between September 11 and November 2001, 'some were identified on the basis of circumstantial links with the attack, but many "were picked up based on tips or were people of Middle Eastern or South Asian descent who had been stopped for traffic violations or for acting suspiciously"' (Zolberg 2002: 296). As Muneer Ahmad describes, after September 11, there was 'an unrelenting, multivalent assault on the bodies, psyches, and rights of Arab, Muslim, and South Asian immigrants' (Ahmad 2002: 101). Indeed, Leti Volpp suggests that the responses to September 11 facilitated 'a new identity category that groups together persons who appear "Middle Eastern, Arab, or Muslim"' (Volpp 2002: 1,575). The recognition of such groups of people as 'could be terrorists' depends upon stereotypes that are already in place, at the same time as it generates a distinct category of 'the fearsome' in the present. We can recall the repetition of stereotypes about the black man in the encounter described by Frantz Fanon: this repetition works by generating the other as the object of fear, a fear which is then taken on by the other, as its own.

Importantly, the word 'terrorist' sticks to some bodies as it reopens histories of naming, just as the word 'terrorist' slides into other words in the accounts of the wars in Afghanistan and Iraq (such as fundamentalism, Islam, Arab, repressive, primitive and so on). Indeed, the slide of metonymy can function as an implicit argument about the causal relations between terms (such as Islam and terrorism), but in such a way that it does not require an explicit statement. The work done by metonymy means that it can remake links – it can stick words like 'terrorist' and 'Islam' together – even when arguments are made that seem to unmake those links. Utterances like 'this is not a war against Islam' coexist with descriptions such as 'Islamic terrorists', which work to restick the words together and constitute their coincidence as more than simply temporal. The sliding between signs also involves 'sticking' signs to bodies: the bodies who 'could be terrorists' are the ones who might 'look Muslim'. Such associations stick precisely insofar as they resist literalisation.

So given that the event functions an object, which allows certain forms of violence and detention of others in the name of defence, what role does security play in the affective politics of fear? Importantly, security is bound up with the 'not' as Michael Dillon has suggested – what is not 'me' or not 'we' (Dillon 1996: 34–5; see also Lipschutz 1995; Krause and Williams 1997; Burke 2001). Security is not simply about securing a border that already exists, nor is fear simply a fear of what we are not. Indeed, I have already shown how anxiety and fear create the effect of borders, and the effect of that which we are not. The transgression of the border is required in order for it to be secured as a border in the first place. As such security involves the securing of 'the not', which paradoxically requires the insecurity of 'the not'. *The insecurity of 'the not' makes it all the more powerful as a security project.* This is why the politics of fear is often narrated as a border anxiety: fear speaks the language of 'floods' and 'swamps', of being invaded by inappropriate others, against whom the nation must defend itself. We can reflect on the *ontology of insecurity* within the constitution of the political: it *must be* presumed that things are not secure, in and of themselves, in order to justify the imperative *to make things secure*.

More specifically, it is through announcing a crisis in security that new forms of security, border policing and surveillance become justified. We only have to think about how narratives of crisis are used within politics to justify a 'return' to values and traditions that are perceived to be under threat. However, it is not simply that these crises exist, and that fears and anxieties come into being as a necessary effect of that existence. Rather, it is the very production of the crisis that is crucial. To declare a crisis is not 'to make something out of nothing': such declarations often work with real events, facts or figures (as we can see, for example, in how the rise in divorce rates is used to announce a crisis in marriage and the family). But the declaration of crisis *reads* that fact/figure/event and transforms it into a fetish object that then acquires a life of its own, in other words, that can become the grounds for declarations of war against that which is read as the source of the threat. Through designating something as already under threat in the present that very thing becomes installed as that which we must fight for in the future, a fight which is retrospectively understood to be a matter of life and death. In other words, to announce a crisis is to produce the moral and political justification for maintaining 'what is' (taken for granted or granted) in the name of future survival.

Indeed, it is fear of death – of the death of oneself, one's loved ones, one's community and one's people – that is generated by such narratives as a means of preserving that which is. So I might fear for myself, for us, or on behalf of others. Indeed, in many of the public outbursts of fear and anxiety around terrorism in Western countries this is precisely the kind of 'collecting together' through fear that takes place. The bodies of the victims become symbolic of that which is under threat not only by terrorists (those who take life), but by all that the possibility of terrorism stands for. Such a possibility has been linked by some commentators not only to the existence of external others, but to internal forms of weakness, such as secularisation, multiculturalism and the decline of social and familial ties. For example, Jerry Falwell in the United States, argued that:

> I really believe that the pagans, and the abortionists, and the
> feminists, and the gays and the lesbians who are actively trying to
> make that an alternative lifestyle . . . all of them who have tried to
> secularise America . . . I point the finger in their face and say 'you
> helped this happen'.[12]

In the United Kingdom, the British National Party's response to September 11 was to posit Islamisation within the UK rather than the Taliban in Afghanistan as the threat to the moral future of the nation itself: 'They can turn Britain into an Islamic Republic by 2025.'[13]

This attribution of the crime of terror to the weakening of religion and community posed by the presence of various others has of course been condemned within mainstream politics, although noticeably with less of a 'disgust reaction' than how some critics of United States foreign policy have been received (see Chapter 4). However, at the same time, a broader set of assumptions around what would be required to defend the nation and the world (strengthening the will of the community in the face of others) both displaces and reworks the narrative logic. Instead of an internal weakness being posited as responsible for the events of September 11, in more moderate discourses, *we have an internal strength being posited as responsible for recovery, survival and moving beyond fear*. As George Bush put it: 'These acts of mass murder were intended to frighten our nation into chaos and retreat. But they have failed; our country is strong.'[14] The response to terror becomes a way of strengthening the bonds of the nation and the global community of free nations: the wound of terror requires 'sticking together' (coherence) and using the values that made the United States and democracy 'strong'.

Indeed, the emphasis on security in Bush's State of the Union Address in 2002 includes the transformation of democratic citizenship into policing: 'And as government works to secure our homeland, America will continue to depend on the eyes and ears of alert citizens.' Citizenship here is translated into a form of Neighbourhood Watch; the citizen must 'look out for suspicious others'.[15] Citizenship works as a way of policing the boundaries of neighbourhoods against others who look suspicious, where such a look is already identified with how others look ('looking Middle-Eastern, Arab, Muslim'). The role of citizens as police is translated as an imperative to love, in which love becomes the foundation of community, as well as the guarantor of our future: 'Our country also needs citizens working to rebuild our communities. We need mentors to love children.'[16] The definition of values that will allow America to prevail in the face of terror – values that have been named as freedom, love, and compassion – involves the defence of particular institutional and social forms against the danger posed by others. Such values function to define not only ideals that supposedly govern war aims and objectives, but also democratic norms of behaviour and conduct, of what it means to be civil, a civil society and a legitimate government. To be brought into international civil society – that is, not to be named as a 'rogue state' or as part of 'the axis of evil' – others must 'mimic' these rules of conduct and forms of governance. Henceforth, the emphasis on values, truths and norms that will allow survival *slides easily into the defence of particular social forms or institutions.*

Following on from my argument in the previous section, the fear of degeneration, decline and disintegration as mechanisms for preserving 'what is', becomes associated more with some bodies than others. The threat of such others to social forms (which are the materialisation of norms) is represented as *the threat of turning and being turned away from the values that will guarantee survival*. These various others come to embody the failure of the norm to take form; it is the proximity of such other bodies that 'causes' the fear that forms of civilisation (the family, the community, the nation, international civil society) have degenerated. What is important, then, is that the narratives that seek to preserve the present, through working on anxieties of death as the necessary consequence of the demise of traditional forms, also seek to locate that anxiety in some bodies, which then take on fetish qualities as objects of fear.

Such bodies also engender even more anxiety, as they cannot be held in place as objects, and threaten to pass by. That is, we may fail to see those forms that have failed to be; it is always possible that we might not be able to 'tell the difference'. The present hence becomes preserved by defending the community against the imagined others, who may take form in ways that cannot be anticipated, a 'not-yet-ness' which means the work of defence is never over. Such a defence is generated by anxiety and fear for the future, and justifies the elimination of that which fails to materialise in the form of the norm as a struggle for survival. Insofar as we do not know what forms other others may take, those who fail to materialise in the forms that are lived as norms, *the policy of continual surveillance of emergent forms is sustained as an ongoing project of survival.*

It is here that we can deepen our reflections on the role of the figure of the international terrorist within the economies of fear. Crucially, the narrative which justifies the expansion of the powers to detain others within the nation and the potentially endless expansion of the war itself to other nations relies on the structural possibility that the terrorist 'could be' anyone and anywhere. The narrative of the 'could be' terrorist, in which the terrorist is the one that 'hides in shadows',[17] has a double edge. On the one hand, the figure of the terrorist is detached from particular bodies, as a shadowy figure, 'an unspecifiable may-come-to-pass' (Massumi 1993: 11). But it is this could-be-ness, this detachment, which also allows the restriction on the mobility of those bodies that are read *as associated with terrorism*: Islam, Arab, Asian, East, and so on. Fear sticks to these bodies (and to the bodies of 'rogue states') that 'could be' terrorist, where the 'could be' extends the power to detain. Although such fear sticks, it also slides across such bodies; *it is the structural possibility that the terrorist may pass us by that justifies the expansion of these forms of intelligence, surveillance and the rights of detention.* Fear works to expand the mobility of some bodies and contain others precisely insofar as it does not reside positively in any one body.

It is important to recognise that the figure of the international terrorist has been mobilised in close proximity to the figure of the asylum seeker. This is certainly clear in the British amendment to the Terrorism Act, which juxtaposes the question of asylum with the question of terrorism (Anti-Terrorism, Crime and Security Act 2001). The amendment merely suggests that the appellant is not entitled to protection when suspected of being an international terrorist. The implicit assumption that governs the juxtaposition in the first place is that *of any body in the nation* (subjects, citizens, migrants, even tourists) the asylum seeker is most likely to be the international terrorist. The slide between these two figures does an enormous amount of work: it assumes that those who seek asylum, who flee from terror and persecution may be bogus *insofar as they could be the agents of terror and persecution*. They, like terrorists, are identified as potential burglars (see Chapter 2); as an unlawful intrusion into the nation. New restrictions on asylum internationally have hence coincided with new terrorism laws. In Australia, for example, the refusal to allow the boat *Tampa* into its waters (with its 433 cargo of asylum seekers, many of whom were from Afghanistan) was retrospectively justified on the grounds that those on board 'could have' been linked to Osama Bin Laden. This violent slide between the figure of the asylum seeker and the international terrorist works to construct those who are 'without home' as sources of 'our fear' and as reasons for new forms of border policing, whereby the future is always a threat posed by others who may pass by and pass their way into our communities. The containment of the bodies of others affected by this economy of fear is most violently revealed in the literal deaths of those seeking asylum in containers, deaths that remain unmourned by the very nations who embody the promise of a future for those seeking asylum. This is a chilling reminder of what is at stake in the global economies of fear.

NOTES

1. We might note here that I have spoken about the object as 'making' us afraid. This needs some qualification. There is nothing in the object that renders fear a *necessary consequence* of the object. As Spinoza put it: 'I saw all the things I feared and which feared me had nothing good or bad in them save insofar as the mind was affected by them' (cited in May 1977: xv). See also my discussion of Descartes and the example of the child and the bear in the introduction to this book.
2. The idea of anxiety as a 'free floating emotion', or as 'generalised', is crucial to Freudian psychoanalysis. Whilst I share the emphasis on anxiety as not 'having' an object, I am suggesting that anxiety tends to generate its objects, and to stick them together. Anxiety is like Velcro: it picks up objects that are proximate to it.
3. In a way, I am suggesting that anxiety generates an object, but that the object itself is absent. This argument might relate to Dominick LaCapra's model. He suggests that the conversion of absence into loss gives 'anxiety an identifiable object – the lost object – and generates the hope that anxiety may be eliminated' (LaCapra 2001: 57).
4. Certainly, in the paper on 'The Unconscious', the argument about 'unconscious emotions' does rely on a model of origins, or the 'true connection' between an idea and a feeling (Freud 1964a: 177).
5. The word 'careful' is interesting, as it reminds us of the link between care and anxiety. To 'have care' (even care for others), can also mean to 'take care', which may engender an anxious relation to the world ('carefulness'). We all know, I suspect, that objects we love make us anxious: we fear we will break them, so we treat them with more care (or

we put the precious objects away, and only use objects that we don't care about). Being careful is an anxious feeling. When we are anxious, we tend to be clumsier with our bodies, as we are hyper-aware of all that can go wrong, and these 'possibilities' become objects of feeling. Hence anxiety and carefulness often lead to the very event they wish to avoid: breakages. We might note here, that femininity is associated with both care and anxiety. A feminine relation to objects could be described as a mode of carefulness, which actually restricts the mobility of the feminine body within domestic space, as well as public space.

6. We see this in responses to September 11. George Bush, for example, claimed in an address to a Joint Session of Congress and the American People: 'Freedom and fear are at war' (http://www.whitehouse.gov/news/releases/2001/09/20010920-8.html Accessed 23 July 2003). As I discuss in the next section, the terrorist attacks were defined as attacks on freedom, which was specifically defined as the freedom to move. To fear would be to give up one's freedom to move. The relation between freedom and fear has been discussed very differently in philosophy. Kierkegaard, for example, associates freedom with fear rather than seeing freedom and fear as opposed. Fear is defined as 'the alarming possibility of *being able*' (Kierkegaard 1957: 40). Kierkegaard shows us that the failure to be fully determined opens up the capacity to act, which itself is 'alarming'. For Kierkegaard, fear is not about restriction, but capacity; we feel afraid because we can act.

7. The speech was posted on http://www.dfat.gov.au/icat/pm_251001_speech.html Accessed 11 November 2002.

8. My analysis of how mobility for some is dependent on the containment of others is informed by feminist and post-colonial critiques of the idealisation of 'mobility' within recent social and cultural theory. For a summary of these critiques see Ahmed et al. (2003).

9. http://www.whitehouse.gov/news/releases/2001/09/20010920-8.html Accessed 23 July 2003.

10. For Arabs, Muslims and South Asians in the United States, displaying the flag might then be read not only as a form of identification with the nation, but as an attempt to 'cover' any signs of difference that might be read as a source of terror. See Ahmad for a wonderful analysis of the 'swap' between the flag and the veil (Ahmad 2002: 110).

11. http://www.whitehouse.gov/news/releases/2002/01/20020129-11.html Accessed 23 June 2002.

12. Jerry Falwell made this comment to Pat Robertson's 700 club on 13 September 2001. He apologised on 14 September.

13. http://www.bnp.org.uk/article92.html; http://www.bnp.org.uk/article87.html Accessed 30 June 2002.

14. http://www.whitehouse.gov/news/releases/2001/09/20010911-16.html Accessed 23 June 2002.

15. For an analysis of how Neighbourhood Watch involves techniques of knowledge, which work to recognise 'strangers' as 'bodies out of place' see Chapter 1 in Ahmed (2000).

16. http://www.whitehouse.gov/news/releases/2002/01/20020129-11.html Accessed 23 July 2003.

17. http://www.whitehouse.gov/response/faq-what.html Accessed 23 July 2003.

CHAPTER 4

The Performativity of Disgust

The term 'disgust', in its simplest sense, means something offensive
to the taste. It is curious how readily this feeling is excited by
anything unusual in the appearance, odour or nature of our food.
In Tierra del Fuego a native touched with his finger some cold
preserved meat which I was eating . . . and plainly showed utter
disgust at its softness; whilst I felt utter disgust at my food being
touched by a naked savage, though his hands did not appear dirty.
(Darwin 1904: 269)

What does it mean to feel 'utter disgust'? Why do some things seem more
disgusting than others? Are we necessarily disgusted by the same things and
can we recognise when another is 'plainly disgusted', by what they do with
their bodies? In the quotation above, the complexity of disgust could not be
more apparent, despite Darwin's emphasis on the almost self-evident nature
of disgust reactions. Beginning with the etymology of the word 'disgust' (bad
taste), he draws his reader into an apparently straightforward encounter, but
one that can take place only given a certain history, a history whereby the
mobility of white European bodies involves the transformation of native
bodies into knowledge, property and commodity. Darwin here reads the
native body as being disgusted by the texture of that which he eats, while he
conveys to the reader his own disgust at the mere proximity of the 'naked
savage' to his own food. That other is not dirty, he admits. The admission is
telling; the other's hands do not 'look dirty' for the proximity of the other to
be felt as disgusting. The other is already seen as dirt, as the carrier of dirt,
which contaminates the food that has been touched. Disgust reads the objects
that are felt to be disgusting: it is not just about bad objects that we are afraid
to incorporate, but the very designation of 'badness' as a quality we assume
is inherent in those objects. Darwin relates 'badness' to anything unusual

about food, that is, to anything that departs from 'the ordinary palate'. This association of what is bad with what is strange or other is significant. The question of what 'tastes bad' is bound up with questions of familiarity and strangeness: here, the proximity of the bodies of others is read as the cause of 'our sickness' precisely insofar as the other is seeable and knowable as stranger-than-me and stranger-to-us in the first place.

Of course, it is significant that this cross-cultural encounter takes place over food, partly because the politics of 'what gets eaten' or consumed is bound up with histories of imperialism (Sheller 2003). Food is significant not only because disgust is a matter of taste as well as touch – as senses that require proximity to that which is sensed – but also because food is 'taken into' the body. The fear of contamination that provokes the nausea of disgust reactions hence makes food the very 'stuff' of disgust. Of course, we must eat to survive. So the very project of survival requires we take something other into our bodies. Survival makes us vulnerable in that it requires we let what is 'not us' in; to survive we open ourselves up, and we *keep the orifices of the body open*. The native touching the white man's food is a sign of the danger that the native will be taken into the white man's body, contaminating the white man's body with its dirt. At the same time, the native is read as being disgusted by the texture of the white man's food, a reading which not only assumes access to the interiority of the native body, but also enables the distantiation necessary to the recovery of the white man's apartness, in the sense that the native's disgust guarantees that he will eat something other than what the white man eats. Disgust does something, certainly: through disgust, bodies 'recoil' from their proximity, as a proximity that is felt as nakedness or as an exposure on the skin surface.

We can see from this example that being disgusted is not simply about 'gut feelings'. Or if disgust is about gut feelings, then our relation to our guts is not direct, but is mediated by ideas that are already implicated in the very impressions we make of others and the way those impressions surface as bodies. Even the apparently simple concept of 'bad taste' gets us into some thorny problems. On the one hand, 'bad taste' suggests that what is bad is something we have eaten (the taste comes from 'what is eaten' rather than the one who eats). Badness might then seem to describe the nature of what gets taken into the orifice of the mouth (the food or object). On the other hand, something tastes bad only within the mouth of the one who tastes (the subject). The inter-corporeal encounter of incorporation or ingestion hence involves the perception of 'badness' as a quality of something only in the event that the badness fills up, as it were, the mouth of the one who tastes. So disgust, even defined simply as bad taste, shows us how the boundaries that allow the distinction between subjects and objects are undone in the moment of their making.

How can we tell the story of disgust in a way that works with the compli-cated relations between bodies, objects and others? In the first section, I will reflect on how disgust is fascinated with the texture and qualities of what is felt to be disgusting, as well as on how disgust affects the surface of the bodies of the disgusted. Secondly, I will examine the relation between disgust and stickiness, and how stickiness becomes an affective quality of objects. And finally, I will reflect on the performativity of disgust, by looking at how disgust involves not just corporeal intensities, but speech acts. My questions are simple: What does it mean to designate something as disgusting? How do such designations work to generate effects? In particular, I will reflect on the generative effects of the responses to the terrorist attacks on September 11 2001, which declare: 'That's disgusting!'

Throughout this chapter, it will be apparent that disgust is deeply ambiva-lent, involving desire for, or an attraction towards, the very objects that are felt to be repellent. As William Ian Miller has put it: 'Even as the disgusting repels, it rarely does so without also capturing our attention. It imposes itself upon us. We find it hard not to sneak a second look or, less voluntarily, we find our eyes doing "double-takes" at the very things that disgust us' (Miller 1997: x). The contradictory impulses of desire and disgust do not necessarily resolve themselves, and they do not take us to the same place. Disgust pulls us away from the object, a pulling that feels almost involuntary, as if our bodies were thinking for us, on behalf of us. In contrast, desire pulls us towards objects, and opens us up to the bodies of others. While the affect of being pulled may feel similar at one level, at another, the *direction* or *orienta-tion* of the pull creates a very different affective relation between the subject and object. In the previous two chapters, I reflected on the processes of 'moving' or 'turning' towards and away from objects and others, and how these processes work to align social and bodily space. I now want to think of 'pulling' *as an intensification of movement as such*. In such an intensification, the objects seem to have us 'in their grip', and to be moving towards us in how they impress upon us, an impression that requires us to pull away, with an urgency that can be undoing.

DISGUST AND ABJECTION

So how else can we tell the story of disgust without assuming some things are inherently disgusting? Paul Rozin and April E. Fallon identify four key elements of the disgust experience: a characteristic facial expression; an appropriate action (distancing of the self from an offensive object); a dis-tinctive physiological manifestation (nausea); and a characteristic feeling state (revulsion) (Rozin and Fallon 1987: 23). This list shows us how disgust involves the 'weightiness' of feelings, the way in which feelings are, in some sense, material; like objects, feelings do things, and they affect what they come into contact with. So feeling 'disgusted' is not simply an inner or psychic state; it works on bodies, by transforming or 'working on' the surfaces of bodies. What is still bypassed in the above list is the question of how some objects come to be felt to be 'offensive' in the first place. We can only ask this question if we assume that offensiveness (and with it disgust) is not an inherent quality of an object, but is attributed to objects partly in the affective response of 'being disgusted'. At the same time, we can only make this observation if we avoid assuming disgust simply comes from within, and then moves out towards others.

We can certainly reflect upon the way in which disgust, as an intense bodily feeling of being sickened, is always directed towards an object. One does not feel disgust in the abstract; one feels disgusted by something in which the thing itself seems to repel us. Or as William Ian Miller puts it: 'Disgust is a feeling *about* something and in response to something, not just raw unattached feeling' (Miller 1997: 8). Disgust is about an object, such that one's feelings of sickness become attributed to the object ('I feel sick, you have sickened me, you are sickening'). We need to account for how it is that the object of disgust impresses upon us, as if the object contained the 'truth' of our own response to it.

Disgust is clearly dependent upon contact: it involves a relationship of touch and proximity between the surfaces of bodies and objects. That contact is felt as an unpleasant intensity: it is not that the object, apart from the body, has the quality of 'being offensive', but the proximity of the object to the body is felt as offensive. The object must have got close enough to make us feel disgusted. As a result, while disgust *over takes* the body, it also *takes over* the object that apparently gives rise to it. The body is over taken precisely insofar as it takes the object over, in a temporary holding onto the detail of the surface of the object: its texture; its shape and form; how it clings and moves. It is only through such a sensuous proximity that the object is felt to be so 'offensive' that it sickens and over takes the body.

Disgust does not end with the proximity of such contact. The body recoils from the object; it pulls away with an intense movement that registers in the pit of the stomach. The movement is the work of disgust; it is what disgust does. Disgust brings the body perilously close to an object only then to pull away from the object in the registering of the proximity as an offence. Or, as Paul Rozin et al. put it: 'Disgust is manifested as a distancing from some object, event or situation, and can be characterized as a rejection' (Rozin et al. 1993: 577). That distancing requires proximity is crucial to the intercorporeality of the disgust encounter. The double movement (towards, away) is forgotten, however, as the body pulls back: it is as if the object moved towards the body, rather than the body having got close enough to the object. Hence the proximity of the 'disgusting object' may feel like an offence to bodily space, as if the object's invasion of that space was a necessary consequence of what seems disgusting about the object itself. Pulling back, bodies that are disgusted are also bodies that feel a certain rage, a rage that the object has got close enough to sicken, and to be taken over or taken in. To be disgusted is after all *to be affected by what one has rejected*. As Silvan S. Tomkins suggests, in disgust: 'Attention is most likely to be referred to the source, the object, rather than to the self or the face. This happens because the response intends to maximise the distance between the face and the object which disgusts the self. It is a literal pulling away from the object' (Tomkins 1963: 128). The pulling away from the object keeps the object at the centre of attention, as a centring which attributes the affect of sickness to the very quality of the object.

But describing the inter-corporeality of disgust encounters does not allow us to understand how some forms of contact between the surfaces of bodies and objects (a contact which produces the effect of surfacing, of skins that shudder and form) are felt as sickening invasions. In order to ask this question of why some forms of contact are felt to be disgusting (and not others), we can examine the relationship between disgust and abjection. Julia Kristeva in *Powers of Horror* provides one of the most influential models of abjection.[1] She argues that, within abjection: 'There looms . . . one of the violent, dark revolts of being, directed against a threat that seems to emanate from an exorbitant outside or inside, ejected beyond the scope of the possible, the tolerable, the thinkable' (Kristeva 1982: 1). Here, the abject threatens, and the threat may come from without or within, as it works to threaten what is thinkable or possible in the first place. But what makes something so threatening? Kristeva shows us that what threatens from the outside only threatens insofar as it is already within: 'It is as if the skin, a fragile container, no longer guaranteed the integrity of one's "own and clean self", but scraped and transparent, invisible or taut, gave way before *the dejection of its contents*' (Kristeva 1982: 53, emphasis added). It is not that the abject has got inside us; the abject turns us inside out, as well outside in.

Kristeva suggests provocatively that, in abjection, it is the border that is transformed into an object (Kristeva 1982: 4). We could return to the racist encounter described in Audre Lorde's *Sister Outsider*, and discussed in Chapter 2. Here, the border between the white woman and black child is transformed into an object: the roach (Lorde 1984: 147–8). The object that makes us 'sick to the stomach' is a substitute for the border itself, an act of substitution that protects the subject from all that is 'not it'. Abjection is bound up with the insecurity of the not; it seeks to secure 'the not' through the response of being disgusted. This extends my argument in Chapter 3: it suggests that what makes 'the not' insecure is the possibility that what is 'not not' (what is 'me' or 'us') can slide into 'the not', a slippage which would threaten the ontology of 'being apart' from others.

The relationship between disgust reactions and the transformation of borders into objects is unclear. On the one hand, it is the transformation of borders into objects that is sickening (like the skin that forms on milk). On the other, the border is transformed into an object precisely as an effect of disgust (spitting/vomiting). Perhaps the ambiguity relates to the necessity of the designation of that which is threatening: borders need to be threatened in order to be maintained, or even to appear *as* borders, and part of the process of 'maintenance-through-transgression' is the appearance of border objects. Border objects are hence disgusting, while disgust engenders border objects. As a result, disgust involves a 'time lag' as well as being generative or futural. It does not make borders (out of nothing), but responds to their making, through a reconfirmation of their necessity. So the subject feels an object to be disgusting (a perception that relies on a history that comes before the encounter) and then expels the object and, through expelling the object, finds it to be disgusting. *The expulsion itself becomes the 'truth' of the reading of the object.* There is a certain truth in the apparently banal statement that border objects are disgusting, while disgust engenders border objects. Is there a route out of this circular economy or is the circularity part of the lure of abjection itself?

For Kristeva, the abject 'is that which opposes the I' (Kristeva 1982: 3). We can also consider how disgust is shaped by the relation *between* objects. Objects come to matter within disgust reactions not simply insofar as they oppose 'the I', *but through their contact with other objects*. As I pointed out in Chapter 1, the word 'contact' is related to the word 'contingency'. Is the object that disgusts 'disgusting' because of its contact with other objects? The way in which disgust is generated by 'contact' between objects is what makes the attribution of disgust dependent on a certain history, rather than being a necessary consequence of the nature of things. It is not that an object we might encounter is inherently disgusting; rather, an object becomes disgusting through its contact with other objects that have already, as it were, been designated as disgusting before the encounter has taken place. It is the dependency of disgust on contact or proximity that may explain its awkward temporality, the way it both lags behind and makes an object.

Disgust hence operates as a contact zone; it is about how things come into contact with other things. As many commentators have argued: 'Anything which has had contact with disgusting things itself becomes disgusting' (Tomkins 1963: 131; see also W. I. Miller 1997: 5 and S. B. Miller 1993: 711). While disgust involves such a metonymic slide, it does not move freely: it sticks to that which is near it; it clings. Furthermore, an object can become disgusting because it resembles another object that is disgusting (Rozin and Fallon 1987: 30; Angyal 1941: 397). Hence, disgust can move between objects through the recognition of likeness. Disgust binds objects together in the very moment that objects become attributed with bad feeling, as 'being' sickening. The slide between disgust and other emotions is crucial to this binding: the subject may experience hate towards the object, as well as fear of the object, precisely as an affect of how the bad feeling 'has got in'. However, the feeling of disgust may resist being fully transferred to the object, even when the object is attributed as the source of the feeling. The object becomes disgusting, in a way that allows the subject to recoil, only after an intimate contact that is felt on the surface of the skin.

We can return to the example of Darwin's disgust at the 'naked savage'. The 'nakedness' of the native body becomes a sign of the risk of proximity. Such proximity is sexualised; it involves contact between skins, without the mediation or distance of cloth or clothing. The nature of the encounter demonstrates that disgust involves not simply distantiation (recoiling), but the intensification of bodily contact that 'disturbs' the skin with the possibility of desire. Such a risky proximity does not involve pulling towards the native's body, in an expression of forbidden desire. Rather natives must get too close for the white man to move away. Furthermore, the feeling that the proximity of this other is disgusting is dependent on past associations, in this case evoked through a negation. The admission that the native body 'is not dirty' works to associate the native body with dirt. The association between the two border objects is very important: the native body 'stands for' dirt (it does not have to be dirty) only insofar as 'dirt' is held in place as the border object. We could argue of course that dirt itself 'stands for' something else; it is not in itself inherently disgusting, but comes to matter 'as matter out of place' (Douglas 1995: 36). But this potential deferral of what is disgusting is *halted or blocked* in the sticking of the objects together. The very process of substitution of objects is halted in the very contingency of the association between 'dirt' and 'native body'. Through sticking these two objects together (adherence), disgust allows the subject to recoil, as if from an object, even given the lack of an inherent quality to the object. It is this metonymic contact between objects or signs that allows them to be felt to be disgusting *as if that was* a material or objective quality.

When thinking about how bodies become objects of disgust, we can see that disgust is crucial to power relations. Why is disgust so crucial to power? Does disgust work to maintain power relations through how it maintains bodily boundaries? The relation between disgust and power is evident when we consider the spatiality of disgust reactions, and their role in the hierarchising of spaces as well as bodies. As William Ian Miller has argued, disgust reactions are not only about objects that seem to threaten the boundary lines of subjects, they are also about objects that seem 'lower' than or below the subject, or even beneath the subject (Miller 1997: 9). We can return here to the question of abject matter. Lower regions of the body – that which is below – are clearly associated both with sexuality and with 'the waste' that is literally expelled by the body. It is not that what is low is necessarily disgusting, nor is sexuality necessarily disgusting. Lowness becomes associated with lower regions of the body as it becomes associated with other bodies and other spaces. The spatial distinction of 'above' from 'below' functions metaphorically to separate one body from another, as well as to differentiate between higher and lower bodies, or more and less advanced bodies. As a result, disgust at 'that which is below' functions to maintain the power relations between above and below, *through which 'aboveness' and 'belowness' become properties of particular bodies, objects and spaces.* Given the fact that the one who is disgusted is the one who feels disgust, then the position of 'aboveness' is maintained only at the cost of a certain vulnerability (Miller 1997: 9), as an openness to being affected by those who are felt to be below. Darwin's disgust keeps the native below, as it makes the native below, but it also signals his own openness to falling below the native.

ON STICKINESS

I suggested in the previous section that we cannot understand disgust without understanding its contingency, defined in terms of the 'contact' between objects. In disgust, contingency is itself intensified; the contact between surfaces engenders an intensity of affect. But it is not just surfaces that materialise through disgust. As one object is substituted for another, or moves into another, a border is temporarily affected, despite the fact that neither object is inherently disgusting. Such objects become sticky as an effect of this substitution.

I have already asked the question 'What sticks?' in this book, but I have yet to address the question of stickiness and how stickiness becomes a quality of some surfaces, objects and signs. Needless to say, the sticky and the disgusting have been linked, if not reduced to each other. As William Ian Miller has argued: 'Horrifying things stick, like glue, like slime' (Miller 1997: 26). We might note already here a slight paradox. It is certainly the case that slimy things might be disgusting, but glue is hardly a substance that is represented as disgusting. So something that is sticky like glue might be disgusting, but glue itself probably isn't. Immediately, we can begin to see that not all sticky things are disgusting. Perhaps glue doesn't bring with it disgusting associations because we think of glue as *something we use to stick other things together*, rather than being something that threatens to stick to us. Glue is also about adherence: and when we remove objects that have been stuck together with glue, typically the stickiness will cease. Perhaps stickiness becomes disgusting *only when the skin surface is at stake such that what is sticky threatens to stick to us.*

We can draw here on a philosophical literature on substances that are not simply solid or liquid. Jean-Paul Sartre, for example, reflects on slime as a quality of surface and feeling, both of which are understood as material in shape and form. He suggests that what is slimy is disgusting because: 'At this instant I suddenly understand the snare of the slimy: it is a fluidity which holds me and which compromises me; I can not slide on this slime, all its suction cups hold me back; it can not slide over me, it clings to me like a leech' (Sartre 1996: 609). The quality of sliminess is that it 'clings'; it neither has the firmness of something solid, nor the flow of something liquid. In between solid and liquid, it takes form only insofar as it sucks at the surface onto which it clings. However, this assumption that sliminess is a repulsive quality in a feeling or substance can be questioned. For the attribution of a quality to substance, although posited as a quality as such (rather than being merely substantial), relies on the figurability of disgust. The quality of slime is described through the use of an analogy: 'It clings to me *like* a leech.' Although sliminess is given the status of a quality as such, the very necessity of figuring that quality through speech suggests its deferral along the chain of signification (figuration without ground). In the last instance, the substance of slime is displaced through the analogy with a leech, which, like the roach in Audre Lorde's narrative, becomes a substitute for an object of disgust.

As Elizabeth Grosz argues, in response to Sartre's work on slime and viscosity, the 'fear of being absorbed into something which has no boundaries of its own' is 'not a property' of something (Grosz 1994: 194). In her terms, such slimy things become disgusting only given the maintenance of an order of things, which allows such absorption to become threatening. Stickiness, like slime, is also not inherently disgusting. Or, to make this point more strongly, stickiness itself might not be a quality that always 'adheres' to an object. Rather than using stickiness to describe an object's surface, we can think of stickiness as an effect of surfacing, *as an effect of the histories of contact between bodies, objects, and signs.* To relate stickiness with historicity is not to say that some things and objects are not 'sticky' in the present. Rather, it is to say that stickiness is an effect. That is, stickiness depends on histories of contact that have already impressed upon the surface of the object.

One could question the relation between being literally sticky (as my finger would be if it brushed against wet paint) or metaphorically sticky (a sign that gets repeated and accumulates affective value: such a sign might seem *like* a sticky finger). However, I do not want to presume an association of the literal with the physical body and the metaphorical with language. Certainly, there are different forms of stickiness. But the sticky surface and the sticky sign cannot be separated through any simple distinction between literal and metaphorical. Rather, stickiness involves a form of relationality, or a 'with-ness', in which the elements that are 'with' get bound together. One can stick by a friend. One can get stuck in traffic. Some forms of stickiness are about holding things together. Some are about blockages or stopping things moving. When a sign or object becomes sticky it can function to 'block' the movement (of other things or signs) and it can function to bind (other things or signs) together. Stickiness helps us to associate 'blockages' with 'binding'.

We could ask an obvious question here: How do surfaces become sticky? Well, at one level an obvious question has an obvious answer: things become sticky as an effect of encountering other sticky things. Such stickiness gets transferred onto other things. As such, a sticky surface is one that will incorporate other elements into the surface such that the surface of a sticky object is in a dynamic process of re-surfacing. The incorporation can lead of course to surfaces becoming less sticky. But the stickiness of that surface *still tells us a history of the object that is not dependent on the endurance of the quality of stickiness*: what sticks 'shows us' where the object has travelled through what it has gathered onto its surface, gatherings that become a part of the object, and call into question its integrity as an object. What makes something sticky in the first place is difficult to determine precisely because stickiness involves such a chain of effects. This does not mean that some substances are not sticky (in the here and the now), but that stickiness is not the property of an object, as it accumulates and affects that which it touches. As a result, to get stuck to something sticky is also to become sticky. In the event of being cut off from a sticky object, an object (including the skin surface) may remain sticky and may 'pick up' other objects. Stickiness then is about what objects do to other objects – it involves a transference of affect – but it is a relation of 'doing' in which there is not a distinction between passive or active, even though the stickiness of one object might come before the stickiness of the other, such that the other seems to cling to it.

We can follow up with a less obvious question: How do signs become sticky? We can return to the example of hate speech discussed in Chapter 2. We could argue signs become sticky through repetition; if a word is used in a certain way, again and again, then that 'use' *becomes* intrinsic; it becomes a form of signing. It is hard then to hear words like 'Pakis' without hearing that word as insulting. The resistance to the word acquiring new meaning is not about the referent; rather the resistance is an effect of these histories of repetition of the word 'Paki'.[2] This repetition has a binding effect; the word works to generate others as 'Paki'; it has particular effects on others who recognise themselves as the object of the address. The 'binding' effect of the word is also a 'blockage': it stops the word moving or acquiring new value. The sign is a 'sticky sign' as an effect of a history of articulation, which allows the sign to accumulate value. The stickiness of the sign is also about the relation or contact between signs. The word 'Paki' becomes an insult through its association with other words, other forms of derision. However, such words do not have to be used once the sign becomes sticky. To use a sticky sign is to evoke other words, which have become intrinsic to the sign through past forms of association. The word 'Paki' might then stick to other words that are not spoken: immigrant, outsider, dirty, and so on. The association between words that generates meanings is concealed: *it is this concealment of such associations that allows such signs to accumulate value*. I am describing this accumulation of affective value as a form of stickiness, or as 'sticky signs'.

What is the relationship between signs and bodies? As I argued in the first section, economies of disgust also involve the shaping of bodies. When the body of another becomes an object of disgust, then the body *becomes* sticky. Such bodies become 'blockages' in the economy of disgust: they slow down or 'clog up' the movement between objects, as other objects and signs stick to them. This is how bodies become fetish objects: as we shall see, feelings of disgust stick more to some bodies than others, such that they become disgusting, as if their presence is what makes 'us sick'.

SPEAKING DISGUST

The question, 'What sticks?', is not simply a question of how objects stick to other objects, but also about how some objects more than others become sticky, such that other objects seem to stick to them. It is important not to neutralise the differences between objects and to recognise that some objects become stickier than others given past histories of contact. In this section, I will address how disgust works performatively not only as the intensification of contact between bodies and objects, but also as a speech act. In other words, I want us to reflect on how disgust can generate effects by 'binding' signs to bodies as a binding that 'blocks' new meanings.

What do I mean here by performative? According to Judith Butler, performativity relates to the way in which a signifier, rather than simply naming something that already exists, works to generate that which it apparently names. Performativity is hence about the 'power of discourse to produce effects through reiteration' (Butler 1993: 20). The temporal dimension of performativity is crucial. On the one hand, the performative is futural; it generates effects in the constitution or materialisation of that which is 'not yet'. On the other hand, performativity depends upon the sedimentation of the past; it reiterates what has already been said, and its power and author-ity depend upon how it recalls that which has already been brought into existence. This model of performativity relates to my argument about the temporality of disgust: it both lags behind the object from which it recoils, and generates the object in the very event of recoiling.

Given this paradoxical temporality, performativity involves iterability (Butler 1993: 13). A performative utterance can only 'succeed' if it repeats a coded or iterable utterance: it works precisely by citing norms and conven-tions that already exist (Butler 1993: 13; see also Chapter 5). Importantly, the historicity of the performative and its role in the generation of effects cannot be separated. If the performative opens up the future, it does so precisely in the process of repeating past conventions, as to repeat something is always to open up the (structural) possibility that one will repeat something with a difference. Significantly, iterability means that the sign can be 'cut off' from its contexts of utterance; that possibility of cutting is structural to the writerly nature of signification (Derrida 1988).

We can relate the question of 'cutting' to the question of stickiness. Think-ing of how signs are sticky – and in particular how they may stick to other signs – also demonstrates the (equally structural) resistance to cutting. This resistance is not inherent within signs, but is dependent on how signs work in relation to other signs, or how the signifier sticks to a signified in a chain of signifiers (see Lacan 1977: 154). Although it is possible that signs will be cut off, the resistance to being cut off, in the stickiness of the sign, relates to the historicity of signification. The resistance is not in the sign, but a 'sign' of how signs are already associated with other signs through metonymic proximity (word-to-word) or metaphoric displacement (word-for-word). While this historicity plays a crucial role in theories of performativity and iterability, it is linked to repetition, to the very fact that signs must be repeat-able, and with them, forms or conventions. I want to expand our under-standing of the historicity implicit to signification, reconceiving historicity in terms of stickiness as well as repetition: stickiness does not relate to conventions that are explicit, but to the attachments that implicitly govern ways in which signs work with other signs. How does the stickiness of signification relate to the performativity of disgust?

To name something as disgusting – typically, in the speech act, 'That's dis-gusting!' – is performative. It relies on previous norms and conventions of speech, and it generates the object that it names (the disgusting object/event). To name something as disgusting is not to make something out of nothing. But to say something is disgusting is still to 'make something'; it generates a set of effects, which *then adhere as a disgusting object*. Indeed, the word 'disgust' is itself a sticky sign, insofar as other signs stick to it ('yuk', 'bad', 'savage'), and insofar as it sticks to some bodies and objects ('the naked savage'), rather than others. To name something as disgusting is to transfer the stickiness of the word 'disgust' to an object, which henceforth becomes generated as the very thing that is spoken. The relationship between the stickiness of the sign and the stickiness of the object is crucial to the performativity of disgust as well as the apparent resistance of disgust reactions to 'newness' in terms of the generation of different kinds of objects. The object that is generated as a disgusting (bad) object through the speech act comes to stick. It becomes sticky and acquires a fetish quality, which then engenders its own effects.

It is not only 'disgusting objects' that are generated by the speech act, 'That's disgusting!' What else does disgust do? We can return to my reflections on abjection. To abject something is literally to cast something out, or to expel something. How can speech acts involve abjection? How do abject bodies and objects relate to abject speech? In disgust reactions, 'words' are also cast out or vomited. The speech act, 'That's disgusting!', can work as a form of vomiting, as an attempt to expel something whose proximity is felt to be threatening and contaminating. That is, to designate something as disgusting is also to create a distance from the thing, which paradoxically becomes a thing only in the act of distantiation. We might recall here that vomiting involves expelling something that has already been digested, and hence incorporated into the body of the one who feels disgust (Rozin and Fallon 1987: 27). Ingestion means that one has already been made disgusting by the perception of something other than me as being disgusting. To name something as disgusting is not only to transfer the stickiness of the word 'disgust' to an object that then comes to stick, but also to the subject. In other words, the disgusted subject is 'itself' one of the effects that is generated by the speech act, 'That's disgusting!'

However, the speech act is never simply an address the subject makes to itself. The speech act is always spoken to others, whose shared witnessing of the disgusting thing is required for the affect to have an effect. In other words, the subject asks others to repeat the condemnation implicit in the speech act itself. Such a shared witnessing is required for speech acts to be generative, that is, for the attribution of disgust to an object or other to stick to others. In addition, the demand for a witness shows us that the speech act, 'That's disgusting!' generates more than simply a subject and an object; it also generates a community of those who are bound together through the shared condemnation of a disgusting object or event. A community of witnesses is generated, whose apparent shared distance from an event or object that has been named as disgusting is achieved through the repetition of the word 'disgust'. Elspeth Probyn in *Carnal Appetites* argues persuasively that others are required to witness the distantiation from an object implicit in naming something as disgusting. As she puts it: 'Through public statements, we want to distance ourselves from this uncomfortable proximity. In uttering the phrase, we call upon others to witness our pulling away' (Probyn 2000: 131). The sharing of the physical processes of both casting out and pulling away means that disgust works to align the individual with the collective at the very moment both are generated. We can examine the way in which such speech acts generate effects by reflecting on how 'That's disgusting!' worked as a response to the events of September 11.

The internet has been a powerful means by which such a community of witnesses to the events of September 11 has been produced, along with other technologies or forms of mediation. On the internet, organisations and individuals have responded to the events on home pages, as well as message boards that have also allowed individuals to respond to each other's responses. This generation of a community of shared witnessing does not require subjects to be co-present, nor does it require that the speech act be made to an addressee who is co-present. The speech act instead takes the form of writing that is posted, with all the risks involved in posting a letter, given that the letter might not reach its destination (Derrida 1987). So what role does disgust have in generating a community in the face of September 11?

In the mediation of the events of September 11, the images seem saturated or even 'full' of affect. The images are repeated, and the repetition seems binding. The signs of the collapse of the buildings, and of bodies falling from the sky, are an invasion of bodies, spaces, homes and worlds. The images that appeared on television screens of the event as it unfolded, and which were repeated after the event, were images of trauma. They were also traumatic images. We did not have to see through the images to witness their trauma. To be a witness to the event through watching the images was to be affected by the images, which is not to say that we were all affected in the same way. As Marusya Bociurkiw puts it:

> The subsequent replaying of the Twin Towers' collapse (every few
> minutes on the first day; every few hours for months afterwards, and
> then every six months) seemed to enact the compulsion to repeat that
> characterizes post-traumatic stress. The compulsive return speaks to
> an unconscious desire to return to the state of trauma. By repeating
> or returning to unpleasurable experiences, the traumatized subject
> unconsciously hopes to achieve mastery, and thus to return to
> pleasure. (Bociurkiw 2003: 21)

The repetition of the images of trauma suggests a need to replay that which has yet to be assimilated into the individual or collective psyche. Critics such as Bociurkiw, Butler and Eng have analysed responses to September 11 in terms of the politics of trauma and grief (see also Chapter 7). Disgust may also be crucial to how the event impacts on others; indeed, the event is often attributed as 'being disgusting'. How does that attribution work? What does it do? Disgust involves a fascination with the event as image, in the desire to get closer to the image as if it were a salient object in the present. Take, for example, the following response to September 11 posted from Urban Outlaw Productions:[3]

> Roughly a month out and the disgusting, damnable events of September 11, 2001 still resonate in my heart and mind daily, if not hourly. I suppose there is some minor consolation in that fact, as for a full week immediately after the attacks, the shell-shocked feeling was omnipresent and inescapable. Not only did every aspect of the media, from television and radio to newspapers and the Internet, saturate us with seemingly every sordid detail of the tragedy, but that was almost all that was heard on the streets, all that we spoke of in private, all that was discussed on an e-group or in chat rooms. It infiltrated almost every facet of our lives. For many I am sure the terrorist incidents curtailed concentration, sleep, and invaded dreams . . . or nightmares.

Here, the object that disgusts has saturated the subjective world; disgust names the penetration of the world by that which is deemed sickening. The 'getting-in-ness' of the disgust reaction constitutes the object only through its proximity, its fatal nearness. The 'disgusting events' have 'invaded' and 'saturated' life itself such that they still resonate in life, even after the attribution of 'That's disgusting!' has been made. Note the slide between what is sickening and the 'shell-shocked feeling'. It is the inability to grasp the event in the present, or even to 'feel its impact', which demands the event is replayed, again and again, as the repetition of the sounds of trauma. This fatal proximity of the event is such that it can register its impact only through a perpetual recontamination of the homes and bodies of 'the disgusted'.

The disgust reaction creates an object, which we can describe as a border or fetish object, insofar as it admits to a prior contamination. The very 'pulling away' from the event is what allows it to acquire this fetish quality. At the same time, the generation of the object also creates the subject. By naming the event as disgusting, the subject 'stands out' in the 'standing apart' or 'pulling away' from the event. The posting is posted to other anonymous net readers; it speaks to an audience who is assumed to share this feeling of disgust and being disgusted. The sharing of disgust (through shared witnessing of that which is designated as disgusting) also becomes a shared rage or anger *about the ingestion of the disgusting* (about the ways in which it saturates one's life, minute by minute).

The ingestion of the disgusting constructs the objects of disgust, by iden-tifying the bodies that 'cause' the event. The posting moves on:

> Those who died have had their lives snuffed out for what is truly an insanely hateful and imprudent cause. This is a cause based on some twisted form of what these terrorists would call religion. These brainwashed, lost and depraved subhuman beasts must be sought out, flushed from the holes in which they cower, and annihilated like the vermin they are.

Here, the bodies of others become the salient object; they are constructed as being hateful and sickening only insofar as they have got too close. They are constructed as non-human, *as beneath and below the bodies of the disgusted.* Indeed, through the disgust reaction, 'belowness' and 'beneathness' become properties of their bodies. They embody that which is lower than human or civil life. The sexualised and militaristic nature of this description is crucial. Hidden in holes, the others threaten through being veiled or covered. The others who are the objects of our disgust must be penetrated or uncovered. We must 'get to them' to 'get away from them'. The proximity of others is here an imperative. They got too close (the event was only possible given this fatal intimacy), but we must get closer, if they are to be expelled. So the word 'disgust' is articulated by the subject, as a way of describing the event, which works to create the event as a border object, as a marker of what we are not and could not be. The word 'disgust' is then transferred from the event to the bodies of those others who are held responsible for the event. But how are those others ingested and expelled? What does this do to the bodies of those who narrate their disgust?

The posting then says: 'And the people, the survivors, and those of us who live, we move forward. We press on into a changed world with a new national mindset that has been violently thrust upon us. It remains to be seen what the ramifications are of the actions perpetuated on us by these Middle Eastern terrorists.' Here, the possibility of 'moving on' is dependent on the origin of terror as coming from another who is recognisable. That is, the transference of affect – such that the disgust is no longer 'in me' or 'ours' – involves an identification of bodies as its object; they are named as 'Middle Eastern terrorists'. Clearly, disgust sticks to the bodies of the others that are named; it is transferred from sign to body. But it can do this work of trans-ference only by sticking together signs. The naming of disgust metonymi-cally sticks these signs together, such that the terror and fear become associated with bodies that are already recognised as 'Middle-Eastern'. It is the association or contact between those signs 'Middle-Eastern' and 'terrorists' that 'blocks' the sticky flow of disgust.

Such 'blocking' means that the 'pulling away' of the disgust reaction simultaneously 'pushes out' the bodies of those others who surface as the objects of disgust. Of course, the 'sticking together' of these signs depends upon an economy of recognition in which some bodies more than others will be identified as terrorist bodies, regardless of whether they have any official links with terrorist organisations. This economy of recognition has become a part of lived reality on the streets in many countries where any bodies who 'look Muslim or Middle-Eastern' have been the victims of racial assault or abuse because they are associated with terrorism, or 'could be' terrorists (see Chapter 3).

Furthermore, the sticking of disgust to some bodies, a sticking which never finishes as the possibility remains open that other bodies 'could be' terrorists, generates other effects. The speech act, 'It's disgusting!' becomes 'They are disgusting,' which translates into, 'We are disgusted by them.' We can see this shift in the final sentence of the posting:

September 11, 2001 should provide a valuable lesson to the world about the tenacity of our safety and the importance of the lives of rational people. People who are adjusted to survive, strive, and cope in a civilized society, something these ghastly, empty, and, basically, sick terrorists forfeited.

This 'we' is named and renamed; first as 'the people', then as 'the survivors', and finally as 'the lives of rational people'. The community of witnesses is named by the speech act, and generated in the act of being named. Such a community comes into being as 'sticking together' in the shared condemnation of the events, a sticking together, that not only spits out the word 'disgusting', but also 'stands for' the spitting out of the bodies of those who become stuck to the word itself ('sick terrorists'). The disgust reaction hence vomits out the words 'Middle-Eastern terrorists', which comes to *stand for* and *slide into* the expulsion of the bodies of such others, who are recognisable as the cause of our sickness, from the community, nation or world. Such an expulsion will never be over given the possibility that other others 'could be' the cause of our disgust; the unfinished nature of expulsion allows its perpetual rejustification: we must be sick, to exclude the sick, again and again. Being sick is performed by the text, which allows the 'word' disgust to become a 'sign' of the other's being.

This is not to say, however, that disgust always sticks, and that the transference of the stickiness from a sign, to an object, to a body and to other signs, always works to affect a community that sticks together: to adhere is not always to cohere. It is clear, of course, that the word 'disgusting' was repeated, again and again, in personal and official responses to the events.

But it is not clear that what was named disgusting was the same thing: each time the attribution 'That's disgusting!' is made, the object, as it were, is remade, but not necessarily in a way that binds the community together. Some disgust reactions named their disgust at the way in which disgust has stuck to the bodies of some others. Take, for example, the following posting: 'The war in Afghanistan is disgusting . . . While the need for increased security is undoubtedly on the minds of the American people, the means being discussed are as disgusting as the terrorist attacks themselves.'[4] Such disgust reactions involve 'pulling away' from the 'pulling away' of the disgust reaction that authorises a community of witnesses. In other words, the speech act 'That's disgusting!' pulls away from the response to the event, which assumes that 'they're disgusting' (in which the 'they' slips between sticky signifiers: terrorists, Middle-Eastern, Muslim) and should be expelled, or vomited out of the nation, the civil world. To put it even more strongly, the disgusting nature of the terrorist attacks is argued to be 'replicated' or 'repeated' in the response to the attacks themselves.

Disgust, therefore, as an imperative not only to expel, but to make that very expulsion stick to some things and not others, does not always work simply to conserve that which is legitimated as a form of collective existence. Disgust can involve disgust at what disgust effects as a form of collective existence (in this case, the war is seen as replicating that which is disgusting about terrorism). The feeling of being disgusted may also be an element in a politics that seeks to challenge 'what is'. However, what the loop of disgust shows us is not simply the possibility of dissent within even the stickiest economies, but also how dissent cannot be exterior to its object. Dissent is always implicated in what is being dissented from. Furthermore, the limits of disgust as an affective response might be that disgust does not allow one the time to digest that which one designates as a 'bad thing'. I would argue that critique requires more time for digestion. Disgust might not allow one to get close enough to an object before one is compelled to pull away.

Of course we must remember that critics of American foreign policy – those who have expressed their disgust at what has been authorised as disgust – have also been met with disgust reactions. One of the most repeated statements about disgust was directed towards Susan Sontag's article in the *New Yorker*, which questioned the representation of the terrorists as cowards and suggested that the act was comprehensible in the sense that hatred towards the US could be explained. Statements such as Sontag's implication that ' "we had it coming" is "disgusting" ' are repeated as a way of resticking disgust to its object.[5] So the economy of disgust does not stop, as it were, with the unsticking of the object of disgust. Disgust reactions that 'pull away' from those that stick a community together can themselves engender other disgust reactions. In pulling away from the pulling away, these disgust reactions work to restick the sign 'disgust' to an object, which becomes salient as an effect of such collective transference. In other words, what gets unstuck can always get restuck and can even engender new and more adhesive form of sticking. Adhesion involves not just sticking to a surface, but giving one's support and allegiance. So we might need to persist with two questions, asked simultaneously. We might need to ask 'What sticks?' (a question that must be posed to ourselves as well as others). But we might pose this question alongside a more hopeful one: How can we stick to our refusal of the terms of allegiance?

NOTES

1. Kristeva's work has especially been taken up by feminist critics interested in how women's bodies are associated with the abject, as well as the monstrous. I will not be engaging with such arguments here, but do wish to signal their importance. See, for example, Creed (1993) and Stacey (1997).
2. I use this example since this is an insult that has been addressed to me, and I remember its effects profoundly.
3. http//:www.urbanoutlaw.com/opinion/100901.html Accessed 2 October 2002. I choose this site from thousands as it builds up a complex narrative around the word 'disgust'. Use a search engine, and type in 'September 11' and 'disgusting' and you can access many comparable web postings, usually on discussion lists.
4. http://gauntlet.ucalgary.ca/a/story/7458 Accessed 2 October 2002.
5. http://www.newyorkmetro.com/news/articles/wtc/flashpoint_speech.htm Accessed 2 October 2002.

CHAPTER 5

Shame Before Others

It should, I think, be apparent to all well-meaning people that true reconciliation between the Australian nation and its indigenous peoples is not achievable in the absence of acknowledgement by the nation of the wrongfulness of the past dispossession, oppression and degradation of the Aboriginal peoples. That is not to say that individual Australians who had no part in what was done in the past should feel or acknowledge personal guilt. It is simply to assert our identity as a nation and the basic fact that national shame, as well as national pride, can and should exist in relation to past acts and omissions, at least when done or made in the name of the community or with the authority of government. (Governor-General of Australia, *Bringing Them Home*, 1996)

What does it mean to claim an identity through shame? How does national shame work to acknowledge past wrongdoings, whilst absolving individuals of guilt? In this chapter, I examine not so much how shame is 'felt' by nations, but how declarations of shame can bring 'the nation' into existence as a felt community. In the quotation above, the nation is represented as having a relation of shame to the 'wrongfulness' of the past. Shame becomes crucial to the process of reconciliation or the healing of past wounds. To acknowledge wrongdoing means to enter into shame; the 'we' is shamed by its recognition that it has committed 'acts and omissions', which have caused pain, hurt and loss for indigenous others. The presumption of an essential relation between recognition and shame is shared by Raimond Gaita, who argues that: 'Shame is as necessary for the lucid acknowledgement by Australians of the wrongs the Aborigines suffered at the hands of their political ancestors, and to the wrongs they continue to suffer, as pain is to mourning' (Gaita 2000a: 278; see also Gaita 2000b: 87–93). Our shame is as necessary as their pain and suffering in response to the wrongs of this history. The proximity of national shame to indigenous pain may be what offers the promise of reconciliation, a future of 'living together', in which the rifts of the past have been healed.

But what kind of recognition and reconciliation are offered by such expressions of national shame? In the preface to *Bringing Them Home*, shame involves movement: the nation, in recognising the wrongfulness of the past, is moved by the injustices of the past. In the context of Australian politics, the process of being moved by the past seems better than the process of remaining detached from the past, or assuming that the past has 'nothing to do with us'. But the recognition of shame – or shame as a form of recognition – comes with conditions and limits. In this first instance, it is unclear who feels shame. The quote explicitly replaces 'individual guilt' with 'national shame' and hence detaches the recognition of wrongdoing from individuals, 'who had no part in what was done'. This history is not personal, it suggests. But if establishing individual guilt may indeed not be the issue, the question remains as to why individual shame is not admitted, even as a possibility, by the document. Wouldn't 'shaming' individuals show how this past injustice lives in the present?

The detachment of shame from individual bodies does a certain kind of work within the narrative. Individuals become implicated in national shame insofar as they already belong to the nation, insofar as their allegiance has already been given to the nation, and they can be subject to its address. Our shame is 'my shame' insofar as I am already 'with' them, insofar as the 'our' can be uttered by me. The projection of what is unjust onto the past allows shame to be represented here as a collective shame that does not affect individuals in the present, even as it surrounds and covers them, like a cloak or skin. Despite its recognition of past wrongdoings, shame can still conceal how such wrongdoings shape lives in the present. The work of shame troubles and is troubling, exposing some wounds, at the same time as it conceals others.

What is striking is how shame becomes not only a mode of recognition of injustices committed against others, but also a form of nation building. It is shame that allows us 'to assert our identity as a nation'. Recognition works to restore the nation or reconcile the nation to itself by 'coming to terms with' its own past in the expression of 'bad feeling'. But in allowing us to feel bad, does shame also allow the nation *to feel better*? What is the relation between the desire to feel better and the recognition of injustice? In this chapter, I want to reflect on the collective politics of shame by examining the role of shame within the discourse of reconciliation in Australia, as well as related conflicts created by the demand made to Europe and the United States for an apology for slavery and colonialism during the third UN conference on racism that took place in South Africa in August and September

2001. I am concerned not only with what it means for a nation 'to feel shame', but also with official speech acts made by governments, including apologies, statements of regret, as well as refusals to apologise. Before investigating such collective forms of shame, however, I will analyse the differences between shame and guilt, and the phenomenological experience of shame in inter-corporeal encounters between others. My argument will suggest that we need to think about what shame *does* to the bodies whose surfaces burn with the apparent immediacy of its affect before we can think about what it means for nations and international civil society to give shame an 'official reality' in acts of speech. Throughout, I will attend to the relation between shame and other affects: including guilt, pride, sorrow and regret.

LIVED EXPERIENCES OF SHAME

Silvan S. Tomkins defines shame as one of the primary 'negative affects'. Shame can be described as an intense and painful sensation that is bound up with how the self feels about itself, a self-feeling that is felt by and on the body. Certainly, when I feel shame, I have done something that I feel is bad. When shamed, one's body seems to burn up with the negation that is per-ceived (self-negation); and shame impresses upon the skin, as an intense feeling of the subject 'being against itself'. Such a feeling of negation, which is taken on by the subject as a sign of its own failure, is usually experienced before another. As Darwin suggests: 'Under a keen sense of shame there is a strong desire for concealment. We turn away the whole body, more espe-cially the shame, which we endeavour in some manner to hide. An ashamed person can hardly endure to meet the gaze of those present' (cited in Epstein 1984: 37). The subject may seek to hide from that other; she or he may turn away from the other's gaze, or drop the head in a sensation more acute and intense than embarrassment. In other words, shame feels like an exposure – another sees what I have done that is bad and hence shameful – but it also involves an attempt to hide, a hiding that requires the subject turn away from the other and towards itself. Or, as Erik H. Erikson describes in shame: 'One is visible and not ready to be visible' (Erikson 1965: 244). To be witnessed in one's failure is to be ashamed: to have one's shame witnessed is even more shaming. The bind of shame is that it is intensified by being seen by others *as* shame.

The very physicality of shame – how it works on and through bodies – means that shame also involves the de-forming and re-forming of bodily and social spaces, as bodies 'turn away' from the others who witness the shame. The 'turning' of shame is painful, but it involves a specific kind of pain. As I argued in Chapter 1, pain can involve the reading of the other as bad ('They hurt me' – 'They are hurtful'– 'They are bad'). In experiences of shame, the 'bad feeling' is attributed to oneself, rather than to an object or other (although the other who witnesses my shame may anger or hurt me, I cannot attribute the other as the cause of bad feeling). The subject, in turning away from another and back into itself, is consumed by a feeling of badness that cannot simply be given away or attributed to another. Shame also involves a different kind of orientation from disgust towards the subject and others (see Chapter 4). In disgust, the subject may be temporarily 'filled up' by something bad, but the 'badness' gets expelled and sticks to the bodies of others (unless we are talking about self-disgust, which is close to shame). In shame, I feel myself to be bad, and hence to expel the badness, I have to expel myself from myself (prolonged experiences of shame, unsurprisingly, can bring subjects perilously close to suicide). In shame, the subject's movement back into itself is simultaneously a turning away from itself. In shame, the subject may have nowhere to turn.

This double play of concealment and exposure is crucial to the work of shame. The word 'shame' comes from the Indo-European verb for 'to cover', which associates shame with other words such as 'hide', 'custody', 'hut' and 'house' (Schneider 1987: 227). Shame certainly involves an impulse to 'take cover' and 'to cover oneself'. But the desire to take cover and to be covered presupposes the failure of cover; in shame, one desires cover precisely because one has already been exposed to others. Hence the word 'shame' is associated as much with cover and concealment, as it is with exposure, vulnerability and wounding (Lynd 1958; Wurmser 1981).[1] On the one hand, shame covers that which is exposed (we turn away, we lower our face, we avert our gaze), while on the other, shame exposes that which has been covered (it un-covers). Shame in exposing that which has been covered demands us to re-cover, such a re-covering would be a recovery from shame.[2] Shame hence conceals and reveals what is present in the present. Shame consumes the subject and burns on the surface of bodies that are presented to others, a burning that exposes the exposure, and which may be visible in the form of a blush, depending on the skin of the subject, which might or might not show shame through this 'colouring'.[3]

The way in which the pain of shame is felt upon the skin surface, at the same time as it overwhelms and consumes the subject, is crucial. Shame involves the intensification not only of the bodily surface, but also of the subject's relation to itself, or its sense of itself as self. In other words, the lived experience of being-itself depends on the intensification of the skin surface. As Jean-Paul Sartre has argued: 'I am ashamed of what I *am*. Shame therefore realises an intimate relation of myself to myself' (Sartre 1996: 221). But, at the same time, Sartre suggests that: 'I am ashamed of myself *as I appear* to the Other' (1996: 222). Shame becomes felt as a matter of being – of the relation of self to itself – insofar as shame is about appearance, about how the subject appears before and to others. Crucially, the individuation of shame – the way it turns the self against and towards the self – can be linked precisely to the inter-corporeality and sociality of shame experiences. The 'apartness' of the subject is intensified in the return of the gaze; apartness is felt in the moment of exposure to others, an exposure that is wounding.

It is the way in which shame fills up the self – becomes what the self is about – that has been interpreted as the difference between shame and guilt at the level of lived and bodily experience. As Donald L. Nathanson argues: 'Whereas guilt refers to punishment for wrongdoing, for violation of some sort of rule or internal law, shame is about some quality of the self. Guilt implies action, while shame implies that some quality of the self has been brought into question' (Nathanson 1987: 4). Shame has been understood, then, as involving 'the whole self' or even 'the global self' by critics working within psychoanalysis, ego psychology and phenomenology (Capps 1993; H. B. Lewis 1971; M. Lewis 1993; Lynd 1958). This is not to say that guilt and shame simply refer to different emotions. As I argued in the introduction to this book, emotions do not have referents, although the recognition of an emotion has effects that could be described as referential. So when we recognise ourselves as shamed, that self-identification involves a different relationship of self to self and self to others from the recognition of ourselves as guilty. In shame, more than my action is at stake: *the badness of an action is transferred to me*, such that I feel myself to be bad and to have been 'found' or 'found out' as bad by others. Shame in this way is bound up with self-recognition: 'It is not an isolated act that can be detached from the self' (Lynd 1958: 50).

However, it is not just anybody that can cause me to feel shame by catching me doing something bad. Only some others can witness my action such that I feel ashamed. Silvan S. Tomkins suggests that shame – as an exposure before another – is only felt given that the subject is interested in the other; that is, that a prior love or desire for the other exists (see also Probyn 2005). Such an interest is not fully annihilated by the other's witnessing of my shame; though that witnessing will certainly affect my relation to the other. As Tomkins argues, shame may involve a complex relay of looks, some of which are partly averted. While the child may be ashamed before another, she or he may also be excited by that very other, such that the child may peep and look at another through the hands that cover the face (Tomkins 1963: 137). In other words, the other can only elicit a response of shame if another has already elicited desire or even love. I may be shamed by somebody I am interested in, somebody whose view 'matters' to me. As a result, shame is not a purely negative relation to another: shame is ambivalent.

Shame as an emotion requires a witness: even if a subject feels shame when she or he is alone, it is the imagined view of the other that is taken on by a subject in relation to herself or himself. I imagine how it will be seen as

I commit the action, and the feeling of badness is transferred to me. Or I remember an action that I committed, and burn with shame in the present, insofar as my memory is a memory of myself. In shame, I am the object as well as the subject of the feeling. Such an argument crucially suggests that shame requires an identification with the other who, as witness, returns the subject to itself. The view of this other is the view that I have taken on in relation to myself; I see myself *as if I were* this other. My failure before this other hence is profoundly a failure of myself to myself. In shame, I expose to myself that I am a failure through the gaze of an ideal other (see Capps 1993: 76; M. Lewis 1992: 34).

We can reflect on the role of idealisation in mediating the relation between the self and others who witness the shame. On the one hand, the idealisation of another is presumed if the other's look matters to me. At the same time, it is 'an ideal' that binds me to another who might be assumed to be 'with me' as well as 'like me' (sharing my ideals). Within psychoanalysis, such an ideal would be defined as an ego ideal, as 'the self' that a self would like to be. Hence the conflict of shame has been characterised as a conflict between ego and ego ideal, in contrast to guilt, where the conflict is between the super-ego and the ego (Jacoby 1994: 3; Piers and Singer 1971: 23).

The 'ideal self' does not necessarily have certain characteristics; the 'content' of the ideal is in some sense empty.[4] Idealisation, which creates the effect of an ideal, is contingent because it is dependent on the values that are 'given to' subjects through their encounters with others. It is the gift of the ideal rather than the content of the ideal that matters. Such an ideal is what sticks subjects together (coherence); through love, which involves the desire to be 'like' an other, as well as to be recognised by an other, an ideal self is produced as an approximation of the other's being. Through love, an ideal self is produced as a self that belongs to a community; the ideal is a proximate 'we' (see Chapter 6). If we feel shame, *we feel shame because we have failed to approximate 'an ideal' that has been given to us through the practices of love*. What is exposed in shame is the failure of love, as a failure that in turn exposes or shows our love.

Shame can reintegrate subjects (Braithwaite 1989) in their moment of failure to live up to a social ideal. Such an argument suggests that the failure to live up to an ideal is a way of taking up that ideal and confirming its necessity; despite the negation of shame experiences, my shame confirms my love, and my commitment to such ideals in the first place. This is why shame has been seen as crucial to moral development; the fear of shame prevents the subject from betraying 'ideals', while the lived experience of shame reminds the subject of the reasons for those ideals in the first place (Hultberg 1988: 115). The story of moral development is bound up with the reproduction of social norms, in particular, with norms of sexual conduct. Shame can work as a deterrent: in order to avoid shame, subjects must enter the 'contract' of the social bond, by seeking to approximate a social ideal. Shame can also be experienced as *the affective cost of not following the scripts of normative existence*.

Loves that depart from the scripts of normative existence can be seen as a 'source' of shame. One may be shamed, for example, by queer desires, which depart from the 'form' of the loving nuclear family. Queer desires become an injury to the family, and to the bodily form of the social norm (see Chapter 7); something to be concealed from the view of others. Shame becomes both a domesticating feeling and a feeling of domestication. The domesticity of shame is telling. Family love may be conditional upon how one lives one's life in relation to social ideals (see Chapter 6). Queer feelings of shame are also signs of an identification with that which has repudiated the queer subject. In this way, shame is related to melancholia, and the queer subject takes on the 'badness' as its own, by feeling bad about 'failing' loved others. Shame secures the form of the family by assigning to those who have failed its form the origin of bad feeling ('You have brought shame on the family'). Indeed, some identities become stigmatised or shaming within the social order, so that the subject in assuming such identities becomes committed to a life that is read by others as shameful. That is, in inhabiting the 'non' normative, queer bodies take on identities that are already read as the origin of 'our shame'.[5] The difficulty of moving beyond shame is a sign of the power of the normative, and the role of loving others in enforcing social ideals.

The intimacy of love and shame is indeed powerful. In showing my shame in my failure to live up to a social ideal, I come closer to that which I have been exposed as failing. This proximity of shame can, of course, repeat the injury (the shamed other may return love through identification with an ideal that it cannot be, so that the return confirms the inhabitance of the 'non'). Shame may be restorative *only when the shamed other can 'show' that its failure to measure up to a social ideal is temporary*. Shame binds us to others in how we are affected by our failure to 'live up to' those others, a failure that must be witnessed, as well as be seen as temporary, in order to allow us to re-enter the family or community. The relationship to others who witness my shame is anxious; shame both confirms and negates the love that sticks us together.

NATIONAL SHAME

The role of shame in confirming our love for others through negation, and the awkward place of the witness in this moment of confirmation, allows us to explain what it means for a nation to express its shame, and to transform shame into an identity. If we reconsider the role of shame in securing the (hetero)normative, then we can see that national shame works as a narrative of reproduction. The nation is reproduced through expressions of shame in at least two ways. First, shame may be 'brought onto' the nation by illegitimate others (who fail to reproduce its form, or even its offspring), such as queer others (see Chapter 7), or asylum seekers (see Chapter 2). Such others are shaming by proxy: they do not approximate the form of the good citizen. As citizens, they are shaming and unreproductive: they cannot reproduce the national ideal. Second, the nation may bring shame 'on itself' by its treatment of others; for example, it may be exposed as 'failing' a multicultural ideal in perpetuating forms of racism (see Chapter 6). These actions get transferred to the national subject; it becomes shamed by itself. In this instance, the nation may even express shame about its treatment of others who in the past were read as the origin of shame. In this section, I want to examine what happens when the normative subject, in this case the white national subject, 'admits' to being shamed.[6]

What do expressions of national shame do? We can return to the role of 'national shame' in *Bringing Them Home*. I suggested that shame requires a witness, one who 'catches out' the failure of the individual to live up to an ego ideal. I have also argued that individual shame is bound up with community precisely because the ideals that have been failed are the ones that 'stick' others together. The individual may also take on the failure of the group or nation to live up to an ideal as a mode of identification with the nation. The subject may feel shame, then, *as* an Australian for the failure of Australia to live up to the national ideal, whereby that failure confirms the subject's love for the nation. In other words, shame can become a form of identification in the very failure of an identity to embody an ideal.

In the preface of *Bringing Them Home*, the nation is described as shameful *because of* the past treatment of indigenous Australians; their wounds (narrated in testimonies of loss, violence and pain) become the reason for shame, and the reason why national identity must be redefined as shameful. In some sense, readers of the document, which is explicitly addressed to white or non-indigenous Australians ('our shame' is about 'their pain') are called upon to bear witness to the testimonies of indigenous Australians. These testimonies are made up of another kind of witnessing – a witnessing of trauma, of a past that lives in the present (see Chapter 1). But readers, who are called upon to witness these other acts of witnessing, are in a double, if not paradoxical, position. They are asked to witness their shame as 'our shame', that is, to be first *and* third party, to be 'caught out' *and* 'catching out'. The implication of such a double position – that white Australians catch out white Australia – is that the national subject, by witnessing its own history of injustice towards others can, in its shame, be reconciled to itself. Reconciliation becomes here a process whereby white Australia is reconciled to itself through witnessing the pain of others.

National shame can be a mechanism for reconciliation as self-reconciliation, in which the 'wrong' that is committed provides the grounds for claiming a national identity, for restoring a pride that is threatened in the moment of recognition, and then regained in the capacity to bear witness. Those who witness the past injustice through feeling 'national shame' are aligned with each other as 'well-meaning individuals'; if you feel shame, you are 'in' the nation, a nation that means well. Shame 'makes' the nation in the witnessing of past injustice, a witnessing that involves feeling shame, as it exposes the failure of the nation to live up to its ideals. But this exposure is temporary, and becomes the ground for a narrative of national recovery. *By witnessing what is shameful about the past, the nation can 'live up to' the ideals that secure its identity or being in the present.* In other words, our shame *means that we mean well*, and can work to reproduce the nation as an ideal.

Ideals can be binding, even when we feel we have failed them; indeed, the emotions that register this failure might confirm the ideals in the first place. Ideals are read as absent or present, or as having been failed or achieved, in the emotions of shame and pride. Such readings do not only respond to how we live up to ideals, they also shape the ideals in the first place. The content of the ideal (for example, the nation as *being* white, or heterosexual, or even as being tolerant, caring, and so on) is an effect of the process of idealisation. In other words, it is not that there is an ideal, which some more than others can approximate or 'measure up to'. The national ideal is shaped by taking some bodies as its form and not others. The pride of some subjects is in a way tautological: *they feel pride at approximating an ideal that has already taken their shape.*

Shame and pride have a similar affective role in judging the success or failure of subjects to live up to ideals, though they make different judgements. The possession of an ideal in feelings of pride or shame involves a performance, which gives the subject or group 'value' and 'character'. We 'show' ourselves to be this way or that, a showing which is always addressed to others. It is the relation of having as being – of having ideals as a sign of being an ideal subject – that allows the 'I' and the 'we' to be aligned. For example, the white subject's involvement in racism does not necessarily undo their success in approximating the national ideal; by showing shame, in fact, such a subject can demonstrate they are ideal subjects ('well-meaning'), and have the ideals that made such shame shameful in the first place. Shame collapses the 'I' with the 'we' in the failure to transform the social ideal into action, a failure which, when witnessed, confirms the ideal, and makes possible a return to pride. In other words, the transference of bad feeling to the subject in shame is only temporary, as the 'transference' can become evidence of the restoration of an identity of which we can be proud (the fact that we are shamed by this past 'shows' that we are now good and caring subjects).

In order to address the complexity of the affective alignments possible in expressions of shame I want to examine the performance of shame in Sorry Books in Australia. Sorry Books are one aspect of the process of reconciliation, which has also included Sorry Days.[7] The Sorry Books involve individual Australians (mostly white, but also some indigenous Australians) writing messages of condolence and support; they are compilations of statements and signatures, which create the effect of a shared narrative of sorrow as well as an account of national shame. Sorry Books have also been created through internet sites, which allow web users to post messages anonymously. The Sorry Books generate a 'we' that is virtual, fantastic and real, through the identification of past injustices and the way that have structured the present for different individuals, who are aligned by the very process of posting messages, even as they tell very different stories, and make different claims. The messages become 'I's', while the 'we' becomes the 'Sorry Book' itself, the mediation of a collective story of sorrow and shame. Such affective and textual alignments do not simply create a 'we', they also testify to its impossibility. I want to reflect on the role of shame in the de-forming and re-forming of the national 'we' through the articulation of the relation between the national subjects and the national ideal. To do this, I will offer a reading of some messages posted on an electronic Sorry Book.

It is important to note that this Sorry Book functions as a petition to the government, so many of the messages are addressed to the Australian Prime Minister John Howard, who has refused to offer an official apology for the Stolen Generation (see Chapter 1). By addressing the Prime Minister in this way, the messages work to identify the refusal to express shame as the source of national shame, as the grounds for an intensification of the shame about the past: 'If you don't, I'll do it for you, and then you'll look a lot worse than what you think you would.'[8] In this way, the Sorry Book functions as a demand to and for the nation to appear ashamed, and to speak the shame on behalf of Australians. The lack of shame becomes another form of national shame witnessed by subjects: 'Disgrace our country no longer, Mr Howard. Recognise past injustice so we can move forward together. Your arrogance on this issue is a national shame!'[9]

Shamed by the shameless, this demand is also a plea that the nation move beyond the past, and enter into a future where pride can itself be 're-covered': 'The failure of our representatives in Government to recognise the brutal nature of Australian history compromises the ability of non indigenous Australians to be truly proud of our identity.'[10] Here, witnessing the government's lack of shame is in itself shaming. The shame at the lack of shame is linked to the desire 'to be truly proud of our country', that is, the desire to be able to identify with a national ideal. The recognition of a brutal history is implicitly constructed as the condition for national pride; if we recognise the brutality of that history through shame, then we can be proud. As a result, shame is posited as an overcoming of the brutal history, a moving beyond that history through showing that one is 'moved by it' or even 'hurt by it'. The desire that is expressed is the desire to move on, where what is shameful is either identified as past (the 'brutal history') or located in the present only as an absence ('the shame of the absence of shame'). Such a narrative allows the national subject to identify with others, so pride itself becomes the emotion that sticks the nation together, an ideal that requires the nation to pass through shame. What is witnessed is not the brutality of this history, but the brutality of the passing over of that history. Ironically, witnessing such a passing over might even repeat the passing over, in the very desire to move beyond shame and into pride.

The complexity of witnessing and its relation to shame structures the genre of 'Sorry Book'. On the one hand, the messages themselves bear witness to the shame of the nation's shame. On the other, they demand that the nation itself becomes a witness to its shame. At the same time, messages evoke other witnesses, those who are witnesses to the shame of the individual subject and the shame of the nation. One message states: 'I think that it is time that we say sorry. People all over the world are comparing us to South African apartheid.'[11] There is a slide from 'I' to 'we' that involves both adherence (sticking to the nation) as well as coherence (sticking together). That 'we' is not idealised in the present; rather the statement asks the 'we' to say sorry, so that it can appear as ideal in the future. Hence the statement evokes others ('people all over the world') as witnesses to Australia's shame; it is the look of the world that makes the subject ashamed, as it 'catches out' the nation by seeing the nation as like other shameful nations ('South African apartheid'). What is shameful about Australia's past is not named; what is shameful is only negatively indicated, in the comparison made to another shameful nation, a comparison that 'shows' Australia to have failed, by making Australia appear *like* other failed nations. Being like the nation that has failed to live up to the ideal hence confirms the ideal as the proper desire of the nation. The fear of being seen as 'like them' structures this shame narrative.

The witness who exposes the shame of the nation – and the shame of its refusal of shame – is here implicitly 'international civil society'. Messages evoke this imagined witness: 'The eyes of the world are upon you. One hundred years from now, how do you want to be remembered?' Being seen as an ideal nation is here defined as that which will pass down in time, not in our memories, but in how we are remembered by others. The desire for shame is here the desire to be seen as fulfilling an ideal, the desire to be 'judged by history' as an ideal nation. The imagined witness to the nation, the one who will record the nation's achievements, is not always presented as exterior to the nation, but as a reflection of its better self: 'How can we point the finger at other countries' abuses and not put a mirror up to our own.'[12] The mirror in which the national subject sees its reflection shows the nation its shame, a 'showing' that allows the national gaze to be directed towards others who have failed the national ideal, to be a witness rather than witnessed. Only when we have seen our own shame in our reflection, the message suggests, can we then 'point the finger' at others. Another message makes a similar declaration: 'Stop telling us to be proud of our country until you take positive steps to remove the source of our great national shame.'[13] Here, pride would be shameful until shame has been expressed, while the expression of shame would justify pride ('until you take'). The politics of shame is contradictory. It exposes the nation, and what it has covered over and covered up in its pride in itself, but at the same time *it involves a narrative of recovery as the re-covering of the nation.*

Such a narrative of recovery, expressed as the demand for government to make shame 'official', becomes an act of identification with the nation through a feeling of injustice. This involves not only a sense that 'past actions and omissions' have been unjust, but also that what makes the injustice unjust is that it has taken pride away; *it has deprived white Australia of its ability to declare its pride in itself to others.* In this way, some of the messages in the Sorry Book seem to mourn the necessity of witnessing shame, as they call for shame to be witnessed such that pride can be returned, and the nation can stick together through a shared embodiment of the national ideal. It is in the name of future generations that shame becomes a way of sticking together, by exposing the failure of the nation to live up to its ideal – described in one message as 'love, generosity, honor and respect for our children'. Another puts it:

> I am an Australian citizen who is ashamed and saddened by the treatment of the indigenous peoples of this country. This is an issue that cannot be hidden any longer, and will not be healed through tokenism. It is also an issue that will damage future generations of Australians if not openly discussed, admitted, apologised for and grieved. It is time to say sorry. Unless this is supported by the Australian government and the Australian people as a whole I cannot be proud to be an Australian.[14]

The utterance, whilst calling for recognition of the 'treatment of the indigenous peoples' does not recognise that subjects have unequal claims 'to be an Australian' in the first place. If saying sorry leads to pride, who gets to be proud? In other words, the ideal image of the nation, which is based on the image of some and not others, is sustained through the conversion of shame to pride.

The desire for pride – for the nation to embody its ideal, which is an effect of some bodies and not others – is crucial to these expressions of shame. What is in question here is not the allegiance of the national subject, but whether or not the nation is seen to be living up to its ideals; whether it does what it is. Exposing the failure of that ideal is politically important – and part of what shame can do and has done – but it can also become the grounds for patriotic declarations of love. In such declarations of love, shame becomes a 'passing phase' in the passage towards being-as-nation, where the ideals that the nation 'has' are transformed into what it does. Nowhere is this clearer than in the message: 'I am an Australian Citizen who wishes to voice my strong belief in the need to recognise the shameful aspects of Australia's past – without that how can we celebrate present glories'.[15] Here, the recognition of what is shameful in the past – what has failed the national ideal – is what would allow the nation to be idealised and even celebrated in the present.

SHAME AND SPEECH ACTS

As my analysis of shame in discourses of reconciliation made clear, the demand for official apologies has become crucial to claims for compensation for injury. Such apologies have been demanded from governments by those who have been victims of past and present atrocities, as well as those who are implicated in those atrocities, and are the potential beneficiaries. Elazar Barkan discusses the politics of apology as a 'new public morality', which defines new grounds of civility for international politics. As he puts it: 'One new measure of this public morality is the growing political willingness, and at times eagerness, to admit one's historical guilt' (Barkan 2000: xxviii). Indeed, reparation has been granted in some cases. Within this account of 'a new moral order', Barkan reflects on the importance of official apologies, which provide 'evidence of the public's distress in carrying the burden of guilt for inflicting suffering and possibly of its empathy with the victims' (Barkan 2000: xxviii). But what does it mean for an apology to be taken as 'evidence' of an affect (whether sorrow, shame or guilt)? What do apologies do? Does an apology show an emotion, or does the 'evidence' that an apology provides come after the act? Does saying sorry 'make' the subject who now exists 'as being sorry' responsible?

As a speech act, the apology can take many forms. I can say: 'I apologise for what I have done', or 'I apologise for hurting you.' Comparing these utterances shows how apologies are conditional. By saying what we apologise for, we delimit the force of the utterance. We also, in the saying, are interpreting what it is that has been done, which is an interpretation that is not necessarily shared. An unconditional apology often does not work because it does not offer an explanation – all I can say is: 'I apologise.' In not saying what I apologise for, the address fails to reach another, whose claim for compensation requires an admission about one's role in a certain history. An apology can take the form of utterances like: 'I am sorry.' Such utterances can work as description ('This is how I feel'), or as polite forms of address ('I am sorry about the delay'). But when addressed to another, and recognisable in fulfilling a certain form (through intonation, gesture, the context of the utterance), the same words can function as an admission of responsibility for an act, in which the other's reception is crucial to the work done by the statement ('I accept your apology'). Of course, the gap between saying sorry and being sorry cannot be filled, even by a 'good performance' of the utterance.

In *How to Do Things with Words*, J. L. Austin considers the apology as a performative utterance. The word 'performative' links 'to perform' with 'an action'; 'It indicates that the issuing of the utterance is the performing of an action' (Austin 1975: 6). Performativity is not a quality of a sign or an utterance; it does not reside within the sign, as if the sign was magical. For an utterance to be performative, certain conditions have to be met (see also Chapter 4). When these conditions are met, then the performative is happy. When they are not met, the performative is unhappy: 'A good many other things have as a general rule to be right and to go right if we are to be said to have happily brought off our action' (Austin 1975: 14).[16] So, for instance, the first performative utterance that Austin discusses, 'I thee wed' only 'acts' – it only weds a couple – when certain conditions have been met. The conditions include not only that the one who utters the utterance is authorised to do so, but also that the one who 'receives' the utterance is legitimated by law as 'marriageable' (see Butler 1997c). In most places, if two women received the utterance, then the utterance would not be happy. The performative conditions for happiness demonstrate that the 'doing' of words is bound up with the rule of law, which legislates social form through positive definition; in this example, by defining the conditions that have to be fulfilled for something 'to be' marriage. A constitutional act can be redefined as 'the making of form': to constitute is to give form to that which is not yet.

Let us return now to the apology as a speech act. Austin does consider the apology as a particular kind of performative, which he calls 'behabitives': 'a kind of performative concerned roughly with reactions to behaviour and with behaviour towards others and designed to exhibit attitudes and feelings' (Austin 1975: 83). Behabitives, he suggests, are not simply statements or descriptions of feeling, although Austin does not discuss what makes them distinct from such utterances (Austin 1975: 160). Behabitives remain curiously ambiguous, and indeed Austin describes them as 'troublesome' (Austin 1975: 151). In order to think about the 'trouble' of apologies we need to explore the relation between the utterance, feeling and action.[17]

Certainly, Austin suggests that apologies can be unhappy, when certain conditions are not met. These conditions in his model relate mainly to the emotions of the speaker: the speaker must feel sorry, if the apology is to work; insincerity would be condition enough for an unhappy apology (Austin 1975: 40, 47). Such a model, however, assumes that emotions are inner states, which are then either expressed or not expressed through words. One can equally imagine that an apology can do something without necessarily being a measure of true feeling; for example, to apologise for my role in hurting another may 'do something' even if I do not feel sorry: the other may accept the apology. Or the apology could become the basis of an appeal for compensation; it could be 'taken up' as evidence of responsibility rather than feeling. The difficulty is that whilst apologies are doing something, it is not clear what they are doing. What would be the condition of happiness or success? Would it be for the other to accept the apology? Or is something more at stake?

This example asks us to think more about what is 'an action'. Here, an action does not simply happen as if by magic. An action also requires a decision; we have to decide what it is that apologies do precisely because the 'action' is not finished in the moment of apologising. Interestingly, Eve Kosofsky Sedgwick includes the apology in her class of explicit performatives, because the verb 'names precisely the act' (Sedgwick 2003: 4). As she puts it, an apology 'apologises'. But the precision of the apology is complicated because the 'action' named by the 'verb' is unfinished. We can see the significance of this point when we consider the relation between the performative and the reception. To receive the utterance 'I thee wed', *if the appropriate conditions have been met*, is to 'become' the verb. 'To wed' is 'to become wed', without the work of any translation (although one still has to give one's signature before the witness). No reading on behalf of the recipient is necessary for the action to be finished. But with an apology, the addressee also has to read the utterance. The utterance is addressed to the other, whose gaze returns to the speaker, who is placed in a history that precedes the utterance. So the receiver has to judge whether the utterance is readable *as* an apology. So the following question becomes intelligible: Does 'this' apology 'apologise'? The action of the apology is curiously dependent on its reception. The apology may 'do something' *in the event that the other is willing to receive the utterance as an apology*, a willingness, which will depend on the conditions in which the speech act was uttered. What the apology does or performs also depends on actions that follow from the apology. If I say that I apologise for an action, then act the same way as before, the force of the 'apology' may be undone.

The unfinished nature of the action of the apology suggests that 'the action' requires a decision; it is an undecided action or a conditional performative. What a speech act does may depend on how it is sent, who receives it, and other contexts of utterance. An apology can certainly do different things, depending on the context. It can declare an emotion, which is not the same thing as having an emotion. Indeed, the apology can stand in for an emotion, when read as a sign of its truth. The apology, when read as a sign of an emotion ('They *are* sorry or ashamed for which they did'), may work on the emotions of others, that is, the 'sign' of an emotion may move others, and hence may succeed, with the act being returned by an acceptance. The success of the sign is not dependent on whether the 'sign' is a sign of inner feeling. An apology can also mean a declaration of responsibility; what it 'does' might be an admission, or be read as an admission. Indeed, if the speech act is differently worded ('I/We apologise for', rather than 'I am sorry') then this action functions as an admission of responsibility, without performing an emotion. Whether an apology is received as a declaration of emotion or an admission of responsibility is dependent on the context in which the statement is given and received as well as on the wording of the utterance. The effects of that declaration depend on who speaks the apology – and what prior authorisation they have – as well as who receives it, and how they are interpellated as witnesses to the speech act. And so what an apology is doing in the moment of its utterance goes through a passage of the undecidable, both opening up the past, and keeping open the future.

And so this question is one that haunts the national imaginary: *What does saying sorry do and what does it commit the nation to?* How will an apology be received by others; that is, how will 'my' or 'our' action be finished by others? It may be anxiety about the unfinished nature of the apology as a social action that makes it such an troublesome topic for official representatives of nation states. An apology may open up the speaker to endless demands, made through repeating the words authorised by the speaker. Despite a noticeable historic shift towards apologies – made by governments as well as royalty for past atrocities and injustices – it is therefore not surprising that some apologies are 'blocked' for fear of what they may do.

We can reflect further on these questions by turning to the controversy about apologies for slavery and colonialism at the 2001 UN conference on racism. At this event, representatives from African countries asked for/demanded an apology from Europe and America for their part in the slave trade. Like all acts of apology, the context mattered. A demand is made by those who feel that they – or the people they represent and stand (in) for – have been damaged, disenfranchised, and oppressed. The perpetrator is then transformed into the addressee – the one who receives the speech act that demands the apology. The addressee – who may also stand (in) for a people, who are hence both present and absent – then becomes the speaker, who either gives or refuses to give the apology. What was being demanded at the UN conference and what was refused when the word 'apology' or 'sorry' was taken out of the final declaration?

In the end, the conflict became a matter of vocabulary – and of the apparent power of words to shape political realities. The European leaders wanted words with less power, *words that did less*. As one newspaper report put it:

> Some African non-governmental organisations have lined up
> behind the governments of Namibia, Zimbabwe, Brazil and several
> Caribbean countries and the powerful African American lobby to
> demand nothing short of an apology and an admission that the
> transatlantic slave trade was a crime against humanity. Such a
> statement in the final declaration of the conference would, the US
> and the four EU countries believe, open up the floodgates for massive
> class actions against leading corporations. (Smith, *The Independent*,
> 4 September 2001)

In this account from a British journalist, an apology is framed as a performative; one that in saying is a doing, which will automatically lead to other doings, which can only be prevented by 'not saying' at all. That is, if the apology that is demanded by others is received as an admission of responsibility – that the past was a crime and that the speaker, or group on whose behalf the speaker is speaking is guilty of the crime – then that would allow the speech act to act anew in courts of law, in appeals for restitution and reparation. Under these conditions, the apology is unutterable and the demand for an apology is refused. The refusal to return the demand for recognition with apology repeats the violence that structures the logic of the demand in the first place:

> As for reparations, they can take many forms but they are necessary.
> The slave trade was wrong. Britain was wrong. What they did was a
> crime against humanity. The Europeans did it for the benefit of their
> own countries. Now they are wanting to keep what they gained on
> the back of colonialism. (Smith, *The Independent*, 4 September 2001)

How did Britain defend its refusal to apologise, a refusal that itself functions as a speech act, as well as an act of violence? A spokesman for Tony Blair said:

> This is an agreed EU position, which was agreed at the (EU foreign ministers') general affairs council in July. That position is that slavery has to be condemned in the present and regretted in the past. It would not be sensible for governments to accept responsibility for the actions of governments so long ago. What is important is what we do in the present.[18]

What is interesting here is that the speech act is justified or justifies itself by referring to a previous authorisation: the EU General Council. In other words, the justification for the decision is deferred to another authorisation. The author of the speech act does not then have either to justify the decision, or claim authority in the name of the decision. The decision and the action are 'decided' by another authorisation that precedes and justifies the present speech. The deferral of authority authorises and justifies the decision ('it was decided') in which the speaker, and who the speaker stands for, can bypass their own responsibility for the act, the decision or the judgement. It simply 'was agreed'.

This bypassing via a reference to a previous authorisation (that refuses to produce an accountable subject: it 'was agreed', rather than 'we agreed') replicates the bypassing of responsibility for historical injustice. Here the grounds for that bypassing relate to what 'makes sense' and is 'common sense' – to what is sensible and therefore intelligible. History is assumed to be 'long ago'; it is cut off from injustice in the present. According to the statement, history was then. We can condemn what is in the present, but only regret the past. We might note here that the refusal to apologise for the past – and the slave trade in particular – relies on the 'cutting off' of the present from the past. It says: 'We were not there then' so 'We cannot be responsible.' Such a delimitation of responsibility assumes the responsibility only takes the form of a direct relation of causality. It works precisely through forgetting that what happened 'long ago' affects the injustices of international politics in the present, in which the world's resources are unequally and unjustly divided between nations and continents. In other words, by cutting the present struggle for justice off from the past, the speech act works to cut off the act of speech from the contexts that surround it.

The speech act of refusing to apologise does its work by cutting off the occasion of speaking – the present of the speech – from the historical struggles for justice that demanded the speech in the first place. The final declaration produced by the conference uses the word 'regret' to describe the relation of the present to the past. Regret is named as a kind of disappointment, an almost polite sense of 'What a shame' rather than 'We are ashamed', or 'We regret what happened, but we cannot condemn it, because it was not us.' As Elizabeth V. Spelman argues, statements of regret do not assume any responsibility (Spelman 1997: 104). The substitution of an apology with regret works powerfully; this is a doing that does what it does by negation. Regret becomes an alternative for responsibility and for reparation; it functions as a sign of an injury, without naming a subject that can be called upon to bear witness, to pay back an unpayable debt, or to compensate for what cannot be compensated.

The implication of my argument is that statements of regret, in bypassing apologies, bypass too much. But how does this argument relate to my earlier critique of shame? We can return to the example of responses to the Stolen Generation in Australia. Here, indigenous others have demanded the government apologise on behalf of the nation. The demand is the utterance, and it is a political action. The demand for an apology exposes the history of violence to others, who are now called upon to bear witness to the injustice. The apology would be the 'return address', although the 'giving' of the apology would not be the only measure of the success of the demand (which was also about making a concealed history visible to others). The Prime Minister, then John Howard, refused to apologise, preferring the word 'regret'. It is not that he has not returned the demand for an apology with an action; he has acted, certainly. The return action is a refusal, and takes the form of 'I/We do not apologise.' This speech act works also as a political action. It 'makes' the nation, by declaring that the nation is not responsible: 'We did not do this,' 'We were not there.' Again, the foreclosure of responsibility does something; it cuts off the speaker and the nation from the histories that shape the present.

My critique of the refusal of an apology, which we could extend to the refusal of shame, helps to complicate my earlier analysis of Sorry Books, by showing how the contexts that surround the speech act, and which shape the position of the speaker, witness and addressee, make a difference. When others, who have been wronged, ask for signs of shame, then the expression of shame does not return ourselves to ourselves, but responds to demands that come from a place other than where we are. The apology in this instance would be a return address, an address to another, whose place we do not inhabit. Saying sorry, as a gesture of return, cannot be a moment in the passage to pride. To return such a speech act, we cannot turn back towards ourselves. We can stay open to hearing the claims of others, only if we assume that the act of speaking our shame does not undo the shame of what we speak. The expressions of national shame in the preface to *Bringing Them Home* and the Sorry Books were problematic, *as they sought within the utterance to finish the action, by claiming the expression of shame as sufficient for the return to national pride.* As such, they did not function as a return address; they blocked the hearing of the other's testimony in turning back towards the 'ideality' of the nation. It remains possible to express shame before others without finishing the act, which refuses this conversion of shame to pride, in an act of shame that is not only before others, but for others.

Of course, we cannot assume any equivalence between statements of shame and acts of apology. Shame is not necessarily evoked by an apology, and nor does it require an apology. An expression of shame can be a substitute for an apology, while an apology can be a substitute for shame. The expression of shame is a political action, which is not yet finished, as it depends on how it gets 'taken up'. Shame, in other words, does not require responsible action, but it also does not prevent it. Indeed, the risk of shame for the nation may be that it *can* do too much work in the uncertainty of the work that it is doing. It is no accident that public expressions of shame try to 'finish' the speech act by converting shame to pride. In this case, *what is shameful is passed over through the enactment of shame.* It is also no accident that in political rhetoric, 'sorry' moves to 'regret' by passing over 'shame'. The affective economies at work, where words are substituted for each other as 'names' and 'acts' of emotion, certainly do something – they re-cover the national subject, and allow recovery for 'civil society', by allowing the endless deferral of responsibility for injustice in the present.

NOTES

1. Of course, the association of shame with exposure and knowledge of that which has been concealed is crucial to the story of Genesis (Broucek 1991). The link between exposure and shame is crucial also to Freud's (rather limited) accounts of shame: it enters into his analysis of dreams of nakedness (Morrison 1989: 22–3). Freud's later work tends to include shame along with guilt and anxiety as defence reactions against tabooed desires such as exhibitionism (Piers and Singer 1971: 17; S. B. Miller 1985: 10).
2. Thanks to Sarah Franklin for this point.
3. If we were to assume that we could all see shame in the redness of blushing skin, we would of course be assuming that only white bodies feel shame. While I experience shame in the burning of my skin, I do not blush. I take some comfort in that others, who might look for the blush as a sign of shame, might overlook my shame, and allow me to pass and move away. At other times, the invisibility of shame experiences in the unavailability of the blush can lead to some people being seen as shameless, and hence as being unaffected by bad deeds ('Have you no shame!'). See Biddle (1997) and Probyn (2005) for discussions of blushing and shame.
4. See Chapter 6 for a qualification of this argument. I point out there that although the ideal is not 'about' its content, it does not follow that the ideal is empty, precisely because the ideal is an effect of the movement of some bodies and not others.
5. Within queer theory, the stigma of shame has been embraced as a condition for political activism. Rather than converting shame to pride, theorists such as Douglas Crimp suggest we should 'stay with shame', that is, we should embrace the emotion that is bound up with the 'non-normative' (for a good summary of this argument, see Barber and Clark 2002: 22–9). Embracing shame means embracing the 'non' rather

than assimilating to the norm. I have a degree of scepticism about this argument. For me, to embrace shame is paradoxical: it still implies a conversion from negative to positive affect. That is, one now feels a kind of pride in not being normative; a pride in being shameful. The 'non' becomes the new ideal, which queer lives might seek to approximate (see Chapter 7 for an extension of this argument). However, I share with Eve Kosofsky Sedgwick and Douglas Crimp a discomfort with discourses of 'queer pride'. In my view, neither pride or shame are 'queer feelings'; rather, the question is how to be affected by one's relation to, and departures from, the normative in a way that opens up different possibilities for living.

6. The implication of this argument is that one can feel shame for occupying the normative position. To go back to the previous section, where I discuss the relation between shame and the heteronormative, one can feel shame for being heterosexual, or for having access to the privileges afforded by this position. Such shame would be a form of discomfort with the comforts of inhabiting the normative. It would hence involve 'seeing' heterosexuality as a form of privilege, rather than 'not seeing' it at all. My argument about the role of shame in the formation of the national subject will suggest that such shame is not necessarily an unlearning of privilege, and can even function as an exercise of privilege. I would speculate that heterosexual shame could also operate in this way. See Chapter 7 for an analysis of comfort/discomfort in heteronormativity.

7. Since May 1998, and on the recommendation of *Bringing Them Home*, annual Sorry Days have certainly brought some Australians together through the shared expressions of sorrow as well as shame about the violence towards indigenous Australians that 'blackens' the past; the history and present of the Stolen Generation. Sorry Days have involved indigenous and non-indigenous Australians marching together in gestures of solidarity, a 'walking with' that promises to open up a different future for Australia, in the recognition that the violence of the past has affected Australia in the present.

8. See http://users.skynet.be/kola/sorry5.htm Accessed 13 December 2002.

9. See http://users.skynet.be/kola/sorry2.htm Accessed 13 December 2002.

10. See http://users.skynet.be/kola/sorry5.htm Accessed 13 December 2002.

11. See http://users.skynet.be/kola/sorry5.htm Accessed 13 December 2002.

12. See http://users.skynet.be/kola/sorry5.htm Accessed 13 December 2002.

13. See http://users.skynet.be/kola/sorry2.htm Accessed 13 December 2002.

14. See http://users.skynet.be/kola/sorry2.htm Accessed 13 December 2002.

15. See http://users.skynet.be/kola/sorry2.htm Accessed 13 December 2002.

16. Austin defines the failure and success of speech acts in terms of happiness and unhappiness. Importantly, this relates the effects of speech acts with 'affects'. So although he discusses emotions as interior states that are expressed, the model also offers a way of considering emotions as effects, which depend on how signs are received by others.

17. For a useful account of the complexity of emotion or 'emotives' as speech acts see Reddy's *The Navigation of Feeling*. He suggests that emotives are like performatives: they 'do things to the world' (Reddy 2001: 105). As such, they are 'themselves instruments for directly changing, building, hiding, intensifying emotions, instruments that may be more or less successful' (Reddy 2001: 105).

18. See http://english.peopledaily.com.cn/200109/04/eng20010904_79267.html Accessed 15 December 2002.

CHAPTER 6

In the Name of Love

Where was Hatewatch during 170 million crimes committed against White Americans over the last 30 years? Hatewatch. What an absurd organisation. But aren't they part of the huge parasitic Infestation which is always trying to destroy anyone who loves liberty and disagrees with the Monsters' plan for the degradation and control of the White Americans of this nation? They steal what they can and target us for government gangsterism and drooling media meatpuppet consumption . . . *Love Watch*. The Wake Up or Die Love Watch is a listing of those who love this nation and our White Racial Family and the alternative to the lists of the parasitic propagandists.[1]

How does politics involve a struggle over who has the right to declare themselves as acting out of love? What does it mean to stand for love by standing alongside some others and against other others? As I pointed out in Chapter 2, it has become common for 'hate groups' to rename themselves as organisations of love. Such organisations claim they act out of love for their own kind, and for the nation as an inheritance of kind ('our White Racial Family'), rather than out of hatred for strangers or others. A crucial part of the renaming is the identification of hate as coming from elsewhere and as being directed towards the 'hate group'. Hate becomes an emotion that belongs to those who have identified hate groups *as* hate groups in the first place. In the above quote, the Hatewatch web site, which lists racist groups on the internet, is juxtaposed with the Lovewatch site, which also lists these organisations, but names them as 'love groups'. Such groups are defined as 'love groups' through an active identification with the nation ('those who love this nation') as well as a core set of values ('anyone who loves liberty'). Love is narrated as the emotion that energises the work of such groups; it is out of love that the group seeks to defend the nation against others, whose presence then becomes defined as the origin of hate. As another site puts it: 'Ask your-self, what have they done to eliminate anything at all? They feed you with, "Don't worry, we are watching the hate groups" and things like this. You know what they do? They create the very hate they purport to try to erase!'[2] It is the critique of racism as a form of hate that becomes seen as the origin of hate; the 'true' hated groups are the white groups who are, out of love, seeking to defend the nation against others, those who threaten to 'steal' the nation away.

It is important to track the cultural significance of this use of 'love' within right-wing fascist groups. What does the language of love do? How does it work? Psychoanalysis has long shown us the ambivalence of love and hate (see Chapter 2). But the representation of hate groups as love groups does not make explicit such ambivalence. On the contrary, the narrative works through conversion: hate is renamed as love, a renaming that 'conceals' the ambivalence that it exercises (we love *rather than* hate). The conversion of hate into love allows the groups to associate themselves with 'good feeling' and 'positive value'. Indeed, such groups become the ones concerned with the well-being of others; their project becomes redemptive, or about saving loved others. These groups come to be defined as positive in the sense of fighting *for* others, and in the name of others. The narrative suggests that it is only this 'for-ness' that makes 'against-ness' necessary. Hence those who identify hate groups as hate groups are shown as failing to protect the bodies of those whose love for the nation makes them vulnerable and exposed. By being *against* those who are *for* the nation (*anti*-racists, *anti*-fascists and so on), such critics can only be *against* the nation; they can only be *against* love. The critics of hate groups become defined as those who hate, those who act out of a sense of 'anti-ness' or 'against-ness', and thus those who not only cannot protect the bodies of white Americans from crimes, but re-enact such crimes in the use of the language of hate. We might note the slide from the crimes against white people committed by unnamed others ('170 million crimes committed') to the crimes committed by Hatewatch ('they steal what they can') in this narrative.

The renaming of hate groups as love groups, and Hatewatch as Love Watch, exercises a narrative of love as protection by identifying white sub-jects as already at risk from the presence of others. Love does not only enter such narratives as a way of being-for-others or being-for-the-nation, but also becomes a property of a particular kind of subject. Love, that is, reproduces the collective as ideal through producing a particular kind of subject whose allegiance to the ideal makes it an ideal in the first place. There has been a proliferation of 'hate group' web sites written by and for women, which argue that women have a particular role in the defence of the nation. This femini-sation of fascism is significant.[3] One web site includes a post by the former

Women's Information Coordinator of the World Church of the Creator, who suggests that:

> The second lesson we have to learn, I believe, is the power a woman can have. Women represent nurturing, LOVE, reaching out, touching, bridging a gap, caring for children, and bringing a gentle, diplomatic approach to the problems at hand. . . . I mean the love borne [sic] of deep racial pride, willing to fight and die, but also willing to share a smile, shake a hand, stroke the hair of a young Aryan child. We need beautiful Aryan women, who can move among the people, speaking, entreating, and LOVING them.[4]

Love becomes a sign of respectable femininity, and of maternal qualities narrated as the capacity to touch and be touched by others. The reproduction of femininity is tied up with the reproduction of the national ideal through the work of love. Here, love relationships are about 'reproducing' the race; the choice of love-object is a sign of the love for the nation. In this posting, Princess Diana as 'a woman of such racial beauty and purity' is condemned for her relations with 'non-Aryan men'. Such a narrative not only confirms heterosexual love as an obligation to the nation, but also constitutes mixed-race relationships as a sign of hate, as a sign of a willingness to contaminate the blood of the race. Making the nation is tied to making love in the choice of an ideal other (different sex/same race), who can allow the reproduction of the nation as ideal in the form of the future generation (the white Aryan child).

In this chapter, I examine how love becomes a way of bonding with others in relation to an ideal, which takes shape as an effect of such bonding. Love is crucial to how individuals become aligned with collectives through their identification with an ideal, an alignment that relies on the existence of others who have failed that ideal. There are, of course, many types of love (familial, friendly, erotic). My concern is not to define 'what is love' or to map the relation between these different kinds of love. Rather, I want to consider how the pull of love towards an other, who becomes an object of love, can be transferred towards a collective, expressed as an ideal or object. I do not want to suggest a one-way relation of transference (when love for a particular other comes to 'stand for' the collective, or when love for a collective 'stands in' for the particular other). Rather, I want to examine how love moves us 'towards' something in the very delineation of the object of love, and how the direction of 'towardness' is sustained through the 'failure' of love to be returned. We could ask: What are we doing when we do something *in the name of love*? Why is it assumed to be better to do the same thing if it is done *out of love*?

My argument about the role of love in shaping collectives could seem rather banal or even obvious; love, after all, has often been theorised as a sticky emotion that sticks people together, for example, in discourses of fraternity and patriotism.[5] But I want to make a more complex argument, partly by thinking through how love works in places where it has been seen as more benevolent, such as in discourses of multiculturalism. Some attempts to critique discourses of racial purity – of narcissistic whiteness – are about finding a love that does not assume love for one's own kind and which does not lead to hatred for others. But does multicultural love work to expand love to include others? Or does this expansion require that other others fail an ideal?

IDENTIFICATION AND IDEALISATION

Within Freudian psychoanalysis, love is ever-present as an affective bond, which is crucial to the formation of subjectivity, sociality and even civilisation. As Freud suggests in *Civilization and Its Discontents*, one of the techniques used in the pursuit of happiness and the avoidance of suffering is to make 'love the centre of everything' (Freud 1961: 29). The logic of this centring is crucial to the psychoanalytical understanding of the intimacy between 'normal' and 'psychotic' subjectivity. For whilst love may be crucial to the pursuit of happiness, love also makes the subject vulnerable, exposed to, and dependent upon another, who in 'not being myself', threatens to take away the possibility of love (Freud 1961: 48; see Chapter 2). Love then becomes a form of dependence on what is 'not me', and is linked profoundly to the anxiety of boundary formation, whereby what is 'not me' is also part of me (see Chapter 3). Love is ambivalent: to love another can also be to hate the power that this love gives to another (Klein 1998: 306–7). The classical scene of this emotional ambivalence is the formation of brotherhood through the murder of the father: the sons love and identify with the father, but in 'not being him', must hate and kill him in order to take his position (Freud 1950: 143). The subject pays for this murder with guilt and fear, taking on the forms of authority as a means of reparation.

Freud offers a theory of love by differentiating between different kinds of love. Take, for instance, Freud's distinction between narcissistic and anaclitic and love. In the former, the self is the primary object of love; and in the latter, external objects are the primary objects of love. Whilst love is seen as in the first instance narcissistic – the child's own body is the source of love – for men, love is assumed to mature into object love, whilst women are assumed to remain narcissistic (Freud 1934a: 45–6). The economy for this differentiation is heterosexual: women's narcissism involves a desire to be loved (to love the love that is directed towards them), while for men, they love to love women who love themselves. The sexual relation becomes a love relation in which the woman becomes the object of her love and the man's love. I will not engage here with the question of whether this model describes or prescribes a heterosexist economy, although I will turn in due course to the heterosexual logic of the couple that organises this distinction.[6] I want to examine this distinction between self-love and object love, which can also be described in terms of a distinction between identification (love as being) and idealisation (love as having).

In Freud's account, identification is the earliest expression of an emotional tie with another person. As he puts it: 'A little boy will exhibit a special interest in his father; he would like to grow like him and be like him, and take his place everywhere' (Freud 1922: 60). In the first place, the boy's identification with the father creates an ideal: his ego ideal. This is the subject the ego would like to be. We should not assume here a linear movement from love to identification (as in the formulation: we identify with those we love). Rather, identification is a form of love; it is an active kind of loving, which moves or pulls the subject towards another. Identification involves the desire to get closer to others by becoming like them. Becoming like them obviously requires not being them in the first place. So identification exercises a distinction between the subject and object of love. At the same time, identification seeks to undo the very distinction that it requires: in becoming more like you, I seek to take your place. But taking the place of the one that is loved is futural: if one were already in their place, then one would not be identifying with them, one would be them. So identification is the desire to take a place where one is not yet. As such, *identification expands the space of the subject*: it is a form of love that tells the subject what it could become in the intensity of its direction towards another (love as 'towardness'). Identification involves *making likeness* rather than being alike; the subject becomes 'like' the object or other only in the future. The other's death is imagined in the desire to take the other's place only insofar as the other is living in the present.

But what is the relation between the boy's identification with the father and his anaclitic love, his love of women as his ideal objects? His secondary love is love for the mother, for what is 'not him': such love works as a form of idealisation, and is based on a relation of having rather than being. Importantly, identification with the father and idealisation of the mother do not take the masculine subject to a different place: the love for the mother is a means by which the identification with the father is performed (one desires what he desires), even if it renders that love ambivalent in its claim to possession. What is at stake, then, is the apparent separation of being and having in terms of objects, *but their contiguity in terms of subject position*: in order to be him, I must have her, whom he has. In other words, identification with the father requires dis-identification with the mother (I must not be her), and desire for the mother (I must have her, or one who can stand in for her). The heterosexual logic of this separation of being from having is clear. In order to approximate the ego ideal, to paraphrase Judith Butler, I must desire an ideal object that is 'not me' in the sense of 'not my gender', whilst I must become 'my gender' by giving up the possibility of taking 'my gender' as a love object (Butler 1997b: 25).[7]

The distinction between identification and desire relates to the distinction between sameness and difference: the heterosexual subject would identify with what is 'like me' and desire what is 'different from me'. The assumption here is that heterosexuality involves love for difference and homosexuality is love for sameness. We can complicate this narrative by rethinking the relation between identification and desire, neither of which are about the nature of the subject or object that one seeks to approximate in relations of being and having. Just as identification leads to the formation of an ego ideal, so too desire creates an ideal object. As Freud argues, desire for an object, which becomes the ideal object, is not determined by the nature of the object. However, Freud's rejection of the nature of the object as determining love still presumes the primary role of the object in the process of idealisation; he differentiates idealisation from sublimation, and describes the former as the over-valuation or exaltation of the object (Freud 1934a: 50). But is it the object which is over-valued? Irving Singer also makes the 'evaluative' aspects of love crucial to his definition of love. He argues that love is a way of valuing something, such that: 'It is the valuing alone that *makes* the value' (Singer 1984: 5). In this way, love creates the ideality of the object, but this ideality does not 'stay with' but 'returns' to the subject.

The 'investment' in the ideal object may work to accumulate value for the subject. As I suggested in Chapter 2, an investment involves the time and labour that is 'spent' on something, which allows that thing to acquire an affective quality (in this case, the 'loveable object'). The idealisation of the object is not 'about' the object, or even directed to the object, but is an effect of the ego. That is, the ideal object, as with the ego ideal, is an effect of the ideal image that the subject has of itself. Renata Salecl speaks to this fit between ego ideal and ideal object when she says:

> The subject simultaneously posits the object of his or her love in the
> place of the Ego Ideal, from which the subject would like to see him-
> or herself in a likeable way. When we are in love, the love object
> placed in the Ego Ideal enables us to perceive ourselves in a new way
> – compassionate, lovable, beautiful, decent, etc. (Salecl 1998: 13)

The subject and the object are hence tied up so that identification and desire, whilst separated by a heterosexual logic (you can't be a man and love a man, or be a woman and love a woman) are connected in their relation to 'an ideal' (what is imagined as loveable or as having value). The ideal joins rather than separates the ego and the object; what one 'has' elevates what one 'is'. One consequence of this argument would be a redefinition of anaclitic love as a sublimated form of narcissism: rather than the male lover being humble, in Freud's terms (Freud 1934a: 55), his exaltation of his beloved is a means of self-exaltation, in which the 'object' stands in for the subject, as a sign of its worth. Emmanuel Levinas puts this well when he says: 'If to love is to love the love the Beloved bears me, to love is also to love oneself in love, and thus to return to oneself ' (Levinas 1979: 266). Or, as Julia Kristeva suggests: 'The lover is a narcissist with an *object*' (Kristeva 1987: 33, emphasis Kristeva's).

So the idealisation of the loved object can allow the subject to *be itself in or through what it has*. The subject approximates an ideal through what it takes as its loved object. I want to suggest that idealisation may also work as the 'creation' or 'making' of likeness: the lover and the object approximate an ideal, an approximation which binds them together. It is hence not sur-prising that heterosexual love may be structured around resemblance and likeness, despite the conflation of heterosexuality with difference. After all, heterosexuality can itself be a bond that two *have in common*. The normative conflation of hetero-sex with reproduction means that the bond gets structured around the desire to 'reproduce well'. Good reproduction is often premised around a fantasy of 'making likeness' by seeing my features reflected back by others, whose connection to me is then confirmed (the ques-tion that is always asked: Who does the child look like?). We may search for signs of likeness on the body. But likeness may also be an effect of proxim-ity. For example, lovers often pick up each other's habits and gestures, becom-ing more alike as an effect of contact and desire. As Ben-Ze'ev describes:

> The desire to be with the beloved often becomes a desire to fuse with
> the beloved and in a sense to lose one's identity. Lovers begin to
> develop similar likes to those of their partners; for example, to enjoy
> music to which they were previously indifferent . . . (Ben-Ze'ev 2000:
> 415; see also Borch-Jacobsen 1988: 86)

Within familial love narratives, proximity in a spatial sense, as an effect of contact, gets collapsed with proximity as an ideological position (we are alike on grounds of character, genetics or belief – this likeness become an 'inher-itance'), which is crucial to the naturalisation of heterosexual love as a famil-ial plot. At the same time, the transformation of proximity into inheritance is concealed by the narrative of heterosexuality as love for difference, a con-cealment which projects sameness onto homosexual love and transforms that very sameness into both perversion and pathology. Commentators such as Michael Warner have critiqued the conflation of homosexuality and sameness (Warner 1990: 202),[8] and the way in which this establishes heterosexuality as normative. I am supplementing this critique by suggesting that heterosexuality cannot be assumed to be 'about' difference or love for difference. The distinction between sameness as that which structures homosexual love, and difference as that which structures heterosexual love, needs questioning on both sides of the distinction. The Freudian model idealises heterosexuality as love-for-difference by transforming homosexuality into a failure to love difference, which in turn conceals the ongoing (psychic and social) investment in the reproduction of heterosexuality.

Furthermore, the distinction of love-as-having from love-as-being secures a restricted domain of loveable subjects, *through the imperative to idealise some objects and not others*, whose ideality 'returns' to me. The imperative to identify with the one who is nearby – where proximity is assumed to be a sign of resemblance that is 'inherited' – also functions as an imperative to have the objects that the subject one loves is assumed to love. The need for approval of a love object from someone with whom one already identifies shows how value 'can be bestowed' only through others, such that the 'bond' of love leads me to others. The object becomes ideal only through approval by loved others; idealisation creates both likeable subjects and loveable objects (see Benjamin 1995). The restriction of ideal objects involves a process of identification. In identifying myself with you, for example, I also delimit who I can love in the sense that I imagine who would be loved by the subject that I would be if I were you. In other words, I ask: Who or what would my ideal idealise? The question shows us how social relations of having can follow from relations of being, even if they take different objects.

Within the narrative of love discussed in my opening, identifying oneself as a white woman and as a white Aryan would mean loving not just men, or even white men, but white men who also identify as Aryan, *who can return the idealised image of whiteness back to oneself.* To love and to be loved is here about fulfilling one's fantasy image of 'who one would like to be' through who one 'has'. Such a love is about making future generations in the image I have of myself and the loved other, who together can approximate a 'likeness', which can be bestowed on future generations. Within this economy, the imperative to love becomes an imperative to extend the 'ideal' that I seek to have onto others, who 'can' return the ideal to me. It is clear from the extension of self in love, or the way in which love orients the subject towards some others (and away from other others), how easily love for another slides into love for a group, which is already imagined in terms of likeness.

THE NATIONAL IDEAL

In *Group Psychology*, Freud offers a theory of how love is crucial to the formation of group identities. Whilst maintaining that the aim of love is 'sexual union', Freud argues that other loves, whilst diverted from this aim, share the same libidinal energy that pushes the subject towards the loved object (Freud 1922: 38). For Freud, the bond within a group relies on the transference of love to the leader, whereby the transference becomes the 'common quality' of the group (Freud 1922: 66). Another way of saying this would be to say that groups are formed through their shared orientation towards an object. More specifically, groups are formed when *'individuals . . . have substituted one and the same object for their ego ideal and have consequently identified themselves with one another in their ego'* (Freud 1922: 80, emphasis Freud's). Now, it is here that Freud complicates the relation between identification and object choice, by showing how one form of love can become the other. In particular, he points to how the ego can assume the characteristics of the lost object of love though introjection (Freud 1922: 64).

In other words, the loss of the object is compensated for by 'taking on' the quality of the object. Mourning and grief become an expression of love; love announces itself most passionately when faced with the loss of the object (see Chapter 8 for an analysis of the role of grief in queer politics). Love has an intimate relation to grief not only through how the subject responds to the lost object, but also by what losses get admitted as losses in the first place. If I can imagine that the person who was lost 'could-have-been me', then the other's grief can also become my grief. This 'could-have-been-ness' is a judgement on whether others approximate the ideals that I have already taken to be 'mine' or 'ours'. So there is an intimate relation between lives that are imagined as 'grievable', in Judith Butler's terms (Butler 2007), and those that are imagined as loveable and liveable in the first place.

Indeed, the impossibility that love can reach its object may also be what makes love powerful as a narrative. At one level, love comes into being as a form of reciprocity; the lover wants to be loved back, wants their love returned (Singer 1984: 6). At another, love survives the absence of reciprocity in the sense that the pain of not being loved in return – if the emotion 'stays with' the object to which it has been directed – confirms the negation that would follow from the loss of the object. Even though love is a demand for reciprocity, it is also an emotion that lives with the failure of that demand often through an intensification of its affect (so, if you do not love me back, I may love you more as the pain of that non-loving is a sign of what it means not to have this love).

We can see how love then may work to stick others together in the absence of the loved object, even when that object is 'the nation'. Love may be especially crucial in the event of the failure of the nation to deliver its promise for the good life. So the failure of the nation to 'give back' the subject's love works to increase the investment in the nation. The subject 'stays with' the nation, despite the absence of return and the threat of violence, as leaving would mean recognising that the investment of national love over a lifetime has brought no value. One loves the nation, then, out of hope and with nostalgia for how it could have been. One keeps loving rather than recognising that the love that one has given has not and will not be returned.

One could even think of national love as a form of waiting.[9] To wait is to extend one's investment and the longer one waits the more one is invested, that is, the more time, labour and energy has been expended. *The failure of return extends one's investment.* If love functions as the promise of return, then the extension of investment through the failure of return works to maintain the ideal through its deferral into the future. It is not surprising that the return of the investment in the nation is imagined *in the form of the future generation* ('the white Aryan child'), who will 'acquire' the features of the ideal white subject. 'The Aryan child' here becomes the object that is 'put in the place of the ego ideal' (Freud 1922: 80). National love places its hope in the next generation; the postponement of the ideal sustains the fantasy that return is possible.

If the failure of return extends one's investment, then national love also requires an 'explanation' for this failure; otherwise, hope would convert into despair or 'giving up' on the loved object. Such explanations work as defensive narratives; they defend the subject against the loss of the object by enacting the injury that would follow if the object was given up. We can see this clearly in the accounts of love in the Lovewatch web site; the nation as loved object has been taken away, and the 'injury' of the theft must be repeated as a way of confirming the love for the nation. In this instance, the fantasy of love as return requires an obstacle; the racial others become the obstacle that allows the white subject to sustain a fantasy that without them, the good life would be attainable, or their love would be returned with reward and value.[10] The failure of return is 'explained' by the presence of others, whose presence is required for the investment to be sustained. The reliance on the other as the origin of injury *becomes an ongoing investment in the failure of return.*

But if the ideal is postponed into the future, as the promise of return for investment, then how does the ideal take shape? I argued in the previous chapter that the 'content' of the national ideal does not matter. The ideal is an effect of the process of idealisation, which elevates some subjects over others. But this does not make the ideal 'empty'. Julia Kristeva writes of the relation between national ideal and ego ideal in *Nations without Nationalism*, when she responds to the 'problem' posed by immigration:

> First there is the interior impact of immigration, which often makes
> it feel as though it had to give up traditional values, including the
> values of freedom and culture that were obtained at the cost of long
> and painful struggles (why accept [that daughters of Maghrebin
> immigrants wear] the Muslim scarf {to school}). (Kristeva 1993:
> 36)

The bracketed sentence evokes the figure of the 'veiled/Muslim woman' who
comes into play as a figure that challenges the values that are felt to be crucial
to the nation (including the values of freedom and culture). These values are
what the nation can give to others. She becomes a symbol of what the nation
must give up to 'be itself', a discourse that would require her unveiling in
order to fulfil the promise of freedom. Kristeva concludes: 'It is possible that
the "abstract" advantages of French universalism may prove to be superior
to the "concrete" benefits of a Muslim scarf' (Kristeva 1993: 47). Kristeva
suggests that the right to wear the scarf (with its multiple meanings) may
give the Muslim women less than the rights afforded by entry into the
abstract idea of the nation. By implication, the abstract includes everybody
as it is not shaped by the concrete specificity of bodies. Others can become
a part of the community of strangers on condition that they give up visible
signs of their 'concrete difference'.

The argument moves from the national idea to a 'national ideal' via an
analogy with the ego ideal. The 'Muslim scarf' is not only 'not' the idea of
freedom 'won' as the freedom of the nation, but it also challenges the image
the nation has of itself: 'That involves a breach of the national image and it
corresponds, on the individual level, to the good image of itself that the child
makes up with the help of the ego ideal and the parental superego' (Kristeva
1993: 36–7). The trauma of the Muslim scarf for the French nation is here
like the trauma of 'failing' to live up to the ego ideal. The nation becomes
depressed when it is faced with the scarf and this shame and depression is
used by the right-wing discourse of anti-immigration: 'Le Pen's nationalism
takes advantage of such depression' (Kristeva 1993: 37). According to this
argument, the task of the radical might be to refuse to celebrate or even
allow the scarf as this would sustain the psychic conditions that enable anti-
immigration and nationalism, as political forms of depression, to flourish.
Kristeva hence suggests that 'a Muslim wish to join the French community'
(Kristeva 1993: 37) might require the elimination of the source of national
shame: the concrete difference of the veil itself. The argument suggests that
by eliminating the veil, the abstract national idea can be returned to an ideal
that is enlarged by the appearance of others.

However, the argument that the national idea is abstract (and the difference of the Muslim woman is concrete) breaks down. The intimacy of the
national idea with an ideal image suggests the national idea takes the shape

of a particular kind of body, which is assumed in its 'freedom' to be unmarked. The ideal is an approximation of an image, which depends on being inhabitable by some bodies rather than others. Such an ideal is not positively embodied by any person: it is not a positive value in this sense. Rather, it accrues value through its exchange, an exchange that is determined precisely by the capacity of some bodies to inhabit the national body, *to be recognisable as living up to the national ideal in the first place*. But other bodies, those that cannot be recognised in the abstraction of the unmarked, cannot accrue value, and become blockages in the economy; they cannot pass as French, or pass their way into the community. The veil, in blocking the economy of the national ideal, is represented as a betrayal not only of the nation, but of freedom and culture itself, as the freedom to move and acquire value.

Love for the nation is hence bound up with how bodies inhabit the nation in relation to an ideal. I would follow Kristeva by arguing that the nation is an effect of how bodies move towards it, as an object of love that is shared. Or more precisely 'the it' of 'the nation' as an ideal or loved object is produced as an effect of the movement of bodies and the direction of that movement (the loved object as an effect of 'towardness'). But, as a result, the promise of the nation is not an empty or abstract one that can then simply be fulfilled and transformed by others. Rather, the nation is a concrete effect of how some bodies have moved towards and away from other bodies, a movement that works to create boundaries and borders, and the 'approximation' of what we can now call 'national character' (what the nation *is like*). Such a history of movement 'sticks', so that it remains possible to 'see' a breach in the ideal image of the nation in the concrete difference of others.

MULTICULTURAL LOVE

What happens when love is extended to others who are recognised as 'being different' in their concrete specificity? In this section, I will analyse how multiculturalism becomes an imperative to love difference and how this extension of love works to construct a national ideal that others fail (a failure that is read both as an injury and a disturbance). To do so, I will refer to the debates on asylum, migration and the race riots in the UK. It is important to acknowledge that within the UK, the nation is imagined as an ideal through the discourse of multiculturalism, which we can describe as a form of conditional love, as well hospitality (see also Chapter 2). The nation becomes an ideal through being posited as 'being' plural, open and diverse; as being loving and welcoming to others.

As Renata Salecl suggests, the pleasure of identifying with the multicultural nation means that one gets to see oneself as a good or tolerant subject (see Salecl 1998: 4). This identification with the multicultural nation, which shapes the 'character' of the multicultural subject, still relies on the structural possibility of the loss of the nation as object. The multicultural nation can itself be taken away by the presence of others – who do not reflect back the good image the nation has of itself – such as intolerant racist others (often conflated with the white working classes, or fascist groups like the British National Party). The nation can also be taken away by migrants or asylum seekers who don't accept the conditions of one's love. *Identifying oneself as British means defining the conditions of the love one can or will give to others.* Indeed, multiculturalism – especially since September 11 – has been viewed as a security threat: those who come into the nation 'could be' terrorists, a 'could-be-ness' that extends the demand for surveillance of others who are already recognisable as strangers (see Chapter 3). The national project hence becomes: How can one identify the nation as open (the national ideal) through the conditions required to inhabit that ideal?

The new conditions require that migrants 'must learn to be British'; that is, migrants must identify themselves as British by taking 'the nation' as their object of love. This becomes a matter of allegiance and adherence; of sticking to the nation in the formation of the ego ideal: 'New immigrants will soon have to pass English exams and formally swear allegiance to the Crown. . . . The Home Secretary believes it is crucial that newcomers to the UK embrace its language, ethos and values' (Hughes and Riddell 2002: 1). Here, migrants must pass as British to pass into the community, a form of 'assimilation' that is reimagined as the conditions for love. Importantly, migrants must become British even at home. Muslim women, in particular, have been asked to speak English at home, so they can 'pass on' the national ideal to the future generation. This ideal is not premised on abstraction (the migrant is not asked to lose her body or even her veil), nor on whiteness, but on hybridity as a form of sociality, as the imperative to mix with others. The others can be different (indeed, the nation is invested in their difference *as a sign of its love for difference*), as long as they refuse to keep their difference to themselves, but instead give it back to the nation, through speaking a common language and mixing with others.

The over-valuation of the nation as a love object – as an object that can reciprocate one's love – hence demands that migrants 'take on' the character of the national ideal: becoming British is indeed a labour of love for the migrant, whose reward is the 'promise' of being loved in return. As Bhikhu Parekh puts it:

A multicultural society cannot be stable and last long without
developing a common sense of belonging among its citizens. The

sense of belonging cannot be ethnic and based on shared cultural, ethnic and other characteristics, for a multicultural society is too diverse for that, but must be political and based on a shared commitment to the political community. Its members do not directly belong to each other as in an ethnic group but through their mediating membership of a shared community, and they are committed to each other because they are all in their own different ways committed to a common historical community. They do and should matter to each other because they are bonded together by the ties of common interest and attachment. . . . The commitment to the political community involves commitment to its continuing existence and well-being, and implies that one cares enough for it not to harm its interests and undermine its integrity. It is a matter of degree and could take such forms as a quiet concern for its well-being, deep attachment, affection, and intense love. (Parekh 1999: 4)

Love here sticks the nation together; it allows cohesion through the naming of the nation or 'political community' as a shared object of love. Love becomes crucial to the promise of cohesion within multiculturalism; it becomes the 'shared characteristic' required to keep the nation together. The emotion becomes the object of the emotion. Or, more precisely, love becomes the object that is 'put in the place of the ego or of the ego ideal' (Freud 1922: 76). It is now 'having' the right emotion that allows one to pass into the community: in this case, by displaying 'my love', I show that I am 'with you'. It is 'love', rather than history, culture or ethnicity that binds the multicultural nation together. Roland Barthes' reflections on the lover's discourse have resonance here: 'It is love the subject loves, not the object' (Barthes 1979: 31).

The 'love for love' is bound up with the making of community. Within the White Paper, *Secure Borders, Safe Haven: Integration with Diversity in Modern Britain*, integration is defined as crucial to the making of community, understood in terms of building 'firmer foundations' for nationhood. Indeed, the foreword to the report suggests that 'confidence, security and trust' are crucial to the possibility that the nation can become an ideal object, a 'safe haven' that is open to others, without being threatened by that opening (Home Office 2002a: 3). In this report, David Blunkett suggests that: 'We need to be secure within our sense of belonging . . . to be able to reach out and to embrace those who come to the UK.' Here, the nation and national subject can only love incoming others – 'embrace' them – if the conditions that enable security are already met. To love the other requires that the nation is already secured as an object of love, a security that demands that incoming others meet 'our' conditions. Such conditions require that others 'contribute' to the UK through labour, or by showing they are not bogus asylum seekers. When such conditions have been met they will 'receive the welcome they deserve'. The asylum system and discourse of citizenship is justified on the grounds that it is only through the intensification of the border that the nation can be secured as an object of love, which can then be given to others.

The ideal constructed by multicultural love also involves the transformation of heterosexuality into good citizenship, and evokes the figure of the ideal woman. Take the following quote from *The Observer*:

> Genevieve Capovilla's father is West Indian. Her mother is Italian.
> And she is British. She has golden skin, and soft, even features. She
> combs her hair into a healthy, curly semi-afro. Her racial mix is
> ambiguous – neither Afro-Caribbean, nor southern European. It is
> no surprise to find that she is a model. She has the enviable quality
> of looking as though she would be at home anywhere in the world.
> And her look is one that will become increasingly familiar, and – in
> the worlds of fashion and beauty – increasingly sought after. . . .
> Genevieve is the new English rose. . . . At the turn of the twenty-first
> century . . . England's rose has become more of a bronzed, burnished
> sunflower, equally at home in the Arabian Gulf, the Caribbean or the
> South China Sea. (Blanchard 2001: 10)

This positing of woman as an image of the nation is not new. As critics such as Nira Yuval-Davis (1997) and Anne McClintock (1995) have shown us, this conflation of the face of the nation with the face of a woman has a long history and points to the gendering of what the nation takes to be as itself (the masculine subject) through what it has (the feminine object). The figure of the woman is associated with beauty and appearance, and through her, the nation appears for and before others. As the new English rose, Genevieve replaces Princess Diana as an ideal image of the nation. White skin becomes golden skin; blonde hair becomes 'curly semi-Afro'. The idealisation of the mixed-race woman allows the nation to accumulate value: as a model, her beauty sells. The exoticisation of mixed-race femininity is also not new, as Lola Young's (1996) work on representations of the mulatto in film demonstrates. What is distinctive is how she gets 'taken in' by the nation: 'the exotic' comes 'home' through her bronzed appearance. As an ideal, she will approximate the fantasy the national subject has of itself: somebody who is hybrid, plural and mobile. In her ideality – 'the new English rose' – she has acquired the features of the national character, which fantasises itself as being 'at home anywhere in the world'. The nation can 'be itself' – a hybrid, mobile nation that loves difference by taking it in – precisely through the objects that it idealises as its objects of love. The object of love is an 'off-spring' of the fantasy of the national subject at stake in the ego ideal, con-firming the role of heterosexuality in the reproduction of the national ideal (Fortier 2008).[11]

This ideal image can be described as a 'hybrid whiteness'; the nation's whiteness is confirmed through how it incorporates and is 'coloured' or 'bronzed' by others. Her ambiguity – 'not quite the same, not quite the other' in Bhabha's (1994) formulation – becomes a sign of the nation, and the promise of the future. This is not to say that mixed-race heterosexual love has become a form of national love. The mixed-race woman 'appears' as a fetish object; she accumulates value only given that her figure is cut off from any visible signs of inter-racial intimacy.[12] In other words, the nation remains the agent of reproduction: she is the offspring of the multicultural love for difference.

The nation here constructs itself as ideal in its capacity to assimilate others into itself; to make itself 'like itself' by taking in others who appear differ-ent. The national ideal is assumed to be reflected in the wishful and hopeful gaze of others: 'Millions of people hear about the UK and often aspire to come here. We should be proud that this view of the UK is held all around the world.' According to the report (*Secure Borders, Safe Haven*), what makes Britain ideal is also what makes it vulnerable to others. A narrative of loss is crucial to the work of national love: this national ideal is presented as all the more ideal through the failure of other others to approximate that ideal. Whilst some differences are taken in, other differences get constructed as vio-lating the ideals posited by multicultural love. A crucial risk posed by migrant cultures is defined as their failure to become British, narrated as their failure to love the culture of the host nation. The failure here is the failure of migrants to 'return' the love of the nation through gratitude.[13] One tabloid headline after the burning down of a detention centre for asylum seekers reads: 'This is how they thank us.'

How are disturbances read as the failure to return the conditions of national love? The race riots that took place in North-West England in 2001 were understood to be a result of a failure to integrate, or 'segregation':

> The reports into last summer's disturbances in Bradford, Oldham
> and Burnley painted a vivid picture of fractured and divided
> communities, lacking a sense of common values or shared civic
> identity to unite around. The reports signalled the need for us to
> foster and renew the social fabric of our communities, and rebuild a
> sense of common citizenship, which embraces the different and
> diverse experiences of today's Britain. (Home Office 2002a: 10)

On the one hand, the riots are read as a disturbance that disturbs the national ideal as they reveal that love has failed to deliver its promise of harmony between others. On the other hand, such an account becomes a demand for love, by suggesting that the violence is caused by the absence of love as nearness and proximity. Rather than segregation being an effect of racism, for example, it now becomes the *origin* of racism and violence. In this way, the narrative assumes that proximity *would mean* harmony between others and the incorporation of others into a national ideal. The narrative goes something like this: *If only we were closer we would be as one.*

The report into the race riots, *Community Cohesion*, makes integration a national ideal. While it suggests there is nothing wrong with people choosing 'to be close to others like themselves' (Home Office 2002b: 12), it then concludes: 'We cannot claim to be a truly multi-cultural society if the various communities within it live, as Cantle puts it, a series of parallel lives which do not touch at any point' (Home Office 2002b: 13). This narrative projects sameness onto 'ethnic minority' communities in order to elevate the national ideal into a love for difference. Difference becomes an ideal by being represented as a form of likeness; it becomes a new consensus that binds us together: 'This needs a determined effort *to gain consensus* on the fundamental issue of "cultural pluralism"' (Home Office 2003: 18, emphasis added). The transformation of pluralism into a consensus is telling. Others must agree to value difference: difference is now what we would have in common. In other words, difference becomes an elevated or sublimated form of like*ne*ss: you must like us – and be like us – by valuing or even loving differences (though clearly this is only about the differences that can be taken on and in by the nation, those that will not breach the ideal image of the nation). The narrative hence demands that migrant communities and working-class white communities must give up their love for each other – a love that gets coded as love-of-themselves, that is, as a perverse form of self-love or narcissism – and love those who are different, if they are to fulfil the image of the nation promised by the ideal and hence if they are to be loved by the nation.

My critique of the distinction between narcissistic and anaclitic love has bearing here. We can now see that the representation within the report works ideologically on two grounds. Firstly, it conceals the investment in the nation within multiculturalism (the nation turns back on itself, or is invested in itself, by positing itself as ideal). That is, it conceals how love for difference is also a form of narcissism; a desire to reproduce the national subject through how it incorporates others into itself. Secondly, the report works to conceal how 'sticking together' for minority communities involves an orientation towards differences; it erases the differences within such communities by positing them as sealed and homogeneous – as 'the same' – in the first place. These communities are constructed as narcissistic in order to elevate the multicultural nation into an ideal, that is, in order to conceal the investment in the reproduction of the nation. This positing of the national ideal requires the projection of sameness onto others and the transformation of sameness into perversion and pathology.

In such a narrative, 'others', including ethnic minorities and white working-class communities, in their perceived failure to love difference, function as 'a breach' in the ideal image of the nation. Their failure to love becomes the explanation for the failure of multiculturalism to deliver the national ideal. At the same time, the failure of 'ethnic minority communities' to integrate – to stick to others and embrace the national ideal – is required to 'show' how that ideal is 'idealisable' in the first place. Multiculturalism itself becomes an ideal by associating the failure to love difference with the origin of racism and violence. Rather than showing how segregation might be a survival tactic for communities who experience racism, deprivation or poverty, and rather than differentiating between the reasons why people might not mix with others who are already constructed as 'unlike' by scripts of racism, this narrative defines segregation as a breach in the image the nation has of itself, and as the origin of violence. The narrative hence places its hope in the integration of difference or in the imperative to mix.

The implications of this narrative is that if migrants or others would 'give' their difference to the nation, by mixing with others, then the 'ideal' would be achieved, and that difference would be 'returned' with love. The promise of multiculturalism is represented as a gift for the future generation (the young mixed-race woman): she may embody the promise of love's return. At the same time, the investment in multiculturalism gets intensified given the failure of return: the multicultural nation is invested in the presence of others who breach the ideality of its image. They become the sign of disturbance, which allows the ideal to be sustained as an ideal in the first place; they 'show' the injury that follows from not approximating an ideal.

In this chapter, I have offered a strong critique of how acting in the name of love can work to enforce a particular ideal onto others by requiring that they live up to an ideal to enter the community. The idea of a world where we all love each other, a world of lovers, is a humanist fantasy that informs much of the multicultural discourses of love, which I have formulated as the hope: *If only we got closer we would be as one.* The multicultural fantasy works as a form of conditional love, in which the conditions of love work to associate 'others' with the failure to return the national ideal.

But having said all this, I am not 'against love', and nor am I saying that love has to work in this way. Whether it is the dizzy, heady and overwhelming feeling of love for a lover, or the warmth and joy at being near a friend who has shared one's struggles, it is our relation to particular others that gives life meaning and direction, and can give us the feeling of there being somebody and something to live for. A politics of love is necessary in the sense that how one loves matters; it has effects on the texture of everyday life and on the intimate 'withness' of social relations. Whilst I do think politics might be about finding another way of loving others by inhabiting loves that do not speak their name, I would be wary of any assumption that love 'makes' politics and decides what form such politics might take. I would hence question Kelly Oliver's attempts to define her political vision as being about love rather than hate: 'Love is an ethics of differences that thrives on the adventure of otherness. This means that love is an ethical and social responsibility to open personal and public spaces in which otherness and difference can be articulated' (Oliver 2001: 20). Love for difference, as we have seen, can work to construct an ideal that others fail at the same time as it conceals the investment in reproduction. The imperative to love difference cannot be separated from negative attachments such as hate, from the relegation of others into signs of injury or disturbance. Indeed, Oliver's alternative to the politics of racism and violence, whilst understandable and even admirable, *speaks too quickly in the name of love* – a speaking position, which as we have seen, can create the conditions that posit others as having failed ideals that have already been taken to be 'mine' or 'ours'.

We might note Kaja Silverman's suggestion that the problem is with 'idealisation' and not love. As she puts it: 'We have consistently argued against idealisation, that psychic activity at the heart of love, rather than imagining the new uses to which it might be put' (Silverman 1996: 2). Silverman examines how the screen has (in her terms) colonised idealisation, by restricting ideality to certain subjects (Silverman 1996: 37). Her solution is described in the following terms: 'The textual intervention I have in mind is one which would "light up" dark corners of the cultural screen, and thereby make it possible for us to identify both consciously and unconsciously with bodies which we would otherwise reject with horror and contempt' (Silverman 1996: 81). Silverman is asking that we learn to put ourselves in the place of those who are abject (which does not mean taking their place as we have already recognised them as 'unlike us'), whose lives are 'uninhabitable' and pushed out from spaces that define what means to have a liveable life. Her vision is of 'any-body', including those bodies that appear different in their concrete specificity, becoming part of a community of lovers and loved. But is such a community possible? I have suggested that the idea of a world where we all love each other is a humanist fantasy that informs much of the multicultural discourse of love (*If only we got closer we would be as one*). Such an ideal requires that some others fail to approximate its form: those who don't love, who don't get closer, become the source of injury and disturbance. Admittedly, Silverman's vision is more complex than this. It is a vision where one learns to love those bodies that have already failed to live up to the collective ideal. I am not sure how I feel about this solution. Part of me questions the 'benevolence' of such good feelings and indeed imagines benevolent intellectuals reaching out to the poor, the dejected and the homeless and offering them their love. Love is not what will challenge the power relations that idealisation 'supports' in its restriction of ideality to some bodies and not others. In fact 'to love the abject' is close to the liberal politics of charity, one that usually makes the loving subject feel better for having loved and given love to someone presumed to be unloved, but which sustains the relations of power that compel the charitable love to be shown in this way (see my discussion of charity discourse in Chapter 1).

I would challenge any assumption that love can provide the foundation for political action, or is a sign of good politics. But what would political vision mean if we did not love those visions? Am I arguing against a visionary politics? If love does not shape our political visions, it does not mean we should not love the visions we have. In fact, we must love the visions we have, if there is any point to having them. We must be invested in them, whilst open to ways in which they fail to be translated into objects that can secure our ground in the world. We need to be invested in the images of a different kind of world and act upon those investments in how we love our loves, and how we live our lives, at the same time as we give ourselves up and over to the possibility that we might get it wrong, or that the world that we are in might change its shape. There is no good love that, in speaking its name, can change the world into the referent for that name. But in the resistance to speaking *in the name of love*, in the recognition that we do not simply act *out of love*, and in the understanding that love comes with conditions however unconditional it might feel, we can find perhaps a different kind of line or connection between the others we care for, and the world to which we want to give shape. Perhaps love might come to matter as a way of describing the very affect of solidarity with others in the work that is done to create a different world. Or as Jodi Dean puts it: 'I present reflective solidarity as that openness to difference which lets our disagreements provide the basis for connection' (Dean 1996: 17). This would be an affectionate solidarity: 'the kind of solidarity that grows out of intimate relationships of love and friendship' (Dean 1996: 17). The final two chapters of the book will turn to this question of the role of emotion and attachment in queer and feminist politics.

NOTES

1. Elena Haskins' Love Watch Site: http://www.wakeupordie.com/html/lovewa1.html Accessed 28 March 2003.
2. About Hate: http://women.stormfront.org/writings/abouthate.html Accessed 28 March 2003.

3. For an excellent collection on the role of women in fascism see Bacchetta and Power 2002.

4. *Lessons from the Death of Princess Diana*: http://women.stormfront.org/Writings/prindi.html Accessed 14 August 2002. The World Church of the Creator lost a legal battle to use this name, and is now known as the Creativity Movement.

5. Indeed, of all the emotions, love has been theorised as crucial to the social bond. More specifically, love has been theorised as central to politics and the securing of social hierarchy. Love has been understood as necessary to the maintenance of authority, in the sense that love of 'the leader' is what allows consent and agreement to norms and rules that do not and cannot guarantee the well-being of subjects and citizens. As Renata Salecl asks: 'How does it happen that people subordinate themselves to the logic of the institution and obey all kinds of social ritual that are supposedly against their well-being?' (Salecl 1998: 16). The crucial paradigm is the love the child has for the parent within the familial setting, and how this love then gets transferred onto other figures of authority. As Jessica Benjamin puts it: 'Obedience to the laws of civilisation is first inspired, not by fear or prudence, Freud tells us, but by love, love for those early powerful figures who first demand obedience' (Benjamin 1988: 5). I also want to ask the question of how love is crucial to the production of forms of subordination and authority. However, I will not argue that the child–parent love is simply transferred into love for authority or figures of authority. Instead, I want to think about love as an investment that creates an ideal, as the approximation of a character that then envelops the one who loves and the loved ('the collective ideal'). Whilst the love the child has for its care takers is crucial, it will not then be theorised as a primary love from which secondary loves necessarily follow.

6. One dimension of this differentiation is that women already take women as their object of desire; narcissism, whilst linked to male homosexuality explicitly by Freud (Freud 1934a: 45), can also be linked to lesbian desire, in which the woman takes herself as object. What makes the heterosexual woman different from the lesbian woman in this model would not be the love object, or who she desires, but who she identifies with/as. The difference would be whether women desires women as self or women as object: the latter possibility is assumed to require a masculine identification. My critique here would not only be a critique of the assumption that masculinity is necessarily taken on by taking women as objects of love, but also a critique of the assumption that women desiring women means taking oneself as the love object: other women are just that, other than oneself. See O'Connor and Ryan (1993: 222–3), who offer an excellent critique of the idea that lesbians are attracted to 'the same gender', and also de Lauretis (1994) for an important account of how lesbian desire can be articulated within a psychoanalytical frame.

7. The term 'gender' works as a form of abbreviation in Butler's account. Whilst I think her argument about the break between identification, desire and loss of a love object (mourning) is important, I think in this formulation she delimits the 'force' of her account by interpreting 'like' and 'unlike' in terms of 'inhabiting' a gender that is already mine ('my gender'). Being like the father/mother cannot be reduced to taking on his/her gender: other forms of familial resemblance might also be at stake. For example, my own experience of having a white English mother and a Pakistani father meant for me that my early points of identification with my mother were bound up with whiteness and the desire to be seen as white, and as part of a white community and even nation. Of course, such an image of whiteness was fantastic, and the fantasy became binding as an effect of the identification. Even when there are not such obvious

'signs' of difference within the familial space, the complex power relations between children and carers (especially when there are two or more primary carers) means that points of similarity and difference are invented (as fantasy) as children make (often temporary) identifications with carers, as ways of negotiating their relation to the world. The relation between identification (wanting to be like) and alliance formation (who I am with or side with) is crucial. For me, the question that remains to be asked is: How does what I take to be 'mine' make 'me' in relation to 'you'?

8. Thanks to Imogen Tyler whose important and critical work on narcissism brought my attention to this essay by Michael Warner.

9. Think of how it feels to be put on hold on the telephone. The longer one waits the harder it is to put the phone down. Giving up becomes harder the longer one does not give up, as the more one has given of oneself (time, energy, money). It does not follow that investments cannot be broken. We have different affective relations to the failure of return. For example, giving up after a lifetime of investment can lead to anger, hatred and despair, which become retrospective readings of the investment itself as the origin of injury. Or, an investment could be sustained by giving up on some objects, but not others, or through the displacement between objects. An example would be a white fascist displacement of loyalty from 'the white nation' to 'the white race'. Thanks to Ella Shohat and Barrie Thorne, whose comments after I presented different versions of this chapter helped me refine my argument about love as a form of waiting.

10. I am indebted here to Lacan's (1984) reading of courtly love, where he shows how it is the 'obstacle' to love that sustains the fantasy that 'love' is possible. See also Žižek's analysis of how 'the block' is projected onto the figure of the Jew: 'Society is not prevented from achieving its full identity because of Jews: it is prevented by its own antagonistic nature, by its own immanent blockage, and it "projects" this internal negativity on the figure of the "Jew"' (Žižek 1989:127). By providing the 'block' or 'obstacle' such figures allow the fantasy of full identity to be sustained.

11. Thanks to Anne-Marie Fortier for her critical work on multiculturalism. Her analysis of multiculturalism foregrounds the role of (hetero)sexuality, and also includes a reading of the mentioned article from *The Observer* race supplement.

12. My suggestion that the mixed-race woman is idealised through being cut off from signs of inter-racial intimacy supports Robyn Wiegman's argument in her article, 'Intimate Publics: Race, Property and Personhood' (2002). Wiegman suggests that 'multicultural kinship' becomes 'detached' from inter-racial intimacy. Her analysis is based on an excellent reading of legal cases involving new reproductive technologies, as well as the film, *Made in America*, which she suggests makes the multiracial family possible 'without the procreative enactment of literal interracial sex' (Wiegman 2002: 873).

13. See Arlie Russell Hochschild's work on the 'economy of gratitude'. As she suggests, gratitude involves not just feelings of appreciation, but also the structural position of indebtedness (Hochschild 2003: 105).

CHAPTER 7

Queer Feelings

> As the immigrant makes visible the processes of production, she also exemplifies the idea that the family is in need of protection because it is losing its viability, increasingly posed in the horrors of the imaginary as needing ever more fierce strategies of security to ensure its ideal of reproducing itself. It is this connection that is hidden – a relation between the production of life (both discursive and reproductive) and global production. (Goodman 2001: 194)

As I argued in the previous two chapters, the reproduction of life itself, where life is conflated with a social ideal ('life as we know it') is often represented as threatened by the existence of others: immigrants, queers, other others. These others become sources of fascination that allow the ideal to be posited as ideal through their embodiment of the failure of the ideal to be translated into being or action. We might note that 'reproduction' itself comes under question. The reproduction of life – in the form of the future generation – becomes bound up with the reproduction of culture, through the stabilisation of specific arrangements for living ('the family'). The family is idealisable through the narrative of threat and insecurity; the family is presented as vulnerable, and as needing to be defended against others who violate the conditions of its reproduction. As Goodman shows us, the moral defence of the family as a way of life becomes a matter of 'global politics'. I have already considered how the defence of the war against terrorism has evoked 'the family' as the origin of love, community and support (see Chapter 3). What needs closer examination is how heterosexuality becomes a script that binds the familial with the global: the coupling of man and woman becomes a kind of 'birthing', a giving birth not only to new life, but to ways of living that are already recognisable as forms of civilisation. It is this narrative of coupling as a condition for the reproduction of life, culture and value that explains the slide in racist narratives between the fear of strangers and immigrants (xenophobia), the fear of queers (homophobia) and the fear of miscegenation (as well as other illegitimate couplings).

These narratives or scripts do not, of course, simply exist 'out there' to legislate the political actions of states. They also shape bodies and lives, including those that follow and depart from such narratives in the ways in which they love and live, in the decisions that they make and take within the intimate spheres of home and work. It is important to consider how compulsory heterosexuality – defined as the accumulative effect of the repetition of the narrative of heterosexuality as an ideal coupling – shapes what it is possible for bodies to do,[1] even if it does not contain what it is possible to be. Bodies take the shape of norms that are repeated over time and with force. The work of repetition involves the concealment of labour under the sign of nature. In this chapter, I want to argue that norms surface *as* the surfaces of bodies; norms are a matter of impressions, of how bodies are 'impressed upon' by the world, as a world made up of others. In other words, such impressions are effects of labour; how bodies work and are worked upon shapes the surfaces of bodies. Regulative norms function in a way as 'repetitive strain injuries' (RSIs). Through repeating some gestures and not others, or through being orientated in some directions and not others, bodies become contorted; they get twisted into shapes that enable some action only insofar as they restrict capacity for other kinds of action.

I would suggest that heteronormativity also affects the surfaces of bodies, which surface through impressions made by others. Compulsory heterosexuality shapes bodies by the assumption that a body 'must' orient itself towards some objects and not others, objects that are secured as ideal through the fantasy of difference (see Chapter 6). Hence compulsory heterosexuality shapes which bodies one 'can' legitimately approach as would-be lovers and which one cannot. In shaping one's approach to others, compulsory heterosexuality also shapes one's own body, *as a congealed history of past approaches.* Sexual orientation is not then simply about the direction one takes towards an object of desire, as if this direction does not affect other things that we do. Sexual orientation involves bodies that leak into worlds; it involves a way of orientating the body towards and away from others, which affects how one can enter different kinds of social spaces (which presumes certain bodies, certain directions, certain ways of loving and living), even if it does not lead bodies to the same places. To make a simple but important point: orientations affect what it is that bodies can do.[2] Hence, the failure to orient oneself 'towards' the ideal sexual object affects how we live in the world, an affect that is readable as the failure to reproduce, and as a threat to the social ordering of life itself.

Of course, one does not have to do what one is compelled to do: for something to be compulsory shows that it is not necessary. But to refuse to be compelled by the narratives of ideal heterosexuality in one's orientation to others is still to be affected by those narratives; they work to script one's orientation as a form of disobedience. The affects of 'not following' the scripts can be multiple. We can consider, for example, the psychic as well as social costs of loving a body that is supposed to be unloveable for the subject I am, or loving a body that I was 'supposed to' repudiate, which may include shame and melancholia (Butler 1997b; Braidotti 2002: 53; see Chapter 5). The negative affects of 'not quite' living in the norms show us how loving loves that are not 'normative' involves being subject to such norms precisely in the costs and damage that are incurred when not following them. Do queer moments happen when this failure to reproduce norms as forms of life is embraced or affirmed as a political and ethical alternative? Such affirmation would not be about the conversion of shame into pride, but the enjoyment of the negativity of shame, an enjoyment of that which has been designated shameful by normative culture (see Barber and Clark 2002: 22–9).

In this chapter, I could ask the question: How does it feel to inhabit a body that fails to reproduce an ideal? But this is not my question. Instead, I wish to explore 'queer feelings' without translating such an exploration into a matter of 'feeling queer'. Such a translation would assume 'queerness' involves a particular emotional life, or that there are feelings that bodies 'have' given their failure to inhabit or follow a heterosexual ideal. Of course, one can feel queer. There are feelings involved in the self-perception of 'queerness', a self-perception that is bodily, as well as bound up with 'taking on' a name. But these feelings are mediated and they are attached to the category 'queer' in ways that are complex and contingent, precisely because the category is produced in relation to histories that render it a sign of failed being or 'non-being'.[3] In examining the affective potential of queer, I will firstly consider the relationship between norms and affects in debates on queer families. I will then discuss the role of grief in queer politics with specific reference to queer responses to September 11. And finally, I will reflect on the role of pleasure in queer lifestyles or countercultures, and will ask how the enjoyment of social and sexual relations that are designated as 'non-(re)productive' can function as forms of political disturbance in an affective economy organised around the principle that pleasure is only ethical as an incentive or reward for good conduct.

(DIS)COMFORT AND NORMS

It is important to consider how heterosexuality functions powerfully not only as a series of norms and ideals, but also through emotions that shape bodies as well as worlds: (hetero)norms are investments, which are 'taken on' and 'taken in' by subjects. To practise heterosexuality by following its scripts in one's choice of some love objects – and refusal of others – is also to become invested in the reproduction of heterosexuality. Of course, one does not 'do' heterosexuality simply through who one does and does not have sex with. Heterosexuality as a script for an ideal life makes much stronger claims. It is assumed that all arrangements will follow from the arrangement of the couple: man/woman. It is no accident that compulsory heterosexuality works powerfully in the most casual modes of conversation. One asks: 'Do you have a boyfriend?' (to a girl), or one asks: 'Do you have a girlfriend?' (to a boy). Queer subjects feel the tiredness of making corrections and departures; the pressure of this insistence, this presumption, this demand that asks either for a 'passing over' (a moment of passing, which is not always available) or for direct or indirect forms of self-revelation ('but actually, he's a she' or 'she's a he', or just saying 'she' instead of 'he' or 'he' instead of 'she' at the 'obvious' moment). No matter how 'out' you may be, how (un)comfortably queer you may feel, those moments of interpellation get repeated over time, and can be experienced as a bodily injury; moments which position queer subjects as failed in their failure to live up to the 'hey you too' of heterosexual self-narration. The everydayness of compulsory heterosexuality is also its affec-tiveness, wrapped up as it is with moments of ceremony (birth, marriage, death), which bind families together, and with the ongoing investment in the sentimentality of friendship and romance. Of course, such sentimentality is deeply embedded with public as well as private culture; stories of hetero-sexual romance proliferate as a matter of human interest. As Lauren Berlant and Michael Warner argue: 'National heterosexuality is the mechanism by which a core national culture can be imagined as a sanitised space of sentimental feeling' (Berlant and Warner 2000: 313).

We can consider the sanitised space as a comfort zone. Normativity is comfortable for those who can inhabit it. The word 'comfort' suggests well-being and satisfaction, but it also suggests an ease and easiness. To follow the rules of heterosexuality is to be at ease in a world that reflects back the couple form one inhabits as an ideal.[4] Of course, one can be made to feel uneasy by one's inhabitance of an ideal. One can be made uncomfortable by one's own comforts. To see heterosexuality as an ideal that one might or might not follow – or to be uncomfortable by the privileges one is given by inhabiting a heterosexual world – is a less comforting form of comfort. But comfort it remains and comfort is very hard to notice when one experiences it. Having uncomfortably inhabited the comforts of heterosexuality for many years, I know this too well. Now, living a queer life, I can reflect on many comforts that I did not even begin to notice despite my 'felt' discomforts. We don't tend to notice what is comfortable, even when we think we do.

Thinking about comfort is hence always a useful starting place for thinking. So let's think about how it feels to be comfortable. Say you are sinking into a comfortable chair. Note I already have transferred the affect to an object ('it is comfortable'). But comfort is about the fit between body and object: my comfortable chair may be awkward for you, with your differently-shaped body. Comfort is about an encounter between more than one body, which is the promise of a 'sinking' feeling. It is, after all, pain or discomfort that return one's attention to the surfaces of the body *as body* (see Chapter 1). To be comfortable is to be so at ease with one's environment that it is hard to distinguish where one's body ends and the world begins. One fits, and by fitting, the surfaces of bodies disappear from view. The disappearance of the surface is instructive: in feelings of comfort, bodies extend into spaces, and spaces extend into bodies. The sinking feeling involves a seamless space, or a space where you can't see the 'stitches' between bodies.

Heteronormativity functions as a form of public comfort by allowing bodies to extend into spaces that have already taken their shape. Those spaces are lived as comfortable as they allow bodies to fit in; the surfaces of social space are already impressed upon by the shape of such bodies (like a chair that acquires its shape by the repetition of some bodies inhabiting it: we can almost see the shape of bodies as 'impressions' on the surface). The impressions acquired by surfaces function as traces of bodies. We can even see this process in social spaces. As Gill Valentine has argued, the 'heterosexualisation' of public spaces such as streets is naturalised by the repetition of different forms of heterosexual conduct (images on billboards, music played, displays of heterosexual intimacy and so on), a process which goes unnoticed by heterosexual subjects (Valentine 1996: 149). The surfaces of social as well as bodily space 'record' the repetition of acts, and the passing by of some bodies and not others.

Heteronormativity also becomes a form of comforting: one feels better by the warmth of being faced by a world one has already taken in. One does not notice this *as a world* when one has been shaped by that world, and even acquired its shape. Norms may not only have a way of disappearing from view, but may also be that which we do not consciously feel.[5] Queer subjects, when faced by the 'comforts' of heterosexuality may feel uncomfortable (the body does not 'sink into' a space that has already taken its shape). Discomfort is a feeling of disorientation: one's body feels out of place, awkward, unsettled. I know that feeling too well, the sense of out-of-place-ness and estrangement involves an acute awareness of the surface of one's body, which appears *as* surface, when one cannot inhabit the social skin, which is shaped by some bodies, and not others. Furthermore, queer subjects may also be 'asked' not to make heterosexuals feel uncomfortable by avoiding the display of signs of queer intimacy, which is itself an uncomfortable feeling, a restriction on what one can do with one's body, and another's body, in social space.[6]

The availability of comfort for some bodies may depend on the labour of others, and the burden of concealment. Comfort may operate as a form of 'feeling fetishism': some bodies can 'have' comfort, only as an effect of the work of others, where the work itself is concealed from view.[7]

It is hence for very good reasons that queer theory has been defined not only as anti-heteronormative, but as anti-normative. As Tim Dean and Christopher Lane argue, queer theory 'advocates a politics based on resistance to all norms' (Dean and Lane 2001: 7). Importantly, heteronormativity refers to more than simply the presumption that it is normal to be heterosexual. The 'norm' is regulative, and is supported by an 'ideal' that associates sexual conduct with other forms of conduct. We can consider, for example, how the restriction of the love object is not simply about the desirability of *any* heterosexual coupling. The couple should be 'a good match' (a judgement that often exercises conventional class and racial assumptions about the importance of 'matching' the backgrounds of partners) and they should exclude others from the realm of sexual intimacy (an idealisation of monogamy, that often equates intimacy with property rights or rights to the intimate other as property). Furthermore, a heterosexual coupling may only approximate an ideal through being sanctioned by marriage, by participating in the ritual of reproduction and good parenting, by being good neighbours as well as lovers and parents, and by being even better citizens. In this way, normative culture involves the differentiation between legitimate and illegitimate ways of living whereby the preservation of what is legitimate ('life as we know it') is assumed to be necessary for the well-being of the next generation. Heteronormativity involves the reproduction or transmission of culture through how one lives one's life in relation to others.

For queer theorists, it is hence important that queer lives do not follow the scripts of heteronormative culture: they do not become, in Judith Halberstam's provocative and compelling term, 'homonormative' lives (Halberstam 2003: 331). Such lives would not desire access to comfort; they would maintain their discomfort with all aspects of normative culture in how they live. Ideally, they would not have families, get married, settle down into unthinking coupledom, give birth to and raise children, join neighbourhood watch, or pray for the nation in times of war. Each of these acts would 'support' the ideals that script such lives as queer, failed and unliveable in the first place. The aspiration to ideals of conduct that is central to the reproduction of heteronormativity has been called, quite understandably, a form of assimilation.

Take, for instance, the work of Andrew Sullivan. In his *Virtually Normal* he argues that most gay people want to be normal; and that being gay does not mean being not normal, even if one is not quite as normal as a straight person (to paraphrase Homi Bhabha, 'almost normal, but not quite'). So he suggests that one can aspire to *have* a heterosexual life without *being* hetero-sexual: the only difference would be the choice of one's love object. As he puts it:

> It's perfectly possible to combine a celebration of the traditional family with the celebration of a stable homosexual relationship. The one, after all, is modelled on the other. If constructed carefully as a conservative social ideology, the notion of stable gay relationships might even serve to buttress the ethic of heterosexual marriage, by showing how even those excluded from it can wish to model themselves on its shape and structure. (Sullivan 1996: 112)

Here, gay relationships are valued and celebrated insofar as they are 'mod-elled' on the traditional model of the heterosexual family. Indeed, Sullivan explicitly defines his project as a way of supporting and extending the ideal of the family by showing how those who are 'not it' seek to 'become it'. Gay relationships, by miming the forms of heterosexual coupling, hence pledge their allegiance to the very forms they cannot inhabit. This mimicry is, as Douglas Crimp (2002) has argued, a way of sustaining the psychic conditions of melancholia insofar as Sullivan identifies with that which he cannot be, and indeed with what has already rejected him. As Crimp remarks, Sullivan is 'incapable of recognising the intractability of homophobia because his melancholia consists precisely in his identification with the homophobe's repudiation of him' (Crimp 2002: 6). Assimilation involves a desire to approximate an ideal that one has already failed; an identification with one's designation as a failed subject. The choice of assimilation – queer skin, straight masks – is clearly about supporting the violence of heteronormative distinctions between legitimate and illegitimate lives.[8]

As Judith Butler has argued, one of the biggest problems in campaigns for gay marriage is precisely the way that they may strengthen the hierarchy between legitimate and illegitimate lives. Rather than the hierarchy resting on a distinction between gay and straight, it becomes displaced onto a new distinction between more and less legitimate queer relationships (Butler 2002: 18). As she asks, does gay marriage 'only become an "option" by extending itself as a norm (and thus foreclosing options), one which also extends property relations and renders the social forms for sexuality more conservative'? (Butler 2002: 21). In other words, if some of the rights of heterosexuality are extended to queers, what happens to queers who don't take up those rights; whose life choices and sexual desires cannot be trans-lated into the form of marriage, even when emptied of its predication on heterosexual coupling? Do these (non-married) queers become the illegiti-mate others against which the ideal of marriage is supported?

Of course, the question of gay marriage remains a political dilemma. For not to support the extension of the right of marriage to gay relationships could give support to the status quo, which maintains the distinction between legitimate and illegitimate lives on the grounds of sexual orientation. As Judith Butler (2002) argues, the social and psychic costs of not having one's relationship recognised by others (whether or not the recognition is determined by law) are enormous especially in situations of loss and bereavement (see the following section). I want to enter this debate by considering how the political choice of being queer or straight (or an assimilated queer) can be contested. Butler herself contests the choice through adopting a position of ambivalence. Whilst I recognise the value of such ambivalence, I want to suggest that more reflection on queer attachments might allow us to avoid positing assimilation or transgression as choices.

To begin with, we can return to my description of what we might call a queer life. I suggested that 'ideally' such lives will maintain a discomfort with the scripts of heteronormative existence. The reliance on this word is telling. For already in describing what may be queer, I am also defining grounds of an ideality, in which to have an ideal queer life, or even to be legitimately queer, people must act in some ways rather than others. We need to ask: How does defining a queer ideal rely on the existence of others who fail the ideal? Who can and cannot embody the queer ideal? Such an ideal is not equally accessible to all, even all those who identify with the sign 'queer' or other 'signs' of non-normative sexuality. Gayatri Gopinath (2003), for example, reflects on how public and visible forms of 'queerness' may not be available to lesbians from South Asia, where it may be in the private spaces of home that bodies can explore homo-erotic pleasures. Her argument shows how queer bodies have different access to public forms of culture, which affect how they can inhabit those publics. Indeed, whilst being queer may feel uncomfortable within heterosexual space, it does not then follow that queers always feel comfortable in queer spaces. I have felt discomfort in some queer spaces, again, as a feeling of being out of place. This is not to say that I have been *made* to feel uncomfortable; the discomfort is itself a sign that queer spaces may extend some bodies more than others (for example, some queer spaces might extend the mobility of white, middle-class bodies). At times, I feel uncomfortable about inhabiting the word 'queer', worrying that I am not queer enough, or have not been queer for long enough, or am just not the right kind of queer. We can feel uncomfortable in the categories we inhabit, even categories that are shaped by their refusal of public comfort.

Furthermore, the positing of an ideal of being free from scripts that define what counts as a legitimate life seems to presume a negative model of freedom; defined here as *freedom from norms*. Such a negative model of freedom idealises movement and detachment, constructing a mobile form of subjectivity that could escape from the norms that constrain what it is that bodies can do. Others have criticised queer theory for its idealisation of movement (Epps 2001: 412; Fortier 2003). As Epps puts it: 'Queer theory tends to place great stock in movement, especially when it is movement against, beyond, or away from rules and regulations, norms and conventions, borders and limits . . . it makes fluidity a fetish' (Epps 2001: 413). The idealisation of movement, or transformation of movement into a fetish, depends upon the exclusion of others who are already positioned as *not free in the same way*. Bodies that can move with more ease may also more easily shape and be shaped by the sign 'queer'. It is for this reason that Biddy Martin suggests that we need to 'stop defining queerness as mobile and fluid in relation to what then gets construed as stagnant and ensnaring' (Martin 1996: 46). Indeed, the idealisation of movement depends upon a prior model of what counts as a queer life, which may exclude others, those who have attachments that are not readable as queer, or indeed those who may lack the (cultural as well as economic) capital to support the 'risk' of maintaining anti-normativity as a permanent orientation.

Queer lives do not suspend the attachments that are crucial to the reproduction of heteronormativity, and this does not diminish 'queerness', but intensifies the work that it can do. Queer lives remain shaped by that which they fail to reproduce. To turn this around, queer lives shape what gets reproduced: in the very failure to reproduce the norms through how they inhabit them, queer lives produce different effects. For example, the care work of lesbian parents may involve 'having' to live in close proximity to heterosexual cultures (in the negotiation with schools, other mothers, local communities), whilst not being able to inhabit the heterosexual ideal. The gap between the script and the body, including the bodily form of 'the family', may involve discomfort and hence may 'rework' the script. The reworking is not inevitable, as it is dependent or contingent on other social factors (especially class) and it does not necessarily involve conscious political acts.

We can return to my point about comfort: comfort is the effect of bodies being able to 'sink' into spaces that have already taken their shape. Discomfort is not simply a choice or decision – 'I feel uncomfortable about this or that' – but an effect of bodies inhabiting spaces that do not take or 'extend' their shape. So the closer that queer subjects get to the spaces defined by heteronormativity the more *potential* there is for a reworking of the heteronormative,[9] partly as the proximity 'shows' how the spaces extend some bodies rather than others. Such extensions are usually concealed by what they produce: public comfort. What happens when bodies fail to 'sink into' spaces, a failure that we can describe as a 'queering' of space?[10] When does this potential for 'queering' get translated into a transformation of the scripts of compulsory heterosexuality?

It is important, when considering how this potential is translated into transformation, that we do not create a political imperative; for example, by arguing that all lesbian parents should actively work to interrupt the scripts of compulsory heterosexuality. As Jacqui Gabb shows, some lesbian parents may perceive their families to be 'just like other families' (Gabb 2002: 6; see also Lewin 1993). Now, is this a sign of their assimilation and their political failure? Of course, such data could be read in this way. But it also shows the lack of any direct translation between political struggle and the contours of everyday life given the ways in which queer subjects occupy very different places within the social order. Maintaining an active positive of 'transgression' not only takes time, but may not be psychically, socially or materially possible for some individuals and groups given their ongoing and unfinished commitments and histories. Some working-class lesbian parents, for example, might not be able to afford being placed outside the kinship networks within local neighbourhoods: being recognised as 'like any other family' might not simply be strategic, but necessary for survival. Other working-class lesbian parents might not wish to be 'like other families': what might feel necessary for some, could be impossible for others. Assimilation and transgression are not choices that are available to individuals, but are effects of how subjects can and cannot inhabit social norms and ideals.[11] Even when queer families may wish to be recognised as 'families like other families', their difference from the ideal script produces disturbances – moments of 'non-sinking' – that will require active forms of negotiation in different times and places.

To define a family as queer is already to interrupt one ideal image of the family, based on the heterosexual union, procreation and the biological tie. Rather than thinking of queer families as an extension of an ideal (and hence as a form of assimilation that supports the ideal), we can begin to reflect on the exposure of the failure of the ideal as part of the work that queer families are doing. As Weeks, Heaphy and Donovan suggest, we can consider families as social practices, and 'more as an adjective or, possibly, a verb' (Week, Heaphy and Donovan 2001: 37). Families are *a doing word and a word for doing*. Indeed, thinking of families as what people do in their intimate lives allows us to avoid positing queer families as an alternative ideal, for example, in the assumption that queer families are necessarily more egalitarian (Carrington 1999: 13). Queer lives involve issues of power, responsibility, work and inequalities and, importantly, do not and cannot transcend the social relations of global capitalism (Carrington 1999: 218). Reflecting on the work that is done in queer families, as well as what queer families do, allow us to disrupt the idealisation of the family form.

This argument seems to suggest that queer families may be just like other families in their shared failure to inhabit an ideal. But of course such an argument would neutralise the differences between queer and non-queer families, as well as the differences between queer families. Families may not 'be' the ideal, which is itself an impossible fantasy, but they have a different relation of proximity to that ideal. For some families the ideal takes the shape of their form (as being heterosexual, white, middle-class, and so on). The 'failure' to inhabit an ideal may or may not be visible to others, and this visibility has effects on the contours of everyday existence. Learning to live with the effects and affects of heterosexism and homophobia may be crucial to what makes queer families different from non-queer families. Such forms of discrimination can have negative effects, involving pain, anxiety, fear, depression and shame, all of which can restrict bodily and social mobility. However, the effects of this failure to embody an ideal are not simply negative. As Kath Weston has argued, queer families often narrate the excitement of creating intimacies that are not based on biological ties, or on established gender relations: 'Far from viewing families we choose as imitations or derivatives of family ties created elsewhere in their society, many lesbians and gay men alluded to the difficulty and excitement of constructing kinship in the *absence* of what they called "models"' (Weston 1991: 116, see also Weston 1995: 93). The absence of models that are appropriate does not mean an absence of models. In fact, it is in 'not fitting' the model of the nuclear family that queer families can work to transform what it is that families can do. The 'non-fitting' or discomfort opens up possibilities, an opening up which can be difficult and exciting.

There remains a risk that 'queer families' could be posited as an ideal within the queer community. If queer families were idealised within the queer community, then fleeting queer encounters, or more casual forms of friendship and alliance, could become seen as failures, or less significant forms of attachment. Queer politics needs to stay open to different ways of doing queer in order to maintain the possibility that differences are not converted into failure. Queer subjects do use different names for what they find significant in their lives and they find significance in different places, including those that are deemed illegitimate in heteronormative cultures. The word 'families' may allow some queers to differentiate between their more and less significant bonds, where significance is not assumed to follow a form that is already given in advance. For others, the word 'families' may be too saturated with affects to be usable in this way. Eve Kosofsky Sedgwick's vision of the family, for instance, is 'elastic enough to do justice to the depth and sometimes durability of nonmarital and/or nonprocreative bonds, same-sex bonds, nondyadic bonds, bonds not defined by genitality, "step"-bonds, adult sibling bonds, nonbiological bonds across generations, etc' (Sedgwick 1994: 71). But hope cannot be placed simply in the elasticity of the word 'family': that elasticity should not become a fetish, and held in place as an object in which we must all be invested. The hope of 'the family' for queer subjects may exist only insofar as it is not the only object of hope (see Chapter 8, for an analysis of hope). If we do not legislate what forms queer bonds take – and presume the ontological difference between legitimate and illegitimate bonds – then it is possible for queer bonds to be named as bonds without the demand that other queers return those bonds in the form of shared investment.

It is, after all, the bonds between queers that 'stop' queer bodies from feeling comfortable in spaces that extend the form of the heterosexual couple. We can posit the effects of 'not fitting' as a form of queer discomfort, but a discomfort which is generative, rather than simply constraining or negative. To feel uncomfortable is precisely to be affected by that which persists in the shaping of bodies and lives. Discomfort is hence not about assimilation or resistance, *but about inhabiting norms differently*. The inhabitance is generative or productive insofar as it does not end with the failure of norms to be secured, but with possibilities of living that do not 'follow' those norms through. Queer is not, then, about transcendence or freedom from the (hetero)normative. Queer feelings are 'affected' by the repetition of the scripts that they fail to reproduce, and this 'affect' is also a sign of what queer can do, of how it can work by *working on* the (hetero)normative. The failure to be non-normative is then not the failure of queer to be queer, but a sign of attachments that are the condition of possibility for queer. Queer feelings may embrace a sense of discomfort, a lack of ease with the available scripts for living and loving, along with an excitement in the face of the uncertainty of where the discomfort may take us.

QUEER GRIEF

The debate about whether queer relationships should be recognised by law acquires a crucial significance at times of loss. Queer histories tell us of inescapable injustices, for example, when gay or lesbian mourners are not recognised as mourners in hospitals, by families, in law courts. In this section, I want to clarify how the recognition of queer lives might work in a way that avoids assimilation by examining the role of grief within queer politics. There has already been a strong case made for how grief supports, or even forms, the heterosexuality of the normative subject. For example, Judith Butler argues that the heterosexual subject must 'give up' the potential of queer love, but this loss cannot be grieved, and is foreclosed or barred permanently from the subject (Butler 1997b: 135). As such, homosexuality becomes an 'ungrievable loss', which returns to haunt the heterosexual subject through its melancholic identification with that which has been permanently cast out. For Butler, this ungrievable loss gets displaced:

heterosexual culture, having given up its capacity to grieve its own lost queer-ness, cannot grieve the loss of queer lives; it cannot admit that queer lives are lives that could be lost.

Simply put, queer lives have to be recognised as lives in order to be grieved. In a way, it is not that queer lives exist as 'ungrievable loss', but that queer losses cannot 'be admitted' as forms of loss in the first place, as queer lives are not recognised as lives 'to be lost'. One has to recognise oneself as having something before one can recognise oneself as losing something. Of course, loss does not simply imply having something that has been taken away. The meanings of loss slide from 'ceasing to have', to suffering, and being deprived. Loss implies the acknowledgement of the desirability of what was once had: one may have to love in order to lose. As such, the failure to recog-nise queer loss *as* loss is also a failure to recognise queer relationships as sig-nificant bonds, or that queer lives are lives worth living, or that queers are more than failed heterosexuals, heterosexuals who have failed 'to be'. Given that queer becomes read as a form of 'non-life' – with the death implied by being seen as non-reproductive – then queers are perhaps even already dead and cannot die. As Jeff Nunokawa suggests, heteronormative culture implies queer death, 'from the start' (Nunokawa 1991: 319). Queer loss may not count *because it precedes a relation of having.*

Queer activism has consequently been bound up with the politics of grief, with the question of what losses are counted as grievable. This politicisation of grief was crucial to the activism around AIDS and the transformation of mourning into militancy (see Crimp 2002). As Ann Cvetkovich puts it: 'The AIDS crisis, like other traumatic encounters with death, has challenged our strategies for remembering the dead, forcing the invention of new forms of mourning and commemoration' (Cvetkovich 2003a: 427). The activism around AIDS produced works of collective mourning, which sought to make present the loss of queer lives within public culture: for example, with the Names Project Quilt, in which each quilt signifies a loss that is joined to others, in a potentially limitless display of collective loss. But what are the political effects of contesting the failure to recognise queer loss by display-ing that loss?

In order to address this question, I want to examine public forms of grief displayed in response to September 11 2001. As Marita Stukern has argued, the rush to memorialise in response to the event not only sought to replace an absence with a presence, but also served to represent the absence through some losses and not others. On the one hand, individual losses of loved others were grieved, and surfaced as threads in the fabric of collective grief. The individual portraits of grief in the *New York Times,* and the memorials to individual losses posted around the city, work as a form of testimony; a way of making individual loss present to others. Each life is painted in order to transform a number into a being, one who has been lost to someone; so the person who is lost *is not only missing, but also missed*. But at the same time, some losses more than others came to embody the collective loss. Sturken suggests that a 'hierarchy of the dead' was constructed: 'The media coverage of September 11 establishes a hierarchy of the dead, with, for instance, the privileging of the stories of public servants, such as firefighters over office workers, of policemen over security guards, and the stories of those with economic capital over those without, of traders over janitors' (Sturken 2002: 383–4). Whilst some losses are privileged over others, some don't appear as losses at all. Some losses get taken in (as 'ours'), thereby excluding other losses from counting as losses in the first place.[12]

Queer losses were among the losses excluded from the public cultures of grief. As David L. Eng has argued, the public scripts of grief after September 11 were full of signs of heteronormativity: 'The rhetoric of the loss of "fathers and mothers", "sons and daughters", and "brothers and sisters" attempts to trace the smooth alignment between the nation-state and the nuclear family, the symbolics of blood relations and nationalist domesticity' (Eng 2002: 90). It is because of this erasure that some queer groups have intervened, by naming queer losses. The president of the National Lesbian and Gay Journalists Association,[13] for example, names queer loss both by naming individual queers who were lost in September 11, and by describing that event as a loss for the queer community. What is interesting about this response is how it addresses two communities: the nation and the queer community, using inclusive pronouns to describe both. The first community is that of all Americans: 'This unimaginable loss has struck at the very core of our sense of safety and order.' Here, September 11 is viewed as striking 'us' in the same place. But even in this use of inclusive language, the difference of GLBT Americans is affirmed: 'Even on a good day, many GLBT Americans felt unsafe or at least vulnerable in ways large and small. Now, that feeling has grown even more acute and has blanketed the nation.' The feelings of vulnerability that are specific to queer communities are first named, and then get extended into a feeling that blankets the nation, covering over the differences. The extension relies on an analogy between queer feelings (unsafety, vulnerability) and the feelings of citizens living with the threat of terrorism (see Chapter 3). The narrative implies that the nation is almost made queer by terrorism: heterosexuals 'join' queers in feeling vulnerable and fearful of attack. Of course, in 'becoming' queer, the nation remains differentiated from those who 'are' already queer.

This tension between the 'we' of the nation and the 'we' of the queer community is also expressed through the evocation of 'hate': 'Like others, our community knows all too well the devastating effects of hate.' This is a complicated utterance. On the one hand, this statement draws attention to experiences of being hated that trouble the national imaginary, which assumes a distinction between tolerant multicultural subjects who 'love' and fundamentalists and racists who 'hate' (see Chapter 6). By showing how queers are a community 'that is hated' by the imagined nation, the statement breaches the ideal image the nation has of itself ('America can hate others (queers), as well as be hated by others'). But at the same time, this narrative repeats the dominant one: the tragedy of the event is the consequence of 'their hate' for 'us' ('Why do they hate us?'). The construction of the queer community as a hated community, which splits the nation, slides into a construction of the nation as 'being' hated by others. The nation is reinstalled as a coherent subject within the utterance: together, we are hated, and in being hated, we are together.

Within this queer response, mourning responds to the loss of 'every life', which includes 'members of our own community'. Individual names are given, and the losses are named as queer losses: 'They include an American Airlines co-pilot on the flight that crashed into the Pentagon; a nurse from New Hampshire; a couple travelling with their 3-year-old son.' Furthermore, the losses are evoked through the language of heroism and courage: 'Father Mychal Judge, the New York Fire Department chaplain, who died whilst administering last rites to a fallen fire fighter, and Mark Bingham, a San Francisco public relations executive, who helped thwart the hijackers'. Certainly, the call for a recognition of queer courage and queer loss works to 'mark' the others already named as losses. That is, the very necessity of identifying some losses *as* queer losses reveals how most losses were narrated as heterosexual losses in the first place. The apparently unmarked individual losses privileged in the media are here marked by naming these other losses *as* queer losses. The risk of the 'marking' is that queer loss is then named as loss *alongside* those other losses; the use of humanist language of individual courage and bravery makes these losses *like the others*. Hence, queer loss becomes incorporated into the loss of the nation, in which the 'we' is always a 'we too'. The utterance, 'we too', implies both a recognition of a past exclusion (the 'too' shows how the 'we' must be supplemented), and a claim for inclusion (we are like you in having lost). Although such grief challenges the established 'hierarchy between the dead' (Sturken 2002: 384), it also works as a form of covering; the expression of grief 'blankets' the nation. Queer lives are grieved *as* queer lives only to support the grief of the nation, which perpetuates the concealment of other losses (such as, for example, the losses in Afghanistan, Iraq, Palestine).

So whilst the NLGJA response to September 11 challenges the way in which the nation is secured by making visible some losses more than others, it allows the naming of queer losses to support the narrative it implicitly critiques. But our response cannot be to suspend the demand for the recognition of queer grief. We have already registered the psychic and social costs of unrecognised loss. The challenge for queer politics becomes finding a different way of grieving, and responding to the grief of others. In order to think differently about the ethics and politics of queer grief, I want to reconsider the complexity of grief as a psycho-social process of coming to terms with loss.

Freud's distinction between mourning and melancholia might help us here. For Freud, mourning is a healthy response to loss, as it is about 'letting go' of the lost object, which may include a loved person or an abstraction which has taken the place of one (Freud 1934b: 153). Melancholia is pathological: the ego refuses to let go of the object, and preserves the object 'inside itself' (Freud 1934b: 153). In the former 'the world becomes poor and empty', whilst in the latter, 'it is the ego itself' (Freud 1934b: 155). Melancholia involves assimilation: the object persists, but only insofar as it is taken within the subject, as a kind of ghostly death. The central assumption behind Freud's distinction is that it is good or healthy to 'let go' of the lost object (to 'let go' of that which is already 'gone'). Letting go of the lost object may seem an ethical as well as 'healthy' response to the alterity of the other.

But the idea that 'letting go' is 'better' has been challenged. For example, the collection *Continuing Bonds*, 'reexamines the idea that the purpose of grief is to sever the bonds with the deceased in order to free the survivor to make new attachments' (Silverman and Klass 1996: 3). Silverman and Klass suggest that the purpose of grief is not to let go, but lies in 'negotiating and renegotiating the meaning of the loss over time' (Silverman and Klass 1996: 19). In other words, melancholia should not be seen as pathological; the desire to maintain attachments with the lost other is enabling, rather than blocking new forms of attachment. Indeed, some have argued that the refusal to let go is an ethical response to loss. Eng and Kazanjian, for example, accept Freud's distinction between mourning and melancholia, but argue that melancholia is preferable as a way of responding to loss. Mourning enables gradual withdrawal from the object and hence denies the other through forgetting its trace. In contrast, melancholia is 'an enduring devotion on the part of the ego to the lost object', and as such is a way of keeping the other, and with it the past, alive in the present (Eng and Kazanjian 2003: 3). In this model, keeping the past alive, even as that which has been lost, is ethical: the object is not severed from history, or encrypted, but can acquire new meanings and possibilities in the present. To let go might even be to kill again (see Eng and Han 2003: 365).

Eng and Han's work points to an ethical duty to keep the dead other alive. The question of how to respond to loss requires us to rethink what it means to live with death. In Freud's critique of melancholia, the emphasis is on a lost external object, that which is other to me, being preserved by becoming internal to the ego. As Judith Butler puts it, the object is not abandoned, but transferred from the external to the internal (Butler 1997b: 134). However, the passage in grief is not simply about what is 'outside' being 'taken in'. For the object to be lost, *it must already have existed within the subject*. It would be too narrow to see this 'insideness' only in terms of a history of past assimilation ('taking in' as 'the making of likeness'), although assimilation remains crucial to love as well as grief, as I have already suggested. We can also think of this 'insideness' as an effect of the 'withness' of intimacy, which involves the process of being affected by others. As feminist critics in particular have argued, we are 'with others' before we are defined as 'apart from' others (Benjamin 1995). Each of us, in being shaped by others, carries with us 'impressions' of those others. Such impressions are certainly memories of this or that other, to which we return in the sticky metonymy of our thoughts and dreams, and through prompting either by conversations with others or through the visual form of photographs. Such 'withness' also shapes our bodies, our gestures, our turns of phrase: we pick up bits and pieces of each other as the effect of nearness or proximity (see Diprose 2002). Of course, to some extent this proximity involves the making of likeness. But the hybrid work of identity-making is never about pure resemblance of one to another. It involves a dynamic process of perpetual resurfacing: the parts of me that involve 'impressions' of you can never be reduced to the 'you-ness' of 'you', but they are 'more' than just me. The creation of the subject hence depends upon the impressions of others, and these 'impressions' cannot be conflated with the character of 'others'. The others exist within me and apart from me at the same time. Taking you in will not necessarily be 'becoming like you', or 'making you like me', as other others have also impressed upon me, shaping my surfaces in this way and that.

So to lose another is not to lose one's impressions, not all of which are even conscious. To preserve an attachment is not to make an external other internal, *but to keep one's impressions alive*, as aspects of one's self that are both oneself and more than oneself, as a sign of one's debt to others. One can let go of another as an outsider, but maintain one's attachments, by keeping alive one's impressions of the lost other. This does not mean that the 'impressions' stand in for the other, as a false and deadly substitute. And nor do such 'impressions' have to stay the same. Although the other may not be alive to create new impressions, the impressions move as I move: the new slant provided by a conversation, when I hear something I did not know; the flickering of an image through the passage of time, as an image that is both your image, and my image of you. To grieve for others is to keep their impressions alive in the midst of their death.

The ethical and political question for queer subjects might, then, not be *whether* to grieve but *how* to grieve. In some queer responses to September 11, the public display of grief installs queer loss as an object, alongside other losses, and in this way constructs the nation as the true subject of grief. But queer subjects can also share their impressions of those they have lost without transforming those impressions into objects that can be appropriated or taken in by the nation. For some, this was precisely the work of the Names Project Quilt, despite the reservations theorists such as Crimp have expressed about the way it sanitised loss for the mainstream audience (Crimp 2002: 196). As Ken Plummer has argued, the Project might matter not because of how it addresses the nation, as an imagined subject who might yet take this grief on as its own, but because of the process of working through loss with others. He suggests that 'stories help organise the flow of interaction, binding together or disrupting the relation of self to other and community' (Plummer 1995: 174). Perhaps queer forms of grief sustain the impressions of those who have been lost by sharing impressions with others. Sharing impressions may only be possible if the loss is not transformed into 'our loss', or converted into an object: when the loss becomes 'ours', it is taken away from others. Not to name 'my' or 'your' loss as 'our loss' does not mean the privatisation of loss, but the generation of a public in which sharing is not based on the presumption of shared ownership. A queer politics of grief needs to allow others, those whose losses are not recognised by the nation, to have the space and time to grieve, rather than grieving for those others, or even asking 'the nation' to grieve for them. In such a politics, recognition does still matter, not of the other's grief, but of the other as a griever, as the subject rather than the object of grief, a subject that is not alone in its grief, since grief is both about and directed to others.[14]

It is because of the refusal to recognise queer loss (let alone queer grief), that it is important to find ways of sharing queer grief with others. As Nancy A. Naples shows us in her intimate and moving ethnography of her father's death, feeling pushed out by her family during her father's funeral made support from her queer family of carers even more important (Naples 2001: 31). To support others as grievers – not by grieving for them but allowing them the space and time to grieve – becomes even more important when those others are excluded from the everyday networks of legitimation and support. The ongoing work of grief helps to keep alive the memories of those who have gone, provide care for those who are grieving, and allow the impressions of others to touch the surface of queer communities. This queer community resists becoming one, and aligned with the patriotic 'we' of the nation, only when loss is recognised as that which cannot simply be converted into an object, and yet is with and for others. Here, your loss would not be translated into 'our loss', but would prompt me to turn towards you, and allow you to impress upon me, again.

QUEER PLEASURES

Of course, queer feelings are not simply about the space of negativity, even when that negativity gets translated into the work of care for others. Queer politics are also about enjoyment, where the 'non' offers hope and possibility for other ways of inhabiting bodies. How do the pleasures of queer intimacies challenge the designation of queer as abject, as that which is 'cast out from the domain of the liveable' (Butler 1993: 9), or even as the 'death' made inevitable by the failure to reproduce life itself? This is a risky question. Whilst queers have been constructed as abject beings, we are also sources of desire and fascination. Michael Bronski explores the tension between 'heterosexual fear of homosexuality and gay culture (and the pleasure they represent) and the equally strong envy of and desire to enjoy that freedom and pleasure' (Bronski 1998: 2). Žižek also examines the ambivalence of the investment in 'the other' as the one 'who enjoys', and whose enjoyment exceeds the economies of investment and return (Žižek 1991: 2). The racist or homophobe tries to steal this enjoyment, which he assumes was taken from him, through the aggression of his hatred (see also Chapters 2 and 6). To speak of queer pleasure as potentially a site for political transformation risks confirming constructions of queerness that sustain the place of the (hetero)normative subject.

Equally though, others can be envied for their lack of enjoyment, for the authenticity of their suffering, their vulnerability, and their pain. I have examined, for example, how the investment in the figure of the suffering other gives the Western subject the pleasures of being charitable (see Chapter 1). Within the Leninist theory of the vanguard party, or the work of the Subaltern Studies group, there also seems to be an investment in the pain and struggle of the proletariat or peasant. Here the investment allows the project of speaking for the other, whose silence is read as an injury (Spivak 1988). In other words, the other becomes an investment by providing the normative subject with a vision of what is lacking, whether that lack is a form of suffering or deprivation (poverty, pain), or excess (pleasure, enjoyment). The other is attributed with affect (as being *in* pain, or *having* pleasure) as a means of subject constitution. I will not suggest that what makes queers 'queer' is our pleasure (from which straight subjects are barred), but will examine how the bodily and social practices of queer pleasure might challenge the economies that distribute pleasure as a form of property – as a feeling we have – in the first place.

In mainstream culture, it is certainly not the case that pleasure is excluded or taboo (there are official events and places where the public is required to display pleasure – where pleasure is a matter of being 'a good sport'). Indeed within global capitalism the imperative is to have more pleasure (through the consumption of products designed to tantalise the senses). And yet along-side this imperative to enjoy, there is a warning: pleasures can distract you, and turn you away from obligations, duties and responsibilities. Hedonism does not get a good press, certainly. Pleasure becomes an imperative only as an incentive and reward for good conduct, or as an 'appropriate outlet' for bodies that are busy being productive ('work hard play hard'). This impera-tive is not only about having pleasure as a reward, but also about having the right kind of pleasure, in which rightness is determined as an orientation towards an object. Pleasure is 'good' only if it is orientated towards some objects, not others. The 'orientation' of the pleasure economy is bound up with heterosexuality: women and men 'should' experience a surplus of plea-sure, but only when exploring each other's bodies under the phallic sign of difference (pleasure as the enjoyment of sexual difference). Whilst sexual pleasure within the West may now be separated from the task or duty of reproduction, it remains tied in some way *to the fantasy of being reproductive*: one can enjoy sex with a body that it is imagined one *could be* reproductive with. Queer pleasures might be legitimate here, as long as 'the queer' is only a passing moment in the story of heterosexual coupling ('queer as an enjoy-able distraction'). The promise of this pleasure resides in its convertability to reproduction and the accumulation of value.

We might assume that queer pleasures, because they are 'orientated' towards an illegitimate object, will not return an investment. But this is not always or only the case. As Rosemary Hennessy has argued, 'queer' can be commodified, which means that queer pleasures can be profitable within global capitalism: the pink pound, after all, does accumulate value (Hennessy 1995: 143). Hennessy argues that money and not liberation is crucial to recent gay visibility. As she puts it: 'The freeing up of sensory-affective capacities from family alliances was simultaneously rebinding desire into new com-modified forms' (Hennessy 2000: 104). The opening up of non-familial desires allows new forms of commodification; the 'non' of the 'non-norma-tive' is not outside existing circuits of exchange, but may even intensify the movement of commodities, which converts into capital (see Chapter 2). Global capitalism involves the relentless search for new markets, and queer consumers provide such a market. The production of surplus value relies, as Marx argued, on the exploitation of the labour of others. The commodifica-tion of queer involves histories of exploitation: the leisure industries that support queer leisure styles, as with other industries, depend upon class and racial hierarchies. So it is important not to identify queer as outside the global economy, which transforms 'pleasures' into 'profit' by exploiting the labour of others.

Such an argument challenges the way in which sexual pleasure is idealised – as almost revolutionary in and of itself – within some versions of queer theory. For example, Douglas Crimp offers a vision of gay male promiscuity as 'a positive model of how sexual pleasures might be pursued' (Crimp 2002: 65), while Michael Warner defines sexual autonomy as 'access to pleasures' (Warner 1999: 7). Michael Bronski sees the 'pleasure principle' as the reason for the fear of homosexuality and also for its power: 'Homosexuality offers a vision of sexual pleasure completely divorced from the burden of reproduction: sex for its own sake, a distillation of the pleasure principle' (Bronski 1998: 8). This idealisation of pleasure supports a version of sexual freedom that is not equally available to all: such an idealisation may even extend rather than challenge the 'freedoms' of masculinity. A negative model of freedom is offered in such work, according to which queers are free to have pleasure as they are assumed to be free *from* the scripts of (hetero)normative existence: 'Because gay social life is not as ritualised and institutionalised as straight life, each relation is an adventure in nearly uncharted territory' (Warner 1999: 115; see also Bell and Binnie 2000: 133). Ironically, such a reading turns queer pleasure into a discovery narrative that is not far off genres that narrated the pleasures of colonialism: as a journey into uncharted territory. Who is the explorer here? And who provides the territory?

And yet, despite the way in which queer pleasures can circulate as commodities within global capitalism, I want to suggest that they can also work to challenge social norms, as forms of investment. To make this argument, we need to reconsider how bodies are shaped by pleasure and take the shape of pleasures. I have already addressed the phenomenology of pain (see Chapter 1), arguing that pain reshapes the surfaces of the body through the way in which the body turns in on itself. Pleasure also brings attention to surfaces, which surface as impressions through encounters with others. But the intensification of the surface has a very different effect in experiences of pleasure: the enjoyment of the other's touch opens my body up, opens me up. As Drew Leder has argued, pleasure is experienced in and from the world, not merely in relation to one's own body. Pleasure is expansive: 'We fill our bodies with what they lack, open up to the stream of the world, reach out to others' (Leder 1990: 75).

Pleasures open bodies to worlds through an opening up of the body to others. As such, pleasures can allow bodies to take up more space. It is interesting to consider, for example, how the display of enjoyment and pleasure by football fans can take over a city, excluding others who do not 'share' their joy, or return that joy through the performance of pleasure. Indeed, the publicness of pleasure can function as a form of aggression; as a declaration of 'We are here.' Beverley Skeggs (1999) shows how the display of pleasure by heterosexuals in queer space can also work as a form of colonisation; a 'taking over' of queer space, which leaves queer subjects, especially lesbians, feeling unsettled, displaced and exposed. These examples demonstrate an important spatial relation between pleasure and power. Pleasure involves not only the capacity to enter into, or inhabit with ease, social space, but also functions as a form of entitlement and belonging. Spaces are claimed through enjoyment, an enjoyment that is returned by being witnessed by others. Recalling my argument in the first section of this chapter, the display of queer pleasure may generate discomfort in spaces that remain premised on the 'pleasures' of heterosexuality. For queers, to display pleasure through what we do with our bodies is to make the comforts of heterosexuality less comfortable.

Further, pleasure involves an opening towards others; pleasure orientates bodies towards other bodies in a way that impresses on the surface, and creates surface tensions. But pleasure is not simply about any body opening up to any body. The contact is itself dependent on differences that already impress upon the surfaces of bodies. Pleasures are about the contact between bodies that are already shaped by past histories of contact. Some forms of contact don't have the same effects as others. Queer pleasures put bodies into contact that have been kept apart by the scripts of compulsory heterosexuality. I am not sure that this makes the genitals 'weapons of pleasure against their own oppression' (Berlant and Freeman 1997: 158). However queer pleasures in the enjoyment of forbidden or barred contact engender the possibility of different kinds of impressions. When bodies touch and give pleasure to bodies that have been barred from contact, then those bodies are reshaped. The hope of queer is that the reshaping of bodies through the enjoyment of what or who has been barred can 'impress' differently upon the surfaces of social space, creating the possibility of social forms that are not constrained by the form of the heterosexual couple.

Queer pleasures are not just about the coming together of bodies in sexual intimacy. Queer bodies 'gather' in spaces, through the pleasure of opening up to other bodies. These queer gatherings involve forms of activism; ways of claiming back the street, as well as the spaces of clubs, bars, parks and homes. The hope of queer politics is that bringing us closer to others, from whom we have been barred, might also bring us to different ways of living with others. Such possibilities are not about being free from norms, or being outside the circuits of exchange within global capitalism. *It is the non-transcendence of queer that allows queer to do its work.* A queer hope is not, then, sentimental. It is affective precisely in the face of the persistence of forms of life that endure in the negative attachment of 'the not'. Queer maintains its hope for 'non-repetition' only insofar as it announces the persistence of the norms and values that make queer feelings queer in the first place.

NOTES

1. I borrow this phrase, of course, from Adrienne Rich. I am indebted to her work, which demonstrates the structural and institutional nature of heterosexuality.

2. A queer phenomenology might offer an approach to 'sexual orientation' by rethinking the place of the object in sexual desire, attending to how bodily directions 'towards' some objects and not others affects how bodies inhabit spaces, and how spaces inhabit bodies.

3. To reflect on queer feelings is also to reflect on 'queer' as a sticky sign. As Butler points put, the word 'queer' is performative: through repetition, it has acquired new meanings (Butler 1997c). Queer, once a term of abuse (where to be queer was to be not us, not straight, not normal, not human) has become a name for an alternative political orientation. Importantly, as a sticky sign, 'queer' acquires new meanings not by being cut off from its previous contexts of utterance, but by preserving them. In queer politics, the force of insult is retained; 'the not' is not negated ('we are positive'), but embraced, and is taken on as a name. The possibility of generating new meanings, or new orientations to 'old' meanings, depends on collective activism, on the process of gathering together to clear spaces or ground for action. In other words, it takes more than one body to open up semantic as well as political possibilities. Furthermore, we should remember that queer still remains a term of abuse, and that not all those whose orientations we might regard as queer, can or would identify with this name, or even be able to 'hear' the name without hearing the history of its use as an injurious term: 'Now, the word *queer* emerges. But other than referring to it in quotations, I will never use the term *queer* to identify myself or any other homosexual. It's a word that my generation – and my companion, who's twenty-five years younger than I am, feels the same way – will never hear without evoked connotations – of violence, gay-bashings, arrest, murder' (Rechy 2000: 319). What we hear when we hear words such as 'queer' depends on complex psycho-biographical as well as institutional histories.

4. See Chapter 5 on shame, where I discuss the way in which normative bodies have a 'tautological' relation to social ideals: *they feel pride at approximating an ideal that has already taken their shape.*

5. My analysis in Chapter 8, section 2, of the relation between wonder and the departure from what is ordinary takes this argument forward.

6. Of course, heterosexual subjects may experience discomfort when faced by queers, and queer forms of coupling, in the event of the failure to conceal signs of queerness. A queer politics might embrace this discomfort: it might seek to make people feel uncomfortable through making queer bodies more visible. Not all queers will be comfortable with the imperative to make others uncomfortable. Especially given that 'families of origin' are crucial spaces for queer experiences of discomfort, it may be in the name of love, or care, that signs of queerness are concealed. Thanks to Nicole Vittelone who helped me to clarify this argument. See also Chapter 5 on shame for a related discussion of queer shame within families.

7. Global capitalism relies on the 'feeling fetish' of comfort: for consumers to be comfortable, others must work hard, including cleaners as well as other manual workers. This division of labour and leisure (as well as between mental and manual labour) functions as an instrument of power between and within nation states. But the 'work' relation is concealed by the transformation of comfort into property and entitlement. We can especially see this in the tourism industry: the signs of work are removed from the commodity itself, such as the tourist package, as a way of increasing its value. See McClintock (1995) for an analysis of commodification and fetishism and Hochschild (1983: 7) for an analysis of the emotional labour that is required for the well-being of consumers.

8. I am, of course, paraphrasing Frantz Fanon's *Black Skin, White Masks*. The analogy has its limits: assimilation into whiteness and assimilation into straightness cannot be assumed to be equivalent, partly given the different relation of race and sexuality to signs of visibility. See Lorde 1984.

9. Thanks to Jackie Stacey whose astute comments during a conversation helped me to formulate this argument.

10. Of course, some queer bodies can pass, which means passing into straight space. Passing as a technology entails the work of concealment: to pass might produce an effect of comfort (we can't see the difference), but not for the subject who passes, who may be feeling a sense of discomfort, or not being at ease, given the constant threat of 'being seen' or caught out. See Ahmed (1999).

11. The debate about queer families has also been defined in terms of the opposition between assimilation and resistance (Goss 1997; Sandell 1994; Phelan 1997: 1; Weston 1991: 2; Weston 1998).

12. Of course, a question remains as to whether 'others' would want collective grief to be extended to them. What would it mean for the ungrieved to be grieved? The other might not want my grief precisely because such a grief might 'take in' what was not, in the first place, 'allowed near'. Would Iraqis, Afghanistanis want the force of Western grief to transform them into losses? Would this not risk another violent form of appropriation, one which claims their losses as 'ours', a claim that conceals rather than reveals our responsibility for loss? Expressions of nostalgia and regret by colonisers for that which has been lost as an effect of colonisation are of course mainstream (see hooks 1992). Recognising the other *as* grieving, as having experienced losses (for which we might have responsibility) might be more ethically and politically viable than grieving for the other, *or claiming their grief as our own*. See my conclusion, 'Just Emotions', for an analysis of the injustice that can follow when the ungrievable is transformed into the grieved.

13. The National Lesbian and Gay Journalists Association 'is an organization of journalists, online media professionals, and students that works from within the journalism industry to foster fair and accurate coverage of lesbian, gay, bisexual and transgender issues. NLGJA opposes workplace bias against all minorities and provides professional development for its members.' Their web site is available on: http://www.nlgja.org/ Accessed 22 December 2003.

14. The political and legal battle for the recognition of queer partners in claims for compensation post September 11 is crucial. However, so far no such recognition has been offered. Recognising queer losses, and queers as the subjects of grief would mean recognising the significance of queer attachments. Bill Berkowitz interprets the 9/11 Victim Compensation Fund, which leaves the determination of eligibility for compensation to states, as follows: 'In essence, in a rather complicated and convoluted decision, families of gays and lesbians will not be given federal compensation unless they have wills, or the states they live in have laws recognizing domestic partnerships, which of course most states do not.' 'Victims of 9/11 and Discrimination', http://www.workingforchange.com/article.cfm?ItemId=13001 Accessed 6 January 2004.

CHAPTER 8

Feminist Attachments

Situating the current political crisis within the context of the ongoing
North/South relations rooted in colonialism and the increasingly
unilateral expansive claims of sovereignty by the U.S. wherever it
decides its interests are being challenged, the speech criticised
American foreign policy and President Bush's racialised construction
of the American nation in mobilising it for war. I argued that
women's groups should oppose the Canadian government's support
for military action and call on it to withdraw support for U.S. foreign
policy. I argued instead for building solidarity with Afghan women's
organizations . . . For articulating the position outlined above, I was
immediately attacked in the media, by the Canadian Prime Minister
in the House of Commons, by the leaders of all the major opposition
parties, and by the Premier of British Columbia. This was followed
by similar attacks from other politicians, editorialists, and media
columnists across the country in the days following the initial reports
of the speech. I began to receive hate mail, harassing phone calls, and
death threats . . . In this climate, the Royal Canadian Mounted Police
(RCMP) chose to make public, through an announcement in the
media, that I was the subject of a 'hate-crime' investigation, an
offence under the criminal code. A complaint had apparently been
made to them alleging that my speech amounted to a 'hate crime'
against Americans. (Thobani 2003: 400, 403)

What happens when feminists speak out against forms of violence, power
and injustice? What role do emotions play in acts of speaking out and in the
'spectacle' of demonstrating against such forms of power? Sunera Thobani,
at a conference on 'Critical Resistance' which took place in Ottawa in October
2001, took the risk of speaking out against the 'war on terrorism'. Bringing

together a feminist and anti-racist critique, Thobani's speech intervened in the discourse around the 'war on terrorism', which had been deployed by Bush and others to attribute danger to 'could-be terrorists', who are already marked by their difference 'from us' (see Chapter 3).

The extremity of the reaction to Thobani's speech demonstrates the risk of speaking out against established 'truths'. Such truths are worlds made through the authorisation of some views over others. Thobani's speech is described as 'hate speech', and is represented as an attack on Americans as well as on America. Her speech is understood as *repeating* the injury or wound that had already been inflicted by terrorists. To be critical of the 'war on terrorism' is to be identified as 'a terrorist'. This narrative – you either support the war or are 'a terrorist' – is of course the narrative exercised by George Bush: 'You are either with us or against us.' Anyone who is not 'with us', is a terrorist, is a friend of terrorists, or *might as well be*.

But what does it mean to 'be with'? To 'be with' in this discursive context is not only to support the war, but to support the very world that the war is identified as defending. Such a world is represented in terms of values of freedom, democracy and even love, whereby these values become 'the truths' that we must defend. So to 'speak out' against 'the war on terrorism' (as the war against 'the axis of evil') is to attack the 'truths' that make this world and give it 'value'. Indeed, to question the distinction, which is naturalised as given, between some forms of violence (committed by legitimate states) and other forms of violence (enacted either by individuals, networks or 'illegitimate states' in a way that is targeted against 'legitimate states') is to betray the very 'foundations' of this world. Such a world requires the 'self-evident' nature of the distinction between terrorism and legitimate violence, and it relies on the repetition of 'our injury' to justify this distinction as a moral as well as a natural one. Any commentary on the violence of US imperialism as the conditions that not only help explain the terrorist attacks (although they do not justify them), but are reproduced through the war itself is unspeakable, indefensible, as well as 'untrue'. The attack on those who attack the war, those who question the very ontological status of the distinction between legitimate (war) and illegitimate violence (terrorism), is crucial to justification of the 'right' to war, as well as the 'right' of war.

But there is more to say here. For what is significant about the attacks on Thobani, as she points out so persuasively in her commentary, is how personalised they became, and how much they focused on delegitimating her very right to speak. Her speech is described as the 'ranting and raving of a "nutty" professor', as 'wingnut ravings', as 'mean-mouthed', as 'sly and sick', as well as 'hate-filled discourse' (Thobani 2003: 401, 405). Such attacks on Thobani's speech worked to exclude it from the register of legitimate speech by constructing her as motivated by a purely negative passion.[1] The attack on the speech translates quickly into an attack on her as an embodied subject. In such attacks, she is also constructed as 'out of place' as an immigrant woman, a woman who has not 'gratefully' received the hospitality or even love that has 'let her into' the 'we' of a civil nation. It is not incidental that it is subaltern women who are posited as 'failing' to 'live up to' the standards of truth in their emotionality. Neither is it incidental that this failure is identified at the very moment in which subaltern women speak about the violence of 'truths', which are made in the making of the worlds in which we live. The appeal then is for her to 'go home', where 'home' is not only constructed as 'elsewhere', but also as the 'where' of terrorism (she is hailed as 'from Afghanistan'). We can see here that the cultural politics of emotion is deeply bound up with gendered histories of imperialism and capitalism, in which violence against the bodies of subaltern women is both granted and taken for granted in the making of worlds.

In this example, we can also identify the risks of considering feminist and anti-racist critique in terms of a politics of emotion. Feminists who speak out against established 'truths' are often constructed as emotional, as failing the very standards of reason and impartiality that are assumed to form the basis of 'good judgement'. Such a designation of feminism as 'hostile' and emotional, whereby feminism becomes an extension of the already pathological 'emotionality' of femininity, exercises the hierarchy between thought/ emotion discussed in the Introduction of this book. This hierarchy clearly translates into a hierarchy between subjects: whilst thought and reason are identified with the masculine and Western subject, emotions and bodies are associated with femininity and racial others. This projection of emotion onto the bodies of others not only works to exclude others from the realms of thought and rationality, but also works to conceal the emotional and embodied aspects of thought and reason. As I have suggested throughout this book, the 'truths' of this world are dependent on emotions, on how they move subjects, and stick them together.

The response to the dismissal of feminists as emotional should not then be to claim that feminism is rational rather than emotional. Such a claim would be misguided as it would accept the very opposition between emotions and rational thought that is crucial to the subordination of femininity as well as feminism. Instead, we need to contest this understanding of emotion as 'the unthought', just as we need to contest the assumption that 'rational thought' is unemotional, or that it does not involve being moved by others. In this chapter, I want us to think about forms of politics that seek to contest social norms, in terms of emotion, understood as 'embodied thought' (Rosaldo 1984). My concern is not only to think about how one becomes attached to feminism, but how feminism involves an emotional response to the world, where the form of that response involves a reorientation of one's bodily relation to social norms.

One can reflect on the role of emotions in the politicisation of subjects. When I think of my relationship to feminism, for example, I can rewrite my coming into being as a feminist subject in terms of different emotions, or in terms of how my emotions have involved particular readings of the worlds I have inhabited. The anger, the anger that I felt about how being a girl seemed to be about what you shouldn't do; the pain, the pain that I felt as an effect of forms of violence; the love, the love for my mother and for all the women whose capacity for giving has given me life; the wonder, the wonder I felt at the way in which the world came to be organised the way that it is, a wonder that feels the ordinary as surprising; the joy, the joy I felt as I began to make different kinds of connections with others and realise that the world was alive and could take new shapes and forms; and the hope, the hope that guides every moment of refusal and that structures the desire for change with the trembling that comes from an opening up of the future, as an opening up of what is possible.

Such emotional journeys are bound up with politicisation, in a way that reanimates the relation between the subject and a collective. But they are bound up with that politicisation in a mediated rather than immediate way. It is not that anger at women's oppression 'makes us feminists': such an anger *already* involves a reading of the world in a particular way, and also involves a reading of the reading; so identifying as a feminist is dependent upon taking that anger as the grounds for a critique of the world, as such. For, as I have already argued, emotions are what move us, and how we are moved involves interpretations of sensations and feelings not only in the sense that we interpret what we feel, but also in that what we feel might be dependent on past interpretations that are not necessarily made by us, but that come before us. Focusing on emotions as mediated rather than immediate reminds us that knowledge cannot be separated from the bodily world of feeling and sensation; knowledge is bound up with what makes us sweat, shudder, tremble, all those feelings that are crucially felt on the bodily surface, the skin surface where we touch and are touched by the world.

So my question in this chapter is how do such attachments to feminism relate to attachments that already exist in the everyday world, including those that are bound up with the reproduction of the very forms of power that feminism seeks to contest. My argument responds to a tendency in some critical feminist literature – a literature to which I am nevertheless indebted – to see attachment as a 'problem' for feminism, as a sign of how it conserves, in its very affective life, a commitment to norms that it might wish to 'let go' in its orientation to the future (Brown 2003: 3, 15). I want to suggest that it is the very assumption that feminism 'could' transcend the objects of its critique that allows feminist attachments to be readable as a sign of failure. Feminist attachments show us precisely that an 'anti-normative' politics does not and cannot suspend the power of social norms.[2] This does mean we should suspend the 'anti', or transform the 'anti' into the 'non'. As I will show, a politics that is critical cannot not be 'anti'; it cannot simply 'overcome' through detachment the affects of the histories of violence, justice and inequality that structure the demand or hope for transformation. Emotions may be crucial to showing us why transformations are so difficult (we remain invested in what we critique), but also how they are possible (our investments move as we move).

FEMINISM AND ANGER

It is not possible to consider the relation between feminism and anger without first reflecting on the politics of pain (see Chapter 1). There is a long history of thinking about the relationship between feminism and pain; women's experiences of violence, injury and discrimination have been crucial to feminist politics (see West 1999). Women's testimonies about pain – for example, testimonies of their experiences of violence – are crucial not only to the formation of feminist subjects (a way of reading pain as a structural rather than incidental violence), but to feminist collectives, which have mobilised around the injustice of that violence and the political and ethical demand for reparation and redress. We could think about feminist therapy and consciousness-raising groups in the 1970s precisely in terms of the transformation of pain into collectivity and resistance (Burstow 1992). Carol Tavris argues that consciousness-raising groups were important because 'to question legitimate institutions and authorities, most people need to know that they are not alone, crazy, or misguided' (Tavris 1982: 246–7). Burstow suggests, in relation to her work on radical feminist therapy: 'The context in which this book is written is the fundamental unhappiness and alienation of women . . . It is that *unnecessary yet unavoidable, individual yet common, suffering born of the patriarchy and other systemic oppression*' (Burstow 1992: viii, emphasis Burstow's). Feminist therapy and consciousness-raising groups allowed women to make connections between their experiences and feelings in order to examine how such feelings were implicated in structural relations of power.

Other feminists, however, have been critical of the emphasis on pain as the condition of membership of a feminist community. We can return to Wendy Brown's critique of the politics of pain (Brown 1995: 55). As she argues, insofar as politics 'makes claims for itself, only by entrenching, restating, dramatising, and inscribing its pain in politics; it can hold out no future – for itself or others – that triumphs over this pain' (Brown 1995: 74). So if pain is what compels feminism into being, then is this a sign of feminism's failure to 'move away' from the site of subordination, or more specifically, to resist transforming that subordination into an identity claim? For example, in Burstow's account of radical feminist therapy described above, pain becomes a means by which women's experience is universalised as an effect of patriarchy, at the same time as it remains individuated at the level of experience. This model is problematic because of its fetishism: the transformation of the wound into an identity cuts the wound off from the complex histories of 'being hurt' or injured, histories which cannot be gathered together under a singular concept such as patriarchy.

Furthermore, when feminism does claim to 'stand for' or even 'stand in for' the pain or suffering of women, which conceals the mediation of that pain, then problematic consequence can follow. For instance, Martha Nussbaum evokes 'the suffering of ordinary women' in her designation of Judith Butler as a 'professor of parody', who 'collaborates with evil'. She argues that Butler's work fails feminism because: 'Hungry women are not fed by this, battered women are not sheltered by it, raped women do not find justice in it, gays and lesbians do not achieve legal protections through it' (Nussbaum 1999). Nussbaum's violent dismissal of Butler's work rests on an implicit claim that feminism *could* simply represent the suffering of ordinary women, which could then be the foundation of political action, without the work of translation. It assumes access to women's suffering to authenticate an ontological distinction between legitimate and illegitimate feminism: women's pain becomes an 'immediate' measure of truth, against which others must fail. The transformation of women's pain into a fetish object can work to delegitimate feminist attempts to understand the complexity of social and psychic life.

There are good reasons, then, to avoid assuming that women's pain provides the foundation for feminism. But this does not mean feminism has nothing to do with pain. As I argued in Chapter 1, our respond to 'wound fetishism' should not be to forget the wounds that mark the place of historical injury. Such forgetting would simply repeat the forgetting that is already implicated in the fetishising of the wound. Rather, our task would be to learn to remember how embodied subjects come to be wounded in the first place, which requires that *we learn to read that pain*, as well as recognise how the pain is already read in the intensity of how it surfaces. The task would not only be to read and interpret pain as over-determined, but also to do the *work* of translation, whereby pain is moved into a public domain, and in moving, is transformed. In order to move away from attachments that are hurtful, we must act on them, an action which requires, at the same time, that we do not ontologise women's pain as the automatic ground of politics.

Experiences of pain may compel the movement towards feminism, as a politics which 'moves' against social and physical hurt. But feminism, as a politics of redress, is also 'about' the pain of others. Feminism's collective project might become then a way of responding to the pain of others, as a pain that cannot be accessed directly, but is only ever approached. Crucially, responding to pain depends on speaking about pain, and such speech acts are the condition for the formation of a 'we', made up of different stories of pain that cannot be reduced to a ground, identity or sameness. Stories of pain can be 'shared' only when we assume they are not the same story, even if they are connected, and allow us to make connections. As bell hooks argues, naming one's personal pain is insufficient and can easily be incorporated into the narcissistic agendas of neo-liberal and therapeutic culture. For hooks, feminism can only move through and with pain into a politics, if it is linked to the 'overall education for critical consciousness of collective political resistance' (hooks 1989: 32). If pain does move subjects into feminism, then it does so precisely by *reading* the relation between affect and structure, or between emotion and politics in a way that undoes the separation of the individual from others.

Furthermore, it is not just that pain compels us to move into feminism – or compels feminism as a movement of social and political transformation. The response to pain, as a call for action, also requires anger; an interpretation that this pain is wrong, that it is an outrage, and that something must be done about it. It is precisely the intimacy of pain and anger within feminism that Wendy Brown critiques as a form of *ressentiment*, as a form of politics that can only 'react' rather than 'act' (Brown 1995: 73). I would argue that a politics which acts without reaction is impossible: such a possibility depends on the erasure and concealment of histories that come before the subject. There is no pure or originary action, which is outside such a history of 'reaction', whereby bodies come to be 'impressed upon' by the surfaces of others.[3]

Feminism involves such histories of contact; feminism is shaped by what it is against, just as women's bodies and lives may be shaped by histories of violence that bring them to a feminist consciousness. If feminism is an emotional as well as ethical and political response to what it is against, then what feminism is against cannot be seen as 'exterior' to feminism. Indeed, 'what' feminism is against is 'what' *gives feminist politics its edge*. If anger is a form of 'against-ness', then it is precisely about the impossibility of moving beyond the history of injuries to a pure or innocent position. Anger does not necessarily require an investment in revenge, which is one form of reaction to what one is against. Being against something is dependent on how one reads what one is against (for example, whether violence against women is read as dependent on male psychology or on structures of power). The question becomes: What form of action is possible *given that reading*?

Within Black feminism, the passion of anger is crucial to what gives us 'the energy' to react against the deep social and psychic investments in racism as well as sexism. Nowhere is this clearer than in the work of Audre Lorde, specifically in her critiques of racism against black women. As she writes so powerfully:

> My response to racism is anger. I have lived with that anger, ignoring it, feeding upon it, learning to use it before it laid my visions to waste, for most of my life. Once I did it in silence, afraid of the weight. My fear of anger taught me nothing . . . [A]nger expressed and translated into action in the service of our vision and our future is a liberating and strengthening act of clarification . . . Anger is loaded with information and energy. (Lorde 1984: 124, 127)

Here, anger is constructed in different ways: as a response to the injustice of racism; as a vision of the future; as a translation of pain into knowledge; and as being loaded with information and energy. Crucially, anger is not simply defined in relationship to a past, but as opening up the future. In other words, being against something does not end with 'that which one is against'. Anger does not necessarily become 'stuck' on its object, although that object may remain sticky and compelling. Being against something is also being for something, but something that has yet to be articulated or is not yet. As Lorde shows us, anger is visionary and the fear of anger, or the transformation of anger into silence, is a turning away from the future (Lorde 1984: 127). So while anger is determined, it is not fully determined. It translates pain, but also needs to be translated. Feminism, as a response to pain and as a form of anger directed against that pain, is dependent then on acts of translation that are moving.

For Audre Lorde, anger involves the naming of various practices and experiences as racism, but it also involves imagining a different kind of world in its very 'energy' (Lorde 1984: 127). If anger energises feminist subjects, it also requires those subjects to 'read' and 'move' from anger into a different bodily world. If anger pricks our skin, if it makes us shudder, sweat and tremble, then it might just shudder us into new ways of being; it might just enable us to inhabit a different kind of skin, even if that skin remains marked or scarred by that which we are against.

Clearly anger involves a reading of pain (which also involves reading): we do not all respond with anger, and to be angry is to assume that something is wrong. However, it is not necessarily the case that something is named or felt to be the cause of anger: there are moments of anger where it is unclear what one is angry about, and all these moments do not necessarily gather together to form a coherent response. Or as Carol Tavris puts it: 'There is no one-to-one correspondence between feeling angry and knowing why' (Tavris 1982: 18). But feminism also involves a reading of the response of anger: it moves from anger into an interpretation of that which one is against, whereby associations or connections are made between the object of anger and broader patterns or structures. This is what allows an object of knowledge to be delineated. The object is not then the ground of feminism (it does not come first, as it were), but is an effect of a feminist response. Anger is creative; it works to create a language with which to respond to that which one is against, whereby 'the what' is renamed, and brought into a feminist world.

This process is dynamic, as can be seen by the different ways feminists have named that which they are against (patriarchy, sexual difference, gender relations or hierarchy, phallocentrism). Indeed, different feminists construct the 'object' of anger quite differently, in ways that are in tension, although they share connections in the 'directionality' of the emotion. So the attachment implicit in the response to anger is not simply about the creation of an object (and to create is not to create something out of nothing, but to produce a name out of a set of differential relations), as the object fails to be secured. Not only have feminists created different names for what they are against, but they have also recognised that what they are against does not have the contours of an object that is given; it is not a positive entity. This lack of residence is implicit in the argument that gender permeates all aspects of social life and that it is in this sense 'worldly'. Anger hence moves us by moving us outwards: while it creates an object, it also is not simply directed against an object, but becomes a response to the world, as such. Feminist anger involves a reading of the world, a reading of how, for example, gender hierarchy is implicated in other forms of power relations, including race, class and sexuality, or how gender norms regulate bodies and spaces. Anger against objects or events, directed against this or that, moves feminism into a bigger critique of 'what is', as a critique that loses an object, and opens itself up to possibilities that cannot be simply located or found in the present.

So it is when feminism is no longer directed towards a critique of patriarchy, or secured by the categories of 'women' or 'gender', that it is doing the most 'moving' work. *The loss of such an object is not the failure of feminist activism, but is indicative of its capacity to move, or to become a movement.* Feminism remains compelled by that which it is against, but no longer is that 'against-ness' delimited as an object. It is the loss of the object, rather than its creation, that allows feminism to become a movement, as it opens up possibilities of action that are not constrained by what we are against in the present.

However, whilst anger as a form of 'against-ness' may give feminist politics its edge, feminism does not necessarily 'stay with' anger. The question remains: What does anger spoken under the 'name' of feminism do? As Marilyn Frye has argued, women's anger and feminist anger are generally 'not well received' (Frye 1983). Let us return to Thobani's response to the war on terrorism. My own view would be that her response is an expression of anger: it is 'against' the war; and it offers 'good reasons' for taking this position. At the same time, the reading of her speech as being angry is what allowed it to be dismissed as motivated by a purely negative passion (as being unreasonable). Indeed, historically, the reading of feminism *as* a form of anger allows the dismissal of feminist claims, even when the anger is a reasonable response to social injustice (Spelman 1989; Campbell 1994). Rather than responding by claiming that feminism is not motivated by anger (which would accept the problematic distinction between anger and reason), we can think instead about anger as a speech act, which is addressed to somebody. As Frye argues: 'Being angry at someone is somewhat like a speech act in that it has a certain conventional force whereby it sets people up in a certain sort of orientation to each other; and like a speech act, it cannot "come off" if it does not get uptake' (Frye 1983: 88). Frye's emphasis on anger as performative is taken up by Brenda R. Silver. She shows how 'the anger of the original speaker' can evoke 'the anger of the person who attempts to silence the upstart through an act of linguistic fiat' (Silver 1991: 340). As Silver suggests, if the anger of the speech act is simply returned by the addressee then a block in communication occurs such that the original speech act 'does not work'. Or to evoke my argument about apologies in Chapter 5, the speech act is made unhappy by how it is 'finished' by others.

As both Frye and Silver suggest, anger as a political act does not always work because the terms of its reception may 'undo' its claim. But at the same time, the performance of anger – as a claim of against-ness – may work; it may 'get uptake', and be received by the addressee. Two strategic questions for feminist activists and scholars are: What are the conditions of possibility for feminist anger to get a just hearing and how could we read the 'sign' of this justice in terms of action? Such questions assume that feminists can intervene in the conditions in which we are received. Of course, we have to have hope in this possibility. The challenge for feminism is to accept that the conditions in which we speak are not of our making. Such a recognition would not signal the futility of naming our anger – but it would mean recognising that the reception of that act might sustain the conditions that compelled the act in the first place. We must persist in explaining why our anger is reasonable, even in the face of others who use this anger as evidence of poor reason. Making public statements, getting heard, writing banners: these remain crucial strategies for feminism, even when they fail to get uptake.

An engaged stance would also require an acknowledgement that we could be in the position of others who 'block' the speech act of anger. How feminists receive the anger of other feminists is a question about the conditions in which it is possible for just hearings to be translated into action. Audre Lorde has shown how white feminists refuse to hear her anger by returning this anger in the form of defensiveness (Lorde 1984: 124).[4] Learning to hear the anger of others, without blocking the anger through a defence of one's own position is crucial. Such a project requires that one accepts that one's own position might anger others and hence allows one's position to be opened to critique by others (it does not then, like guilt or shame, turn the self back into itself by 'taking' that anger as one's own). As Berenice Fisher argues: 'The voices that make us most uncomfortable and the feelings that accompany them constitute a built-in critique of our ideals' (Fisher 1984: 206).

The fact of resistance within feminism to hearing the anger of some feminists is a 'sign' that what 'we are against' cannot be relegated to the outside. We need to take care not to install feminist ideals as ideals that others must embody if they are to pass into feminism. Such a reification of political ideals would position some feminists as 'hosts', who would decide which others would receive the hospitality of love and recognition, and would hence remain predicated on a differentiation between natives and strangers (see Ahmed 2000). To avoid such a politics, we may need to stay uncomfortable within feminism, even when we feel it provides us with a home. This discomfort, as I discussed in the previous chapter, means 'not sinking' into the spaces in which we live and work, and it means always questioning our own investments.

Of course, a politics of discomfort does not necessarily avoid such differentiations between natives and strangers given that we do not tend to feel our comforts. Allowing that which we do not tend to feel to surface within politics can only be an imperative for the future, something we work for or reach towards, rather than an achievement in the present.

FEMINISM AND WONDER

The question of how feminist attachments might open up different possibilities of living reminds us that feminism cannot be reduced to that which it is against, even if what it is against is irreducible. Feminism is also 'for' something other, a 'for-ness' that does not simply take the shape of what it is against. Whilst I have shown that the negation of anger is creative (a 'sure sign' of its ambivalence), it does not then follow that the attachment to the negative is the only means by which other possibilities are opened up. In what other ways do the emotions that bring us into feminism also take us to a different relation to the world in which we live?

My relationship to feminism has never felt like one of negation: it has never been reducible to the feelings of pain, anger or rage, which have nevertheless, at times, given my politics a sense of urgency. It has felt like something more creative, something that responds to the world with joy and care, as well as with an attention to details that are surprising. Descartes' 'The Passions of the Soul' describes 'wonder' as the first and primary emotion, as it is about being surprised by that which is before us (Descartes 1985: 350). As he elaborates:

> When our first encounter with some object surprises us and we find it novel, or very different from what we formerly knew or from what we supposed it ought to be, this causes us to wonder and to be astonished at it. Since all this may happen before we know whether or not the object is beneficial to us, I regard wonder as the first of all the passions. (Descartes 1985: 350)

Wonder here seems premised on 'first-ness': the object that appears before the subject is encountered for the first time, or *as if* for the first time. It is hence a departure from ordinary experience; or, by implication, the ordinary is not experienced or felt at all. We can relate this non-feeling of ordinariness to the feeling of comfort, as a feeling that one does not feel oneself feel, which I described in Chapter 7. Wittgenstein also discusses the ordinary – or, in his terms, the familiar – as that which we do not experience (Wittgenstein 1964: 127). What is ordinary, familiar or usual often resists being perceived by consciousness. It becomes taken for granted, as the background that we do not even notice, and which allows objects to stand out or stand apart. Wonder is an encounter with an object that one does not recognise; or wonder works to transform the ordinary, which is already recognised, into the extraordinary. As such, wonder expands our field of vision and touch. Wonder is the precondition of the exposure of the subject to the world: we wonder when we are moved by that which we face.

So wonder, as an affective relation to the world, is about seeing the world that one faces and is faced with 'as if' for the first time. What is the status of the 'as if'? Does such an impulse to wonder require an erasure of history, by forgetting that one has seen the world before, or even that the world precedes the impulse to wonder? It could be assumed that the 'as if' functions as a radical form of subjectivism, in which the subject forgets all that has taken place before a given moment of contemplation. But I would suggest that wonder allows us to see the surfaces of the world *as made*, and as such wonder opens up rather than suspends historicity. Historicity is what is concealed by the transformation of the world into 'the ordinary', into something that is already familiar, or recognisable. The ordinariness of the world is an effect of reification, as Marx has shown us. I would describe Marxism as a philosophy of wonder: what appear before consciousness, as objects of perception, are not simply given, but are effects of history: 'Even the objects of the simplest "sensuous certainty" are only given him through social development, industry and commercial intercourse' (Marx and Engels 1965: 57; see also Gramsci 1971: 422–3). To learn to see what is ordinary, what has the character of 'sensuous certainty', is to read the effects of this history of production as a form of 'world making'.

Historicity is negated by the assumption that the world is 'already there', whereby its 'thereness' is taken for granted as the background of action in the present. To see the world *as if* for the first time is to notice that which is there, is made, has arrived, or is extraordinary. Wonder is about learning to see the world as something that does not have to be, and as something that came to be, over time, and with work. As such, wonder involves learning. As Philip Fisher argues: 'Being struck by something is exactly opposite to being struck dumb. The tie between wonder and learning is clear . . .' (Fisher 1998: 21; see also Fisher 2002: 1).

The surprise of wonder is crucial to how it moves bodies. Luce Irigaray emphasises this relation between wonder and movement: 'Wonder is the motivating force behind mobility in all its dimensions' (Irigaray 1993: 73). Sometimes how we feel and what we think is contained within the reproduction of the ordinary. Nothing noticeable happens, and repetition, while it creates desire, sometimes just goes on and on. But then something happens, which is out of the ordinary – and hence a relation to the ordinary – and that something surprises us. The philosophical literature on wonder has not focused on wonder as a corporeal experience, largely because it has been associated with the sublime and the sacred, as an affect that we might imagine leaves the materiality of the body behind. But for me the expansion of wonder is bodily (see Midgley 1989). The body opens as the world opens up before it; the body unfolds into the unfolding of a world that becomes approached as another body. This opening is not without its risks: wonder can be closed down if what we approach is unwelcome, or undoes the promise of that opening up. But wonder is a passion that motivates the desire to keep looking; it keeps alive the possibility of freshness, and vitality of a living that can live as if for the first time. This first-time-ness of wonder is not the radical present – a moment that is liveable only insofar as it is cut off from prior acts of perception. Rather, wonder involves the radicalisation of our relation to the past, which is transformed into that which lives and breathes in the present.

Wonder is what brought me to feminism; what gave me the capacity to name myself as a feminist. Certainly, when I first came into contact with feminism, and began to read my own life and the lives of others differently, everything became surprising. At the time, this felt like moving out of false consciousness, though now I see that I was not moving into the truth as such, but just towards a reading that explained things better. I felt like I was seeing the world for the first time, and that all that I took for granted as given – as a question of the way things are – had come to be over time, and was contingent. It is through wonder that pain and anger come to life, as wonder allows us to realise that what hurts, and what causes pain, and what we feel is wrong, is not necessary, and can be unmade as well as made. Wonder energises the hope of transformation, and the will for politics.

I want to suggest that feminist pedagogy can be thought of in terms of the affective opening up of the world through the act of wonder, not as a private act, but as an opening up of what is possible through working together. The role of emotions within the feminist classroom has been the subject of much discussion. For example, Janet Lee discusses the role of anger in Women's Studies, suggesting that anger functions as 'an important source of energy for the movement from personal experience to being able to contextualise this everyday reality in the politics of institutional systems' (Lee 1999: 19). Other emotions discussed include love and the erotic (hooks 1994: 115), discomfort (Boler 1999), as well as betrayal and disappointment (Wiegman 1999: 109). Within this diverse literature, it is accepted that the emotions are always 'at the surface' of Women's Studies' classrooms not only because objects of study typically include questions of violence, injury and injustice, but also because of the way in which investments in feminism can operate to 'undo' any easy separation of bodies from 'work'.

As Megan Boler and Elspeth Probyn have both argued, for some critics, the emotionality of feminist teaching is risky and dangerous. Boler describes how feminist teaching is dismissed as 'touchy-feely' in a way that other forms of critical pedagogy are not (Boler 1999: xxiii). To counter this representation of 'feeling feminism', she points to how emotions involve critical and public forms of inquiry, rather than simply being psychological givens or 'raw data' (Boler 1999: 112–17). Emotion work within the classroom is uncomfortable work, which invites students and teachers to live 'at the edge' of their skins (Boler 1999: 200). Likewise, Elspeth Probyn (2001) detects an 'anxiety' about 'the live subject' and with her, emotion and affect, within Women's Studies' classrooms. She examines how the intrusion of emotions such as rage and anxiety within the classroom – importantly, around the question of race – is viewed as 'a block' to learning and the acquisition of knowledge. Probyn and Boler both try to counter this anxiety about emotion by showing how it can lead to new forms of knowledge (Boler 1999), or can open up conversations about how cultural objects affect us (Probyn 2001).

I want to follow on from Boler and Probyn by suggesting that emotions are crucial to feminist pedagogy. As their works show us, emotions do not only operate as blockages, they can also open up lines of communication. To make this claim is not to idealise emotions as 'good' or necessary to critical thinking or learning. Indeed, emotions should not become the preferred 'outcome' of teaching. This would transform emotions into a bank, to evoke Freire's (1996) classic metaphor for instrumental and conservative practices of teaching. If emotions were to become the 'outcome' of feminist teaching (rather than part of a process), then the task of the feminist teacher would be to '"fill" the students with' the right emotions, hence 'turn[ing] them into "containers"' in an 'act of depositing' (Freire 1996: 52–3). Here, emotions would be transformed into fetish objects, which we assumed had meaning in advance of their naming. Emotions might matter in teaching insofar as they cannot be translated into an outcome, which would be knowable in advance of the pedagogic encounter. I suggest this makes 'wonder' a key affective possibility within the Women's Studies' classroom.

The politics of teaching Women's Studies, in which feminist pedagogy becomes a form of activism as a way of 'being moved', is bound up with wonder, with engendering a sense of surprise about how it is that the world has come to take the shape that it has. Feminist teaching (rather than teaching feminism) begins with this opening, this pause or hesitation, which refuses to allow the taken-for-granted to be granted. In the Women's Studies classroom, students might respond firstly with a sense of assurance ('This is the way the world is'), then with disbelief ('How can the world be like this?') and towards a sense of wonder ('How did the world come to take this shape?'). The critical wonder that feminism involves is about the troubling affect of certain questions: questions like 'How has the world taken the shape that it has?', but also 'Why is it that power relations are so difficult to transform?', 'What does it mean to be invested in the conditions of subordination as well as dominance?', and so on.

What is striking about feminist wonder is that the critical gaze is not simply directed outside; rather, feminist wonder becomes wonder about the very forms of feminism that have emerged here or there. So we might stop and think, 'How is it that feminism comes to take form the way that it does?', 'How is it that Women's Studies has taken this shape?', and 'How can feminism work to transform the world in this way or that?' This critical wonder is about recognising that nothing in the world can be taken for granted, which includes the very political movements to which we are attached. It is this critical wonder about the forms of political struggle that makes Black feminism such an important intervention, by showing that categories of knowledge (such as patriarchy, or 'women') have political effects, which can exclude others from the collective (Lorde 1984; hooks 1989). Black feminism demonstrates the intimacy between the emotional response of wonder, critical thinking and forms of activism that try and break with old ways of doing and inhabiting the world.

The passion of wonder can be passed between the bodies that make up the cramped spaces of Women's Studies. It is a passion that allows the historicity of forms of life to emerge – in the perception of the intimacy of norms and forms.[5] The world cannot stay the same when forms are no longer simply forms of life. But this is not to say that all students get to the same place through wonder, or that Women's Studies could be about 'making feminists' through wonder. What is shared is rather the capacity to leave behind the place of the ordinary. Capacity is not something we simply have, as if it were an inherent quality of this or that body. As Spinoza (1959) and Deleuze (1992) teach us, capacities do not belong to individuals, but are about how bodies are affected by other bodies. As a result: 'You do not know beforehand what a body or a mind can do, in a given encounter, a given arrangement, a given combination' (Deleuze 1992: 627). The capacity for wonder is the space of opening up to the surprise of each combination; each body, which turns this way or that, impresses upon others, affecting what they can do. Wonder opens up a collective space, by allowing the surfaces of the world to make an impression, as they become see-able or feel-able *as* surfaces. It is not so much that the feeling of wonder passes (so that I feel wonder, in the face of your wonder). Rather, the very orientation of wonder, with its open faces and open bodies, involves a reorientation of one's relation to the world. Wonder keeps bodies and spaces open to the surprise of others. But we don't know, with such bodies, what we can do.

FEMINISM AND HOPE

We must stay with this question, this impossible question: What can we do? Or where we can go? What kind of future might we imagine for feminism? Does feminism have a future? We need to ask the question of the future, to pose the future as a question, with the carefulness that such a question demands. The future is both a question mark and a mark of questioning. In some sense, what feminists share is a concern with the future, that is, a desire that the future should not simply repeat the past, given that feminism comes into being as a critique of, and resistance to, the ways in which the world has already taken shape. When we think the question of feminist futures, we also need to attend to the legacies of feminist pasts; what we have inherited from past feminists, in terms of ways of thinking the very question of what it would mean to have a world where feminism, as a politics of transformation, is no longer necessary. As such, the question of the future is an affective one;

it is a question of hope for what we might yet be, as well as fear for what we could become.

My own relationship to feminism has always been imbued with hope, a hope that things can be different, and that the world can take different forms. Politics without hope is impossible, and hope without politics is a reification of possibility (and becomes merely religious). Indeed, it is hope that makes involvement in direct forms of political activism enjoyable: the sense that 'gathering together' is about opening up the world, claiming space through 'affective bonds' (Roseneil 1995: 99). Hope is crucial to the act of protest: hope is what allows us to feel that what angers us is not inevitable, even if transformation can sometimes feel impossible. Indeed, anger without hope can lead to despair or a sense of tiredness produced by the 'inevitability' of the repetition of that which one is against.

But hope is not simply about the possibilities of the future implicit in the failure of repetition (what Judith Butler, amongst others, has called 'iterability', the structural possibility that things will be repeated with a difference (1993)). It would be tempting to say that it is in the failure of the past to repeat itself that the conditions for political hope might exist. But such an argument would empty politics of work and it would allow us to sit back and do nothing. I would argue instead that hope involves a relationship to the present, and to the present as affected by its imperfect translation of the past. It is in the present that the bodies of subjects shudder with an expectation of what is otherwise; it is in the unfolding of the past in the present. The moment of hope is when the 'not yet' impresses upon us in the present, such that we must act, politically, to make it our future. If hope impresses upon us in the present rather than being merely futural (see Benjamin 1997), then hope requires that we must act in the present, rather than simply wait for a future that is always before us.

What do we hope for when we place our hope in feminism? When we hope we usually hope for something; hope is intentional and directed towards the future only in relation to an object that is faced in the present. Such hope is a form of investment, which assumes that an object, if achieved, will promise the fulfilment of the hope, and return our investment. But can we maintain hope? Should we have hope, as we face this world in the early twenty-first century, where the revolutionary politics of the left seems so hard to imagine even in the future? Can we maintain hope when 'the war on terror' is justified as an ethical right, and is conducted in the name of love and liberation? What would it mean to be hopeful in this world, here and now? For what, and for whom, do we have hope?

Within much of the critical literature, hope is assumed to be the engine of change and transformation. Hope is described as 'a decisive element in any attempt to bring about social change in the direction of greater aliveness, awareness, and reason' (Fromm 1968: 6), and as 'the ability to make expectations fluid and not be overcome by the absoluteness of the present' (Farran et al. 1995: 8). In the first, hope is represented as a collective project of working for change; in the latter, it is an individual's hope that can keep the future open. If we give up hope, of course, then there is no hope. So the emotion of hope keeps something open. William F. Lynch defines hope as a 'sense of *the possible*' (Lynch 1965: 32). We could return to my argument about fear in Chapter 3. I suggested emotions involve readings of the openness of bodies to being affected. Fear reads that openness as the possibility of danger or pain; hope reads that openness as the possibility of desire or joy. These readings reshape bodies. Whilst fear may shrink the body in anticipation of injury, hope may expand the contours of bodies, as they reach towards what is possible. As Ernst Bloch suggests: 'The emotion of hope goes out of itself, makes people broad instead of confining them' (Bloch 1986: 3).

To give up hope would be to accept that a desired future is not possible. Without hope, the future would become impossible: bodies would not reach for it. But thinking along these lines shows how the politics of hope may be frustrated precisely by its over-estimation of the individual will; as if the future were dependent upon whether or not I felt it to be possible. Hope can slide from a reading of what is possible to a disposition: 'a disposition to be confident in the face of the future' (Hage 2003: 25).[6] It could be assumed that being hopeful was enough to create the conditions of possibility for the future that one hopes for. This is the implication of Averill, Catlin and Chon's argument: 'by projecting themselves into the future . . . With hope, we can begin to realise the possibilities inherent both in the situation and in ourselves' (Averill et al. 1990: 105). But, as J. Pieper suggests: 'No one says he hopes for a thing that he can make or bring about himself' (Pieper 1969: 21). Being hopeful may be necessary for something to stay possible, but it is not sufficient grounds for the determination of the future.

So what if I stay hopeful in order to keep open the future when the situation is beyond hope? Is this hope just about making me feel better? Anna Potamianou, for example, suggests that hope can function as a stubbornness (Potamianou 1997: 2), which may actually foreclose transformation insofar as it maintains an investment in something that has already been lost. As she argues: 'Whereas hope is usually regarded as an affect that promotes development and change, here it is in the service of a series of fixations which transform its aims' (Potamianou 1997: 2). Indeed, she suggests that the emotion of hope can take the place of lost objects: one has hope in hope, only insofar as the object of hope has already been given up (Potamianou 1997: 4). The investment in hope, she suggests, can be a way of maintaining one's ego ideal, even when one has failed to live up to the ideal. *The attachment then gets in the way of a process of moving on.*

Potamianou's critique of hope is important. For instance, we can see that hope can work to extend investments in social norms precisely in the failure of the investment to be returned (see Chapter 6). The nation, for example, could be installed as an object of hope: the nation may promise that it will return one's investment, as a return that has to be endlessly deferred into the future if the investment is to be sustained. Here, the emotion of hope is sustained by transforming hope into a lost object, as a transformation that encrypts the object, and blocks more creative forms of political and personal action. But I want to suggest that hope can be sustained in ways that allow the animation rather than encrypting of its object. Rethinking the role of hope in feminism might allow us to explore this distinction.

As I have already suggested, for feminists, the hope might be for a world in which feminism itself is no longer necessary (see Brown 2003: 4), although how we would recognise such a world might be a difficult matter. This is a revolutionary hope, certainly. The difficulty for feminism is produced by the force of its own critique of gender as a form of subordination that 'goes all the way down'. The hope that was invested in programmes of 'de-gendering' that informed some 1970s and 1980s feminist politics – including work based on object relations psychoanalysis around changing the social relations of parenting – now seems at best naïve. Such hopes seemed to underestimate the attachments that govern the reification of gender as an attribute. The wish and hope of de-gendering – that gender could be overcome if we changed this or that practice, or once we knew 'it was just gender' – may now even seem complicit with the liberal assumption that we can will away power simply through recognising its force. Furthermore, the feminist hope for a gender-free world has been cruelly translated into a post-feminist vision of a present in which gender has been overcome, a neo-liberal vision in which it is assumed that gender, as with other forms of power, no longer makes a difference. In this vision of the present, women are not oppressed; feminism is no longer necessary; and so on. This world is not the world we hoped for, but a continuation of what we were against under our name.

The translation of feminist hope into a politics of concealment is not a necessary consequence of that hope. It would be premature to mourn for the loss of hope: such mourning would simply transform hope into a lost object. The fact that hope can be 'taken up' by others to undo the promise it embodies is a sign of the necessary risks of anticipating the future in the uncertainty of the present. To express hope for another kind of world, one that is unimaginable at present, is a political action, and it remains so even in the face of exhaustion and despair. The existence of risks does not suggest we should 'block' an action, but it does mean that we should recognise that political actions can be taken up in ways that undo their force (see the first section of this chapter).

At the same time, I would suggest that Wendy Brown's vision of a feminism that lets 'our objects fly' (Brown 2003: 15) might let go of too much. Brown's model of a feminism that lets its objects fly is hopeful. She suggests that a feminism that keeps hold of its objects is one that is delimited by the wish for its own reproduction, or one that is invested in 'its own career advancement' (Brown 2003: 15). She offers us a model of feminist hope in which the 'objects' of feminism (such as sex or gender) do not block new forms of action in the present. Indeed, she calls for a feminism that lets go of itself, 'becoming part of a larger order of transformative politics' (Brown 2003: 15), partly by letting its objects fly, almost as if they were birds released into the indeterminate air. I want to make an alternative argument, one which respects the hopefulness of this vision of flight: feminism can fly not by letting its objects go, or by releasing them into the air, but by keeping them close, or even by getting closer to them.

We can return to my analysis of queer grief in Chapter 7. Here, I suggested that such grief refuses to 'let go' of the object, and that this refusal allows the loved object to remain alive as an impression, an 'aliveness' that lives through the sharing of impressions. I have also argued that it is the failure of the object of feminism to be secured that allows feminism to become a movement. We can now link these arguments together. It is by turning towards the objects of feminism, that we keep hope in feminism alive. Such a 'turning towards' does not hold the objects of feminist critique in place; rather, it is the condition of possibility for their movement. The hope we install in feminism is not about transforming feminism into a lost object: to preserve our attachment to the objects of feminism is to allow 'feminism' to move, to be shaped by the contact between those bodies that gather under its name. Keeping the objects of feminism alive means allowing them to acquire new shapes and forms as we reach for what is possible. To let the objects of feminism go would be to allow those objects to become encrypted, as relics of a past that we assume is behind us. As present attachments, the objects of feminism move, as we move. To stay open to feminism is both to critique the world, which we face in the present, and to encounter the objects of feminism anew, as that hope for the 'not yet', in the here and the now.

The hope that brings me to feminism comes from my conviction that 'what I am against' is not inevitable. At the same time, hope implies that what I am for might not happen (Pieper 1969: 20). To have hope in feminism is to recognise that feminist visions of the future have not been realised in the present. The hope of feminism can stay alive, as that which moves and allows movement, not by letting the objects of feminist critique go, but by turning towards those very objects, *as signs of the persistence of that which we are against in the present*. As such, placing hope in feminism is not simply about the future; it is also about recognising the persistence of the past in the present.[7]

One must persist because of this persistence, by keeping feminism alive in the present. In fact, some degree of stubbornness in relation to one's hopes may be important: one can struggle for one's investments, even if one is open to the possibility of giving them up. For feminists, a political and strategic question remains: When should we let go? And what should we let go of? Such a question has no immediate resolution: we must decide, always, what to do, as a decision that must be made again, and again, in each present we find ourselves in. This decision is not mine, or even yours – we have to think about how decisions can be made with or for others. Making a decision – which means refusing to allow 'things' to be already decided – might also mean questioning one's investments, although this does not require suspending one's investments. One can be invested and open to those investments being challenged through the contact we have with others. That contact keeps us open; being affected by others is crucial to the opening up of feminism to the uncertainty of the future.

This opening is an interval in time, and that interval is the time for action: it is now, when we must do the work of teaching, protesting, naming, feeling, and connecting with others. The openness that gathers in the struggle against 'what is' involves the coming together of different bodies in this present time. It is here that the feminist 'we' becomes affective. For the opening up of that which is possible does not just take place in time, in that loop between present and future. The opening up also *takes time*. The time of opening is the time of collecting together. One does not hope alone, but for others, whose pain one does not feel, but whose pain becomes a thread in the weave of the present, touched as it is by all that could be. Through the work of listening to others, of hearing the force of their pain and the energy of their anger, of learning to be surprised by all that one feels oneself to be against; through all of this, a 'we' is formed, and an attachment is made. This is a feminist attachment and an attachment to feminism and it is moving. I am moved by the 'we', as the 'we' is an effect of those who move towards it. It is not an innocent 'we', or one that stands still. It is affected by that which it is against, and hence also by that which it is for, what it enables, shapes, makes possible. Here, you might say, one moves towards others, others who are attached to feminism, as a movement away from that which we are against. Such movements create the surface of a feminist community. In the forming and deforming of attachments: in the writing, conversations, the doing, the work, feminism moves, and is moved. It connects and is connected. More than anything, it is in the alignment of the 'we' with the 'I', the feminist subject with the feminist collective, an alignment which is imperfect and hence generative, that a new grammar of social existence may yet be possible. The 'we' of feminism is not its foundation; it is an effect of the impressions made by others who take the risk of inhabiting its name. Of course, this 'hopeful' narrative has another edge: the 'we' of feminism is shaped by some bodies, more than others.

It is hence important that we don't install feminism as the object of hope, even if feminism is what gives us hope. Returning to the opening of this chapter, feminists who speak out against forms of social violence are often dismissed as motivated by negative passion. The risks of foregrounding the emotions of feminism are clear. Some risks are, of course, worth taking. Feminists who have spoken out against the war on terrorism have done so in a way that expresses hope for another kind of world, another kind of way of inhabiting the world with others. The hope for 'transnational solidarity', to use Chandra Talpade Mohanty's (2003) term, might lie in taking a feminist orientation, a way of facing the world, which includes facing what we might not recognise, with others we do not yet know. When feminists spoke out against the 'war on terror', they claimed such solidarity. In speaking against the war as a form of terrorism, they spoke for something, in speeches that were reaching out for another orientation to the world. What we 'speak for' when 'we speak against' is not always available to us, as an object that can be delineated in the present. Indeed, speaking for something, rather than someone, often involves living with the uncertainty of what is possible in the world that we inhabit. Solidarity does not assume that our struggles are the same struggles, or that our pain is the same pain, or that our hope is for the same future. Solidarity involves commitment, and work, as well as the recognition that even if we do not have the same feelings, or the same lives, or the same bodies, we do live on common ground.

NOTES

1. Of course, this image of the angry black woman has a long history. See Lorde (1984), Moreton-Robinson (2003), as well as Thobani (2003: 401).
2. We could rethink, for example, the relation between femininity and feminism. On the one hand, feminist politics involves the recognition of femininity as a social norm that is linked to the subordination of women. Feminism hence reads the 'naturalness' of femininity as an effect of power (Butler 1990). However, this does not mean identifying as a feminist necessarily means transcending or giving up on femininity. One's investment in femininity *as if it were* an ideal does not necessarily dissipate in the moment of recognising its normative function in policing gendered bodies. We can also understand investment in terms of how value accrues: being 'good' at femininity for women can give you value, and to give up on femininity can be to risk losing value that one has accrued over time, which can be especially significant if one feels under-valued in other ways. To be invested in an attribute that is linked to one's subordination is an effect of subordination: one's value becomes dependent on how one lives up to that ideal, even if the ideal is what restricts possibilities for gendered subjects. What is clear here is that even when we consciously recognise something, and disagree with

something, our investments in what embodies that something cannot simply be willed away. *It takes time to move on and to move away;* given how investments in norms surface in bodies, then one's bodily relation to the world, and especially to those one loves, is reorientated if one wishes not to embody a norm in the same way.

3. This argument clearly has implications for theories of agency. To deconstruct the opposition between action and reaction is not to say that agency is impossible. But it is to relocate agency from the individual to the interface between individuals and worlds; agency is a matter of what actions are possible given how we are shaped by our contact with others. In this model, I would not be an agent insofar as I am not enacted upon (the classical liberal model). I would be an agent insofar as that which affects me does not determine my action, but leaves room for a decision. Politics is the space left between the surfaces of reaction and the necessity of a decision about what to do. This model contrasts with Lois McNay's argument, which links agency with the creativity of action, where the capability for action is defined as a pre-disposition and originary (McNay 2000: 3, 18, 22). Whilst my work leaves room for creative action (to be shaped is not to have one's course of action be fully determined), it also suggests that there is no original action, which is not already a form of reaction, or shaped by the contact we have with others. *To react is not always to be reactionary.*

4. In interpersonal communication, the blocking of an emotion can lead to the intensification of emotions: your inability to 'hear' my anger may make me angrier. Blockages aren't only effects of defensive behaviours, but are also effects of emotional collisions. For example, if I express my anger, and someone returns that anger with reasonableness, indifference or even happiness, then the feeling of anger is intensified. Or the anger could slide into another emotion: despair, frustration, bitterness. As I suggested in the Introduction to the book, emotions involve tension and they can be in tension: *the miscommunication of emotions involves a process of intensification.* Thanks to Mimi Sheller for helping me formulate this point.

5. I am very indebted to Lauren Berlant, whose insightful question, 'When do norms become forms?' has provided an inspiration for my work.

6. Ghassan Hage offers an excellent analysis of the political economy of hope in *Against Paranoid Nationalism* (2003). He suggests that hope and hopefulness are distributed, and that in paranoid nationalism, there is not enough hope to go around. Subjects hence don't have any hope to give to others (Hage 2003: 9). Whilst I find this argument convincing, it is in danger of supporting a model of hope as something we must have. Hage suggests that if subjects were at home, 'cuddled', felt cared for, *then* they would be more hospitable to others. This is surprisingly close to New Labour's version of multicultural Britain: the nation must take care of itself, and have enough for itself, *before* it can be generous to others. Our task might be to challenge the idea that access to care and hope for some are necessary conditions for being generous towards others.

7. There is a tendency to privilege the future in some feminist theory, see, for example, Grosz (1999: 15). For a critique of this tendency and how it can forget the ethical significance of the past, see Ahmed (2002) and Kilby (2002).

Conclusion: Just Emotions

> Brave Ali, 13, takes his first steps to recovery after losing arms in
> Baghdad bomb blast . . . Ali's suffering was a symbol of the pain of
> the Iraqi people, innocent victims of a cruel dictator and a cruel war.
> Now his recovery is a new symbol – of fresh hope for a broken
> nation. (Smith and Williams 2003: 5)

In this book I have examined the cultural politics of emotion by asking the
question: What do emotions do? The 'doing' of emotions, I have suggested,
is bound up with the sticky relation between signs and bodies: emotions work
by working through signs and on bodies to materialise the surfaces and
boundaries that are lived as worlds. In conclusion, I want to consider the
relation between emotions and (in)justice, as a way of rethinking what it is
that emotions do. We can ask: How are emotions bound up with stories of
justice and injustice? How do emotions work through texts not only to 'show'
the effects of injustice, in the form of wounds and injury, but also to open
up the possibility of restoration, repair, healing and recovery? Is a just
response to injustice about having more 'just emotions', or is justice never
'just' about emotions?

One way of examining the role of emotions in responding to injustice is
to consider the politics of grief. In Chapters 6 and 7, I showed how emotions
work to differentiate between others precisely by identifying those that *can
be* loved, those that *can be* grieved, that is, by constituting some others as the
legitimate objects of emotion. This differentiation is crucial in politics as it
works to secure a distinction between legitimate and illegitimate lives. For
example, Judith Butler (2005) has argued that the distinction between lives
that are grievable and ungrievable is necessary if the 'war on terrorism' is to
be justified as a recovery from terror, rather than a repetition of terror. The
legitimacy of the war is inferred from the 'legitimacy' of some losses over

others. The 'injustice' of war, and the injustices that are legitimated through the narrating of war as a mission of love, depend upon the exclusion of others from the emotional response of grief. But what happens when those who have been designated as ungrievable are grieved, and when their loss is not only felt as a loss, but becomes a symbol of the injustice of loss? Is to grieve for the ungrieved to convert an injustice to a justice?

In Chapter 7, I examined queer responses to September 11, and suggested that to add queer loss onto the losses already mourned by the nation would remain complicit with the erasure of other losses that remain ungrievable. So what would it mean for 'other losses' to become the object of grief? In my opening quote, for example, a life that might be assumed to be ungrievable from the point of view of the British reader, the life of an Iraqi child, is grieved. The loss of Ali's arms becomes a loss that is visible to the British reader, who is asked to mourn for this loss. But does mourning for Ali's injury repair the injustice of the injury? How do others become available to us as 'lives to be mourned'? When such 'others' are constructed as grievable it is often through the sentimentalisation of loss, so that what makes us alike, *is now the bond of loss*. Indeed, the rescue of the child is what allows grief to be extended, but it is also what allows the erasure of other losses to be sustained in the very 'time' of the extension. The child stands for, and stands in for, the pain of the nation. The other others too numerous to name who have lost or been lost are erased both by the rescue of the child as a singular figure, and by the absent presence of what the child represents ('the nation').

So what does feeling grief for this other do? How does it move the subject into a relationship with this other? We can return to my argument about how pain works in charity discourses in Chapter 1 as a way of 'moving' the subject. The face of the suffering child places the British subject in a position of charitable compassion. In being moved by this pain, I show myself to be full of love in the midst of the violence: 'One story above all others touched the British people during the Iraq war' (*The Mirror*, 7 June 2003: 7). Lauren Berlant examines how compassion has become the new face of conservatism (2003). To be moved by the suffering of some others (the 'deserving' poor, the innocent child, the injured hero), is also to be elevated into a place that remains untouched by other others (whose suffering cannot be converted into my sympathy or admiration). So it is not a coincidence that it is a child's suffering that touches the nation. The child represents the face of innocence; through the child, the threat of difference is transformed into the promise or hope of likeness. That child *could be* mine; his pain is universalised through the imagined loss of *any* child as a loss that could be my loss. The child's pain is what brings us closer to the others, because I can identify with the pain another must feel when faced by the child's pain: 'Back at home, Ali's sister and aunt impatiently await his return' (*The Mirror*, 7 June 2003: 7). We can be 'with them' in the face of this pain.

Within this narrative, compassion for the other's suffering becomes a gift that can be extended to others: the promise of this gift becomes the hope of the Iraqi nation. Through our compassion, the suffering of others can be repaired, and the nation can be 'restored' or 'healed'. Here, we can rescue those who suffer, and embody the hope of those who have been refused entry into the 'we' of civil life. Importantly, if our hope is a gift, then the other remains indebted to us. The position of indebtedness is the position of gratitude (Hochschild 2003): the other must be grateful for being saved or being brought into civil society. The story was extended in August with a quote from Ali, which forms the headline: 'I'm going to ask the Queen if I can stay in Britain for ever' (*The Mirror*, 9 August: 9). The 'hope of the nation' gets quickly translated into the promise of becoming British.

This story tells us a lot about the difficult relation between (in)justice and emotion. It shows us that justice and injustice cannot be 'read' as signs of good and bad feeling: to transform bad feeling into good feeling (hatred into love,[1] indifference into sympathy, shame into pride, despair into hope) is not necessarily to repair the costs of injustice. Indeed, this conversion can repeat the forms of violence it seeks to redress, as it can sustain the distinction between the subject and object of feeling, which is repeated by the extension of feeling to some others. But what about the other's feelings? Isn't the reality of the other's suffering a sign of injustice?

The relation between injustice and feeling bad is complicated. Lauren Berlant has argued that injustice cannot be reduced to pain, or feeling bad (Berlant 2000: 35). Although pain and injustice cannot be reduced, they also cannot be separated: the fact of suffering, for example, has *something to do* with what is 'wrong' about systematic forms of violence, as relations of force and harm (see Chapter 1). The effects of violence are something to do with why violence can be judged as 'bad'. Now, this is not to say that what makes violence bad *is* the other's suffering. To make such a claim is dangerous: it makes the judgement of right and wrong dependent upon the existence of emotions.[2] The reduction of judgements about what is bad or wrong to experiences of hurt, pain or suffering would be deeply problematic. For the claim would allow violence to be sustained in the event that the other claimed not to suffer, or that I claimed the other did not suffer. We must remember that some forms of violence remain concealed *as* violence, as effects of social norms that are hidden from view. Given this, violence itself could be justified on the grounds of the absence of consciously-felt suffering. The reduction of injustice to emotions also 'justifies' claims of access to the interiority of the feelings of others. We have probably all heard arguments that justify power relations through the claim that this other is in fact 'not hurting', or might even be 'content', or 'happy'.³ Indeed, I could make this claim about myself: 'I do not hurt, I am happy, therefore it is not wrong.' But emotions are not transparent, and they are not simply about a relation of the subject to itself, or even the relation of the subject to its own history.

For example, my chapters on hate and fear show the way in which emotions circulate through objects: emotions are not a positive form of dwelling, but produce the effect of surfaces and boundaries of bodies (see Chapters 2 and 3). It is not simply that the subject feels hate, or feels fear, and nor is it the case that the object is simply hateful or is fearsome: the emotions of hate and fear are shaped by the 'contact zone' in which others impress upon us, as well as leave their impressions. Throughout this book, I have considered examples of racism as a particular form of contact between others. A white racist subject who encounters a racial other may experience an intensity of emotions (fear, hate, disgust, pain). That intensification involves moving away from the body of the other, or moving towards that body in an act of violence, and then moving away. The 'moment of contact' is shaped by past histories of contact, which allows the proximity of a racial other to be perceived as threatening, at the same time as it reshapes the bodies in the contact zone of the encounter. These histories have already impressed upon the surface of the bodies at the same time as they create new impressions. So while emotions may be experienced as 'inside out' or 'outside in', they actually work to generate the distinction between inside and outside, partly by rehearsing associations that are already in place. I have thus described emotions as performative: they both generate their objects, and repeat past associations (see Chapter 4). The loop of the performative works powerfully: in reading the other as being disgusting, for example, the subject is filled up with disgust, as a sign of the truth of the reading.

I have associated emotions not with individuals, and their interior states or character, nor with the quality of objects, but with 'signs' and how they work on and in relation to bodies. Of course, emotions have often been linked to the power of language. But they are often constructed as an instrument: as something that we use simply to persuade or seduce others into false belief (emotion as rhetoric, rhetoric as style without content). Such a view constructs emotion as a possession, at the same time that it presumes that emotions are a lower form of speech. This presumption in turn elevates reasonableness or detachment into a better address, one that does not seek to stir up trouble. I have offered an alternative view of emotions as operating precisely where we don't register their effects, in the determination of the relation between signs, a relation that is often concealed by the form of the relation: the metonymic proximity between signs. In Chapter 4, I called this determination 'stickiness', examining how 'signs' become sticky or saturated with affect. My discussion of emotive language was not then a discussion of a special class or genre of speech, which can be separated from other kinds of speech. Rather this model of 'sticky signs' shows how language works as a form of power in which emotions align some bodies with others, as well as stick different figures together, by the way they move us.

If emotions are not possessions, then the terrain of (in)justice cannot be a question of 'having' or 'not having' an emotion. Interestingly, in moral and political philosophy, those who argue that emotions are relevant to justice, often do so via a model of character and virtue. Robert C. Solomon, for example, following from a classical view of justice as virtue, and David Hume's and Adam Smith's concept of moral sentiments, argues that: 'Justice is first of all a function of personal character, a matter of ordinary, everyday feeling' (Solomon 1995: 3). Justice becomes a form of feeling, which is about 'fellow-feeling', a capacity to feel for others, and to sympathise with their pain (Solomon 1995: 3, see also Smith 1966: 10). We have already seen the risks of justice defined in terms of sympathy or compassion: justice then becomes a sign of what I can give to others, and works to elevate some subjects over others, through the reification of their capacity for love or 'fellow-feeling' (see Chapters 1 and 6). But we must also challenge the view that justice is about having the right kind of feelings, or being the right kind of subject. Justice is not about 'good character'. Not only does this model work to conceal the power relations at stake in defining what is good-in-itself, but it also works to individuate, personalise and privatise the social relation of (in)justice. Character is, after all, an effect rather than a ground of social life. Emotions then cannot be installed as the 'truth' of injustice, partly as they do not simply belong to subjects.

But our response to the model of just emotions as virtue should not be to say that emotions have nothing to do with justice and injustice. This argument would support the attempt to detach justice and indeed morality from emotions, which was crucial to the universalism of the Kantian and post-Kantian ethical traditions. Such a tradition relies on a distinction between emotion and reason, which constructs emotions as not only irrelevant to judgement and justice, but also as unreasonable, and as an obstacle to good judgement. Indeed, it is the hierarchies established by such models, which allow women and racial others to be seen as less moral, as less capable of making judgements: it is such others, of course, who are often presented as being 'swayed by their emotions', as I discussed in Chapter 8. The model which empties all emotion out of the process of making judgements is also the model that justifies the relegation of others to the sphere of nature. In other words, this model justifies 'injustice' as a sign of the rule of law.

In this book, I have challenged this opposition between emotion and reason partly by examining how emotional responses to others also work as forms of judgement (see Chapter 1). But my thesis has not then installed emotion as a form of access to truth, or indeed as a 'better' form of judgement. Emotions, I have suggested, are effects rather than origins: they hence cannot be taken as 'the ground' of judgement (to be a 'form' is not a 'ground'). Instead, I have argued that emotions are not only about the 'impressions' left by others, but that they involve investments in social norms (see Chapter 7). Injustice may work precisely through sustaining particular kinds of affective relations to social norms through what we do with our bodies. As I argued in the chapters on queer feelings and feminist attachments, challenging social norms involves having a different affective relation to those norms, partly by 'feeling' their costs as a collective loss. This argument certainly makes 'feeling' crucial to the struggle against injustice, but in a way that does not take feeling as the ground for action, but as an effect of the repetition of some actions rather than others. Relatedly, although injustice cannot be measured by the existence of suffering, some suffering is an effect of injustice. There are other affects that are possible, including anger, rage and resentment, all of which are not necessary consequences of these injustices. As I pointed out in Chapters 2 and 4, the non-necessity of the affective consequences of violence does not mean those affects are not determined: for example, in the case of hate speech, histories are already in place that render some words 'sticky', and more likely to cause harm and hurt to others. The contingency of the relation between injustice and emotion reminds us that injustice also involves the proximity of the contact zone (see Chapter 1): injustice is a question of how bodies come into contact with other bodies. We need to respond to injustice in a way that shows rather than erases the complexity of the relation between violence, power and emotion.

If injustice is not simply about feeling bad, then justice is not simply a matter of feeling good: it is not about the overcoming of pain, or even about the achievement of happiness. That is, being happy is not itself a sign of justice.[4] The risk that 'happiness' is installed as the 'truth' of justice is partly that happiness can be promised as a return for investment in social norms. Lauren Berlant calls this fantasy of happiness a stupid form of optimism: 'the faith that adjustment to certain forms or practices of living and thinking will secure one's happiness' (Berlant 2002: 75). Such optimism does not originate from a subject, but is generated through promises made to the subject, which circulate as 'truths' within public culture. The nation, for example, is installed as the 'hope' of the subject, insofar as it guarantees the 'pursuit of happiness' as its originary goal. The 'happiness' promised by the nation is what sustains investment in the nation in the absence of return, a 'happiness' that is always deferred as the promise of reward for good citizenship. Indeed, as I argued in Chapter 6, it is the failure of return for investment that extends one's attachment to the nation: the endless deferral of happiness takes the form of waiting. So 'justice' becomes the promised return for investment in the nation, but one that must not be realised for the investment to be sustained. The nation, in other words, becomes the 'agent' of justice, the one that *can* deliver justice through happiness, but this *capacity is sustained only through its failure to be actualised in the present.*

Furthermore, the desire to feel good or better can involve the erasure of relations of violence. In Chapter 5, for example, I examined how expressions of shame about histories of violence work not only as narratives of 'recovery', but also as a form of 'covering over'. Shame becomes an expression of 'bad feeling', which can be 'about' feeling better in the present. Interestingly, in Susie Orbach's work, psychotherapy is not defined as the 'overcoming' of bad feeling, but as entering into a different kind of relation to bad feeling. As she puts it: 'Psychotherapy is not so much about turning bad feelings into good ones as about staying with and accepting the bad feelings long enough to make a personal sense of them' (Orbach 1999: 52). Orbach suggests that overcoming bad feeling is not a measure of healing. Indeed, if 'bad feeling' is also an effect of injustice, then to overcome bad feeling can also be to erase the signs of injustice. We saw this in my chapter on shame, where the shame became a narrative of conversion: white Australians express sorrow, sympathy and shame in order that they can 'return' to their pride in the nation, as an affective relation to nationhood, which was itself the proper scene of the violence. Is the struggle against injustice about having a different kind of relation to bad feeling, in which 'bad feeling' is not installed as a sign of the truth of injustice, and is not that which we seek to overcome?

To reflect on this question we can consider the idea of 'restorative justice'. Restorative justice has allowed the return of 'emotions' to the scene of justice in a way that is about dealing with the complex effects of injustice on social life as well as individual lives. The idea partly came out of criminology and the challenge to the model of justice as retribution as a punishment for an offence.[5] It begins as a response to crime, which views crime not as a violation of legal rules, but as a violation of 'a *person* by another person' (Johnstone 2002: ix). If crime is personal, it could be argued, then justice must be too. Hence, within the restorative model, justice is about making offenders 'feel' the costs of their crime: 'our primary concerns should be to make offenders aware of the harm they have caused' (Johnstone 2002: ix). This emphasis on making offenders feel the consequence of their crime, involves arranging for the offenders to face their victims in conferences or family courts. As such, victim's communicate their feelings: including feelings of anger, fear and suffering (Johnstone 2002: 66). The restoration promised by this model of justice is not simply the repair of injury for victims, but the restoration of community, by 'bringing' the offender back into the community (Daly 2000: 36), and asking them to face the emotional consequence of the crime. Restoration is symbolised by the expression of remorse from the offender, which itself might make the victim feel better. The remorse may even be returned by the victim through an expression of forgiveness, which is understood as a gift rather than a duty within restorative justice (Braithwaite 2002: 15). Forgiveness is also the hope of restorative justice, a sign that justice has been restored in the reconciliation between those torn apart by crime, as a restoration of the community.[6] As Hudson and Galaway put it: 'The aim of the criminal justice process should be to create peace in communities by reconciling the parties and repairing the injuries caused by the dispute' (Hudson and Galaway 1996: 2).

I am sympathetic with the emphasis on the personal: the depersonalising of justice can make injuries disappear, and protect those who harm others. The dictum 'don't take it personally' fails because it allows the harmful action to be justified through the concealment of its effects, which are effects on somebody. The effects of crime, and indeed of injustice, are personal, even if they are not simply 'about' a person. But of course, to reduce crime or injustice to the realm of the personal has its risks: the personalising of crime can conceal its public and systematic dimensions. The personal is complicated, and mediated by relations that make any person embody more than the personal, and the personal embody more than the person. When emotions are seen as only personal, or about the person and how they feel, then the systematic nature of their effects is concealed. There could be a lot to say here about the reliance on emotions as 'signs' of justice, in particular, the assumption that 'remorse' works to overcome injury. The apology, as we saw in Chapter 5, is not simply 'about' the expression of emotion, but can 'stand in for' an emotion, *when read as a sign of its truth*. The 'exchange' of emotions within this idealisation of justice surely assumes the 'expression' of emotions as a transparent measure of 'true feeling'. This is not to say that expressions of emotions must be read as insincere or inauthentic. But the circulation of 'signs' of emotions may indeed be a 'sign' of something else.

The 'signs' of emotion return us to the 'promise' of community. In Braithwaite's model, for example, the restoration of the community also takes place through 'reintegration' of the offender. For Braithwaite, reintegration is enabled not by empathy, but by what he calls 'reintegrative shaming', which 'shames while maintaining bonds of respect or love, that sharply terminates disapproval with forgiveness, instead of amplifying deviance by progressively casting the deviant out' (Braithwaite 1989: 12–13). Shame would not be about making the offender feel bad (this would install a pattern of deviance), so 'expressions of community disapproval' are followed by 'gestures of reacceptance' (Braithwaite 1989: 55). Note, this model presumes the agents of shaming are not the victims (who might make the offender feel bad), but the family and friends of the offender. It is the love that offenders have for those who shame them, which allows shame to integrate rather than alienate. Braithwaite concludes that: 'The best place to see reintegrative shaming at work is in loving families' (Braithwaite 1989: 56).

This idealisation of the family is not incidental. What is presumed in the literature on restorative justice is that injustice is caused by the failure of the social bond. The restoration of the social bond (the family, the community, the nation) is hence read as a sign of justice.[7] What this leaves out is the relation between injustice and the social bond, the ways in which, for example, the idealisation of the family requires the determination of others *as* others, such as queers, who have already failed its form (see Chapter 7). The making of the social bond involves conditions of love, which others will have failed, in their failure to live up to an ideal (see Chapter 6).

In the restorative justice literature, justice becomes not only a matter of restoring social bonds (which may be linked to violence), but is assumed to be about 'having' good relationships. I would argue that the struggle against injustice cannot be transformed into a manual for good relationships without concealing the injustice of how 'relationships' work by differentiating between others. Justice might then not be simply about 'getting along', but may preserve the right of others not to enter into relationships, 'not to be with me', in the first place. The other, for example, might not want my grief, let alone my sympathy, or love. The idealisation of the social bond quickly translates into the transformation of relationship itself into a moral duty, which others fail. We saw this with the idealisation of multiculturalism as a social bond: ethnic minorities and white working-class communities fail precisely in their refusal 'to mix' more intimately with others (see Chapter 6). Proximity becomes here the 'truth' of justice and a sign of healing (the 'rift' between communities is explained as a consequence of distance). But peace and harmony cannot be linked without the transformation of proximity into a duty that requires others to mimic the very forms of community, which produce violence against others.

Of course, the language of justice as healing has a much longer history, and a much wider circulation than simply in theories of restorative justice. Braithwaite in his later work says: 'Because we are hurt, there is a need to heal; there is a need for others to listen to the stories of our hurts before we can all move on to solve the problem' (Braithwaite 2002: x; see also Kiss 2000: 72; Sullivan and Tifft 2001; Rotberg 2000: 7; Minow 1998). The motif of healing links discourses of therapy with the national politics of reconciliation and reparation. The 'travel' of the motif between those domains should not allow us to reduce them. But the relation between individual and collective healing needs to remain a question. The risk is, of course, that the collective comes to be read 'as if it were' an individual, as a subject that 'has' feelings. For Minow, the work of healing is bound up with the complexity of emotional life. As she puts it: 'To be healing, the act of narrating an experience of trauma needs to move beyond a plain statement of facts to include also the survivor's emotional and bodily responses and reactions of others who mattered to the individual' (Minow 2000: 245). Minow suggests then that politics should leave room for therapy (Minow 2000: 245), which does not mean that politics should be reduced to therapy. The key to ensuring this non-reduction would be to challenge any model of emotions as the property of individuals or collectives, as something that 'I' or 'we' simply have.

Within the politics of reparation, and in the truth commissions that have been set up in response to trauma and historical injustice, telling the story of injury has become crucial. My emphasis in Chapter 1 was on the importance of testimony as a form of healing for indigenous communities. This is not to say that 'telling' a story of pain and injury is necessarily therapeutic. The telling is also about witnessing, which makes demands on others to hear, but which does not always get a just hearing. Responses to testimonies of injury can 'cover over' the injury, for example, by claiming it as 'our own' (appropriation). We should not conclude that testimonial forms of politics fail in such failures to hear, or in such refusals of recognition. Testimonies about the injustice of colonisation, slavery and racism are not only calls for recognition; they are also forms of recognition, in and of themselves. Injustice is irreducible to injury, though it does involve injuries. To recognise the injustices of colonisation as a history of the present is to rewrite history, and to reshape the ground on which we live, for we would recognise the ground itself as shaped by such histories. If the violence of what happened is recognised, as a violence that shapes the present, then the 'truths' of history are called into question. Recognition of injustice is not simply about others becoming visible (though this can be important). Recognition is also about claiming that an injustice did happen; the claim is a radical one in the face of the forgetting of such injustices. Healing does not cover over, but exposes the wound to others: *the recovery is a form of exposure*. The visibility produced by recognition is actually the visibility of the ordinary and normative or the visibility of what has been concealed under the sign of truth.

The work of exposure is not over in the moment of hearing: often such testimonies have to be repeated, again and again. Doing the work of exposure is hence both political and emotional work. The demand for recognition can risk exposing too much, and 'defences' against 'hearing' the claim are often already in place (which can include guilt, shame and anger as well as denial and indifference), and those defences can, but do not always, block the message. Political struggle is about learning to deal with such blockages, and finding ways to get through.

Political struggle can be a struggle, for what we struggle against can diminish our resources, our capacities for action, our energy – even take lives. This is why justice has to leave room for feeling better, even if it is not *about* feeling better. For those whose lives have been torn apart by violence, or those for whom the tiredness of repetition in everyday life becomes too much to bear, feeling better does and should matter. Feeling better is not a sign that justice has been done, and nor should it be reified as the goal of political struggle. But feeling better does still matter, as it is about learning to live with the injuries that threaten to make life impossible. The projects of reconciliation and reparation are not about the 'nation' recovering: they are about whether those who are the victims of injustice can find a way of living in the nation that feels better through the process of speaking about the past, and through exposing the wounds that get concealed by the 'truths' of a certain history. Feeling better might be an effect of telling one's story, or of finding a more liveable way of sustaining silence, or of having those who committed the crime apologise, or of receiving material forms of compensation, or other modes of recognition of an injury. Feeling better might be about having the room left to think and feel, or to dance on the ground; it might be about having space and time apart from others. Feeling better might be about having sufficient materials to sustain life in one's body; it might be about having energy, shelter, warmth, light, or air to breathe. We cannot know in advance what makes others (or even ourselves) feel better about the injustices that have shaped lives and worlds.

Indeed, feeling better for some might involve expressing feelings of anger, rage and shame as feelings in the present about a past that persists in the present. The emotions that have often been described as negative or even destructive can also be enabling or creative, often in their very refusal of the promise of the social bond. For example, as I argued in Chapter 8, anger against injustice can move subjects into a different relation to the world, including a different relation to the object of one's critique. The emotional struggles against injustice are not about finding good or bad feelings, and then expressing them. Rather, they are about how we are moved by feelings into a different relation to the norms that we wish to contest, or the wounds we wish to heal. Moving here is not about 'moving on', or about 'using' emotions to move away, but moving and being moved as a form of labour or work, which opens up different kinds of attachments to others, in part through the recognition of this work *as* work.

In conclusion, I want to suggest that we can rethink our relation to scars, including emotional and physical scars. It is a truism that a good scar is one that is hard to see. We would praise the surgeons for the expertise of their stitching. The skin looks almost as it did before the injury. We can even maintain the fiction that the injury did not take place as the scar does not remind us of the wounding. But perhaps we need to challenge the truism. Let me offer an alternative. A good scar is one that sticks out, a lumpy sign on the skin. It's not that the wound is exposed or that the skin is bleeding. But the scar is a sign of the injury: a good scar allows healing, it even covers over, *but the covering always exposes the injury, reminding us of how it shapes the body.* Our bodies have been shaped by their injuries; scars are traces of those injuries that persist in the healing or stitching of the present. This kind of good scar reminds us that recovering from injustice cannot be about covering over the injuries, which are effects of that injustice; signs of an unjust contact between our bodies and others. So 'just emotions' might be ones that work *with* and *on* rather than *over* the wounds that surface as traces of past injuries in the present.

Emotions tell us a lot about time; emotions are the very 'flesh' of time. They show us the time it takes to move, or to move on, is a time that exceeds the time of an individual life. Through emotions, the past persists on the surface of bodies. Emotions show us how histories stay alive, even when they are not consciously remembered; how histories of colonialism, slavery, and violence shape lives and worlds in the present. The time of emotion is not always about the past, and how it sticks. Emotions also open up futures, in the ways they involve different orientations to others. It takes time to know what we can do with emotion. Of course, we are not just talking about emotions when we talk about emotions. The objects of emotions slide and stick and they join the intimate histories of bodies, with the public domain of justice and injustice. Justice is not simply a feeling. And feelings are not always just. But justice involves feelings, which move us across the surfaces of the world, creating ripples in the intimate contours of our lives. Where we go, with these feelings, remains an open question.

NOTES

1. One almost 'queer moment' occurred on Valentine's Day in 2003, when *The Mirror* had as its front page an image of George Bush and Tony Blair kissing in a pink love heart, with the words 'Make love not war'. *The Mirror*'s anti-war stance repeats the slogan of the peace movement, whilst queering that slogan into a visual display of male homoeroticism. Of course, as an imperative the slogan fails: the justification of the war evoked precisely the language of love (see Chapter 6). We can supplement my analysis of the politics of love by reflecting on how love became a 'bond' between Blair and Bush, and how their bond was represented as the bond of friendship between the United States and Britain. The love between Blair and Bush was over-represented, certainly. The homoerotic might not have been crucial to that love (hence the 'joke' of the image), but it certainly involved the idealisation of male friendship premised not even on fraternity, but on the form of the couple. The love was visually represented by the handshake, and verbally evident through repeated statements of admiration for each other. For many, this was a sickening display or performance of love, and a historically tragic coupling.

2. The criteria we use to make judgements about 'what is bad' involve norms as well as affects: we cannot use emotions to bypass the normative sphere. But it is also important that the normative should not bypass the affective. The process of deciding what is bad or wrong involves affects, and indeed the affective dimension helps us to remember that norms are provisional decisions, which must remain open to being challenged (see Ahmed 1998: 51–8). The affective dimension to the normative sphere also helps remind us that actors involved in normative decision are embodied, and located in history, and that the rational does not transcend the emotional. See Benhabib (1992) and Young (1990), who in developing feminist critiques of communicative rationality, link the affective and normative.

3. As Patricia J. Williams puts it: 'We must get beyond the stage of halting conversations filled with the superficialities of hurt feelings and those "my maid says blacks are happy" or "whites are devils" moments' (Williams 1995: 24).

4. I have not had time to explore happiness as an emotion in any depth. See McGill (1967) for an excellent review of philosophical writings on happiness. See also Spaemann (2000) and Sumner (1996).

5. Nietzsche (1969) provides a powerful critique of the emotional logic of retribution as the desire for revenge. See also Brown (1995).

6. I have not explored forgiveness as an emotion in this book. For an analysis of forgiveness, which explores its ambivalent relation to virtue, see Murphy (1988). For an analysis of political forgiveness, which separates forgiveness from emotion and considers it as a speech act, see Digeser (2001). See also Minow (1998) who relates the question of forgiveness to historical injustice.

7. Indeed, heteronormativity could be reread as a narrative of restoration and injury. Many classic narratives depend on the drama of the 'break-up' of the traditional nuclear family and the 'hurt' of this break, which is often narrated as a form of personal injury as well as social loss. The story becomes restorative insofar as the family itself is restored as the 'condition' of happiness. Indeed, the experience of injury is often recuperated as enabling a better version of familial or romantic love.

Afterword: Emotions and Their Objects[1]

I am delighted to have the opportunity to reflect back on *The Cultural Politics of Emotion*. I wrote this book between 1999 and 2003, a period in which I was co-Director and then Director of the Institute for Women's Studies at Lancaster University, an experience that probably had more impact on some of the arguments I developed in the book than I realised at the time. All my scholarly writing up to and including *The Cultural Politics of Emotion* had been inspired by my participation in Women's Studies as an intellectual project and I have no doubt that many of my concerns in this book with questions of embodiment and difference were shaped by conversations I had at Lancaster. How the book took shape, through my own immersion in a feminist collective, is reflected in some of the arguments of the book about the complex, mediated and affective relation between bodies and worlds.

I did not begin this project with the aim of developing a theory of how emotions work. Rather I turned to emotion in order to explain how worlds are reproduced; in particular, I wanted to reflect on how social norms become affective over time. I originally thought of the project as a development of a feminist concern with how gender and sexuality become *investments*, or with what Judith Butler called 'the psychic life of power' (1997b). Following from my concern with 'stranger danger' in *Strange Encounters* (2000) I also wanted to explore how racism worked through emotions, but in such a way that did not psychologise racism by assuming emotions as psychological. When I began to read the vast interdisciplinary literatures on emotion (including not only the psychology of emotion, but also the sociology and anthropology of emotion, as well as philosophical literatures[2]), my attention was somewhat redirected. *The Cultural Politics of Emotion* represented a turning point in my own intellectual trajectory: it was doing the research for this book that reignited my interest in the history of ideas.[3] I became fascinated by the differences in how emotions had been thought, and began to appreciate how feminist theory in offering an approach to norms as investments could contribute to theories of emotion, as such.

I write this afterword to the second edition of *The Cultural Politics of Emotion* with two main aims: firstly, to explain how the book relates to some of the other key works in the emergent field of affect studies; and secondly, to show how the book formed part of my own intellectual trajectory – how the main arguments developed the insights of *Strange Encounters: Embodied Others in Post-Coloniality*, published in 2000, and were then subsequently developed in *The Promise of Happiness*, published in 2010. It was a most affective decade! When I returned to the book in 2013, in preparation for writing this afterword, I felt that the introduction did not give as much information to the reader as it might have done about how I arrived at this project. I now think of books themselves as stepping stones, ways of pausing on an intellectual journey, ways of gathering not only words and thoughts, but also ourselves, before we begin our travels again.

THE AFFECTIVE TURN

Since *The Cultural Politics of Emotion* was published, there have been many publications that have announced 'an affective turn', a declaration that often takes the form of simultaneously participating in the creation of what is being declared. It is worth noting the description 'affective turn' was already in use whilst I was writing this book: I first heard this expression from Anu Koivunen at a conference on 'Affective Encounters' that took place at Turku, Finland in September 2001. If at the time I did not explicitly think of the book as part of an affective turn, it nevertheless provided an important intellectual horizon for my own work. This affective turn has gathered momentum: numerous edited books and journals, as well as individual research monographs, have been published on affect and emotion, such that we have a witnessed the unfolding of a conversation in time.

In her preface to the book that came out of the conference mentioned above, *Affective Encounters: Rethinking Embodiment in Feminist Media Studies*, Anu Koivunen describes how 'in many disciplines, scholars have introduced affects, emotions and embodied experience as timely research topics' (2001: 1). In particular she notes how 'in feminist criticism, the interest in affect has in a sense a long history: the conceptual links between woman, body and emotion is a recurrent issue' (1). More recently, Ann Cvetkovich in *Depression: A Public Feeling* also refers to this long history as a reason for her reluctance to use the expression 'affective turn'. She explains: 'I have to confess I am somewhat reluctant to use the term *affective turn* because it implies that there is something new about the study of affect when in fact . . . this work has been going on for some time' (2012: 4, emphasis in original). Later when Cvetkovich reflects on feminism as 'an affective turn' she notes, again in a cautionary manner, that it 'doesn't seem particularly new to me' (8).

We could contrast these accounts of an affective turn as having a 'long history' within feminism with Michael Hardt's preface to Patricia Ticineto Clough's edited collection, *The Affective Turn*, published six years after Koivunen's preface in 2007. Hardt describes feminist approaches to the body and queer approaches to emotion as 'the two primary precursors to the affective turn' (2007: ix). For Hardt, 'A focus on affect certainly does draw attention to the body and emotions, but it also introduces an important shift' (ix). Hardt suggests that the turn to affect requires a different 'synthesis' than the study of the body and emotions because affects 'refer equally to the body and mind' and because they 'involve both reason and the passions' (ix).

When the affective turn becomes a turn to affect, feminist and queer work are no longer positioned as part of that turn. Even if they are acknowledged as precursors, a shift *to* affect signals a shift *from* this body of work.[4] Affect is given a privileged status in commentaries such as Hardt's, becoming almost like a missionary term that ushers in a new world, as a way of moving beyond an implied impasse, in which body and mind, and reason and passion, were treated as separate. I would like both to challenge this argument and to offer an alternative history. The implication of Hardt's framing is that we had to turn to affect (defined primarily in Deleuze's Spinozian terms) in order to show how mind is implicated in body; reason in passion. But feminist work on bodies and emotions *challenged from the outset* mind-body dualisms, as well as the distinction between reason and passion. It was this feminist work on emotion – key examples would include work by Alison Jaggar (1996), Elizabeth Spelman (1989), Sue Campbell (1994, 1997), Marilyn Frye (1983), Arlie Hochschild (1983), bell hooks (1989) and Audre Lorde (1984) – that provided the intellectual inspiration for *The Cultural Politics of Emotion*.[5] Feminist theories of emotion opened up a critical space to rethink the relation between mind and body; and much work in feminist theory (some of which is also explicitly engaged with philosophical debates about minds and bodies) did precisely the kind of work that Hardt seems to assume that affect as a concept was required in order to do.

In some hands, then, the affective turn is understood as a turn away from emotion. It has become clearer over time how scholars have become invested not only in affect as such, but in the gradual sharpening and refinement of a distinction between affect and emotion. We can detect this treatment of affect as other than or beyond emotion in Gregory Seigworth and Melissa Gregg's introduction to *The Affect Theory Reader*:

Affect, at its most anthropomorphic, is the name we give to those forces – visceral forces beneath, alongside, or generally *other than* conscious knowing, vital forces insisting *beyond* emotion – that can serve to drive us toward movement, toward thought and extension, that can likewise suspend us (as if in neutral) across a barely registering accretion of force-relations, or that can even leave us overwhelmed by the world's apparent intractability. (2010: 1, second emphasis added)

It is implied here that affect in taking us beyond conscious knowing and emotion is what allows movement, what enables us to go beyond a subject, even though an 'us' that is somehow attuned to vital force relations is given here in words.

The affective turn has thus come to privilege affect over emotion as its object, and considerable effort has been directed toward making affect into an object of study with clear boundaries, such that it now makes sense to speak of 'affect studies'. Scholars such as Brian Massumi (2002) have even described affects as having a 'different logic' than that of emotion, as pertaining to a different order. These two terms are not only treated as distinct but have, at least by some, come to be defined against each other. For Massumi, if affects are pre-personal and non-intentional, emotions are personal and intentional; if affects are unmediated and escape signification; emotions are mediated and contained by signification. Feminist ears might prick up at this point. A contrast between a mobile impersonal affect and a contained personal emotion suggests that the affect/emotion distinction can operate as a gendered distinction.[6] It might even be that the very use of this distinction performs the evacuation of certain styles of thought (we might think of these as 'touchy feely' styles of thought, including feminist and queer thought) from affect studies.

The Cultural Politics of Emotion challenges this use of this distinction between affect and emotion, although for the most part this challenge was indirect and implicit.[7] However, I took emotion as my starting point not as deliberate choice (in the other words, I did not choose emotion *over* affect in a conscious way) but because I thought of the book as in conversation with other work on emotion (especially but not only feminist literatures and work in queer studies on 'public emotions') and because emotion is the term used in everyday life to describe what I wanted to give an account of. Even though my own contribution took emotion rather than affect as my organising term or starting point I have sometimes been described as an 'affect theorist' (for example East 2013: 176). At other times, I have been read as not working on affect because I work with emotion. For example, Lauren Berlant in her introduction to *Cruel Optimism,* and in reference to my later book *The Promise of Happiness*, suggests that I am 'not really working on affect but emotion' (Berlant 2011: 12–13).[8]

I would suggest that my own attempt to re-theorise emotions includes analysis of those processes that some have used the term 'affect' to describe. Emotions, in other words, involve bodily processes of affecting and being affected, or to use my own terms, emotions are a matter of how we come into contact with objects and others. I was drawn from the outset to seventeenth-century philosophers of the passions, including Descartes and Locke as well as Spinoza:[9] however much they offer contrasting models, they all describe how a judgement of something can be a matter of how we are affected by that thing. Something might be judged as good if it affects us in a good way. As Susan James describes in her helpful study of passions in seventeenth-century philosophy, 'the evaluations of good and harm contained in passions directed to objects outside the mind are therefore not in the world, waiting to be read' (1997: 103). I turned to emotions as they help me to explain not only how we are affected in this way or that, by this or that, but also how those judgements then hold or become agreed as shared perceptions, though I was not then (and I am still not now) interested in distinguishing affect and emotion as if they refer to different aspects of experience. If anything, it was important for working through my argument not to assume or create separate spheres between consciousness and intentionality, on the one hand, and physiological or bodily reactions on the other (please note I am not sug-gesting that affect theorists assume this separation, but that the creation of a distinction between affect and emotion *can carry this implication*). Borrowing David Hume's[10] favoured word 'impressions', I wanted to explore not only how bodies are 'pressed' upon by other bodies, but how these presses become impressions, feelings that are suffused with ideas and values, however vague or blurry (in the sense of 'having an impression' of something).

We might note as well how the turn to affect, and the designating of affect as what moves us beyond emotion, allows the reduction of emotion to per-sonal or subjective feeling. It was precisely this model that I hoped to chal-lenge in *The Cultural Politics of Emotion*. As Rei Terada suggests in *Feeling in Theory*, 'Championing affect is not the best way to debunk the supposed connection between emotion and subjectivity, in other words, because pro-ponents of the subject are willing to compromise on affect' (2001: 7). Terada carefully explores how theorising emotion is one way of signalling the death of the subject. In *The Cultural Politics of Emotion*, I hoped to develop a model of emotion that involves subjects but is not reducible to them; drawing on psychoanalysis (probably more than I would if I was writing this book now), I wanted to show how emotions are not transparent; so much follows when we do not assume we always know how we feel, and that feelings do not belong or even originate with an 'I', and only then move out toward others.

When affect is used as a way of going beyond the perceived limitations of an intentional model of emotion, the emotions can be easily reduced to intentionality, as Ruth Leys (2011) has shown very persuasively in her critique of the turn to affect in critical theory. Phenomenology has certainly introduced the language of intentionality, and was a key influence on the development of my own model with its emphasis on objects.[11] A phenomenological model of emotions explores how emotions are directed toward objects. We feel fear *of* something. I will explore in due course how I attempted to rethink emotions through rethinking the status (and specifically the sociality) of their objects. But what I want to stress here is how showing that emotions are not simply about objects, or that they, to use a different but related language, involve cognitive appraisals of objects does not require introducing another term (such as affect) that belongs to a different order. In fact, it helps to use the same term. A great deal of phenomenological work has not been based on a description of cognition or even of consciousness as a consciousness of things, but on affectivity as receptivity, as we can see in Heidegger's work on mood, and in Husserl's work on passive synthesis.

Rather than turning to affect to explain how emotions move beyond subjects, I thus returned to emotion. Drawing on the etymology of the word, I became interested in emotions as how we are moved, as well as the implied relationship between movement and attachment, being moved *by* as a connection *to*. Following many other feminist theorists, I am deeply concerned with how in feeling a body is moved: who could even think of feeling without also recalling physical impressions: the sweatiness of skin, the hair rising; or the sound of one's heartbeat getting louder? I also wanted to explore how emotions do things in other ways; how to be affected by something is an orientation or direction toward that thing that has worldly effects.

The book thus brings together a concern with how we are affected *by* things with a more phenomenological concern with intentionality *about* things. To be affected by something, such that we move toward or away from that thing, is an orientation toward something.[12] It is in the intensity of bodily responses to worlds that we make judgements about worlds; and those judgements are directive even if they do not follow narrative rules of sequence, or cause and effect. Those judgements are enacted: they do not lead to actions; they *are* actions. For instance to feel hate towards another (to be affected by that other with hate such that the other is given the quality of being hateful) is to be moved in such a way that one moves away from that other, establishing corporeal distance, as my reading of Audre Lorde's powerful description of racism on the subway in New York City attempted to show. This is what I mean when I describe emotions as *doing things*. Emotions involve different movements towards and away from others, such that they shape the contours of social as well as bodily space. One of the reasons I took different emotions as points of entry was not because I presumed the existence of these as 'basic emotions'[13] but rather to explore how different emotions, once experienced, identified and named as such, involve different orientations toward objects and others. In other words, starting with different emotions was a way of exploring different aspects of experience: from physical sensations such as pain to declarations of shame as a national feeling.

My work thus explores the *messiness of the experiential*, how bodies unfold into worlds, and the *drama of contingency*, how we are touched by what comes near (Ahmed 2010: 22). Messiness is a good starting point for thinking with feeling: feelings are messy such that even if we regularly talk about having feelings, as if they are mine, they also often come at us, surprise us, leaving us cautious and bewildered. When experiences (human or otherwise) are messy, making distinctions that are clear can mean losing our capacity for description.[14] One problem with constantly refining our conceptual distinctions is that arguments can then end up being *about* those distinctions. I have never found intellectual conversations about definitions particularly inspiring in part as they often end up as self-referential, as being about the consistency or inconsistency of our own terms.

Of course, sometimes we need to make distinctions to make sense of the complexity of worlds; we often sort things out by separating things. Perhaps it would be useful to think of 'separate' as a verb rather than noun. We have to separate elements when they are not separate, even if they are separable. The activity of separating affect from emotion could be understood as rather like breaking an egg in order to separate the yolk from the white. We can separate different parts of a thing even if they are contiguous, even if they are, as it were, in a sticky relation. We might have different methods for performing the action of separation. But we have to separate the yolk from the white *because* they are not separate. And sometimes we 'do do' what we 'can do' because separating these elements, not only by treating them as separable but by modifying their existing relation, or how they exist in relation, allows us to do other things that we might not otherwise be able to do. That we *can* separate them does not mean they *are* separate. Given that it was the contiguity between different aspects of experience (sensation, thought, feeling, judgement), how they stick together that I was trying to explore, without assuming the subject as the origin of this coherence, it did not make sense to proceed by separating affect from emotion. I recognise, however, that there are other ways of proceeding.

In order to explore further how my original argument developed, I will now draw on two examples. I hope to show how as well as why *The Cultural Politics of Emotion* was concerned with articulating not only a different approach to how emotions work as a form of cultural politics (beyond thinking of emotion as rhetorical instruments that can be used to bind people together, which is not to say emotions are not used in this way) but an alternative approach to the *sociality of emotion*, focusing on the circulation of objects, rather than the circulation of affects, as such.

STRANGER DANGER

It was following the figure of the stranger that led me on the path to writing *The Cultural Politics of Emotion*. In my earlier book *Strange Encounters* I explored how the stranger as a figure appears through the very acquisition of a charge.[15] The stranger, we might assume, is anybody we do not know. I became interested in the techniques (we might think of these as bodily as well as disciplinary techniques) whereby some bodies are recognised *as* strangers, as bodies out of place, as not belonging in certain places. These techniques are formalised in Neighbourhood Watch or in discourses of child protection, in which the stranger is the one who the citizen/child must recognise in order to protect themselves (their property, their bodies). Recognising strangers becomes a moral and social injunction. Indeed, *The Cultural Politics of Emotion* explored how this injunction is extended as a national project: citizens are called to defend national borders against those who are suspicious, who 'could be terrorists'.

Rather than the stranger being anyone we do not recognise, *some bodies are recognised as strangers*, as bodies out of place. To recognise somebody as a stranger is an affective judgement: a stranger is the one who seems suspicious; the one who lurks. I became interested in how some bodies are 'in an instant' judged as suspicious, or as dangerous, as objects to be feared, a judgement that can have lethal consequences. There can be nothing more dangerous to a body than the social agreement that *that* body is dangerous.

There are so many cases, too many cases. Just take one: Trayvon Martin, a young black man fatally shot by George Zimmerman on 26 February 2012. Zimmerman was centrally involved in his Neighbourhood Watch programme. He was doing his civic neighbourly duty: looking out for what is suspicious. As George Yancy has noted in his important piece, 'Walking While Black', we learn from Zimmerman's call to the dispatcher how Trayvon Martin appeared to him. Zimmerman says:

> 'There's a real suspicious guy.' He also said 'This guy looks like he's
> up to no good or he's on drugs or something.' When asked by the
> dispatcher, he said, within seconds, that, 'He looks black.' Asked what
> he is wearing, Zimmerman says, 'A dark hoodie, like a gray hoodie.'
> Later, Zimmerman said that 'now he's coming toward me. He's got his
> hands in his waist band.' And then, 'And he's a black male.' (Yancy
> 2013: n.p.)

Note the sticky slide: suspicious, 'up to no good', coming at me, looking black, a dark hoodie, wearing black, being black. The last statement makes explicit *who* Zimmerman was seeing right from the very beginning. That he was seeing a Black man was already implied in the first description 'a real suspicious guy'. Let me repeat: there can be nothing more dangerous to a body than the social agreement that *that* body is dangerous. And later, when Zimmerman is not convicted, there is a retrospective agreement with that agreement: that Zimmerman was right to feel fear, that his murder of this young man was self-defence because Trayvon was dangerous, because he was, as Yancy describes so powerfully, 'walking while black', already judged, sentenced to death, by the how of how he appeared as a Black man to the white gaze.

The stranger is a dark shadowy figure. I use the word 'darkness' deliberately here: it is a word that cannot be untangled from a racialised history. To use this word as if it can be disentangled from that history is to be entangled by that history.[16] The racialisation of the stranger is not immediately apparent – it is disguised, we might say, by the strict anonymity of the stranger, the one who after all, we are told from childhood, could be anyone. We witness from this example how this 'could be anyone' is *pointed*: the stranger as a figure points to some bodies more than others. This 'could be anyone' thus only appears as an open possibility, stretching out into a horizon, in which the stranger reappears as the one who is always lurking in the shadows. Frantz Fanon (1986) taught us to watch out for what lurks, seeing himself *in* and *as* the shadow, the dark body, always passing by, at the edge of social experience.

To explore how bodies are perceived as dangerous *in advance of their arrival* requires not beginning with an encounter (a body affected by another body) but asking how encounters come to happen in this way or that. The immediacy of bodily reactions is mediated by histories that come before subjects, and which are at stake in how the very arrival of some bodies is noticeable in the first place. The most immediate of our bodily reactions can thus be treated as pedagogy: we learn about ideas by learning how they become quick and unthinking. Somewhat ironically, perhaps, there is nothing more mediated than immediacy.

In the conscious recognition of a feeling as a feeling, all sorts of complicated and messy processes are at stake, not all of which are revealed or available to consciousness; it is these complicated processes that I hoped to explore. This is not to say that every time a body responds fearfully, all of these processes are always at stake; but it is to say that the careers of feelings are not independent of the careers of their objects, which is how just thinking of a feeling can bring up certain objects (in thinking of fear, an object might be what comes to mind); or how thinking of an object can just bring up certain feelings. To think of emotions as a cultural politics is to attend to *what comes up*.

Learning to understand how the figure of the stranger 'comes up' returns us with a difference to affect studies. As I noted in my original introduction, a key aspect in the history of thought on emotion is that emotions not only have an evolutionary function but are this function. Fear is probably one of the emotions that has most been thought in these terms: fear as the body in flight, fear as a way of signalling to the body that there is danger.[17] In the work of neuroscientists such as Antonio Damasio, whose work has been quite influential in affect studies, we can see the function of this model of fear as function. In his account of feelings and emotions in *The Feeling of What Happens* (2003), Damasio talks explicitly about suspicion. He refers to the case of patient S who suffers from amygdala damage, alongside other unnamed cases. He then discusses the findings of an experiment where patients are required to look at faces and make judgements about them.[18] It seems that when patients have amygdala damage, then the person does not feel suspicious when they should feel suspicious, that is, when they don't feel suspicious about faces that are suspicious:

> when they looked at faces of which you and I would be suspicious,
> faces of persons that we would try to avoid, they judged them
> as equally trustworthy . . . The inability to make sound social
> judgements, based on previous experience, of situations that are or
> are not conducive to one's welfare has important consequences for
> those who are so affected. Immersed in a secure Pollyanna world,
> those individuals cannot protect themselves against simple and
> not-so-simple social risks, and are thus more vulnerable and more
> independent than we are. Their life histories testify to the chronic
> impairment as much as they testify to the paramount importance of
> emotion in the governance of not just simple creatures but of humans
> as well. (2003: 67)

We can see here the problem with not offering a theory of mediation at the level of the object: it is assumed that certain faces are suspicious, as if that is an inherent quality of the faces, such that there is an error of judgement if the patient is not affected rightly; if they do not feel suspicious. Daniel M. Gross comments rather wryly in *The Secret History of Emotions*, 'you don't have to be a classical humanist or critical race theorist to find all this a bit unsettling' (2006: 31). He expands: 'It is no accident that trustworthiness gets stripped of its essentially social quality' (32). Ruth Leys is also critical of this same passage in similar terms. She notes that 'the concepts of "trustworthiness" and "untrustworthiness" have been stripped of all context in order to treat these traits as objective, identifiable features of persons that are immediately and universally and unambiguously readable in the human face' (2012b: 75).[19]

It is the absence of a social understanding that leads to affects being understood as both intrinsic to subjects (who if they are not suspicious, are lacking something) and objects (that are suspicious). What we might conclude instead is that over time, in a set of processes that might bypass conscious recognition (and are all the more affective *given* this bypassing), some objects (and an object can be anything that a feeling is directed toward) become suspicious, such that affect almost comes to reside as a quality of this or that object. Once an affective quality has come to reside in something, it is often assumed as without history. We need to give this residence a history. One of Michel Foucault's definitions of genealogy was precisely this: a way of recording what 'we tend to feel is without history' (1997: 39), which would, we might add, include a history of the felt. When we are affected by those things in the right way, there is a confirmation that is not often registered as such. Emotions that are apparently universal and innate (that are necessary for either human welfare or wellbeing) are thus directed in certain ways, such that when feelings 'agree' with this direction, they become background. We tend to notice emotions that are in disagreement and to represent them as the origin of danger (stranger danger is then translated into: the danger of not recognising strangers). Indeed, what has been described as automatic describes the effects of a set of techniques, which have become habits, directing bodily matter as well as how things matter.

It is also worth noting how Silvan S. Tomkins' monumental volumes on affect also exercise the figure of the stranger. This fact is picked up by Eve Kosofsky Sedgwick and Adam Frank in their introduction to Tomkins' work: 'The emphasis in this account on the *strange*', they suggest points both away from the repressive hypothesis and toward a 'phenomenology of shame' (1995: 5, emphasis in original). If we return to Tomkins' writing, we find that the figure of the stranger is rather fraught, even ambivalent, and might allow us to explore the gap between his model of affect as a universal and biological program that functions independently of cognition and culture (or at least can function independently), and his actual examples and observations on children and parenting. In some instances, Tomkins refers to responses to strangers as 'almost universal innate'. This 'almost' can be read as a qualification of an argument that nevertheless allows that argument to be made. Tomkins suggests that the recognition of strangers works as a differentiation: the face of the mother is differentiated from the face of the stranger (by implication, here, the stranger is not-mother), or in the case of children brought up in orphanages, the differentiation is between the familiar and the unfamiliar (by implication the stranger is an automatic registering of the not familiar). We are close to the usual sense of the stranger as anyone we do not know.

The argument that this differentiation is 'almost innate' sits uncomfortably with the emphasis throughout on the considerable effort of parents to teach the child how to respond to strangers. Indeed the implication is that the child's curiosity about strangers must be dampened by affective training: the child is taught for example 'that it is impolite to stare earnestly at the face of the stranger' (327). I will return to this idea of 'affective training' in the following section. Tomkins notes: 'The child who is burning with excitement to explore the face of the stranger is nonetheless vulnerable to shame just because the other is perceived as strange' (627). The stranger is not simply someone we don't know but someone who is perceived *as* strange. Tomkins in his emphasis on the role of scripts in affective life shows how cognition and affect are entangled. But affect scripts work only to contain and to manage affects that are themselves unlearned: he can thus argue that one does not learn to be afraid in the same way one does not learn the pain of hunger (12). He then argues that one can learn to be afraid of anything. The affect 'fear' in other words can become attached to anything. I would argue that the (however provisional) separation of an affect such as fear from the objects to which it becomes attached could lead to an underdescription of how learning works through the body. You learn to fear by learning what to fear. What Tomkins's own arguments about the strange and the stranger imply for me is that scripts not only manage or contain the affects, they generate them. The child must be affected by strangers in the right way, one that is deemed necessary for their survival (and well-being or even happiness as I will discuss in due course), a learning that if successful creates fear. It is in this sense that it can make sense to say that affects are learned; learning is precisely how being affected is being directed.

I find Silvan S. Tomkins's work useful at the level of description probably because his descriptions push against his own model. We end up with a set of descriptions of the techniques for differentiating between classes of beings in terms of how then enable or threaten individual or social welfare and wellbeing. Racism is one such affective technique. The encounters I discussed, such as those offered by Frantz Fanon and Audre Lorde, are bodily and intercorporeal encounters that take place on trains and subways – those intense spaces of transitory sociality. But it is important to note that if some bodies become containers of affect, these containers spill. As I tried to show, it is the possibility that fear is not contained by an object that makes fear all the more frightening. The very perception of others is thus an impression of others, in which to appear as other or stranger is to be blurred. I have since described racism as a blunt instrument, which is another way of making the same argument (Ahmed 2012: 181). Stop and search, for example, is a technology that makes this bluntness into a point: Stop! You are brown! You could be Muslim! You could be a terrorist! The blurrier the figure of the stranger *the more bodies can be caught by it.*

Given my focus on intercorporeality and what I called in my earlier book *Strange Encounters* 'economies of touch', how we are touched differently by different others, it is worth explaining why in *The Cultural Politics of Emotion* I not only focused on texts, but framed the argument in terms of 'the emotionality of texts'. I placed a strong focus on language in part at least, as I wanted to intervene in some of the debates about hate speech (Chapter 2) and because I was interested in the role of speech acts such as apologies in staging a relation to traumatic histories (Chapter 5). I focused on language *because* I was interested in bodies. I wanted to explore, following Fanon, how a body can become a sign, a sign of danger for instance; these judgements of the body work precisely because they are affective. So although I did emphasise the significance of how words become sticky, I stressed how feelings are directed towards certain bodies; how feelings stick to those bodies in everyday encounters, or what I previously called 'strange encounters' between embodied others.[20]

I think it is important as well that the focus on texts is at once a focus on materials that derive from experiences, whether it was Audre Lorde and Frantz Fanon's experiences of racism, or materials gathered that documented the violence against Indigenous peoples in Australia, or the materials that treated others as disgusting in response to events such as September 11th. I think on reflection that I was responding to the possibility that a critique of the psychology of emotion (that emotions are mine, that they belong to me) could lead to a presumption that the feelings of others could be accessed directly: that if my feelings are not mine, hers are also not hers. Such implied claims to access the feelings of others would amount to a repetition of violence, a way of emptying the place of others by assuming that place. It is noteworthy for example that Saidiya Hartman in her extraordinary work on the archives of slavery foregrounds the opacity of the materials. She describes her task as 'to give full weight to the opacity of these texts wrought by toil, terror and sorrow' (1997: 35–6). We could think as well of Gayatri Chakravorty Spivak's (1995) important work on translation and subalternity with its emphasis on the politics of secrets: translations are important for what they do not and cannot reveal. Both Hartman and Spivak show how concealment can be a form of resistance.

It is important not to assume the equivalence between texts and the histories they keep alive. But whatever methods we use, whether we read documents that already exist in the public domain, as memory traces of histories that are with us, or whether we conduct interviews (including with those for whom these histories are constantly in front, as what is being confronted), or do ethnography, this opacity is not something we can overcome. I remain firmly committed to this viewpoint. Since the publication of the first edition of *The Cultural Politics of Emotion*, I have myself engaged in ethnographic research on diversity work, a project which led to a book, *On Being Included:*

Racism and Diversity in Institutional Life (2012). Even if *The Cultural Politics of Emotion* did not draw on qualitative research, it became a useful tool for this subsequent research, allowing me to explore how emotions can work in practice by circulating through words and figures and by sticking to bodies.

Through the study I began to appreciate how the charged figure of the stranger is one we encounter in the room, as a way of encountering how you might appear to others. The charged figure of stranger might even be 'in the room' *before* a body enters that room. When you are caught up in its appearance, emotions become work: you have to manage your own body by not fulfilling an expectation. Let me share with you two quotes from the study. Let me share with you two quotes from interviews with black male diversity trainers:

> The other point as well about being a black trainer is that I've got
> to rapport build. Do I do that by being a member of the black and
> white minstrel show or do I do that by trying to earn respect with my
> knowledge? Do I do it by being friendly or do I do it by being cold,
> aloof and detached? And what does all this mean to the people now?
> From my point of view, it probably has nothing to do with the set of
> people that are in that room because actually the stereotype they've got
> in their heads is well and truly fixed. (Ahmed 2012: 160)

Building rapport becomes a requirement because of a stereotype, as that which is fixed, no matter who you encounter. The demand to build rapport takes the form of a perpetual self-questioning; the emotional labour of asking yourself what to do when there is an idea of you that persists, no matter what you do. Indeed, the consequences of racism are in part managed as a question of self-presentation: of trying not to fulfil a stereotype:

> Don't give white people nasty looks straight in their eyes; don't show
> them aggressive body positions. I mean, for example I am going to
> go and buy a pair of glasses because I know the glasses soften my face
> and I keep my hair short because I'm going bald, so I need something
> to soften my face. But actually what I am doing, I am countering a
> stereotype, I'm countering the black male sexual stereotype and yes,
> I spend all my time, I counter that stereotype, I couch my language
> behaviour and tone in as English a tone as I can. I am very careful, just
> very careful. (Ahmed 2012: 160)

Being careful is about softening the very form of your appearance so that you do not appear 'aggressive' because you are already assumed to be aggressive before you appear. The demand not to be aggressive might be lived as a form of body-politics, or as a speech politics: you have to be careful what you say, how you appear, in order to maximise the distance between you and their idea of you, which is at once how you are the cause of fear ('the black male sexual stereotype'). The *encounter* with racism is experienced as the intimate labour of *countering* their idea of you. The experience of being a stranger in the institutions of whiteness is an experience of being on perpetual guard: of having to defend yourself against those who perceive you as somebody to be defended against. Once a figure is charged, it appears not only outside but *before* the body it is assigned to. This is how, for some, to arrive is to receive a charge.

Institutions too can create strangers; bodies out of place, or not in the right place, those who come to embody diversity. Diversity work is not only the work we do when we aim to transform the norms of the institution, but the work we do when we not quite inhabit those norms. This work can require working on one's own body in an effort to be accommodating. The effort to rearrange your own body becomes an effort to rearrange the past. This past is not only difficult to budge, but it is often what those, to whom you appear, do not recognise as present.

HAPPY OBJECTS

My focus on the sociality of emotions in this book described objects rather than feelings themselves as what circulates for a number of related reasons. One of the primary models of the sociality of affect is contagion (see Izard 1977; Sedgwick 2003),[21] which can be related to what Teresa Brennan (2004) was to describe as 'transmission' in a book published the same year as *The Cultural Politics of Emotion*. Whilst I have no doubt that affects can and do pass between bodies, I was concerned that these models tended to assume they pass rather smoothly. Social feeling is thus implicitly understood as shared feeling such that if shame is contagious we are both caught up by shame. The sociality of emotion, for me, can also refer to the situations in which we feel quite differently; when we do not even share a feeling though something is shared (it might even be a disagreement). We do not, as I pointed out in my original introduction, even feel the same way about an atmosphere, or even feel an atmosphere in the same way, even when or if the atmosphere can be something that we are 'in', like being in air made thick by smog.[22] It was probably the fact that I was writing the book whilst being head of a Women's Studies programme (one that was struggling just to exist), and of being 'the feminist at the table', that made me attuned to how social experience involves tension, disagreement and perversion.

Rather than focusing on feeling as circulating between bodies, I thus attended to objects: objects which circulate accumulate affective value. An object of fear (the stranger's body as a phobic object of instance) becomes shared over time, such that the object, in moving around, can generate fear in the bodies of those who apprehend it. Fear does then 'in effect' move around through being directed toward objects. It remains possible that bodies are not affected in this way; for example, someone might not be suspicious of a body that has over time been agreed to be suspicious (there is nothing more affective, as I have already implied, than an agreement, precisely because what is in agreement does not tend to be registered by consciousness[23]).

Of course there is so much left out from this analysis: including a more precise description of the mechanisms whereby some feelings pass through objects; and others do not. I want to explore in this section how thinking through positive affects and emotions such as happiness might allow us to think more explicitly about these mechanisms. *The Cultural Politics of Emotion* offered a model of 'affective economies' primarily through working with emotions that are regarded as negative, such as hate and fear (see Chapters 2 and 3).[24] What might be useful is to explore the role of feeling in making things good and bad, in other words, to explore the relationship between affective and moral economies.

We are now ready to turn to the question of happiness, which has only relatively recently (from the eighteenth century onwards) been thought of in affective terms, as an emotion or good feeling. Working on the idea of happiness in *The Promise of Happiness* (2010) helped me develop an argument that was implied in *The Cultural Politics of Emotion*: feelings in being directed toward objects *become directive*. We might note for instance how some of the models of affect discussed in the previous section are framed in terms of whether objects threaten or support human survival and/or human wellbeing or happiness. To be affected, I have suggested, establishes relations of proximity and distance between bodies. We might aim to be proximate to what is judged to bring happiness; at a distance from what is judged to compromise happiness. Happiness after all has often been thought of as an end point, as the aim of life or as what makes a life good.

This idea of happiness as the end of life is central to quite different intellectual traditions, from classical thought (happiness as *eudemonia*) to utilitarianism, even if happiness is thought quite differently in each of these traditions. An object of emotion can simultaneously be an end. Many have reflected upon the significance of happiness as an end point or *telos*. But we can explore the significance of this idea of happiness for other things: some things become good as happiness-means, as what we might do, or what we might have, to reach happiness. Certain things become good *because they point toward happiness*.

All sorts of consequences follow this most simple of observations. Firstly, some things can become associated with happiness before they are even encountered (as things that are necessary for a good life). Just think of the wedding day, which is often described as 'the happiest day of your life', before it happens, which might be *how* it happens. We can thus anticipate an affect without being retrospective: objects acquire the value of proximities that are not derived from our own experience. The example of stranger danger also taught us this. Some things are encountered as 'to-be-feared' before they arrive.[25] We can also anticipate that an object will cause happiness in advance of its arrival; the object becomes available within a horizon of possibility because it has already been given positive affect. The judgement that some things are good not only precedes our encounter with things, but directs us toward those things. Even if happiness appears to point forward, it can thus depend on histories of associations that have become 'sticky', to use the term I employed in *The Cultural Politics of Emotion*. Certain objects are attributed as the cause of happiness, which means they already circulate as social goods before we 'happen' upon them, which is why we might happen upon them in the first place.

We can call these objects 'happy objects'. When happy objects circulate, it is not necessarily the feeling that passes. In her classic book, *The Managed Heart*, Arlie Hochschild explores emotional labour, the work that is done to narrow the gap between who one does feel and how one should feel. One of her examples is the bride who does not feel happy on the wedding day, that is, she is not affected happily on the day that is meant to be happiest. If the bride is not happy on the wedding day and even feels 'depressed and upset' then she is experiencing an 'inappropriate affect' (2003: 59), or is being affected inappropriately. She has to save the day by feeling right: 'Sensing a gap between the ideal feeling and the actual feeling she tolerated, the bride prompts herself to be happy' (61). The capacity to 'save the day' depends on the bride being able to persuade herself to be affected in the right way or at least being able to persuade others that she is being affected in the right way. To correct feelings is to become disaffected from a former affectation: the bride makes herself happy by stopping herself being miserable. We also learn from this example that it is possible not to inhabit fully one's own happiness, or even to be alienated from one's happiness, if the former affection remains lively, or if one is made uneasy by the labour of making oneself feel a certain way. Uneasiness might persist in the very feeling of being happy, as a feeling of unease *with* the happiness you are in.

Once you have closed the gap between how you do feel and how you should feel, the happiness of a situation would be preserved. The experience of this gap, however, does not always lead to corrections that close this gap. We might be disappointed if we do not achieve the happiness expected. Disappointment can also involve an anxious narrative of self-doubt (why I am not made happy by this, what is wrong with me?), or a narrative of rage, where the object that is supposed to make us happy is attributed as the cause of disappointment. Your rage might be directed against the object that fails to deliver its promise, or spill out towards those who promised you happiness through the elevation of some things as good. We become strangers, or what I call 'affect aliens', in such moments.

Thinking through happiness allows me to reflect in another way on the charged nature of the figure of stranger. It is worth noting here that within the specific field of 'happiness studies' there has been a strong emphasis on contagion as an explanation of how happiness works. For example, James H. Fowler and Nicholas A. Christakis's study published in the *BMJ* in 2008 (which was very widely reported in the global media under the heading 'happiness is contagious' in December 2008) examines how happiness can spread from person to person within social networks, creating 'clusters of happy and unhappy people' (2008: 1). In their analysis of happiness distributions, they suggest that 'people at the core of their local networks seem more likely to be happy, while those on the periphery seem more likely to be unhappy' (6). The happiness of the centre is presumed to be a sign that happy people are drawn to each other. The authors of the study admit that the data does not allow them to make conclusions about the causal mechanisms behind happiness clusters. They speculate that happy people might 'share their good fortune', or 'change their behavior towards others' or 'merely exude an emotion that is genuinely contagious'. In an interview about this research, Fowler and Christakis evoke for us an image of a party: 'Imagine a birds-eye view of a party: "You may see some people in quiet corners talking one-on-one," Fowler says. Others would be at the center of the room having conversations with lots of people. According to the study findings, those in the center would be among the happiest.'[26] What is noticeable here is how the happiness map 'maps' onto other kinds of maps: the edges, here narrated as 'quiet corners', are presumed to be less happy.

One way to think through how emotions are involved in the creation of edges that are nevertheless populated by bodies is to take up the question of 'attunement', which has become another key term in affect studies. Attunements are often related to moods, which have been understood as distinct from emotions insofar as they have less distinct objects.[27] Rene Rosfort and Giovanni Stanghellini for example suggest moods 'attend to the world as a whole, not focusing on any particular object or situation' (2009: 208). Martin Heidegger's discussion of mood or attunement (*Stimmung*) might help us to think through attunements as a form of sociability. For Heidegger a mood is not something specific that belongs to me first; it is *not* possible *not* to be in a mood. Mood or attunement 'makes manifest "how one is and coming along"' (1995: 127). He further specifies:

A human being who – as we say – is in good humour brings a lively atmosphere with them. Do they, in so doing, being about an emotional experience which is then transmitted to others, in the manner in which infectious germs wander back and form from one organism to another? We do indeed say that attunement or mood is infectious. Or another human being is with us, someone who through their manner of being makes everything depressing and puts a dampener on everything; no-body steps out of their shell. What does this tell us? Attunements are *not side-effects*, but are which in advance determine our being with one another. It seems as though attunement is in each case already there, so to speak, like an atmosphere in which we first immerse ourselves in each case and which then attunes us through and through. (1995: 66–7)[28]

A mood is thus rather like an atmosphere: it is not that we catch a feeling from another person but that we are caught up in feelings that are not our own. Note the implication here that an atmosphere is what is with someone, or around them; if a body might bring a lively atmosphere *with* them, that situation becomes lively. If an atmosphere is around, it is still generated by those who are around, becoming something that can be 'put down' as well as 'picked up' by others. Heidegger does consider what he calls the 'lack of attunement'. He says of this lack: 'in which we are neither out of sorts nor in a "good" mood' (1995: 68). By implication a lack of attunement is a mood that is neither bad nor good. What is this lack? It is here that Heidegger seems almost to stumble or fall over: a lack of attunement is 'seemingly hard to grasp', such that it 'seems to be something apathetic and indifferent' and yet it is 'not like this at all'. And then he adds: 'There is only ever a change of attunement' (1995: 68). Heidegger is not able to say what a lack of attunement is other than what it is not. Perhaps one consequence of the argument that attunement is fundamental is that a lack of attunement becomes hard to register.

Attunement might register *that* we are affected by what is around, but it does necessarily decide *how* we are affected. Max Scheler in *The Nature of Sympathy* suggests that 'infection' has been assumed too quickly as the mechanism for how feelings become sociable (2008: 15–17). Max Scheler does not argue that infection does not happen: he notes how we might enter a situation in hope that we will be infected by good humour, or how we might avoid a situation in fear of being infected by bad humour. It is given this possibility of infection that feelings become consciously regulated. Scheler differentiates infection from 'communities of feeling' when we both experience a feeling in relation to an object that is shared: we might both be sad because we have lost someone we loved (2008: 12). He also introduces a class of social emotions called 'fellow feeling' in which one person shares the feeling of another person, but not the object of their feeling (2008: 13): in the case of when we are both sad because you have lost someone I did not know, my sadness refers to your sadness; I am sad because you are sad.

Fellow feeling can be experienced as crisis: you might be made happy by another person's happiness, but not be made happy by what makes them happy. A crisis might be *how objects matter*. It is through crisis that an object of feeling becomes more clear or distinct. Attunements are not always or only happy: we can be attuned in moments of sadness. To be attuned in sadness might still be experienced happily; you might experience a sense of harmony that one wants to persist in the face of what does not persist. In sad moments, when the sadness is shared, we might fear that we will laugh, or speak or act in a way that breaks the precarious solemnity of the attunement. What happens when one is attuned to happiness and one loses this attunement? I might enter a situation that is cheerful, and 'pick up' that good cheer in becoming cheerful, without reference to anything, only to realise that this is not a situation I would find cheerful. Say people are laughing at a joke. I might start laughing too; perhaps I start laughing before I hear the joke. When we are laughing, we are facing each other; our bodies are mirroring each other. I might hear the joke, and when I register what has been said, I might find that I do not it funny, or even that I find it offensive. When I hear the joke, it becomes a crisis; I might hear it even more clearly and distinctly. To find this joke offensive would not only be to lose my good cheer, but to become affectively 'out of tune' with others. If I stop laughing, I withdraw from a bodily intimacy. I might break that intimacy; it can shatter like a jug. I might be left having to pick up the pieces. Sometimes we keep laughing because we fear causing a breakage. Or if we stop laughing, we might experience the loss of attunement as rage or shame, a feeling that I can direct towards myself (how did I let myself be caught up by this?).

We learn from this loss of attunement about the nature of attunement. To be attuned to each other is not only to share in emotions (good or bad, lively or unlively), or to share an orientation toward objects (as being good or bad), but to share leanings. Attunement is not exhaustive: to be attuned to some bodies might simultaneously mean not to be attuned to others, those who do not share our leanings. We can close off our bodies as well as ears to what is not in tune. An experience of *non-attunement* refers then to how we can be in a world with others when we are not in a responsive relation: we do not tend to 'pick up' on how they feel. This sense of not being in harmony might not even register to consciousness. A happy or cheerful mood might be shared by turning away from, or screening out, what or who would compromise that mood. When this screening is *not* successful, those bodies (and the moods they might bring with them) become registered as what or who causes the loss of attunement. Attunement might create strangers not necessarily or only by making the stranger into an object of feeling but as the effect of not leaning that way. No wonder strangers seem to appear at the edges of a room, dimly perceived, or not quite perceived, lurking in the shadows, those quiet corners where the unhappy ones are assumed to reside. No wonder a stranger is a rather vague impression. If in *The Cultural Politics of Emotion*, I focused on how to feel *with* is to feel *about* (both editions, 41), I am now suggesting feeling can be *about with*, and thus also about *not with*.

For those deemed strangers, for those whose arrival is noticeable, who are registered dimly as those we are not with, attunement requires emotional labour: you have to work to be attuned to those who are already 'in the room', perhaps by closing a (perceived) gap between how they feel and how you feel. There has been a considerable attention to rooms as *affective containers* within scholarship and activism by feminists of colour (even if this attention has not been expressed in quite these terms). Listen to this description from bell hooks of what happens when a woman of colour enters a feminist room:

> A group of white feminist activists who do not know one another may
> be present at a meeting to discuss feminist theory. They may feel
> bonded on the basis of shared womanhood, but the atmosphere will
> noticeably change when a woman of color enters the room. The white
> women will become tense, no longer relaxed, no longer celebratory.
> (56)

In this example, bell hooks shows how meetings can be full of light and cheerful mood because of who is there, and who is not there, which provides content for discussion (bonding over shared womanhood). A woman of colour can just enter the room and the atmosphere becomes tense. Not to cause tension would require working to make others comfortable with the very fact of your arrival. I explored in my chapter, 'Queer Feelings', how comfort is a feeling that tends not to be consciously felt. Those who do not sink into spaces, whose bodies are registered as not fitting, often have to work to make others comfortable. Much of what I have called earlier 'diversity work' is thus emotional work.

It follows that if happiness is assumed as a good thing, and some things are made into goods by being associated with happiness, then those who are not made happy by these things are not only alienated by virtue of their affections but become those who alienate others. The affect alien is thus often a killjoy: the one who gets in the way of the happiness of others or, more simply, the one gets in the way. I have found in the rather animated figure of the killjoy, or to be more specific, the feminist killjoy (as well as the angry woman of colour as the killer of feminist joy) a certain kind of political potential and energy. To be willing to become a killjoy, to be willing to accept this assignment, is to be willing to get in the way of any happiness that does not have your agreement.

From the figure of the killjoy, we learn more about the sociality of emotion. It is not simply that feelings pass from one body to another. Some feelings are blocked (or there is an attempt to block their transmission) if the expression of those feelings would challenge the rights of others to occupy spaces. After all, as I explored in my chapter on feminist attachments, some anger is not well-received. Indeed, some bodies are treated as blockage points: where the smooth transmission of communication stops. Rather than assuming feelings pass smoothly from one to another, we need to give an account of the mechanisms which explain *how some feelings do not pass*. Some feelings might not pass if we do not agree with them (which is not to say that feelings do not pass around that do not have our agreement). I might be enraged by your happiness, if I feel it is inappropriate, or I might, in feeling happy, avoid you, in fear your sadness would get in the way of my happiness.

The means by which emotions flow or are blocked take us back to fundamental social and political questions about how spaces are organised around certain bodies. If certain bodies come first, then their happiness comes first. We can thus re-describe citizenship as a technology for deciding whose happiness comes first.

CONCLUSION: EMOTION AND RHETORIC

In *The Cultural Politics of Emotion* I developed my arguments primarily through a reading of texts, including what we would conventionally call 'rhetoric'. I want in concluding this afterword to show how my examples of stranger danger and happiness can also help us with an analysis of political rhetoric. What does it do to declare national danger or national happiness? *The Cultural Politics of Emotion* explored how multiculturalism becomes an injunction that the 'would-be' or 'could-be' citizens must love the nation and its values (law, liberty, tolerance, democracy, modernity, diversity and equality – all these terms are presented as if they are attributes of a national body). The national body can then appear to love diversity *at the very same time* as requiring those who embody diversity to give their allegiance to its body. Note how multiculturalism appears to make belief into the primary bond, and thus appears to separate nation from race: you can become part of the nation if you share these beliefs.

Today this idea of a loving multiculturalism seems far removed from political vocabularies regularly exercised across Europe. Multiculturalism has itself been sentenced to death: as if the act of welcoming diverse others endangered the security and well-being of the nation. When the British

Prime Minister David Cameron called for a 'muscular liberalism' in 2011, echoing and echoed by other political leaders, we could witness a narrowing of the gap between mainstream and fascist uses of political love. It is *out of love*, according to Cameron, that we must exercise our muscles; that we must stand up against those who have stopped us from standing up, those forms of political correctness, that have prevented us from defending our values and beliefs.[29] And here Cameron re-attaches beliefs quite explicitly to race: 'When a white person holds objectionable views, racist views for instance, we rightly condemn them. But when equally unacceptable views or practices come from someone who isn't white, we've been too cautious frankly – frankly, even fearful – to stand up to them.' Racism becomes understood as something that is 'rightly' condemned. But the immediate implication is that the tendency to condemn racism in white people is the same tendency as the one that does not object to what is unacceptable in 'someone who isn't white'.

The speech carefully creates the impression that racism in white culture is not acceptable (it is this very idea that participates in *obscuring the very ordinary nature of acceptable racism*) whilst implying again that 'our tolerance' of others has stopped those others from being more tolerable, more acceptable in terms of their beliefs. This nervous white subject who is unable to stand up to the non-white others then becomes a national subject:

> A passively tolerant society says to its citizens, as long as you obey the law we will just leave you alone. It stands neutral between different values. But I believe a genuinely liberal country does much more; it believes in certain values and actively promotes them. Freedom of speech, freedom of worship, democracy, the rule of law, equal rights regardless of race, sex or sexuality. It says to its citizens, this is what defines us as a society: to belong here is to believe in these things.
> Now, each of us in our own countries, I believe, must be unambiguous and hard-nosed about this defence of our liberty.

A muscular liberal is the one who is hard about belief: who demands that others believe as we do. And we note the nervous slide between the individual and collective subject: it is the nervousness that creates a bond, implying that the national subject is the white subject, the one who must regain its nerves, becoming more 'hard-nosed' about others. (*The Cultural Politics of Emotion* began with the image of the 'soft touch' nation, as the nation that is easily bruised by incoming others.)

At the time of the speech the security minister Baroness Neville-Jones said to the *Today* radio programme on BBC 1: 'There's a widespread feeling in the country that we're less united behind values than we need to be.' Speeches like Cameron's are affective because they pick up on feelings, and give them form. In giving them form, they direct those feelings in specific ways. Feelings of nervousness or anxiety might be prevalent; they might even be widespread (we are living in times which make such feelings *make sense*). Political discourse transforms feeling by giving that feeling an object or target. We could call this projection: negative feelings are projected onto outsiders, who then appear to threaten, from without, what is felt as precariously within. But projection is not the right word insofar as it implies an inside going out. I think these feelings are in some way *out and about*. They circulate at least in part through being understood as in circulation (the speech act which says the nation feels this or that way does something, it becomes an injunction to feel that way in order to participate in a thing being named, such that to partici-pate in the feeling or with feeling becomes a confirmation of feeling).

Let's return to the question of tension as atmosphere. In naming or describ-ing an atmosphere, whether to ourselves or others, we also give it form. If there is tension we might search for an explanation: someone or something becomes *the cause of tension*. Some attributions 'take hold', becoming shared explanations for an event or situation. Once someone or something is agreed to be the cause of tension, then shared feelings are directed toward that cause. Something 'out there' which is sensed and real, but also intangible, is made tangible. In 'finding' cause, feelings can become even more forceful. Political discourse is powerful as it can turn intangible feelings into tangible things that you can do things with. If we feel nervous, we can do something by eliminating what is agreed to be making us nervous. I still think the Marxist model of com-modity fetishism helps to describe these mechanisms: feelings come to reside in objects, magically, as if they are qualities of or in things, only by cutting those objects off from a wider economy of labour and production. It is then as if fear originates with the arrival of others whose bodies become *containers* of our fear. Given that containers spill, fear becomes the management of crisis.

When a feeling becomes an instrument or a technique it is not that some-thing is created from nothing. But something is being created from some-thing: a wavering impression of nervousness can strengthen its hold when we are given a face *to be nervous about*. To track how feelings cohere as or in bodies, we need to pay attention to the conversion points between good and bad feelings. As I have suggested, a politics that directs hatred towards others (that creates others as objects to be hated as well as feared) often pre-sents itself as a politics of love. But there are many other kinds of conversion points. It was noteworthy in the UK that when anger about cuts to public spending (justified under the affective language of austerity – of shared peril) moved people to march onto the streets, the government responded by calling for a happiness index.[30] Is happiness here a technique of distraction, a way of covering the nation with the warmth of a blanket? After all, at the very moment public anger was being expressed as demonstration, there was an announcement of a Royal Wedding. The Prime Minister said immediately 'everyone would want to put on record the happy news that was announced yesterday' and opened for public debate whether there should be a national holiday.[31] Happiness became a gift to the nation, one that was given as a counter-gift, a way of countering a sense of national exhaustion and misery (and note even the idea of a tired miserable nation was a way of pacifying the potency of the signs of rage[32]). Those who did not participate in this national happiness were certainly positioned as affect aliens or killjoys, alienated from the nation by virtue of not being affected in the right way.[33]

Like all weddings, this one was always meant to be a happy occasion. It was a celebration of the love of a heterosexual couple (this is a love *we can believe in*, a love we are happy to love). And not just any couple, of course: an especially shiny white couple. In anticipation of the event, one commentator noted: 'They will help form our collective imagination. They are now part of what we are as a nation, how we define ourselves as individuals, and how we are seen by foreigners.' The love for the couple becomes a form of national membership resting quite explicitly on self-consciousness about how we appear to those deemed 'foreigners'. The same writer concludes his article with a flourish:

> But the monarchy is also about magic. It sets Britain apart. It reminds
> us that this is a very antique nation, with a history and an identity
> which goes back for thousands of years. Just as a royal funeral is a
> moment of collective national sadness and mourning, a royal wedding
> is a moment of overwhelming joy and renewal. We all share in it.
> When the marriage itself takes place on an as-yet-unspecified date next
> year, the nation will take to the streets, rejoicing.[34]

An institution that has been reproduced over time becomes magic: cut off from the labour of its own reproduction. And note as well how description (this is a happy occasion) becomes evaluation (this is good for the nation) and command (be happy, rejoice!). To share in the body of the nation requires that you place your hopes for happiness in the right things.

The wedding in 2011 was followed by the Royal Jubilee and the flags came out again. In both national events, the cause for celebration took us back to history, to class as heritage, to class as continuity, to class solidarity rather than antagonism. Commentators again claimed in advance that the event would be a day of national happiness: 'It will be marked by great national happiness – and hopefully by good weather.'[35] If good weather can only be hoped for (in the UK, much happiness is gained by moaning about weather), great national happiness is given the safety and wisdom of prediction. And this happiness is tied directly to the singularity of a Royal body, a body who has survived the comings and goings, the ups and downs, of national demo-cratic time.

> The jubilee is an opportunity to have a party amid hard times,
> but it should also be an opportunity to debate the institution more
> thoughtfully – because it defines this country and it will have to
> change after Elizabeth II's reign is over. Yet it would be churlish
> not to acknowledge that the principal public feeling this weekend
> is respect for a woman who has done her strange, anachronistic and
> undemocratic job with tact and judgment for far longer than most of
> the rest of us could ever contemplate doing ours.[36]

The singular body becomes an object of shared feeling, a way the national body can cohere in recognition of the longevity of a history it can call its own. A bond of belief still turns upon a body, one that can concretise or 'hold' that belief and convert it into memory.

The investment in national happiness has much to teach us about the emo-tional politics of citizenship. Citizenship becomes a requirement to be sympa-thetic: as an agreement with feeling. To be a sympathetic part is to agree with your heart. After all, who could fail to be touched by the endlessly repeated images of the young queen coming to the throne after the death of her father? Who could fail to be touched by the memory of the young prince following the coffin of his dead mother? Here, being touched into citizenship is to be touched by the trauma of a past and the prospect of its conversion. Not to feel happiness in reaching these points is to become not only unsympathetic but also hostile, as if this unfeeling masks a disbelief in the national good, a will to destroy the nation. To be part of the nation is to remember these histories of national trauma: to recall them on route to national pride. To be part of the nation, to participate in the national body, was to right a wrong, to feel right having felt wronged. National feeling was predicated quite specifically on *the happiness of this conversion*.

One of my hopes in the re-issuing of *The Cultural Politics of Emotion* is that we become more attuned to the requirements to participate in national culture through feeling right. There are wrongs in this right. This book describes some of them.

NOTES

1. One of the sections of my original introduction was entitled 'Emotions and Objects'. In adding a 'their' I am hoping to extend my analysis of how the career of emotions is not independent of the career of objects. This 'their' in other words signifies an inter-relation

rather than a possessive relation. One could thus also reverse the formulation: 'objects and their emotions'.

2. I think that the introduction did not refer as fully as it could or should have to this vast interdisciplinary archive. In particular, the psychology and sociology of emotion are introduced too schematically (by being summarised as 'inside out' and 'outside in' models) such that you do not get a sense of the internal debates within each of these fields. It is worth noting that these diverse literatures are drawn upon more closely in the following chapters that take specific emotions as their point of entry, even if they are not cited and framed in disciplinary terms (as psychological, sociological or anthropological ways of approaching emotion). I would argue that I could not have developed the argument on emotion as a form of cultural politics without travelling across and between disciplines.

3. The history of ideas (along with literature) was a part of my initial training at Adelaide University, but I had become frustrated with the ways in which it was taught (ideas were treated as effects of histories that happened elsewhere). Since *The Cultural Politics of Emotion*, my engagement with history of ideas as a field has taken a somewhat different turn: my tendency is now to follow word-concepts (such as orientation, happiness, will, and in my current research project, utility) in and out of their intellectual histories.

4. We need to be explicit here: when the affective turn is translated into a turn to affect, male authors are given the status of originators of this turn. This is a very familiar and very clear example of how sexism works in or as citational practice.

5. No work by these writers is referred to by Hardt, which might be explained by how he refers to feminist work on bodies, and queer work on emotions rather than feminist work on emotions. Only one of these important feminist works on emotion (Hochschild's *The Managed Heart*) is referred to in the edited collection as a whole. In this model of 'the affective turn' feminism, prefaced as precursor, has disappeared. My argument would be that this disappearance is made possible by the translation of an affective turn into a turn to affect.

6. Somewhat ironically, of course if we give a word-concept to what cannot be contained, then that word-concept becomes a container (for what cannot be contained). I would argue that affect has become a container in exactly this way.

7. In the original introduction I suggested that the distinctions between sensation and emotion 'can only be analytic'. I follow on by claiming that the word 'impression' is what 'allows me to avoid making analytic distinctions between bodily sensation, emotion and thought as if they could be "experienced" as distinct realms of human "experience"' (both editions, 6). The challenge to the use of the distinction between affect and emotion is made explicit in one endnote (both editions, 40). In this note I equated 'sensation' with 'affect', a confusion of terms which probably did not help me to articulate my case in the strongest terms. I also challenged the use of the distinction in one endnote in *The Promise of Happiness* (2010: 230).

8. Interestingly, one reviewer of *The Promise of Happiness* suggests that affect rather than emotion is given privileged status such that 'the discursive tide of affect triumphs' (Cefai 2011: 346). So if you are read as working with emotion, you are read as not working on affect; if you are read as working with affect, you are read as not working on emotion. I hope for an intellectual horizon in which emotion and affect are not taken as choices that lead us down separate paths.

9. I refer both to Descartes and Spinoza in *The Cultural Politics of Emotion* and had read but did not refer to Locke. Although Spinoza's *Ethics* is the crucial reference point in

affect studies, in *The Promise of Happiness* I drew on John Locke's *An Essay in Human Understanding* to develop my thesis of happy objects.

10. In the original introduction, I contrasted approaches in terms of whether emotions are 'tied primarily' to bodily sensations or cognition (both editions, 5) and suggested that Hume could be identified in terms of the former. Whilst this is not strictly incorrect (after all Hume explicitly refutes the idea of passions as having representational qualities in *Treatise of Human Nature*), I would now tend to stress how many approaches, including Humes' own, are hybrid models: differences relate as much to *how* emotions are tied to bodily sensation and cognition as to *whether* they are primarily tied to one or the other. This is very clear in Hume's case from his own consideration of passions in relation to morality and thus motivation. See also my contrasting of David Hume and Adam Smith's models of the sociality of emotion in *The Promise of Happiness* (2010: 28).

11. I (probably mistakenly) removed at the last minute a section on phenomenology of emotion from the introduction of *The Cultural Politics of Emotion* (2004) when preparing the manuscript for publication. In this section I had made explicit how my argument related to Sartre's thesis on emotions as magical transformations and to Heidegger's discussions of mood. My gradual inclination to rethink emotion as orientation is what led me on a path to *Queer Phenomenology* (which I began researching in 2004) in which orientation becomes the explicit thematic.

12. I was beginning to understand the project in terms of this combining of concepts of affection and orientation toward the end of the research. I made this suggestion in note 7, Chapter 1, though I put it differently: 'the object with which I have contact is the object I have a feeling about' (both editions, 17). I refined this argument in *Queer Phenomenology* (2006) and *The Promise of Happiness* (2010).

13. In Margaret Wetherell's critique of *The Cultural Politics of Emotion*, in the concluding pages of her recent exploration of affect and emotion, she notes the consistency of the emotions I take as points of entry and 'basic emotions' as a paradigm in psychology: 'the list of emotions Ahmed explores in her book pretty much reproduces the basic emotions of traditional psychobiology' (2013: 158). They are also emotions that are *ordinarily* recognised as emotions.

14. Making overly clean distinctions also tends to generate what I would call 'clean concepts'. When I was reading many of the texts on affect, I noticed how often the concept was treated almost like a subject with agency, even when affect was assumed to take us away from a subject. Scholars often say 'affect is x' or 'affect does x'. If we attribute agency to concepts we tend to block our capacity for description.

15. The route taken from *Strange Encounters* to *The Cultural Politics of Emotion* can also be explained through my use of Kristeva's model of abjection. In the former text I offered a political model of abjection by rethinking how some bodies become abject (border objects); my argument was then developed in my chapter, 'The Performativity of Disgust', by focusing more on the affective dimensions of Kristeva's model of abjection.

16. This is why some recent uses of 'dark' in critical theory (for example in so-called 'dark materialism') are extremely problematic.

17. In questioning functionalist models I am not saying that emotions do not have a function: for instance, as I point out in Chapter 1, not to experience pain can make the world very dangerous. But the reduction of feeling to function simplifies feelings by assuming they are governed by ends defined in advance. Later, in questioning how happiness becomes a telos, what is assumed in advance as what life is directed towards, I was to return to this problem by another route (Ahmed 2010). It is noticeable to me how Damasio's work not only reduces feeling to its evolutionary function but assumes happiness (as well as

flourishing and well-being) as the 'point' of human existence. He thus rewrites Spinoza in American terms: 'I hold these truths to be self-evident, that humans are created such that they tend to preserve their life and seek well-being, that their happiness becomes from the successful endeavour to do so and that the foundation of virtue rests on these facts' (2004: 171).

18. Damasio is influenced here by Paul Ekman's work on 'facial expression' as 'innate and universal to our species' (Ekman 2007: 1). Ekman was in turn influenced by his mentor Silvan S. Tomkins. For discussion of the relationship between Silvan S. Tomkin's and Paul Ekman's work see the debate between Ruth Leys (2012a) and Adam Frank and Elizabeth Wilson (2012).

19. Whilst it has become somewhat fashionable to chastise social and cultural theorists for the absence of an engagement with the sciences, my own reading of the neuroscience of emotion brought home to me how much scientists would benefit from an engagement with social and cultural theory.

20. It is worth me noting here that some critics have tended to describe my argument as being about signs *more than* or even *rather than* bodies (see Puar 2007; Wetherell 2012). Whilst Puar's critique is cautious and careful, Wetherell's critique (with which she ends her own book) is rather less so. Wetherell writes: 'To focus just on the circulation of signs is to risk over-idealizing, and paradoxically, as we have seen, bodies completely disappear from the study of affect' (2012: 160), such that, in her view, my book generates an 'almost completely disembodied account' (160). Wetherell seems mainly to be referring here to the section, 'affective economies' in Chapter 2. The following section is entitled 'hated bodies' and describes racism as an embodied and lived encounter. Wetherell argues that political rhetoric that mobilises hate follows 'a very different compositional logic' than 'the everyday practices of hate in everyday life' (159). The examples of racism (which I described in terms of love as well as hate) show us how the political and everyday cannot be assumed as if they are distinct domains; how the making of strangers into the cause of hatred and fear becomes form of address not only in politics but in the worlds *into which bodies are thrown*.

21. For a very useful genealogical approach to the emergence of affect as well as the concept of affective contagion see Blackman (2012).

22. See also Ahmed (2010: 38–45) for a development of my argument originally made in *The Cultural Politics of Emotion* on tension and atmosphere.

23. I work with this idea that agreement is what does not tend to be registered by consciousness in my most recent book, *Willful Subjects* (2014), drawing on the work of Arthur Schopenhauer.

24. Although I did not explore happiness in depth in *The Cultural Politics of Emotion*, I do describe happiness as a promise, showing how the deferral of this promise extends an investment (both editions, 196). It is this idea of happiness as promissory that I was to develop in subsequent work. See also Lauren Berlant's *Cruel Optimism* (2011), which offers a compelling analysis of how objects of desire can be rethought as 'clusters of promise'.

25. Furthermore, some objects might *not* be encountered because they are already associated with negativity (the avoidance of what is socially negated). This is why an encounter (affecting and being affected) is not for me the starting point, as it is for example in Deleuze's essay on Spinoza, where in describing how Pierre encounters Paul, he asks whether it is a good or bad encounter, whether they are affected well or not by each other (1978: 6). I discuss Deleuze's example in the conclusion to *The Promise of Happiness* (2010: 211–14). Affective histories include the histories of what or who is allowed close

enough to this or that body for this or that body to be affected in the first place (this is not to say the techniques for determining proximity and distance are always or only successful). Gentrification could be described in these terms: the gradual removal of 'eye-sores' (people and things) in order that those who reside in these spaces are not negatively affected by them; such that they do not have to encounter what would get in the way of the happiness of their occupation.

26. See: http://www.npr.org/templates/story/story.php?storyId=97831171

27. Again, I would be cautious about making too clear a distinction between emotions and moods, as this would allow us not to register how emotions can also involve less clear or less distinct objects.

28. One of the texts often cited in studies of affect and attunement is Daniel Stern's *The Interpersonal World of the Infant*, which as a study of developmental psychology, focuses on the 'affective attunement' between mother and child (2000: 138–69). It is important for me to note that Stern does refer to misattunements, which he describes as 'troublesome' (211). In forthcoming work, I will develop these arguments about misattunements and their implications for the sociality of affect and emotion.

29. For the written copy of Cameron's 2011 Speech, see: http://www.number10.gov.uk/news/pms-speech-at-munich-security-conference/ Last accessed 4 March 2014.

30. http://www.guardian.co.uk/news/datablog/2011/dec/01/happiness-index-david-cameron Last accessed 4 March 2014.

31. http://www.bbc.co.uk/news/uk-politics-11791929 Last accessed 4 March 2014.

32. The pacification of the potency of rage has been an important part of the media and political response to the protests. The anger was typically projected onto militant outsiders, those who were intent on destroying the march for others, rather than being understood as what compelled people to march in the first place. It is almost as if the media 'willed' the marches *to be of tired rather than angry feet*. For further discussion see Chapter 4, *Willful Subjects* (2014).

33. http://swns.com/killjoy-post-office-bosses-ban-royal-wedding-flags-281501.html Last accessed 4 March 2014.

34. http://blogs.telegraph.co.uk/news/peteroborne/100064013/prince-william-and-kate-middleton-to-marry-we-all-have-a-stake-in-this-couple%E2%80%99s-future/ Last accessed 4 March 2014.

35. http://www.guardian.co.uk/commentisfree/2012/jun/01/editorial-queen-jubilee-diamond Last accessed 4 March 2014.

36. http://www.theguardian.com/commentisfree/2012/jun/01/editorial-queen-jubilee-diamond Last accessed 4 March 2014.

References

Ahmad, M. (2002), 'Homeland Insecurities: Racial Violence the Day after September 11', *Social Text* 72, 20 (3): 101–15.

Ahmed, S. (1998), *Differences that Matter: Feminist Theory and Postmodernism*, Cambridge: Cambridge University Press.

—— (1999), 'Passing Through Hybridity', *Theory, Culture and Society* 16 (2): 87–106.

—— (2000), *Strange Encounters: Embodied Others in Post-Coloniality*, London: Routledge.

—— (2002), 'This Other and Other Others', *Economy and Society* 31 (4): 558–72.

—— and Stacey, J. (2001), 'Testimonial Cultures: An Introduction', *Cultural Values* 5 (1): 1–6.

—— (2006), *Queer Phenomenology: Orientations, Objects, Others*, Durham: Duke University Press.

—— (2010), *The Promise of Happiness*, Durham: Duke University Press.

—— (2012), *On Being Included: Racism and Diversity in Institutional Life*, Durham: Duke University Press.

—— (2014), *Willful Subjects*, Durham: Duke University Press.

Ahmed, S., Castañeda, C., Fortier, A.-M. and Sheller, M. (eds) (2003), *Uprootings/Regroundings: Questions of Home and Migration*, Oxford: Berg.

Allport, G. W. (1979), *The Nature of Prejudice*, Reading, MA: Addison-Wesley Publishing Company.

—— (1992), 'The Nature of Hatred' in R. M. Baird and S. E. Rosenbaum (eds), *Bigotry, Prejudice and Hatred: Definitions, Causes and Solutions*, Buffalo, NY: Prometheus Books.

Althusser, L. (1971), *Lenin and Philosophy*, trans. B. Brewster, New York: Monthly Review Press.

Angyal, A. (1941), 'Disgust and Related Aversions', *Journal of Abnormal and Social Psychology* 36: 393–412.

Aristotle (2003), 'From *Rhetoric*' in R. C. Solomon (ed.), *What is an Emotion? Classic and Contemporary Readings*, 2nd edn, Oxford: Oxford University Press.

Austin, J. L. (1975), *How to Do Things with Words*, J. O. Urmson and M. Sbisà (eds), Oxford: Oxford University Press.

Averill, J. R., Catlin, G. and Chon, K. K. (1990), *Rules of Hope*, New York: Springer-Verlag.

Bacchetta, P. and Power, M. (eds) (2002), *Right Wing Women: From Conservatives and Extremists around the World*, New York: Routledge.

Baird, R. M. and Rosenbaum, S. E. (1992), 'Introduction' in R. M. Baird and S. E. Rosenbaum (eds), *Bigotry, Prejudice and Hatred: Definitions, Causes and Solutions*, Buffalo, NY: Prometheus Books.

Barber, S. M. and Clark, D. L. (2002), 'Queer Moments: The Performative Temporalities of Eve Kosofsky Sedgwick' in S. M. Barber and D. L. Clark (eds), *Regarding Sedgwick: Essays on Queer Culture and Critical Theory*, New York: Routledge.

Barkan, E. (2000), *The Guilt of Nations: Restitution and Negotiating Historical Injustices*, Baltimore: Johns Hopkins University Press.

Barthes, R. (1979), *A Lover's Discourse: Fragments*, trans. R. Howard, London: Jonathan Cape.

Beck, U. (1992), *Risk Society: Towards a New Modernity*, trans. M. Ritter, London: Sage.

Bell, D. and Binnie, J. (2000), *The Sexual Citizen: Queer Politics and Beyond*, Cambridge: Polity.

Bendelow, G. and S. J. Williams (eds) (1998), *Emotions in Social Life: Critical Themes and Contemporary Issues*, London: Routledge.

Bending, L. (2000), *The Representation of Bodily Pain in Late Nineteenth-Century English Culture*, Oxford: Clarendon Press.

Benhabib, S. (1992), *Situating the Self: Gender, Community and Postmodernism in Contemporary Ethics*, Cambridge: Polity Press.

Benjamin, A. (1997), *Present Hope: Philosophy, Architecture, Judaism*, London: Routledge.

Benjamin, J. (1988), *The Bonds of Love: Psychoanalysis, Feminism, and the Problem of Domination*, New York: Pantheon Books.

—— (1995), *Like Subjects, Love Objects: Essays on Recognition and Sexual Difference*, New Haven: Yale University Press.

Ben-Ze'ev, A. (2000), *The Subtlety of Emotions*, Cambridge, MA: The MIT Press.

Berlant, L. (1997), *The Queen of America Goes to Washington City: Essays on Sex and Citizenship*, Durham: Duke University Press.

—— (2000), 'The Subject of True Feeling: Pain, Privacy and Politics' in S. Ahmed, J. Kilby, C. Lury, M. McNeil and B. Skeggs (eds), *Transformations: Thinking Through Feminism*, London: Routledge.

—— (2002), 'Two Girls, Fat and Thin' in S. M. Barber and D. L. Clark (eds), *Regarding Sedgwick: Essays on Queer Culture and Critical Theory*, New York: Routledge.

—— (2003), 'Capitalism and Compassion', paper presented at the 'Class Outings: Rethinking the Relation between Gender and Class' dayschool, Institute for Women's Studies, Lancaster University, 6 June.

—— and Freeman, E. (1997), 'Queer Nationality' in L. Berlant, *The Queen of America Goes to Washington City: Essays on Sex and Citizenship*, Durham: Duke University Press.

—— and Warner, M. (2000), 'Sex in Public' in L. Berlant (ed.), *Intimacy*, Chicago: University of Chicago Press.

—— (2011), *Cruel Optimism*, Durham: Duke University Press.

Bhabha, H. K. (1994), *The Location of Culture*, London: Routledge.

Biddle, J. (1997), 'Shame', *Australian Feminist Studies* 12 (26): 227–39.

Bird, J. and Clarke, S. (1999), 'Racism, Hatred, and Discrimination Through the Lens of Projective Identification', *Journal for the Psychoanalysis of Culture and Society* 4 (2): 332–5.

Blackman, L. (2012), *Immaterial Bodies: Affect, Embodiment and Mediation*, London: Sage.

Blackman, L. and Walkerdine, V. (2001), *Mass Hysteria: Critical Psychology and Media Studies*, Palgrave: Macmillan.

Blanchard, T. (2001), 'Model of a Modern Briton', *The Observer*, 25 November: 10. Bloch, E. (1986), *The Principle of Hope*, vol. 1, trans. N. Plaice, S. Plaice and P. Knight, Oxford: Basil Blackwell.

Bociurkiw, M. (2003), 'Homeland (In)Security: Roots and Displacement, from New York, to Toronto, to Salt Lake City', *Reconstruction: An Interdisciplinary Culture Studies Community* 3 (3), http://www.reconstruction.ws/033/bociurkiw.htm

Boler, M. (1999), *Feeling Power: Emotions and Education*, New York: Routledge.

Bollas, C. (1995), 'Loving Hate', *Annual of Psychoanalysis*, vol. 12 (13): 221–37.

Borch-Jacobsen, M. (1988), *The Freudian Subject*, trans. C. Porter, Stanford: Stanford University Press.

—— (1993), *The Emotional Tie: Psychoanalysis, Mimesis, and Affect*, Stanford: Stanford University Press.

Braidotti, R. (2002), *Metamorphoses: Towards a Materialist Theory of Becoming*, Cambridge: Polity Press.

Braithwaite, J. (1989), *Crime, Shame and Reintegration*, Cambridge: Cambridge University Press.

—— (2002), *Restorative Justice and Responsive Regulation*, Oxford: Oxford University Press.

Brennan, T. (2004), *The Transmission of Affect*, Ithaca: Cornell University Press.

Brentano, F. (2003), 'From *On the Origin of Our Knowledge of Right and Wrong*' in R. C. Solomon (ed.), *What is an Emotion? Classic and Contemporary Readings*, 2nd edn, Oxford: Oxford University Press.

Bringing Them Home: Report of the National Inquiry into the Separation of Aboriginal and Torres Strait Islander Children from their Families, 1996, http://www.austlii.edu.au/au/special/rsjproject/rsjlibrary/hreoc/stolen/website

Bronski, M. (1998), *The Pleasure Principle: Sex, Backlash, and the Struggle for Gay Freedom*, New York: St Martin's Press.

Broucek, F. J. (1991), *Shame and the Self*, New York: Guilford Publications.

Brown, W. (1995), *States of Injury: Power and Freedom in Late Modernity*, Princeton: Princeton University Press.

—— (2003), 'Women's Studies Unbound: Revolution, Mourning, Politics', *Parallax* 9 (2): 3–16.

Burke, A. (2001), *In Fear of Security: Australia's Invasion Anxiety*, Annandale, NSW: Pluto Press.

Burns, B., Busby, C. and Sawchuk, K. (1999), 'Introduction' in B. Burns, C. Busby and K. Sawchuk (eds), *When Pain Strikes*, Minneapolis: University of Minnesota Press.

Burstow, B. (1992), *Radical Feminist Therapy: Working in the Context of Violence*, Newbury Park: Sage.

Butler, J. (1990), *Gender Trouble: Feminism and the Subversion of Identity*, New York: Routledge.

—— (1993), *Bodies that Matter: On the Discursive Limits of 'Sex'*, New York: Routledge.

—— (1997a), *Excitable Speech: A Politics of the Performative*, New York: Routledge.

—— (1997b), *The Psychic Life of Power: Theories in Subjection*, Stanford: Stanford University Press.

—— (1997c), 'Critically Queer' in S. Phelan (ed.), *Playing with Fire: Queer Politics, Queer Theories*, London: Routledge.

—— (2002), 'Is Kinship Always Already Heterosexual?' *Differences: A Journal of Feminist Cultural Studies* 13 (1): 14–44.

—— (2005), *Precarious Life: The Powers of Mourning and Violence*, London: Verso.

Campbell, D. (1998), *Writing Security: United States Foreign Policy and the Politics of Identity*, Minneapolis: University of Minnesota Press.

Campbell, S. (1994), 'Being Dismissed: The Politics of Emotional Expression', *Hypatia* 9 (3): 46–65.

—— (1997), *Interpreting the Personal: Expression and the Formation of Feeling*, Ithaca: Cornell University Press.

Capps, D. (1993), *The Depleted Self: Sin in a Narcissistic Age*, Minneapolis: Fortress Press.

Carrington, C. (1999), *No Place Like Home: Relationships and Family Life Among Lesbians and Gay Men*, Chicago: University of Chicago Press.

Castañeda, C. (2002), *Figurations: Body, Child, World*, Durham: Duke University Press.

Cefai, S. (2011), 'Unhappy Families', *Cultural Studies Review* 17 (1): 339–48.

Chapman, C. R. (1986), 'Pain, Perception, and Illusion' in R. A. Sternbach (ed.), *The Psychology of Pain*, New York: Raven Press.

Collins, R. (1990), 'Stratification, Emotional Energy, and the Transient Emotions' in T. D. Kemper (ed.), *Research Agendas in the Sociology of Emotions*, Albany, NY: State University of New York Press.

Cowan, J. L. (1968), *Pleasure and Pain: A Study in Philosophical Psychology*, London: Macmillan.

Creed, B. (1993), *The Monstrous-Feminine: Film, Femininity, and Psychoanalysis*, New York: Routledge.

Crimp, D. (2002), *Melancholia and Moralism: Essays on AIDS and Queer Politics*, Cambridge, MA: The MIT Press.

Cvetkovich, A. (1992), *Mixed Feelings: Feminism, Mass Culture and Victorian Sensationalism*, New Brunswick, NJ: Rutgers University Press.

—— (2003a), 'Legacies of Trauma, Legacies of Activism: ACT UP's Lesbians' in D. L. Eng and D. Kazanjian (eds), *Loss: The Politics of Mourning*, Berkeley: University of California Press.

—— (2003b), *An Archive of Feelings: Trauma, Sexuality, and Lesbian Public Cultures*, Durham: Duke University Press.

—— (2012), *Depression: A Public Feeling*, Durham: Duke University Press.

Daly, K. (2000), 'Revisiting the Relationship between Retributive and Restorative Justice' in H. Strang and J. Braithwaite (eds), *Restorative Justice: Philosophy to Practice*, Aldershot: Ashgate.

Damasio, A. (2003), *The Feeling of What Happens: Body, Emotion and the Making of Consciousness*, London: Vintage.

Darwin, C. (1904), *The Expression of the Emotions in Man and Animals*, ed. F. Darwin, London: John Murray.

Dean, J. (1996), *Solidarity of Strangers: Feminism after Identity Politics*, Berkeley: University of California Press.

Dean, T. and Lane, C. (2001), 'Homosexuality and Psychoanalysis: An Introduction' in T. Dean and C. Lane (eds), *Homosexuality and Psychoanalysis*, Chicago: University of Chicago Press.

De Lauretis, T. (1994), *The Practice of Love: Lesbian Sexuality and Perverse Desire*, Bloomington: Indiana University Press.

Deleuze, G. (1978), 'Lecture Transcripts on Spinoza's Concept of Affect', http://www.goldsmiths.ac.uk/csisp/papers/deleuze_spinoza_affect.pdf, 1–28.

—— (1992), 'Ethology: Spinoza and Us' in J. Crary and S. Kwinter (eds), *Incorporations*, New York: Zone.

Denzin, N. K. (1984), *On Understanding Emotion*, San Francisco: Jossey-Bass Publishers.

Der Derian, J. (1995), 'The Value of Security: Hobbes, Marx, Nietzsche, and Baudrillard' in R. D. Lipschutz (ed.), *On Security*, New York: Columbia University Press.

Derrida, J. (1987), *The Post Card: From Socrates to Freud and Beyond*, trans. A. Bass, Chicago: University of Chicago Press.

—— (1988), 'Signature Event Context' in *Limited Inc*, trans. S. Weber and J. Mehlman, Evanston, IL: Northwestern University Press.

—— (1992), 'Force of Law: The "Mystical Foundation of Authority" ' in D. Cornell, M. Rosenfeld and D. G. Carlson (eds), *Deconstruction and the Possibility of Justice*, New York: Routledge.

Descartes, R. (1985), 'The Passions of the Soul', *The Philosophical Writings of Descartes*, vol. 1, trans. J. Cottingham, R. Stoothoff and D. Murdoch, Cambridge: Cambridge University Press.

Digeser, P. E. (2001), *Political Forgiveness*, Ithaca: Cornell University Press.

Dillon, M. (1996), *Politics of Security: Towards a Political Philosophy of Continental Thought*, London: Routledge.

Diprose, R. (2002), *Corporeal Generosity: On Giving with Nietzsche, Merleau-Ponty, and Levinas*, New York: SUNY Press.

Ditton, J. and Farrall, S. (2000), *The Fear of Crime*, Aldershot: Ashgate.

Douglas, M. (1995), *Purity and Danger: An Analysis of the Concepts of Pollution and Taboo*, London: Routledge.

Dunant, S. and Porter, R. (eds), (1996), *The Age of Anxiety*, London: Virago.

Durkheim, E. (1966), *The Rules of Sociological Method*, trans. S. A. Solovay and J. H. Mueller, New York: The Free Press.

—— (1976), *The Elementary Forms of the Religious Life*, trans. J. W. Swain, London: George Allen and Unwin.

East, S. (2013), 'Tracing the Future: Child's Play and the Freefall of Imagination' in T. Winter (ed.), *Shanghai Expo: An International Forum on the Future of Cities*, Abingdon: Routledge.

Eisenstein, Z. (1994), 'Writing Hatred on the Body', *New Political Scientist*, vol. 30/31: 5–22.

Ekman, P. (2007), *Emotions Revealed: Recognizing Faces and Feelings to Improve Communication and Emotional Life*, London: Macmillan.

Elias, N. (1978), *The Civilizing Process: The History of Manners*, trans. E. Jephcott, Oxford: Blackwell.

Eng, D. L. (2002), 'The Value of Silence', *Theatre Journal* 54 (1): 85–94.

—— and Han, S. (2003), 'A Dialogue on Racial Melancholia' in D. L. Eng and D. Kazanjian (eds), *Loss: The Politics of Mourning*, Berkeley: University of California Press.

—— and Kazanjian, D. (2003), 'Introduction: Mourning Remains' in D. L. Eng and D. Kazanjian (eds), *Loss: The Politics of Mourning*, Berkeley: University of California Press.

Epps, B. (2001), 'The Fetish of Fluidity' in T. Dean and C. Lane (eds), *Homosexuality and Psychoanalysis*, Chicago: University of Chicago Press.

Epstein, A. L. (1984), 'The Experience of Shame in Melanesia: An Essay in the Anthropology of Affect', *Occasional Paper No. 40*, London: Royal Anthropological Institute of Great Britain and Ireland.

Erikson, E. H. (1965), *Childhood and Society*, rev. edn, Harmondsworth: Penguin Books.

Erikson, K. (1995), 'Notes on Trauma and Community' in C. Caruth (ed.), *Trauma: Explorations in Memory*, Baltimore: Johns Hopkins University Press.

Fanon, F. (1986), *Black Skin, White Masks*, trans. C. L. Markmann, London: Pluto Press.

Farran, C. J., Herth, K. A. and Popovich, J. M. (1995), *Hope and Hopelessness: Critical Clinical Constructs*, Thousand Oaks, CA: Sage.

Fischer, W. F. (1970), *Theories of Anxiety*, New York: Harper and Row.

Fisher, B. (1984), 'Guilt and Shame in the Women's Movement: The Radical Ideal of Action and its Meaning for Feminist Intellectuals', *Feminist Studies* 10 (2): 185–212.

Fisher, P. (1998), *Wonder, the Rainbow, and the Aesthetics of Rare Experiences*, Cambridge, MA: Harvard University Press.

—— (2002), *The Vehement Passions*, Princeton: Princeton University Press.

Fortier, A-M. (2003), 'Making Home: Queer Migrations and Motions of Attachment' in S. Ahmed, C. Castañeda, A.-M. Fortier and M. Sheller (eds), *Uprootings/Regroundings: Questions of Home and Migration*, Oxford: Berg.

—— (2008), *Multicultural Horizons: Diversity and the Limits of the Civil Nation*, London: Routledge.

Foucault, M. (1997), *The Politics of Truth*, ed. Slyvere Lotringer and Lysa Hochroth, New York: Semiotexte.

Fowler, J. H. and N. A. Christakis (2008), 'Dynamic Spread of Happiness in a Large Social Network: Longitudinal Analysis over 20 years in the Framingham Heart Study' *BMJ*, 337: a2338 doi.1136/bmj.a2338 Last accessed 4 March 2014.

Frank, A. and Wilson, E. (2012), 'Like-Minded', *Critical Enquiry* 38: 870–8.

Freire, P. (1996), *Pedagogy of the Oppressed*, trans. M. B. Ramos, rev. edn, Harmondsworth: Penguin Books.

Freud, S. (1922), *Group Psychology and the Analysis of the Ego*, trans. J. Strachey, London: The International Psycho-Analytical Press.

—— (1934a), 'On Narcissism: An Introduction', *Collected Papers*, vol. 4, ed. E. Jones, trans. J. Riviere, London: The Hogarth Press.

—— (1934b), 'Mourning and Melancholia', *Collected Papers*, vol. 4, ed. E. Jones, trans. J. Riviere, London: The Hogarth Press.

—— (1950), *Totem and Taboo: Some Points of Agreement between the Mental Lives of Savages and Neurotics*, trans. J. Strachey, London: Routledge and Kegan Paul.

—— (1961), *Civilization and Its Discontents*, trans. and ed. J. Strachey, London: Norton.

—— (1964a), 'The Unconscious', *The Standard Edition of the Complete Psychological Works of Sigmund Freud*, vol. 14, trans. J. Strachey, London: The Hogarth Press.

—— (1964b), 'The Ego and the Id', *The Standard Edition of the Complete Psychological Works of Sigmund Freud*, vol. 19, trans. J. Strachey, London: The Hogarth Press.

—— (1964c), 'Beyond the Pleasure Principle', *The Standard Edition of the Complete Psychological Works of Sigmund Freud*, vol. 18, trans. J. Strachey, London: The Hogarth Press.

—— (1964d), 'Inhibitions, Symptoms and Anxiety', *The Standard Edition of the Complete Psychological Works of Sigmund Freud*, vol. 20, trans. J. Strachey, London: The Hogarth Press.

Fromm, E. (1968), *The Revolution of Hope: Toward a Humanised Technology*, New York: Harper and Row.

Frye, M. (1983), *The Politics of Reality: Essays in Feminist Theory*, Trumansburg, NY: The Crossing Press.

Furedi, F. (1997), *Culture of Fear: Risk-taking and the Morality of Low Expectation*, London: Cassell.

Gabb, J. (2002), 'Telling Tales: Troubling Sexuality within Analyses of the "Lesbian Community" and "Lesbian Families" ', paper presented at 'Re-Imagining Communities' conference, Lancaster University, May 2002.

Gaita, R (2000a), 'Guilt, Shame and Collective Responsibility' in M. Grattan (ed.), *Reconciliation: Essays on Australian Reconciliation*, Melbourne: Bookman Press.

—— (2000b), *A Common Humanity: Thinking About Love and Truth and Justice*, London: Routledge.

Gibbs, A. (2001), 'Contagious Feelings: Pauline Hanson and the Epidemiology of Affect', *Australian Humanities Review*, http://www.lib.latrobe.edu.au/AHR/archive/Issue-December-2001/gibbs.html

Goleman, D. (1995), *Emotional Intelligence: Why It Can Matter More Than IQ*, London: Bloomsbury.

Goldberg, D. T. (1995), 'Afterword: Hate, or Power?' in R. K. Whillock and D. Slayden (eds), *Hate Speech*, Thousand Oaks, CA: Sage.

Goodman, R. T. (2001), *Infertilities: Exploring Fictions of Barren Bodies*, Minneapolis: University of Minnesota Press.

Gopinath, G. (2003), 'Nostalgia, Desire, Diaspora: South Asian Sexualities in Motion' in S. Ahmed, C. Castañeda, A.-M. Fortier and M. Sheller (eds), *Uprootings/Regroundings: Questions of Home and Migration*, Oxford: Berg.

Goss, R. E. (1997), 'Queering Procreative Privilege: Coming Out as Families' in R. E. Goss and A. A. S. Strongheart (eds), *Our Families, Our Values: Snapshots of Queer Kinship*, New York: The Harrington Park Press.

Gramsci, A. (1971), *Selections from the Prison Notebooks of Antonio Gramsci*, eds and trans. Q. Hoare and G. N. Smith, London: Lawrence and Wishart.

Greenspan, P. (2003), 'Reasons to Feel' in R. C. Solomon (ed.), *What is an Emotion? Classic and Contemporary Readings*, 2nd edn, Oxford: Oxford University Press.

Gross, D. M. (2006), *The Secret History of Emotion: From Aristotle's* Rhetoric *to Modern Brain Science*, Chicago: University of Chicago Press.

Grosz, E. (1994), *Volatile Bodies: Toward a Corporeal Feminism*, Bloomington: Indiana University Press.

—— (1999), 'Thinking the New: Of Futures Yet Unthought' in E. Grosz (ed.), *Becomings: Explorations in Time, Memory, and Futures*, Ithaca: Cornell University Press.

Gutiérrez-Jones, C. (2001), *Critical Race Narratives: A Study of Race, Rhetoric, and Injury*, New York: New York University Press.

Hage, G. (2003), *Against Paranoid Nationalism: Searching for Hope in a Shrinking Society*, Annandale, NSW: Pluto Press.

Halberstam, J. (2003), 'What's That Smell? Queer Temporalities and Subcultural Lives', *International Journal of Cultural Studies* 6 (3): 313–33.

Hanmer, J. and Saunders, S. (1984), *Well-Founded Fear: A Community Study of Violence to Women*, London: Hutchinson.

Hardt, M. (2007), 'Foreword: What Affects are Good For' in P. Clough (ed.), *The Affective Turn*, Durham: Duke University Press.

Hartman, S. V. (1997), *Scenes of Subjection: Terror, Slavery and Self-Making in Nineteenth Century America*, New York: Oxford University Press.

Heidegger, M. (1962), *Being and Time*, trans. J. Macquarie and E. Robinson, London: SCM Press.

—— (1995), *The Fundamental Concepts of Metaphsyics: World, Finitude, Solitude*, trans. W. McNeill and N. Walker, Bloomington: Indiana University Press.

Heller, A. (1979), *A Theory of Feelings*, Assen: Van Gorcum.

Hennessy, R. (1995), 'Queer Visibility in Commodity Culture' in L. Nicholson and S. Seidman (eds), *Social Postmodernism: Beyond Identity Politics*, Cambridge: Cambridge University Press.

—— (2000), *Profit and Pleasure: Sexual Identities in Late Capitalism*, New York: Routledge.

Hobbes, T. (1991), *Leviathan*, Cambridge: Cambridge University Press.

Hochschild, A. R. (1983), *The Managed Heart: Commercialisation of Human Feeling*, Berkeley: University of California Press.

—— (2003), *The Commercialisation of Intimate Life: Notes from Home and Work*, Berkeley: University of California Press.

Holbrook, D. (1972), *The Masks of Hate: The Problem of False Solutions in the Culture of an Acquisitive Society*, Oxford: Pergamon Press.

Home Office (2002a), *Secure Borders, Safe Haven: Integration with Diversity in Modern Britain*, London: Stationery Office.

—— (2002b), *Community Cohesion: A Report of the Independent Review Team*, http://www.homeoffice.gov.uk/docs2/pocc.html

—— (2003), *Community Cohesion: A Report of the Independent Review Team*, http://www.homeoffice.gov.uk/docs2/comm_cohesion.html

hooks, b. (1989), *Talking Back: Thinking Feminist, Thinking Black*, London: Sheba Feminist Publishers.

—— (1992), *Black Looks: Race and Representation*, Boston: South End Press.

—— (1994), 'Eros, Eroticism and the Pedagogical Process' in H. A. Giroux and P. McLaren (eds), *Between Borders: Pedagogy and the Politics of Cultural Studies*, New York: Routledge.

Hudson, J. and Galaway, B. (1996), 'Introduction' in B. Galaway and J. Hudson (eds), *Restorative Justice: International Perspectives*, Monsey, NY: Criminal Justice Press.

Hughes, D. and Riddell, M. (2002), 'Migrants Must Learn to Be British', *Daily Mail*, 7 February, p. 1.

Hultberg, P. (1988), 'Shame – A Hidden Emotion', *Journal of Analytical Psychology* 33: 109–26.

Hume, D. (1964), *The Philosophical Works: A Treatise of Human Nature and Dialogues Concerning Natural Religion*, vol. 2, London: Scientia Verlag Aalen.

Irigaray, L. (1993), *An Ethics of Sexual Difference*, trans. C. Burke and G. C. Gill, London: The Athlone Press.

Izard, C. E. (1977), *Human Emotions*, New York: Plenum Press.

Jacobs, J. B. and Potter, K. (1998), *Hate Crimes: Criminal Law and Identity Politics*, New York: Oxford University Press.

Jacoby, M. (1994), *Shame and the Origins of Self-Esteem: A Jungian Approach*, trans. D. Whitcher, London: Routledge.

Jaggar, A. M. (1996), 'Love and Knowledge: Emotion in Feminist Epistemology' in A. Garry and M. Pearsall (eds), *Women, Knowledge, and Reality: Explorations in Feminist Philosophy*, New York: Routledge.

James, S. (1997), *Passion and Action: The Emotions in Seventeenth Century Philosophy*, Oxford: Oxford University Press.

James, W. (1890), *The Principles of Psychology*, vol. 2, New York: Dover Publications.

Johnstone, G. (2002), *Restorative Justice: Ideas, Values, Debates*, Devon: Willan Publishing.

Jureidini, R. (2000), 'Origins and Initial Outcomes of the Racial Hatred Act 1995', *People and Place*, http://elecpress.monash.edu.au/pnp/pnpv5nl/jureidin.htm

Katz, J. (1999), *How Emotions Work*, Chicago: University of Chicago Press.

Kemper, T. D. (1978), *A Social Interactional Theory of Emotions*, New York: John Wiley and Sons.

Kemper, T. D. (ed.) (1990), *Research Agenda in the Sociology of Emotions*, Albany: SUNY Press.

Kierkegaard (1957), *The Concept of Dread*, trans. W. Lowrie, Princeton: Princeton University Press.

Kilby, J. (2002), 'Redeeming Memories: The Politics of Trauma and History', *Feminist Theory* 3 (2): 201–10.

Kiss, E. (2000), 'Moral Ambition within and beyond Political Constraints: Reflections on Restorative Justice' in R. I. Rotberg and D. Thompson (eds), *Truth v. Justice: The Morality of Truth Commissions*, Princeton: Princeton University Press.

Klein, M. (1998), *Love, Guilt and Reparation and Other Works 1921–1945*, London: Vintage.

Kleinman, A., Das, V. and Lock, M. (1997), 'Introduction' in A. Kleinman, V. Das and M. Lock (eds), *Social Suffering*, Berkeley: University of California Press.

Koivunen, A. (2001), 'Preface: An Affective Turn?' in A. Koivunen and S. Passonen (eds), *Affective Encounters: Rethinking Embodiment in Feminist Media Studies*, University of Turku, School of Art, Literature and Music, Media Studies, Series A.

Kotarba, J. A. (1983), *Chronic Pain: Its Social Dimensions*, Beverly Hills: Sage.

Krause, K. and Williams, M. C. (eds) (1997), *Critical Security Studies: Concepts and Cases*, London: UCL Press.

Kristeva, J. (1982), *Powers of Horror: An Essay on Abjection*, trans. L. S. Roudiez, New York: Columbia University Press.

—— (1987), *Tales of Love*, trans. L. S. Roudiez, New York: Columbia University Press.

—— (1993), *Nations without Nationalism*, trans. L. S. Roudiez, New York: Columbia University Press.

Lacan, J. (1977), *Écrits: A Selection*, trans. A. Sheridan, London: Tavistock.

—— (1984), *Feminine Sexuality*, ed. Juliet Mitchell, trans. Jacqueline Rose, New York: W. W. Norton and Co.

LaCapra, D. (2001), *Writing History, Writing Trauma*, Baltimore: Johns Hopkins University Press.

Laing, R. D. (1960), *The Divided Self: A Study of Sanity and Madness*, London: Tavistock.

Laplanche, J. and Pontalis, J.-B. (1988), *The Language of Psycho-Analysis*, trans. D. Nicholson-Smith, London: Karnac Books.

Leder, D. (1990), *The Absent Body*, Chicago: University of Chicago Press.

Lee, J. (1999), 'Teaching Feminism: Anger, Despair, and Self Growth', *Feminist Teacher* 7 (2): 15–19.

Levinas, E. (1979), *Totality and Infinity: An Essay on Exteriority*, trans. A. Lingis, The Hague: Martinus Nijhoff Publishers.

Lewin, E. (1993), *Lesbian Mothers: Accounts of Gender in American Culture*, Ithaca: Cornell University Press.

Lewis, H. B. (1971), *Shame and Guilt in Neurosis*, New York: International Universities Press.

Lewis, M. (1992), *Shame: The Exposed Self*, New York: The Free Press.

—— (1993), 'Self-Conscious Emotions: Embarrassment, Pride, Shame, and Guilt' in M. Lewis and J. M. Haviland (eds), *Handbook of Emotions*, New York: Guilford Press.

Lewis, M. and Haviland, J. M. (eds) (1993), *Handbook of Emotions*, New York: Guilford Press.

Leys, R. (2011), 'The Turn to Affect: A Critique', *Critical Inquiry* 37: 434–72.

—— (2012a), 'Facts and Moods: Reply to my Critics', *Critical Inquiry* 38: 882–91.

—— (2012b), 'How Did Fear Become a Scientific Object and What Kind of Object is it?' in B. Lazier (ed.), *Fear: Across the Disciplines*, Pittsburgh: University of Pittsburgh Press.

Lipschutz, R. D. (ed.) (1995), *On Security*, New York: Columbia University Press.

Little, G. (1999), *The Public Emotions: From Mourning to Hope*, Sydney: Australian Broadcasting Corporation Books.

Lorde, A. (1984), *Sister Outsider: Essays and Speeches*, Trumansburg, NY: The Crossing Press.

Lupton, D. (1998), *The Emotional Self: A Sociocultural Exploration*, London: Sage.

Lutz, C. A. (1988), *Unnatural Emotions: Everyday Sentiments on a Micronesian Atoll and Their Challenge to Western Theory*, Chicago: University of Chicago Press.

Lutz, C. A. and Abu-Lughod (1990), *Language and the Politics of Emotion*, Cambridge: Cambridge University Press.

Lynch, W. F. (1965), *Images of Hope: Imagination as Healer of the Hopeless*, Notre Dame: University of Notre Dame Press.

Lynd, H. M. (1958), *On Shame and the Search for Identity*, New York: Harcourt, Brace and Company.

McClintock, A. (1995), *Imperial Leather: Race, Gender and Sexuality in the Colonial Contest*, New York: Routledge.

McGill, V. J. (1967), *The Idea of Happiness*, New York: Frederick A. Praeger.

McGurran, A and Johnston, J. (2003), 'The Homecoming: It's too Painful: Martin's Sad Return to Farm', *Daily Mirror*, 9 August: 4–5.

Machiavelli, N. (1950), *The Prince and the Discourses*, New York: The Modern Library.

McNay, L. (2000), *Gender and Agency: Reconfiguring the Subject in Feminist and Social Theory*, Cambridge: Polity Press.

Martin, B. (1996), *Femininity Played Straight: The Significance of Being Lesbian*, New York: Routledge.

Marx, K. (1975), *Early Writings*, trans. R. Livingstone and G. Benton, Harmondsworth: Penguin Books.

—— (1976), *Capital: A Critique of Political Economy*, vol. 1, trans. B. Fowkes, Harmondsworth: Penguin Books.

—— and Engels, F. (1965), *The German Ideology*, trans. and ed. S. Ryazanskaya, London: Lawrence and Wishart.

Massumi, B. (1993), 'Everywhere You Want to Be: Introduction to Fear' in B. Massumi (ed.), *The Politics of Everyday Fear*, Minneapolis: University of Minnesota Press.

—— (2002), *Parables for the Virtual: Movement, Affect, Sensation*, Durham: Duke University Press.

Matsuda, M. J. (1993), 'Public Response to Racist Speech: Considering the Victim's Story' in M. J. Matsuda, C. R. Lawrence, R. Delgads, *Words That Wound: Critical Race Theory, Assaultive Speech, and the First Amendment*, Boulder: Westview Press.

May, R. (1977), *The Meaning of Anxiety*, rev. edn, New York: Norton.

Melzack, R. and Wall, P. D. (1996), *The Challenge of Pain*, Harmondsworth: Penguin Books.

Merleau-Ponty, M. (1962), *Phenomenology of Perception*, trans. C. Smith, London: Routledge and Kegan Paul.

Midgley, M. (1989), *Wisdom, Information, and Wonder: What Is Knowledge For?* London: Routledge.

Miller, S. B. (1985), *The Shame Experience*, Hillsdale, NJ: The Analytic Press.

—— (1993), 'Disgust Reactions: Their Determinants and Manifestations in Treatment', *Contemporary Psychoanalysis* 29 (4): 711–35.

Miller, W. I. (1997), *The Anatomy of Disgust*, Cambridge, MA: Harvard University Press.

Minow, M. (1998), *Between Vengeance and Forgiveness: Facing History after Genocide and Mass Violence*, Boston: Beacon Press.

Mohanty, C. T. (2003), ' "Under Western Eyes" Revisited: Feminist Solidarity Through Anticapitalist Struggles', *Signs*, 28 (2): 499–538.

Moreton-Robinson, A. (2003), 'Tiddas Talking up to the White Woman: When Huggins et all took on Bell' in M. Grossman (ed.), *Blacklines: Contemporary Critical Writing by Indigenous Australians*, Carleton: Melbourne University Press.

Morrison, A. P. (1989), *Shame: The Underside of Narcissism*, Hillsdale, NJ: The Analytic Press.

Murphy, J. (1988), 'Forgiveness and Resentment' in J. G. Murphy and J. Hampton, *Forgiveness and Mercy*, Cambridge: Cambridge University Press.

Naples, N. A. (2001), 'A Member of the Funeral: An Introspective Ethnography' in M. Bernstein and R. Reimann (eds), *Queer Families, Queer Politics: Challenging Culture and the State*, New York: Columbia University Press.

Nathanson, D. L. (1987), 'A Timetable for Shame' in D. L. Nathanson (ed.), *The Many Faces of Shame*, New York: Guilford Publications.

Nicoll, F. (1998), 'B(l)acklash: Reconciliation after Wik', *Meanjin* 57 (1): 167–83.

Nietzsche, F. (1969), *On the Genealogy of Morals* and *Ecce Homo*, trans. W. Kaufmann and R. J. Hollingdale, New York: Vintage Books.

Nunokawa, J. (1991), ' "All the Sad Young Men": AIDS and the Work of Mourning' in D. Fuss (ed.), *Inside/Out: Lesbian Theories, Gay Theories*, New York: Routledge.

Nussbaum, M. C. (1999), 'The Professor of Parody', http://www.tnr.com/archive/0299/022299/nussbaum022299.html

—— (2001), *Upheavals of Thought: The Intelligence of Emotions*, Cambridge: Cambridge University Press.

O'Connor, N. and Ryan, J. (1993), *Wild Desires and Mistakes Identies: Lesbianism and Psychoanalysis*, London: Verso.

Oliver, K. (2001), *Witnessing: Beyond Recognition*, Minneapolis: University of Minnesota Press.

Orbach, S. (1999), *Towards Emotional Literacy*, London: Virago Press.

Packer, G. (2001), 'Recapturing the Flag', *New York Times Magazine*, 30 September: 15–16.

Parekh, B. (1999), 'What Is Multiculturalism?', http://www.india-seminar.com/1999/484/484%20parekh.htm

Parkinson, B. (1995), *Ideas and Realities of Emotion*, London: Routledge.

Phelan, S. (1997), 'Introduction' in S. Phelan (ed.), *Playing with Fire: Queer Politics, Queer Theories*, London: Routledge.

Pieper, J. (1969), *Hope and History*, trans. R. and C. Winston, London: Burns and Oates.

Piers, G. and Singer, M. B. (1971), *Shame and Guilt: A Psychoanalytic and a Cultural Study*, New York: Norton.

Plummer, K. (1995), *Telling Sexual Stories: Power, Change and Social Worlds*, London: Routledge.

Potamianou, A. (1997), *Hope: A Shield in the Economy of Borderline States*, trans. P. Slotkin, London: Routledge.

Probyn, E. (2000), *Carnal Appetites: FoodSexIdentities*, London: Routledge.

—— (2001), 'Affect in/of Teaching: What Can a Body Do in a Gender Studies' Classroom?', paper presented at the 'Interdisciplinary and Feminist Pedagogy Series', Lancaster University.

—— (2005), *Blush: Faces of Shame*, Minneapolis: University of Minnesota Press.

Prosser, J. (1998), *Second Skins: The Body Narratives of Transsexuality*, New York: Columbia University Press.

Puar, J. K. (2007), *Terrorist Assemblages: Homonationalism in Queer Times*, Durham: Duke University Press.

Pugmire, D. (1998), *Rediscovering Emotion: Emotion and the Claims of Feeling*, Edinburgh: Edinburgh University Press.

Rachman, S. (1998), *Anxiety*, Hove: Psychology Press.

Rechy, J. (2000), Comments in 'The Final Frontier: A Roundtable Discussion', moderator T. Modleski, in J. A. Boone, M. Dupuis, M. Meeker, K. Quimby, C. Sarver, D. Silverman and R. Weatherston (eds), *Queer Frontiers: Millennial Geographic, Genders, and Generations*, Madison: The University of Wisconsin Press.

Reddy, W. M. (2001), *The Navigation of Feeling: A Framework for the History of Emotions*, Cambridge: Cambridge University Press.

Rey, R. (1995), *The History of Pain*, trans. L. E. Wallace, J. A. Cadden and S. W. Cadden, Cambridge, MA: Harvard University Press.

Rosaldo, M. Z. (1984), 'Toward an Anthropology of Self and Feeling' in R. A. Shweder and R. A. LeVine (eds), *Culture Theory: Essays on Mind, Self, and Emotion*, Cambridge: Cambridge University Press.

Roseneil, S. (1995), *Disarming Patriarchy: Feminism and Political Action at Greenham*, Buckingham: Open University Press.

Rosfort, R. and Stanghellini, G. (2009), 'The Person between Moods and Affects', *Philosophy, Psychiatry and Psychology*, 16 (3): 251–36.

Rosga, A. (1999), 'Policing the State', *The Georgetown Journal of Gender and the Law* 1: 145–71.

Rotberg, R. I. (2000), 'Truth Commissions and the Provision of Truth, Justice, and Reconciliation' in R. I. Rotberg and D. Thompson (eds), *Truth v. Justice: The Morality of Truth Commissions*, Princeton: Princeton University Press.

Rozin, P. and Fallon, A. E. (1987), 'A Perspective on Disgust', *Psychological Review* 94 (1): 23–41.

Sacco, V. F. and Glackman, W. (2000), 'Vulnerability, Loss of Control and Worry about Crime' in J. Ditton and S. Farrall (eds), *The Fear of Crime*, Dartmouth: Ashgate.

Said, E. W. (1978), *Orientalism*, London: Routledge and Kegan Paul.

Salecl, R. (1998), *(Per)versions of Love and Hate*, London: Verso.

Sandell, J. (1994), 'The Cultural Necessity of Queer Families', *Bad Subjects* 12: http://eserver. org/bs/12/sandell. html

Sartre, J.-P. (1962), *Sketch for a Theory of the Emotions*, trans. P. Mairet, London: Methuen and Co.

—— (1996), *Being and Nothingness: An Essay on Phenomenological Ontology*, trans. H. E. Barnes, London: Routledge.

Scarry, E. (1985), *The Body in Pain: The Making and Unmaking of the World*, New York: Oxford University Press.

Scheff, T. J. (1994), *Bloody Revenge: Emotions, Nationalism, and War*, Boulder: Westview Press.

Scheler, M. (1954), *The Nature of Sympathy*, trans. P. Heath, London: Routledge and Kegan Paul.

—— (2008), *The Nature of Sympathy*, 5th edn, New Brunswick, NJ: Transaction Publishers.

Schneider, C. D. (1987), 'A Mature Sense of Shame' in D. L. Nathanson (ed.), *The Many Faces of Shame*, New York: Guilford Publications.

Sedgwick, E. K. (1994), *Tendencies*, London: Routledge.

—— (2003), *Touching Feeling: Affect, Pedagogy, Performativity*, Durham: Duke University Press.

Sedgwick, E. K. and Frank, A. (1995), 'Introduction' in E. K. Sedgwick and A. Frank (eds), *Shame and its Sisters: A Silvan Tomkins Reader*, Durham: Duke University Press.

Seigworth, G. and Gregg, M. (2010), 'Introduction: An Inventory of Shimmers', in M. Gregg and G. Seigworth (eds), *The Affect Theory Reader*, Durham: Duke University Press.

Sheller, M. (2003), *Consuming the Caribbean: From Arawaks to Zombies*, London: Routledge.

Silver, B. R. (1991), 'The Authority of Anger: *Three Guineas* as Case Study', *Signs: Journal of Women in Culture and Society* 16 (2): 340–70.

Silverman, K. (1996), *The Threshold of the Visible World*, New York: Routledge.

Silverman, P. R. and Klass, D. (1996), 'Introduction: What's the Problem?' in D. Klass, P. R. Silverman and S. L. Nickman (eds), *Continuing Bonds: New Understandings of Grief*, Philadelphia: Taylor and Francis.

Singer, I. (1984), *The Nature of Love: 1. Plato to Luther*, Chicago: University of Chicago Press.

Skeggs, B. (1999), 'Matter out of Place: Visibility and Sexualities in Leisure Spaces', *Leisure Studies* 18: 213–32.

Smith, A. (1966), *The Theory of Moral Sentiments*, New York: Augustus M. Kelley.

Smith, A. D. (2001), 'EU Nations Left in the Spotlight over Slavery Apologies', *The Independent*, 4 September.

Smith, J. and Williams, A. (2003), 'I'm OK Now', *The Mirror*, 7 June, p. 4–5.

Solomon, R. C. (1995), *A Passion for Justice: Emotions and the Origins of the Social Contract*, Lanham, MD: Rowman and Littlefield Publishers.

—— (ed.) (2003), *What is an Emotion? Classic and Contemporary Readings*, Oxford: Oxford University Press.

Spaemann, R. (2000), *Happiness and Benevolence*, trans. J. Alberg, Notre Dame: University of Notre Dame Press.

Spelman, E. V. (1989), 'Anger and Insubordination' in A. Garry and M. Pearsall (eds), *Women, Knowledge, and Reality: Explorations in Feminist Philosophy*, Boston: Unwin Hyman.

—— (1997), *Fruits of Sorrow: Framing our Attention to Suffering*, Beacon Press: Boston.

Spinoza, B. (1959), *Spinoza's Ethics: And on the Correction of the Understanding*, trans. A. Boyle, London: Everyman's Library.

Spivak, G. C. (1988), 'Can the Subaltern Speak?' in C. Nelson and L. Grossberg (eds), *Marxism and the Interpretation of Culture*, Urbana: University of Illinois Press.

Spivak, G. C. (1995), trans. Preface and Afterword, *Imaginary Maps: Three Stories*, New York: Routledge.

Stacey, J. (1997), *Teratologies: A Cultural Study of Cancer*, London: Routledge.

Stanko, E. (1990), *Everyday Violence: How Women and Men Experience Sexual and Physical Danger*, London: Pandora.

Stern, D. N. (2000), *The Interpersonal World of the Infant*, New York: Basic Books.

Strongman, K. T. (2003), *The Psychology of Emotion: From Everyday Life to Theory*, West Sussex: John Wiley and Sons.

Sturken, M. (2002), 'Memorialising Absence' in C. Calhoun, P. Price and A. Timmer (eds), *Understanding September 11*, New York: The New Press.

Sullivan, A. (1996), *Virtually Normal: An Argument about Homosexuality*, New York: Vintage Books.

Sullivan, D and Tifft, L. (2001), *Restorative Justice: Healing the Foundations of Our Everyday Lives*, Monsey, NY: Willow Tree Press.

Sumner, L. W. (1996), *Welfare, Happiness, and Ethics*, Oxford: Clarendon Press.

Suttie, I. D. (1963), *The Origins of Love and Hate*, Harmondsworth: Penguin Books.

Tavris, C. (1982), *Anger: The Misunderstood Emotion*, New York: Simon and Schuster.

Terada, R. (2001), *Feeling in Theory: Emotion After the 'Death of the Subject'*, Cambridge, MA: Harvard University Press.

Thobani, S. (2003), 'War and the Politics of Truth-Making in Canada', *International Journal of Qualitative Studies in Education* (16) 3: 399–414.

Tomkins, S. S. (1963), *Affect, Imagery, Consciousness: The Negative Affects*, vol. 2, New York: Springer.

Trigg, R. (1970), *Pain and Emotion*, Oxford: Clarendon Press.

Valentine, G. (1996), '(Re)Negotiating the "Heterosexual Street": Lesbian Productions of Space' in N. Duncan (ed.), *Bodyspace: Destabilising Geographies of Gender and Sexuality*, London: Routledge.

Volpp, L. (2002), 'The Citizen and the Terrorist', *UCLA Law Review* 49 (5): 1,575–1,600.

Warner, M. (1990), 'Homo-Narcissism; or, Heterosexuality' in J. A. Boone and M. Cadden (eds), *Engendering Men: The Question of Male Feminist Criticism*, New York: Routledge.

—— (1999), *The Trouble with Normal: Sex, Politics, and the Ethics of Queer Life*, Cambridge, MA: Harvard University Press.

Weeks, J., Heaphy, B. and Donovan, C. (2001), *Same Sex Intimacies: Families of Choice and Other Life Experiments*, London: Routledge.

West, T. C. (1999), *Wounds of the Spirit: Black Women, Violence, and Resistance Ethics*, New York: New York University Press.

Weston, K. (1991), *Families We Choose: Lesbians, Gays, Kinship*, New York: Columbia University Press.

—— (1995), 'Forever is a Long Time: Romancing the Real in Gay Kinship Ideologies' in S. Yanagisako and C. Delaney (eds), *Naturalizing Power: Essays in Feminist Cultural Analysis*, New York: Routledge.

—— (1998), *Long Slow Burn: Sexuality and Social Science*, London: Routledge.

Wetherell, M. (2012), *Affect and Emotion: A New Social Science Understanding*, London: Sage.

White, G. M. (1993), 'Emotions Inside Out: The Anthropology of Affect' in M. Lewis and J. M. Haviland (eds), *Handbook of Emotions*, New York: Guilford Publications.

Wiegman, R. (1999), 'Feminism, Institutionalism, and the Idiom of Failure', *Differences: A Journal of Feminist Cultural Studies* 11 (3): 107–36.

—— (2002), 'Intimate Publics: Race, Property, and Personhood', *American Literature* 74 (4): 859–85.

Williams, P. J. (1995), *The Rooster's Egg: On the Persistence of Prejudice*, Cambridge, MA: Harvard University Press.

Williams, S. J. (2001), *Emotion and Social Theory: Corporeal Reflections on the (Ir)Rational*, London: Sage.

Wilson, E. A. (1999), 'Introduction: Somatic Compliance – Feminism, Biology and Science', *Australian Feminist Studies* 14 (29): 7–18.

Wittgenstein, L. (1964), *Preliminary Studies for the 'Philosophical Investigations': Generally Known as The Blue and Brown Books*, Oxford: Basil Blackwell.

Wurmser, L. (1981), *The Mask of Shame*, Baltimore: Johns Hopkins University Press.

Yancy, G. (2013), 'Walking While Black', *New York Times*, 1 September.

Young, I. M. (1990), *Justice and the Politics of Difference*, Princeton: Princeton University Press.

Young, L. (1996), *Fear of the Dark: 'Race', Gender and Sexuality in the Cinema*, London: Routledge.

Yuval-Davis, N. (1997), *Gender and Nation*, London: Sage.

Zajonc, R. B. (1994), 'Emotional Expression and Temperature Modulation' in S. H. M. Van Goozen, N. E. Van de Poll and J. A. Sergeant (eds), *Emotions: Essays on Emotion Theory*, Hillsdale, NJ: Lawrence Erlbaum Associates.

Žižek, S. (1989), *The Sublime Object of Ideology*, London: Verso.

—— (1991), *For They Know Not What They Do: Enjoyment as a Political Factor*, London: Verso.

Zolberg, A. R. (2002), 'Guarding the Gates' in C. Calhoun, P. Price and A. Timmer (eds), *Understanding September 11*, New York: The New Press.

Index